Poetics and Politics

Poetics and Politics

Net Structures and Agencies in Early Modern Drama

Edited by
Toni Bernhart, Jaša Drnovšek, Sven Thorsten Kilian,
Joachim Küpper, Jan Mosch

DE GRUYTER

This book is published in cooperation with the project DramaNet, funded by the European Research Council

Early Modern European Drama
and the Cultural Net

European Research Council
Established by the European Commission

ISBN 978-3-11-070946-9
e-ISBN (PDF) 978-3-11-053669-0
e-ISBN (EPUB) 978-3-11-060352-1

This work is licensed under the Creative Commons Attribution-NonCommercial-NoDerivs 4.0 License. For details go to http://creativecommons.org/licenses/by-nc-nd/4.0/.

Library of Congress Cataloging in Publication Control Number: 2018017860

Bibliographic information published by the Deutsche Nationalbibliothek
The Deutsche Nationalbibliothek lists this publication in the Deutsche Nationalbibliografie; detailed bibliographic data are available on the Internet at http://dnb.dnb.de.

© 2020 Toni Bernhart, Jaša Drnovšek, Sven Thorsten Kilian, Joachim Küpper, Jan Mosch, published by Walter de Gruyter GmbH, Berlin/Boston
This volume is text- and page-identical with the hardback published in 2018.
Typesetting: Meta Systems Publishing & Printservices GmbH, Wustermark
Printing and binding: CPI books GmbH, Leck
Cover illustration: photodeedooo/iStock/Thinkstock

www.degruyter.com

Acknowledgements

This book is a collection of papers presented at an international conference at Freie Universität Berlin on 29–30 April 2015. Bringing together experts of early modern drama and music, the event was a wonderful example of transnational and interdisciplinary collaboration in the academy. We would like to thank everybody who participated for the insightful talks and stimulating discussions.

The conference was organized within the framework of a European Research Council Advanced Grant Project entitled Early Modern European Drama and the Cultural Net (DramaNet). We wish to extend our warmest thanks to our friends and colleagues in this project, whose friendly support and constructive feedback has informed our own research over the years. We would also like to register our grateful acknowledgement of the ERC's funding of outstanding research in the arts and humanities, without which neither the conference nor this volume would have been possible.

We owe a debt of gratitude to the project coordinators, Konstanze Ameer and Agnes Kloocke, whose dedication and organizational skills ensured that the creative process ran smoothly at all times. Furthermore, our thanks go to Orla Mulholland, who revised the following essays with a keen eye for detail and astute remarks, as well as to Ulrike Krauß, Gabrielle Cornefert and the team at de Gruyter.

European Research Council
Established by the European Commission

Contents

Acknowledgements —— v

Introduction —— 1

Joachim Küpper
'National Literatures'? —— 19

Stephen G. Nichols
American Presidential Candidates at the Court of Charles V: How Political *Theory* Trumped Political *Theology* in Fourteenth-Century Paris —— 37

Sandra Richter
Cross-Cultural Inventions in Drama on the Basis of the Novel in Prose, or World Literature before World Literature: The Case of Fortunatus —— 53

Esther Schomacher
Sex on Stage: How Does the Audience Know? (Dovizi da Bibbiena, *La Calandra*, III.10; Shakespeare, *Henry V*, V.2) —— 69

Stefano Gulizia
Castiglione's 'Green' Sense of Theater —— 101

Bernhard Huss
Luigi Groto's *Adriana*: A Laboratory Experiment on Literary Genre —— 119

Cristina Savettieri
The Agency of Errors: *Hamartia* and its (Mis)interpretations in the Italian Cinquecento —— 149

Stephanie Bung
Playful Institutions: Social and Textual Practices in Early Spanish Academies —— 169

Franz Gratl
The Role of Music in Folk Drama: An Investigation Based on Tyrolean Sources —— 185

Erika Fischer-Lichte
From a Rhetorical to a 'Natural' Art of Acting: What the Networks of the Seventeenth and Eighteenth Centuries Achieved —— 199

Jaša Drnovšek
Early Modern Religious Processions: The Rise and Fall of a Political Genre —— 215

Igor Grdina
Directions, Examples, and Incentives: Slovenian Playwriting in the Second Half of the Eighteenth Century —— 225

DS Mayfield
Variants of *hypólepsis*: Rhetorical, Anthropistic, Dramatic (With Remarks on Terence, Machiavelli, Shakespeare) —— 233

Index —— 275

Introduction

Poetics and Politics: Net Structures and Agencies in Early Modern Drama

Without the textual and institutional models of the early modern period, the current landscape of European theater would look very different. Early modern theater, in turn, could not have prospered without the occurrence of those dynamic and productive processes that are frequently subsumed under the rubrics of influence, contamination, hybridization, or fertilization. Their effects can be detected in virtually every early modern genre: comedy and tragedy, Italian Renaissance and French Reformation plays, religious pieces and German popular drama, to name but a few pertinent examples. It is therefore not too bold a claim that no truly pan-European history of theater will be written until these phenomena have been widely studied and taken into account. But if the results of the intertextual constellations are evident, their mechanics have so far proved more elusive. A comprehensive theory ought to embrace indirect connections between texts, which the narrow concept of influence, oblivious to shifts and delays, fails to factor in. As a consequence, the revised narrative of the history of theater, even as it does justice to drama's remarkable scope in space and time, will have to allow for periods of stagnation that would undermine any linear account. What is more, since the circulation of forms and contents is often tied to the existence of specific practices and organizations, such as wandering actors' companies, the movements need to be carefully described and conceptualized. In their failure to meet any or all of these demands, the familiar metaphors soon reach their heuristic and epistemological limits. The concept of exchange, for example, would seem to presuppose existing institutions on a lateral basis, whereas "transfer" implies a "colonial" relationship in the widest sense. Similarly, the economic or biological connotations of terms such as "borrowing," "debt," "hybrid," "virus," and "rhizome" are either infelicitous, because they imply illness and a pseudo-Darwinian struggle for life, or misleading, as the development of culture is not predetermined by a DNA blueprint.

It is with a view to these theoretical problems and conceptual challenges that the essays collected in this anthology examine early modern drama from a thoroughly comparative and transnational perspective. In doing so, they draw attention to cultural production as the creative interplay between people and pre-existing cultural artifacts, which are posited here as "floating material" without any ties to a specific group or territory. The guiding metaphor of the "cultural net" was developed and theoretically substantiated by Joachim Küpper;[1] its applicability to early modern drama was further explored by scholars who carried out studies within the framework of the ERC-funded research project "DramaNet: Early Modern European Drama and the Cultural Net" (Freie Universität Berlin, 2011 to 2016).[2]

The net metaphor theorizes culture as a virtual network; cultural artifacts are treated as mobile entities that "float" on the net, where they remain available at different times and places and can be freely "withdrawn," i.e. re-used or creatively appropriated and adapted. The net is a virtual construct because it is an idealized representation of the myriads of contacts between human beings and non-autochthonous cultural artifacts. This, to be sure, does not efface the need for a hypothesis of how the material in question travels from one point to the next; however, emphasis is primarily placed on the net rather than its material substrate. In other words: whether cultural artifacts are encoded in books or brains, and whether these material containers travel by ship or stagecoach is, by and large, of less import than the fundamental mobility of the ideational contents themselves. These observations may already have established two other properties of the net: its re-configurability and its spatio-temporal dimension. It will be evident that the net widens its scope when people enter new places, but it can also be curbed, if only to a degree, by political decisions (isolationist policies, censorship, etc.) that hinder the flow of cultural material. Regarding the net's extension across space and time, two early modern examples may serve as cases in point: a bestseller such as *Don Quixote* was distributed across Europe in a matter of months or years; conversely, when the humanists went "book hunting," they were searching for ancient texts that had survived for centuries in monastic libraries – not least, of course, due to the mobility of the material and its extraction from the net by Arab scholars who had written translations and commentaries.

For a full appreciation of the issues raised above, we recommend that readers also consult the multifaceted publications that have, along with the present book, resulted from the DramaNet research project. The following introduction will focus on elucidating the principal tenet of the present volume, that is, that literature is produced in a nexus of power relations, agency, and the cultural net. It will also comment on the paradigmatic status that early modern drama (which appears, crucially, in a pre-national context) can achieve for the theori-

---

[1] Joachim Küpper. *The Cultural Net: Early Modern Drama as a Paradigm*. Berlin: de Gruyter, 2018.
[2] www.fu-berlin.de/erc-dramanet. Accessed 13 February 2018.

zation of cultural production, before concluding with an outline of the essays in this anthology.

By subtitling this book *Net Structures and Agencies*, we wish to call attention to two important steps that are involved in literary production. On the one hand, cultural material needs to be afloat on the net. This may come about as the result of a conscious effort to disseminate this or that cultural unit, but is more often than not a side effect of other human activities: trade, warfare, travel, and so on. On the other hand, material needs to be extracted from the net and used by a human being. This may be the case when the material meets a certain demand, e.g. by responding to pressing psychological needs or by providing answers to moral questions that are pertinent in a given sociohistorical context. Thus, in the most general terms, we posit culture-as-net as the enabling force of literary production, combined with the author as the executive force.

As our main title, *Poetics and Politics*, underlines, we do not aim for naïve universalism or the resurrection of Barthes's dead author. In fact, all of the following chapters endorse the assumption that cultural practices are beset by political, institutional, and social practices that need to be taken into account in the analysis of literary texts. At the same time, though, it would be a mistake to ignore the relevance of contingent encounters and individual agency. Within our collection, Cristina Savettieri's investigation of the productive (mis-)reading of Aristotle in early modern Italy and Bernhard Huss's analysis of the "experiments" conducted in Luigi Groto's literary "laboratory" provide just two examples of creative ingenuity that cannot be seamlessly reduced to the effects of power and discourse. As Edward Said memorably put it, writing, for the author, "is a series of decisions and choices expressed in words"[3] – even if we might add that it is often worthwhile to look at the root causes of these choices.

A comprehensive rehearsal of the weal and woe of the self in the academy could fill entire books of its own, of course. To put it succinctly, we acknowledge the manifold attempts to exorcize "the spectre of the Cartesian subject," in Slavoj Žižek's ironic formulation,[4] whilst also insisting on the unclaimed spaces and potential for subversion that discursive formations – rarely totalizing, often internally inconsistent – must produce. Not least due to the religious

---

[3] Edward W. Said. *Humanism and Democratic Criticism*. New York: Columbia University Press, 2004, p. 62.
[4] Slavoj Žižek. *The Ticklish Subject: The Absent Centre of Political Ontology*. New edition. London: Verso, 2008, p. xxiii. – Žižek gives a concise, if playful, overview of the 'exorcisms,' citing deconstruction, Habermasian communication, Heideggerian 'Being,' cognitive science, Deep Ecology, post-Marxism, and feminism.

pluralization, early modern literature follows two divergent trajectories: the staging of power and authority (of the king, the church, etc.) on the one hand,[5] and the search for a stable relationship between the proto-individual and the world on the other.[6] In order to do justice to the plurality of early modern literature,[7] we have settled upon the term "agencies" to indicate that we are not talking about the self-transparent "bourgeois" self, nor about the author as origin and center of the text, but that we do wish to uphold ideas about choice and initiative without which the cultural net would hardly be imaginable. Culture in this sense retains traces of the transitive verb *colere*: working the land, shaping the world, adorning; it is a fundamental and indeed inescapable mode of being human in the world. In any case, however, the DramaNet approach is non-reductive with regard to modes of textual criticism. As indicated in the above remarks about literary production as a two-step process, the approach posits the cultural net as a *conditio sine qua non* of cultural production, but does not prescribe any one method for analyzing why a specific text is created and how it is functionalized. Thus, the notion of the cultural net is compatible, on the level of literary theory, with any mode of textual interpretation, from biographical criticism to poststructuralism and beyond. This adapt-

---

[5] An example from this book is the chapter by Jaša Drnovšek, who demonstrates how the practice of religious processions was disseminated throughout Europe by Catholic orders, how it was functionalized by proponents of the counter-Reformation to strengthen not just piety, but also the authority of the church, and how philosophers of the Enlightenment attacked the practice precisely because of its political aims. – One anthology to rise from the DramaNet project has focused specifically on the ways in which plays (and theatrical productions) fashioned and manipulated their audiences: *Dramatic Experience: The Poetics of Drama and the Early Modern Public Sphere(s)*, edited by Katja Gvozdeva, Tatiana Korneeva, and Kirill Ospovat. Leiden: Brill, 2017.

[6] One fascinating text in that regard, albeit outside the domain of drama, is Thomas Browne's *Religio Medici*, in which the author seeks to justify his metaphysical idiosyncrasies, critically engaging with Catholicism and Roman Antiquity as well as blending Anglicanism with various folk beliefs in angels, witches, and the devil. The *Religio* is arguably not conceivable without Montaigne and the early modern essay. – Cf. also Scott Black's notion of the early modern essay as a trial not of one's self and the world, but of one's self and one's reading: "One reads in order to get material to work with, but one must digest what one reads, making it one's own. One writes in order to aid this process of digestion." (Scott Black. *Of Essays and Reading in Early Modern Britain*. New York: Palgrave Macmillan, 2007, p. 33.)

[7] Verena Olejniczak Lobsien, for example, has persuasively argued that the ideologically fraught attempts to assign texts to the camp of either autonomy or heteronomy should be abandoned in favor of analyzing their interrogative and tentative properties when it comes to delineating the contours of selfhood. – Verena Olejniczak. "Heterologie: Konturen frühneuzeitlichen Selbstseins jenseits von Autonomie und Heteronomie." *Zeitschrift für Literaturwissenschaft und Linguistik*, no. 101, 1996, pp. 6–36.

ability is reflected by the chapters in this volume: some of them focus on creative individuals, others on networks and academies as collective producers of knowledge, others again on the ways in which spectators are fashioned as (moral) subjects through sensory effects and embodied cognition.

The net metaphor enables scholars to conceive of a wide range of relationships between texts; rather than focus on linear "influences," it becomes possible to theorize a connection between texts that are remote in space and time by focusing on parallels in the use of cultural artifacts (a phenomenon that includes both larger conceptual entities such as genres and plots and smaller conceptual items such as ideologemes). The fact that we envision a dyadic process of literary creation – the transnational content on the net, combined with the creational dispositive of a given sociohistorical context – sets this approach apart from transcultural studies, which have latterly been gaining in strength as the cultural studies of the globalized age. While we share the impetus "to de-link literatures from their national-territorial-ethnic loci and at the same time to offer 'an alternative to the dichotomic paradigm of postcolonialism,'"[8] the metaphor of culture-as-net focuses on culture as a general human activity; there is, according to this model, only one cultural net. By contrast, transcultural studies focus on particular cultures as separate entities, albeit entities with a tendency to converse and mingle: "cultures are no longer seen as monolithic entities or as mutually exclusive absolutes, but are perceived as hybridizing organisms in constant dialogue with each other."[9] As a consequence, transcultural studies are currently predominantly interested in neo-nomadic literatures, which result from migratory experience or tell of uprooted individuals. As fascinating as those studies are, the metaphor of the cultural net that is championed here has a much wider scope, treating any and every text as the result of the drift of inherently transnational cultural material. It is therefore not limited at all to texts that acknowledge difference, alterity, etc. on the content level, even though individuals who are on the move or who are at home in different places do, of course, play an important role in maintaining the material substrate of the cultural net.

Another critical tension exists between the idea of the cultural net and the notion of the author as origin and creator, which ultimately links literary theorists as diverse as Plato, the neurobiologist Wolf Singer, and the Romantics. Where the latest theories enlist neuroscience to understand works of art as

---

[8] Arianna Dagnino. "Transcultural Literature and Contemporary World Literature(s)." CLCWeb: Comparative Literature and Culture, vol. 15, no. 5, 2013, pp. 1–11, p. 4. https://doi.org/10.7771/1481-4374.2339. Accessed 13 February 2018.
[9] Ibid.

world-models that are fabricated by self-reflexive brains and communicated to other brains as part of the evolutionary game (but are quiet on how this communication occurs),[10] the oldest theories turned dependably to the gods. In Plato's *Ion*, Socrates maintains that a poet's abilities do not constitute either knowledge or skill (*epistêmê* or *technê*), because a poet cannot apply them invariably at all times and across all genres; therefore, inspiration must be a "divine power" that moves him like a magnetic force:

> [E]ach [poet] is able only to compose that to which the Muse has stirred him, this man dithyrambs, another laudatory odes, another dance-songs, another epic or else iambic verse; but each is at fault in any other kind. For not by art do they utter these things, but by divine influence; since, if they had fully learnt by art to speak on one kind of theme, they would know how to speak on all. (534c)[11]

Socrates' argument for the heteronomous character of inspiration is a double bind: it renders the poet immune to criticism, but it also forecloses any discussion of how and why authors compose what they compose. This unaccountability of the origin finds a belated echo in the expressivist poetics of the Romantics, who substitute individual nature for Socrates' Muse. As Earl Wasserman has shown with regard to English Romanticism, the Romantic poem is supposed to "both formulate its own cosmic syntax and shape the autonomous poetic reality that the cosmic syntax permits; 'nature', which was once prior to the poem and available for imitation, now shares with the poem a common origin in the poet's creativity."[12] Final and efficient causes collapse into one: the expression of nature is the poem's raison d'être, and nature creates the poem. This line of thinking becomes problematic as soon as it is elevated from the individual to the tribal level: As Charles Taylor argues, the Romantic shift to the sovereignty of the individual poet had its analogue in

> Rousseau's notion that the locus of sovereignty must be a people, that is, an entity constituted by a common purpose or identity, something more than a mere 'aggregation'. This root idea is developed further in Herder's conception of a *Volk*, the notion that each people has its own way of being, thinking, and feeling, to which it ought to be true; that

---

[10] Wolf Singer. "Neurobiologische Anmerkungen zum Wesen und zur Notwendigkeit von Kunst." *Der Beobachter im Gehirn: Essays zur Hirnforschung*. Frankfurt: Suhrkamp, 2002, pp. 211–234.
[11] Plato. *Ion. Plato in Twelve Volumes*, vol. 9, translated by W. R. M. Lamb. London: William Heinemann, 1925.
[12] Earl Wasserman. *The Subtler Language*. Baltimore: Johns Hopkins University Press, 1968, p. 10. Cf. also Stuart Peterfreund. "Earl Wasserman: A Critical (Re-)Reading." *The Wordsworth Circle*, vol. 37, no. 2, 2006, pp. 64–67.

> each has a right and a duty to realize its own way and not to have an alien one imposed on it.[13]

Thus, the idea of the poet's unique individuality merges with the idea of a 'national character' and gains a normative standing vis-à-vis cultural production: "Different *Völker* [peoples] have their own way of being human, and shouldn't betray it by aping others," or so Taylor paraphrases Herder.[14]

The Romantic example shows how easily theories of cultural production can transgress the line between description and prescription, disowning – in postulating autonomy on the individual and the national level – any knowledge about the transnational character of cultural goods. By contrast, early modern writers, the first subjects of a culture of print, were often acutely aware that they were writing in a larger discursive space – and of how that space tended to grow day by day. In every field of scientific and artistic production in the early modern period, the abundance of texts and the forms of their availability was reflected upon, welcomed, rejected, or problematized. What emerged is therefore not only and not essentially a material question, but the destabilization of the concept of textual tradition and authority. Complaints about the "scribbling age" were common, and the physician Thomas Browne came close to condemning the printing press altogether (which, inaccurately, he alleged to be one of three German inventions, along with gunpowder and the pocket watch):

> I have heard some with deepe sighs lament the lost lines of Cicero; others with as many groanes deplore the combustion of the Library of Alexandria; for my owne part, I thinke there be too many in the world [...]. Pineda quotes more Authors in one worke, than are necessary in a whole world. Of those three great inventions of Germany, there are two which are not without their incommodities. (Sect. 24)[15]

There is a certain irony involved when Browne denounces intertextuality *avant la lettre* and still cannot avoid it (as his exasperated allusion to Pineda's *Monarchia Ecclesiastica* betrays) in a tract that he purportedly intends as a personal meditation on religion and free thinking. Clearly, authors do not fully 'own' their texts. William Shakespeare's *Midsummer Night's Dream* is among those early modern dramas in which the uneasy negotiation of originality and discur-

---

[13] Charles Taylor. *Sources of the Self: The Making of the Modern Identity*. Cambridge: Harvard University Press, 1989, p. 415.
[14] Ibid., p. 376.
[15] Thomas Browne. *Religio Medici. The Prose of Sir Thomas Browne*, edited by Norman Endicott. New York: W. W. Norton, 1967, pp. 1–90.

siveness can be retraced. Late in the play, when the Athenian king Theseus finally hears about the marvelous events outside his city – fairy encounters, love potions, and even metamorphoses –, he baffles his entourage with a diatribe against the excesses of fancy:

> The poet's eye, in a fine frenzy rolling,
> Doth glance from heaven to earth, from earth to heaven,
> And as imagination bodies forth
> The forms of things unknown, the poet's pen
> Turns them to shapes, and gives to airy nothing
> A local habitation and a name. (5.1.12–17)[16]

How authoritative – in fact: how 'authorial' are these observations? Since Theseus' wife Hippolyta is the only one who dares to contradict him (arguing, quite sensibly, that the reports from the woods do add up after all), the impromptu lecture on madness and literary inventions remains largely uncontested on the level of character speech. Arguably, though, the king's dismissal of recent events as "[m]ore strange than true" (5.1.2) threatens to invalidate the better part of the previous stage action, and it is this tension that prompts the audience to question the reliability of Theseus' claims.

In his monologue, the king sketches the image of a writer who, in a fit of mania, will tap into a well of "airy nothing" somewhere between this world and the next. As metapoetic comments go, this one is fraught with philosophical implications, but might just seem familiar enough. On the one hand, the passage suggests a creation out of nothing[17] and posits, in its metonymical

---

16 All quotations from Shakespeare are from *The Norton Shakespeare: Based on the Oxford Edition*, edited by Stephen Greenblatt, Walter Cohen, Jean E. Howard, et al. Second edition. New York: W. W. Norton, 2008.

17 The concept of nothingness is a staple of Shakespeare criticism. Two of the most suggestive lines are Iago's "I am nothing if not critical" (*Othello* 2.1.121), which can be read as essentializing Iago's destructiveness, and Lear's "Nothing can come of nothing" (*The History of King Lear* 1.1.79), which seemingly contradicts Genesis 1:1. There is a real danger of reading too much into such passages, which represent a natural use of language: "nothing if not" simply means "very," and Lear's response to Cordelia has a decidedly proverbial ring, with the old king merely stating that his daughter will get nothing (no part of the kingdom) as long as she gives him nothing (no public avowal of devotion). That said, the Christian insistence on God the creator, the rediscovery of Lucretius' *De rerum natura* with its argument that "ex nihilo nihil fit," and the wide adoption of Hindu-Arabic numerals, including "0," leads to some fascinating constellations in the Renaissance. – Nothingness in Shakespeare, with a view to the mathematical revolution, has recently been explored in R. S. White. "Making Something out of Nothing in Shakespeare." *Working with Shakespeare*, edited by Peter Holland. Cambridge: Cambridge University Press, 2013, pp. 232–245. The relevance of Lucretius has been argued for by Stephen Greenblatt. *The Swerve: How the World Became Modern*. New York: W. W. Norton, 2011.

emphasis on the poet's eye, imagination, and pen, the human being as a point of origin rather than a receptacle for divine whispers. On the other hand, any celebration of autonomy is contained by the fact that Theseus makes his points with the sole intention of proving the equivalence (and equivalent untrustworthiness) of lovers, madmen, and poets. Therefore, his rationalization of the *furor poeticus* could well be seen as innocuous: a Greek character in an early modern play argues for a Greek concept[18] that has – during its early modern handling[19] by Boccaccio, Ficino, Landino, Vadian, the Pléiade, etc. – been mostly stripped of its apologetic value and become a secular trope for the contingency of art.[20] Even the claim about mad lovers and poets is perfectly in keeping with the poetological discourse.[21]

Therein, however, lies the rub. Theseus, too, is a character in a work of art, and if none of his lines represent "things unknown" that were fabricated by the author's frenzied imagination, the text establishes a clear contradiction between its metapoetic content and its own modus operandi. This argument is borne out, for example, by Barbara Mowat's analysis of the hypertextual construction of the play. As she demonstrates, Theseus,

> woven from rhetorically oppositional texts, [...] re-presents Chaucer's "noble duc," Plutarch's legendary figure of military and sexual prowess, Ovid's "most valiant Prince," and, at the same time, [Reginald] Scot's opposing passages [in his critique of fiction and credulity, *The Discoverie of Witchcraft*] that hold up to scorn all such antique fables.[22]

The argument could be taken further by comparing the Elizabethan understanding of the mental faculties, based on the Aristotelian theory of the soul, with the views articulated by Theseus. Here, however, it may suffice to point out that the character's description of poetic fervor closely matches contemporary observations; the poet John Davies, for one, writing in 1599, declares that "if a frenzy do possess the brain; / It so disturbs and blots the forms of

---

18 E. N. Tigerstedt. "*Furor Poeticus*: Poetic Inspiration in Greek Literature before Democritus and Plato." *Journal of the History of Ideas*, vol. 31, no. 2, 1970, pp. 163–178.
19 Christoph J. Steppich. *Numine afflatur: Die Inspiration des Dichters im Denken der Renaissance*. Wiesbaden: Harrassowitz, 2002.
20 Philipp Jeserich. "Legitimität und Kontingenz: Zur Lehre vom *furor poeticus* in der französischen Renaissance-Poetik (Sebillet, Du Bellay, Ronsard, Peletier du Mans)." *Romanistisches Jahrbuch*, vol. 60, 2009, pp. 108–144.
21 Alexander Cyron. "Amor als Gott der Dichter: Zur Poetologie in Cristoforo Landinos *Aeneis*-Allegorese." *Das diskursive Erbe Europas: Antike und Antikenrezeption*, edited by Dorothea Klein and Lutz Käppel. Frankfurt: Peter Lang, 2008, pp. 259–271.
22 Barbara A. Mowat. "'A local habitation and a name': Shakespeare's Text as Construct." *Style*, vol. 23, no. 3, 1989, pp. 335–351, p. 347.

things."²³ In fact, Elizabethan interest in the relationship between the imagination and "the shape of things," or the "the formes of things," – these phrases are drawn from Stephen Batman,²⁴ and Richard Surphlet's translation of André DuLaurens,²⁵ respectively – is so wide that the debate tends to turn circuitous and formulaic. Theseus' explanation of inspiration, then, is far from inspired – and its derivative occurrence in a work of literature undermines the surface meaning of the paragraph. Like Polonius in *Hamlet*, who tries to squeeze the output of the (implicitly Elizabethan) stage into the humanist's absurd analytical corset of "tragical-comical-historical-pastoral" drama (2.2.381), Theseus ranks among those Shakespearean characters who are well-educated and assertive, but betray – certainly in the eyes of a theater professional – a decisive lack of understanding of literary craftsmanship.

As Leonard Barkan reminds us, we will never be sure of the contents of Shakespeare's library; the best we can do is retrace his "reading," which for Barkan encompasses specific source texts as well as what Barthes calls the "mirage of citations" – the intertextual codes that, according to Barthes's model of the "déjà lu," dwell in every subject of language.²⁶ Likewise, the passage from the *Dream* cannot function as a literary 'statement of intent,' and it would be hazardous to use its subversion of authorial originality in any positivist attempt to reconstruct Shakespearean poetics. Nevertheless, the lines are remarkable for their negotiation of the boundaries of self and other, originality and influence. Early modern literature is frequently haunted by the ambiguities of this debate; one well-known example is the beginning of Philip Sidney's sonnet cycle, *Astrophil and Stella*, in which the Petrarchan subject finds himself "turning others' leaves" in search of inspiration until he is told by his muse to "look in thy heart and write."²⁷ Shakespeare's play, by contrast, ultimately seems to concede that the secret of creation is in the recombination of con-

---

23 John Davies. *Nosce Teipsum*. Quoted in William Rosky. "Imagination in the English Renaissance: Psychology and Poetic." *Studies in the Renaissance*, vol. 5, 1958, pp. 49–73. – Rosky's detailed analysis of contemporary sources remains a useful starting point, implicitly also demonstrating the formulaic quality of the debate.
24 Stephen Batman. *Batman uppon Bartholome*. [London, 1599.] Quoted in Rosky, "Imagination," p. 51.
25 André DuLaurens. *A Discourse of the Preservation of the Sight: of Melancholike Diseases* [...] *of Old Age*. [Translated by Richard Surphlet. London, 1599.] Quoted in Rosky, ibid.
26 Leonard Barkan. "What did Shakespeare Read?" *The Cambridge Companion to Shakespeare*, edited by Margreta de Grazia and Stanley Wells. Cambridge: Cambridge University Press, 2006, pp. 31–48, p. 45.
27 Philip Sidney. "Loving in Truth." *Astrophil and Stella*. *The Major Works*, edited by Katherine Duncan-Jones. Oxford: Oxford University Press, 2008, pp. 153–211, p. 153.

cepts, not the elusive invention of "airy nothing." In that, it is comparable to the famous passage from Francis Burton's *Anatomy of Melancholy*, where Burton, in the guise of Democritus Junior, verbosely and playfully informs the reader: "*Omne meum, nihil meum,* 'tis all mine and not mine. As a good housewife out of divers fleeces weaves one peece of Cloath, [...] I have laboriously collected this *Cento* out of divers Writers [...]. The matter is theirs most part, and yet mine, [...] the method only is mine own."[28]

In the face of such early modern self-reflections, the continuing strength of the paradigm of originality (fading, to be sure, in terms of authorial autonomy, but certainly recognizable behind the study of – implicitly distinct – national literatures) ought to come as a surprise. As recently as 2008, for example, Patrick Cheney set out to explore "the full, original, and compound form of Shakespearean authorship in a national setting."[29] Part of the problem may be that even though the stark valorization of the national begins at a later date,[30] early traces of the emphasis on the individual and the national, which Romanticism merged and developed into a critical and poetic theory, may already be found in Shakespeare's lifetime. Much like Sidney's sonnet cycle, whose speaker pretends that he is writing "from the heart," the *Midsummer Night's Dream* betrays its double vision when it comes to recognizing the transnational properties of cultural goods whilst valorizing the self over the other.

Theseus' speech in the *Dream* raises an important question: how does "the poet's pen" conspire with the poet's imagination to "give a local habitation and a name" to something immaterial – to mental constructs? We posit that the answer must leave room for three pertinent forces: culture as a net, which means that cultural artifacts are simultaneously available as the products of culture and as the raw material for continued cultural production; the power relations that determine the conditions of writing; and the author as a person or subject whose agency is liable to historical change. As a consequence, "the poet's pen" might well be read as shorthand for a nexus of poetics and politics, net structures and agencies. The analysis of these constituent parts of the poet's pen is as complex as it is rewarding, and the essays in this collection rise to the challenge by casting new light on literary production and the links between alleged national cultures. Originally presented as papers at an inter-

---

28 Francis Burton. *The Anatomy of Melancholy*, vol. 1, edited by Thomas C. Faulkner, Nicolas K. Kiessling, and Rhonda L. Blair. Oxford: Oxford University Press, 1989, p. 11.
29 Patrick Cheney. *Shakespeare, National Poet-Playwright*. Cambridge: Cambridge University Press, 2008, p. 10.
30 Michael Dobson. *The Making of the National Poet: Shakespeare, Adaptation and Authorship, 1660–1769*. Oxford: Oxford University Press, 1994.

national conference organized by the DramaNet research group at Freie Universität Berlin in April 2015, the following chapters reflect the contributors' wide range of interests and expertise; to name but a few topics, they deal with academies and religious processions, Aristotelian poetics and the theory of embodiment, acting techniques and political theory. Each text stands on its own and can be read as an illuminating case study. However, in taking us across Europe from Spain to Slovenia and Italy to England, all contributions share a deep conviction that early modern drama was a transnational enterprise, and they furnish proof that the history of early modern drama cannot be adequately told without a net theory of culture.

The collection opens with Joachim Küpper's critique of the concept of national literatures, which may be read as a programmatic essay which elaborates many of the theoretical points that could only be touched upon above. The collection then proceeds chronologically from the Cinquecento to the Enlightenment in order to illuminate sections of the cultural net in various sociopolitical constellations. While the main focus is on early modern drama, which serves as a paradigmatic test case for the application of the net theory of culture, Stephen Nichols's chapter opens up further perspectives: his account of political reform in fourteenth-century France demonstrates how the cultural net facilitated a felicitous collaboration between a late medieval king, a theologian, and an ancient Greek philosopher. The collection concludes with DS Mayfield's argument for *hypólepsis* – the discursive moment of 'tying in with' something that 'everybody knows' – as perhaps the most fundamental of human practices.

Joachim Küpper's "'National Literatures'?" offers a sustained theoretical reflection on the origin and functionalization of the paradigm of national culture and its continued application in the study of national literatures in the humanities. Analyzing the blind spots of any theory that envisions cultural material as having irreducibly autochthonous characteristics, i.e. 'roots,' Küpper engages in a critical discussion of Johann Gottfried Herder and demonstrates that the idea of a 'national literature' that is connected to a certain territory and tribe is willfully ignorant of historical realities, such as migratory movements. Küpper then argues for the necessity of a new conceptualization of cultural production, and illustrates the theory of the cultural net, thereby giving a programmatic overview that resonates with all of the subsequent case studies in this volume.

The title of Stephen Nichols's "American Presidential Candidates at the Court of Charles V: How Political Theory Trumped Political Theology in Fourteenth-Century Paris" is clearly an allusion to Mark Twain. Unlike Twain, however, Nichols is not interested in time travel – unless, of course, one counts the transtemporal enterprise of culture. Rather, he uses current misconceptions about populism as the vanishing point of his analysis of the far-reaching social reforms implemented by Charles V of France. Nichols argues that the first election of a French chancellor, which was held in 1372, constitutes a crucial step in the transition from divine-right theory to secular and participatory governance. In order to implement this shift, that is, in order to find a model that was practically suitable and ideologically sound, the French king relied on Nicole Oresme, whom he had tasked with a vernacular translation of Aristotle's works. As Nichols's comparative study shows, the king's strategy of using Aristotelian political precepts to minimize discontent within the social order was successful because it was able to make use of a textual network (which imbued the reforms with ancient *auctoritas*) even as it adapted Aristotle, in the translator's glosses and choices, to the needs of the present.

Sandra Richter's "Cross-Cultural Inventions in Drama on the Basis of the Novel in Prose: The Case of Fortunatus" offers a transnational and intermedial perspective on a "large narrative complex [...]" that consists of "strong characters, recurring plots and scenes, and moral questions relevant to their audiences." Through the Fortunatus complex – a three-generation family story that entails many travels, brushes with death, and a purse that can produce riches beyond belief –, Richter explores a constellation that has largely been neglected in literary histories: the relevance of English drama in the German-speaking parts of early modern Europe, and the contributions of English wandering actors' groups to the professionalization of German theater. Tracing the Fortunatus material across countries and genres, from a 1509 German prose novel to Thomas Dekker's "pleasant comedy" in the seventeenth century, and then back to Germany and to multiple European "Fortunati" in the eighteenth century, Richter makes a strong case for the Fortunatus artifacts as floating material. She also demonstrates how the extraction of the material from the net was interlaced with the writers' context-driven changes to the story, e.g. Thomas Dekker's supplementation of an Anglican perspective.

Esther Schomacher's "Sex on Stage: How Does the Audience Know?" introduces a comparison of two seemingly unrelated scenes: Act III, Scene 10 of Dovizi da Bibbiena's *La Calandra* and Act V, Scene 2 of Shakespeare's *Henry V*. Both scenes stage sexual relations; however, this superficial similarity is of less importance to Schomacher than the divergent ways in which the scenes shape the audience's perception and create "particular relationships" between the spectators and the action represented on the stage. Out of the early modern debate for and against the theater, Schomacher distils several questions that guide her interpretation: Are stage illusions bad, or can they impart some form of (moral) truth? Does the (moral) understanding of a play rest upon cognition, or is sensory perception important to 'make sense' of a play? Schomacher's interpretation of her examples reveals that the plays actualize conflicting stances from these contemporary discussions: *La Calandra* comes down on the side of uninvolved, detached observation, whereas *Henry V* presumes that the audience must understand the action through emotional involvement and "participatory sense-making." As a consequence, *Henry V* addresses its spectators as embodied subjects. Suggesting a new perspective with regard to the function of the two scenes, the essay stresses the influence of politics, i.e. the moral and anthropological debate, on the poetics of the theater.

Like Schomacher's contribution, Stefano Gulizia's "Castiglione's 'Green' Sense of Theater" investigates the importance of embodiment in the theatrical context. In a letter to the bishop Ludovico Canossa, Castiglione describes his production of Dovizi's *La Calandra* in Urbino in 1513. Gulizia interprets this "unusual engagement as a stage-manager" as "a representative instance of networks and public-making in early modern Italy." Finding in the letter "a genuine concern for 'media effects,'" Gulizia proceeds to analyze the precepts behind Castiglione's evident concern for the material reality of the theatrical space and its effects on the audience. The author of *The Courtier* seems fascinated by the notion of theater as an affair of the body that banks on the five senses through decoration and stage machinery, noise, involuntary laughter, or one neighbor's reactions. In Gulizia's reading of the letter to Canossa, Castiglione is far from affecting *sprezzatura* in the face of his somewhat grubby duties as stage manager. Rather, he seems to feel pride in his managerial tasks, his supervision of the actors and craftsmen, the installation of "greenery" in the theater hall. Gulizia therefore concludes that the letter is deeply engaged in negotiations of personhood and public appearance: "the groups of workers that [Castiglione] moves around as the show's director express the necessary relationship between publicity and personhood." A careful reading of the letter makes it possible "to localize the discrete publics or interest groups that made up the theatrical polity in the early modern period."

Bernhard Huss's "Luigi Groto's *Adriana*: A Laboratory Experiment on Literary Genre" introduces Groto (1541–1585) as one of the most renowned literary mannerists of the Secondo Cinquecento. A member of several academies and a frequent supervisor of the productions of his own plays, Groto was known for testing the breaking point of contemporary poetological tenets; his work in different genres – tragedies, comedies, pastoral plays – served as an "experimental set-up [...] designed to put the existing ingredients under pressure." Huss's main example, Groto's tragedy *La Hadriana* (1578), presents a sad love story and concentrates on the creation of compassion while it virtually eliminates the second tragic affect, i.e. fear. Huss's analysis reveals how Groto takes on Pietro Bembo's postulate that poetry (including verse drama) should be modelled on the diction of Petrarch's *Canzoniere*. The result, Huss finds, is a tragedy that is saturated with the stylemes of lyrical Petrarchism: a drama whose action tends to stand still. By writing play that so pointedly tests the limits of the tragic genre, Groto, as Huss argues, puts the role of the author as experimenter to the fore.

This series of assessments of the Italian sixteenth century is completed by Cristina Savettieri's paper entitled "The Agency of Errors: *Hamartia* and its (Mis)interpretations in the Italian Cinquecento." Savettieri traces how the Aristotelian concept was remodeled and thus sketches what could be called a net of interconnecting poetological positions that functions as a theoretical substratum to the artistic productions and experiments mentioned beforehand. The authors she scrutinizes range from Sperone Speroni and Giovan Battista Giraldi Cinzio to Francesco Robortello, Lodovico Castelvetro, and Giason Denores. In addition to her contributing to the more specific philological debate within the field of Italian Studies, Savettieri gives a deep insight into the early modern concern about human responsibility and suffering that still informs our modern and postmodern dealing with tragedy.

The title of Stephanie Bung's "Playful Institutions: Social and Textual Practices in Early Spanish Academies" points to a dichotomy in the history of the academies: the venerable state-sponsored institutions such as the Académie Française (1635) and the Real Academia Española (1713) were only established long after the Renaissance; for quite some time, "academy" was an ambiguous term that could refer to occasional gatherings as much as to permanent institutions. With respect to Golden Age Spain, this relative degree of freedom is borne out by the (somewhat unfortunate) fact that the early academies are poorly documented. It is on the basis of this fragile textual evidence that the Academia de los Nocturnos (1591) is often cited as a paradigm, not least because it has some structural resemblance to the academies of the following centuries. Bung's comparative analysis of the statutes of the Nocturnos and La Pítima (1608), however, identifies divergent models of what an academy could be. Even after they had been signed, the *instituciones* of La Pítima were, as Bung shows, expanded and contested for "the sheer pleasure of invention" and "the pleasure of writing." Bung argues that this textual fluidity suggests a playfulness which may well be rooted in medieval tournaments and jousts and which formed an important part of the idea of the academy in Golden Age Spain. Thus, the essay offers an important perspective on cultural networking whilst also emphasizing how easily linear trajectories (from Italian humanism to the Nocturnos to the chartered academies in France and Spain) can lead to misrepresentations of textual and institutional interconnections.

Franz Gratl's "Music in Folk Drama: An Investigation of Tyrolean Sources" explores a topic that is located somewhere "between" theater studies and musicology and consequently all too often neglected. Departing from the observation that the scarcity of research into music in folk drama by no means reflects the historical importance of music in folk theater, Gratl outlines several desiderata: What did the music sound like? Was it folk music, as one might be inclined to expect? Who composed (or arranged) it? Who performed it? What were its functions? Gratl analyzes three main sources to find answers: the Joseph Play of Axams (1677), the Christmas Play of Matrei, and the Mariahilf Play, the latter two both from the eighteenth century. After discussing some of the problems that beset research into music in folk drama (drama is often preserved in the form of the actors' scripts, which lack the musical score), Gratl is able to introduce recent discoveries in Tyrolean archives that may remedy the situation in the future. Most fascinatingly, perhaps, Gratl is able to identify instances of art music (arias, recitatives, etc.) in folk plays, and so comes to the conclusion that there are important connections between folk theater, the Baroque opera, and the German singspiel – with obvious implications for the analysis of folk theater as a constituent of the cultural net, rather than an expressivist, 'authentic' form of literature tied to local folk culture.

Erika Fischer-Lichte's "From a Rhetorical to a 'Natural' Art of Acting: What the Networks of the Seventeenth and Eighteenth Centuries Achieved" compares two interest groups that were very successful in shaping the theory (and hence practice) of acting at their time: a Jesuit network in the seventeenth century, which included artists, philosophers, and scholars of Antiquity, and an eighteenth-century network comprised of leading artists and intellectuals in England, France, Germany, and beyond. Both networks were acutely interested in finding the best way to represent a sentiment in such a way that the same feeling would be triggered in the spectator. Comparing the approaches to acting championed by the two networks, Fischer-Lichte identifies three common areas of interest: the "conceptualization of feelings" (e.g. the Jesuits' belief in a limited number of affects that seize the human subject from outside); the sources that were used "to determine and describe the most efficient representation of each feeling" (e.g. the Jesuits' reliance on Quintilian's teachings about rhetoric); and "the definition of the aims of the art of acting and theater in general" (e.g. the Jesuits' aim to create "deeply moved men" as part of the larger aim to fight back against the Reformation). Analyzing the changes from one century to the next, Fischer-Lichte connects the older Jesuit precepts to Norbert Elias's concept of the civilizing process and the pacification of the (aristocratic) body. The essay moves on to a discussion of the new ideas of sensibility and 'natural behavior' that were engendered by the rise of the bourgeois mentality. Drawing upon rich textual material to trace the cross-European discussion of empathy, Fischer-Lichte elucidates what was at stake when 'natural' acting became the norm.

Jaša Drnovšek's "Early Modern Religious Processions: The Rise and Fall of a Political Genre" locates religious processions firmly in the field of politics *sensu lato*, arguing that processions, while not unknown in Late Antiquity, became a common practice of the Roman Catholic Church only as late as the sixteenth century. Leaving behind the conventional heuristic concept of piety, Drnovšek shows that the golden age of religious processions is, not by chance, the age of Catholic renewal; therefore, he argues that processions like the one held in Montepulciano in 1539 must be seen in the context of the politics of the Tridentine church. The essay connects the spread of religious processions across (Catholic) Europe to the transnational mobility of religious orders, in particular the Society of Jesus and the Capuchin Friars Minor. Having thus tied the spread of this genre to its political capital and its institutional prerequisites (the agencies and the net structures that characterize the dyadic model suggested in our book), Drnovšek concludes his chapter with an investigation of the passion play of the Slovenian town of Škofja Loka (1725–1727). The play is remarkable not least because the whole codex including the dramatic manuscript is still extant, and Drnovšek's analysis reveals how the procession play could stage power by producing a "closed crowd" (Canetti). The anti-procession satires of Enlightenment philosophers like Anton von Bucher serve as final proof of the early modern recognition of the political value of this genre – and as an early signal of its demise, at least as a supremely political tool.

Igor Grdina's "Directions, Examples, and Incentives: Slovenian Playwriting in the Second Half of the eighteenth century" focuses on a formative period for the national identity of Slovenia and analyzes its repercussions for literary production. Grdina shows that there had been no autochthonous dramatic tradition in Slovenia before the eighteenth century, which makes evident one central claim of this book: the idea of a national culture as somehow rooted in territory and essentialized ethnicity is a Romantic fiction that obscures the inherently transnational traits of culture. Turning to the paradigmatic case of Anton Tomaž Linhart (1756–1795), Grdina discusses various aspects of the uneasy negotiation of national identity in the project of an original national literature. He shows how Linhart progressed to drama in the Slovene language, having previously written in German. The *Sturm und Drang* play *Miss Jenny Love* (1780) serves as a case in point; one might add that Linhart had even picked up the anglophilia of the likes of Goethe and Karl Philipp Moritz. In any case, and notwithstanding its lack of success, Linhart's project, as Grdina argues, always remained one of synthesis: the adaptation of cultural material from across Europe to a local context.

DS Mayfield's "Variants of *hypólepsis*: Rhetorical, Anthropistic, Dramatic (With remarks on Terence, Machiavelli, Shakespeare)" explores *hypólepsis* as the textual, discursive movement of 'picking up' what 'everyone knows,' or implicitly referring to 'what is commonly said.' Mayfield engages critically with various definitions of the term, rejecting the claim that it is a "controlled variation" (Jan Assmann) in favor of Odo Marquard's description of "Anknüpfung" ('tying in with'). This 'tying in' was envisioned by Aristotle, who used the concept of *hypólepsis* to emphasize "that philosophy takes its initial assumptions and terms from common ken, (linguistic) conventions." It is therefore evident that *hypólepsis* constitutes an important effect of the cultural net: it uses something that is "common currency," i.e. material floating in the net, and it "may also involve longer distances between the time when a notion enters cultural circulation (in a context or discourse of emittance), and when it is (randomly, non-systematically) taken up again from common knowledge." Mayfield cites anthropology as one domain in which *hypólepsis* is particularly prevalent because the question "what is a human being" is capable of producing an infinite number of replies. It is no surprise, then, that it has often been answered with statements of the hypoleptic type: "man is what everyone knows." Turning to early modern drama, Mayfield finds in Shakespeare frequent "hypoleptic allusions to the Aristotelizing 'human invariant' of man as the 'animal rationale,'" for example in *Hamlet* and *King Lear*. Moreover, Antony's speech in *Julius Caesar*, which subtly undermines the previous speech by Brutus, is cited as a "striking example as to how a concrete 'tying in with' need not share the same assumptions (to say nothing of 'principles'), nor have exclusively textual implications." Concluding his phenomenistic approach with observations on Terence, Mayfield argues that the best definition of a human being might be self-affirming: we are, as will hopefully become evident in all chapters in this volume, the "hypoleptic animal" that "takes up, ties in with, and varies".

Toni Bernhart, Jaša Drnovšek, Sven Thorsten Kilian,
Joachim Küpper and Jan Mosch

Joachim Küpper
'National Literatures'?

When we are doing literary scholarship, we almost automatically move within the frame of the concept of "national literatures." This notion is, at least to a certain extent, in contradiction to the theoretical assumption at the basis of the research project that organized this conference: namely, that literary artifacts originate in a withdrawal of material and a subsequent synthetization of material floating in a universal virtual network of cultural items.[1] But where does this notion originate, and what conclusions may – or should – we derive from the context of its emergence?

The Greeks of the classical period (like many or, perhaps, all ancient civilizations) did not care about the question to what extent their great texts were essentially "Greek" – for the simple reason that they did not deem the literary production on the part of other tribes or communities worth the effort of considering them. To put it in current terms, they were strict communitarians; universalism was a concept so far removed from their intellectual framework that they did not even compare their culture to that of the "others," the *bárbaroi*.[2] – As a first point concerning the entire debate at issue here, this observation yields the insight that the emergence of a concept like "national literatures" presupposes universalism as its background. Only if humans consider other humans as in principle equal does the question of how to define one's "own" culture with regard to the cultural products of the "others" become a relevant point.[3] – It is precisely this latter feature which is absent from

---

[1] For details see my book *The Cultural Net: Early Modern Drama as a Paradigm*. Berlin: de Gruyter, 2018; the above deliberations are taken from the manuscript of that publication.
[2] Is it necessary to make explicit that this generalizing assessment is (like all generalizing statements within the humanities) relative, that is, that it needs to be understood in relation to our modern Western situation? Since ancient Greeks maintained close economic relations with limitrophic tribes and empires, and also engaged them in military activities as early as archaic times, there was, consequently, a certain knowledge about the barbarian cultures (in contrast, for example, to the relative ignorance of the "other" in traditional China, and also to the absolute ignorance in this respect conditioned by geological factors [communities living on islands far removed from other islands (Australia); small communities living scattered in vast territories difficult to traverse (Brazil)]). But as can be inferred from emblematic literary figures – Medea, for instance – there was nothing that could compare to the relations of exchange on an equal level and the ensuing mutual esteem that are characteristic of cultural relations in the West from with the Middle Ages onwards.
[3] The above point may also be of a certain relevance with regard to the other early high civilization, China – a community that preserved its communitarian attitude of self-centeredness much longer than Greece (which, as part of the Roman Empire, adopted universalism in

the system of a classical school of thought that has been very influential in Western modernity, and which is frequently seen as a precursor of modern universalism: the Skeptics. Their tolerance of the "views" (manners, social codes, artworks) of any imaginable other tribe is not based on the assumption of equality; it emanates rather from a less aggressive interpretation of the concept of barbarism than the one to be found in Aristotle (who deemed it legitimate to treat barbarians in just the same way as wild beasts).[4] For the Skeptics, the "others" and their culture are without any importance. It is indifference and disinterest which characterizes their attitude towards foreign cultures. Since alien communities are consigned to (total) dis-consideration, there is no need to theorize what one's own culture may be in contrast to that of the "barbarians." – According to current clichés, Greek culture and its self-conception underwent a radical change in the period when the various tribes were (violently) unified and then made to spread in warfare into regions hardly known to them before. Hellenism is, on the one hand, a period of cultural imperialism, which, on the other, goes hand in hand with a partial integration of cultural patterns of the subjugated into a "new" and more comprehensive Greek culture. Still, the processes occurring in this period did not provoke reflection upon what is or was Greek (vs. non-Greek). The civilizational gap between the conquered territories and the Greek mother-land was so great that the encounter with the "others" did not pique Greek self-reflection's pre-existing self-sufficiency. Just as was the case in later times – in the period of the Western penetration into sub-Saharan Africa for example – no need for self-reflection or self-problematization emerged; the difference was cast as hierarchical, and, in addition, as categorical; as long as they did not adopt Greek culture, the conquered remained the *bárbaroi* as theorized by Aristotle: intermediate beings between animals and "real" humans, meaning Greeks. – In addition to the abovementioned feature, tribal self-consciousness ("nationalism") seems to have a second prerequisite: the presence of various tribes of an approximately comparable civilizational level within a territory that is physically – as well as

---

the fourth century CE), in fact up to the period when it was forced to "open" itself by military intervention on the part of the Western powers. Within traditional Chinese culture, there is not the slightest interest in "foreign" art works and, consequently, no need to reflect what the (dichotomously conceived) "essence" of one's "own," Chinese art is.

4 See Plutarch's summary of Aristotle's advice in this respect to his pupil Alexander (*De Alexandri magni fortuna aut virtute* I 6). There is much controversy regarding the authenticity of the passage, but such discussions seem somewhat superfluous. In his authorized works, Aristotle equates passim *bárbaroi* and *douloi* (slaves, who were most frequently of "barbarian" provenance); the juridical status of the latter was to be objects, instruments, without any human dignity or rights (see *Politics* 1252a 30 ff., and 1253b 30 ff.).

conceptually – manageable under a given standard of technological development.

Things are at first sight different, though ultimately the same, with the Romans. The Romans adopted Greek culture and literature as their own after conquering the peninsula – partly translating or emulating in Latin the basic texts, partly preserving them in their original formulation. They chose the path of self-Hellenization. There was a "strong" concept of Rome as a power and as regards its mission, but there was no specific concept of an autochthonous cultural identity linked to it.[5] One might speculate about the reasons for this quasi-absence of a *cultural* "national" identity. As occurred in Late Antiquity (when the barbaric conquerors of the empire adopted Roman culture), the difference in terms of civilizational level may have appeared so immense that the idea of casting a Roman cultural identity in contrast to Greek culture may have seemed senseless; and the inverse relation in terms of physical power may have facilitated acceptance of the narcissistic injury that accompanied the adoption of a cultural model that was not the Romans' own. – This feature of the absence of a "national" cultural identity was reinforced when Rome spread its rule over the entire Mediterranean world, integrating innumerable tribes and peculiar traditions into its empire; it was given another strong impulse through the reception of Stoicism by parts of the population and their adoption of its universalizing implications; it became definitive when the empire finally embraced, in the fourth century, the first universalistic religion ever, Christianity – thus converting the universalizing claims and speculations proffered by the Stoics into a divinely revealed truth, that is, an incontestable view.

According to a widespread belief, the situation radically changed about 1000 years later, namely with Dante's theorizing of "volgare" – that is, of the variant of classical Latin that had become the language of daily communication in Tuscany – as an instrument that is (at least on the level Dante calls "volgare illustre") no less dignified than Latin as language for literary texts. As is well known, Dante even wrote a treatise, *De vulgari eloquentia*, concerning his postulate; but it is quite telling that he wrote it in Latin.[6] Dante's views have, finally, little in common with what we currently understand by the term

---

[5] The central text establishing the rising empire's self-conception with regard to its "origins," Virgil's *Aeneid*, presents Rome as a product not of autochthony, but of transfer.
[6] In anticipation of my argument above, I should stress that the treatise is written for people writing and discussing literary texts, that is, the educated only, whereas Dante's most important text, the *Commedia* (1307–1321), is a didactic text, that is, it is conceived for general divulgation.

"national literature."[7] The dichotomy he discusses is not that of Latin vs. Italian; it is the dichotomy of "grammatica" vs. "vulgaris sermo" – that is, the standardized language of script[8] vs. the flexible and non-standardized language of oral communication. It was not Dante himself, but another of the "tre corone," namely Boccaccio, who made explicit the reasons for this claim to an equal linguistic dignity: the knowledge of "grammatica" was limited to a very restricted circle of educated people (less than 1% of the population), whereas the "volgare," in oral presentation at least, was accessible to everyone.[9] There was no ambition involved to assert a particular Italian national identity, which did not exist at the time;[10] the question at issue is that of an extremely limited vs. a general (potential) audience.

---

7 On this point see Dante's explicit rejection of every sort of "nationalism" or claims to the supremacy of one tribe over another, as resulting from a lack of reason and from the state of being uncultured ("Nam quicunque tam obscene rationis est ut locum sue nationis delitiosissimum credat esse sub sole, hic etiam pre cunctis proprium vulgare licetur, idest maternam locutionem, et per consequens credit ipsum fuisse illud quod fuit Ade. Nos autem, cui mundus est patria velut piscibus equor, quanquam Sarnum biberimus ante dentes et Florentia adeo diligamus ut, quia dileximus, exilium patiamur iniuste, rationi magis quam sensui spatulas nostri iudicii podiamus." / "For whoever is so misguided as to think that the place of his birth is the most delightful spot under the sun may also believe that his own language, his mother-tongue, that is, is pre-eminent among all others; and, as a result, he may believe that his language was also Adam's. To me, however, the whole world is a homeland, like the sea to fish; though I drank from the Arno before my teeth grew, and love Florence so much that, because I loved her, I suffer exile unjustly, I will weight the balance of my judgement more with reason than with sentiment." (*De vulgari eloquentia*, Liber primus, VI, 2–3).
8 Etymologically, *grammatica* derives from Greek *gramma*, 'letter.' Grammars or grammar books, in the modern sense of the term, are a collection of rules applicable to the written version of the language, whose limits may be transgressed (and are indeed transgressed) in oral communication.
9 I am referring to the preface of the *Decameron* where Boccaccio gives expression to the idea that his collection is written in view of a primarily female audience and, for this reason, makes use of the *volgare* instead of the *grammatica*.
10 I should like to recall, that as concerns politics Dante was a partisan of the idea of the Holy Roman Empire, and hence expected the emperor to settle the situation of civil war in Italy to which Dante had fallen victim. – In order not to get lost in details, I leave it to my readers to extrapolate how I would respond to less important objections to my above arguments (I will be addressing the more important ones, however). I shall just give one example relevant to the above postulate: there is, of course, a piece like Petrarch's famous *canzone* "Italia mia." When nineteenth-century Italians were fighting the Spaniards, the French, and the Austrians in order to accede to the state of political nation, it is not astonishing at all that this poem was read along Herderian lines, that is, as testimony to the fact that "Italians" had been longing for national unity as early as the Middle Ages (Dante's abovementioned ideas thus being neglected, however). Reading Petrarch's poem without any nationalistic emphasis, the text turns out to be anything but a dichotomous commitment; its essence is nostalgia, the

I am not sure that the situation changed substantially in the centuries we usually call the Renaissance or the Early Modern Age. The "grammaticalization" of the vernaculars – meaning their standardization, which started with Antonio de Nebrija's grammar of Castilian Spanish (1492), and which was continued in the work done by the Académie française – did indeed have implications for a concept that links cultural products mediated by language to political units. Language standardization was one important aspect in the establishment of what we call the modern state, that is, political organizations governed by rules and norms universally applicable in a certain, given territory. Yet it was not the assumption of "blood bonds" between its inhabitants that formed the basis of these territories. As may be inferred from the history of Spain in the age of the "Reyes católicos," or from that of the fragmented German principalities of that age, the rationale of early modern state-building was dynastic constellations. The concept of the nation, meaning people united not only politically – that is, by bonds or constraints of power – but also by bonds of birth, by natural bonds,[11] did not exist in that period; the link between soil, blood, and culture became a widely accepted, quasi-natural concept only in later times.

It may at first sight seem astonishing that the idea as such was not developed in the most pervasively homogenized state of the time, that is, France. The concept of *Volkskultur* is linked to the name of Johann Gottfried Herder (1744–1803). Yet if we consider the idea that not only fiction, but also the modeling of "realities," may – to a large extent – obey the imperative of compensation, it is not difficult to devise reasons why the concept of nation as a unitary culture was first developed in the German-speaking territories. There was no political unit called "Germany" at the time, and there was no prospect of creating such a unit (the modern German state was founded only around a century later by Bismarck). The concept of a "cultural nation" may have been the only way to confer unity upon a fragmented territory which seemed somewhat belated in its political development in comparison to the other important European communities (England, France, Spain).

---

longing for a period past and for the *topoi* where this period of the speaker's life took place; nostalgia, however, is a universal feeling; it emanates from our incapacity to revivify the past in ways other than by remembering. Memory is always and by necessity impregnated by nostalgia, by the feeling of loss.

11 The Latin noun *natio*, from which our modern term "nation" stems in terms of etymology, derives from the verb *nasci*, meaning "to be born."

Herder's theorizing of culture, and in particular of culture as language, that is, literature,[12] formed the basis of the Romantic concept of "national culture" throughout Europe. Whereas this approach to culture was relegated to the background in the age of avantgardism, the emergence of "new" nations after the end of colonialism revitalized it in a most remarkable way. As happened in Europe at the beginning of the nineteenth century, the process of nation-building was accompanied by a discourse aimed at delimiting what is one's own from that which belongs to others; or, to put it in current terminology, it was accompanied by an identity discourse.

Vernaculars are indeed different – this is a fact. As such, however, they are not sufficient to substantiate the postulate of identity. The long-lasting practice of vernacular plurilingualism, widespread amongst the nobility and the educated parts of the middle class, may have resulted in the impression that language alone could be an all too frail basis for postulating a cultural "identity" in a substantialist fashion. Herder's concept of *Volksliteratur* ('national literature') seemed suitable to supplement the lack. According to Herderian conceptualization, popular culture, and literature especially, is not the creation of singular geniuses; it is the collective creation of the common people, amongst whom it first emerged. By narrating and re-narrating the stories or "songs" again and again for thousands of years before the texts were put in writing in the way known to us, these texts became – according to Herder – the direct expression of the *Volksseele* (literally: 'national soul,' in the sense of national character), that is, of the entire mental cast of the people concerned. The texts were thus conceived as no less "rooted" than the people, meaning the common people (and not the highly mobile nobility and intellectual class) who were, in times before the liberation of the third estate, "rooted," just like trees and plants.

The – at first sight striking – evidence of this conceptualization seems to be further confirmed by the fact that there are features of human culture directly contingent upon the conditions that obtain in a specific habitat. The architecture of houses as well as dresses and dress-styles, nutrition, etc., are indeed

---

[12] Specialists on Herder's work will not be satisfied by the following portrayal of his positions; but my argument does not address specialists. The concession I would be ready to make is that Herder's argumentation is self-contradictory with regard to many problems (as I shall point out in the course of this paper). But the "racist" component that I will be foregrounding is undeniably a most prominent element of his entire thinking. In addition, I should stress that it is not my intention to give an adequate and balanced precis of Herder's theorizing in its entirety, nor to offer speculations regarding the question what he might "really" have thought. When it comes to the *reception* of Herder's ideas, that is, to their resonance, the point here stressed seems indeed to be by far the most relevant one.

dependent on climate and on geological factors (mountains, plains, the shore, etc.). Since literary texts were apparently different in different regions – the indicator of difference being the difference in language – it seemed self-evident to transpose this concept of the rootedness of cultural practices onto literary texts, with popular texts given first place, and so to arrive at the well-known and still virulent notion of *Volksliteratur* as an expression of *Volksseele*.[13]

One might add a detail of German cultural history touched upon in passing above: the entire theorizing of Herder had one aim, which shines through on almost every page of his tracts. German eighteenth-century culture was under a strong influence from France. Noblemen, as well as intellectuals, mainly communicated in French. German seventeenth-century – that is, baroque – literature was conceived of as "barbaric"; it is indeed somewhat odd, linguistically, as well as conceptually. The treasures of medieval Middle High German literature were largely unknown at the time. Herder is one of those people – such as exist in all tribes and at all times, including the present – who, for whatever reason, were opposed to this early vogue of "globalization," that is, the absorption of cultural entities performing less well by those that perform better. He was a communitarian. In order to stake his claim that German culture is worthy of being valorized, he could not do other than postulate that there is an "essential" difference between French *civilisation* on the one hand, and an "authentic" German *Kultur* on the other.

It is striking, however, to see the innumerable logical twists that this highly learned man is obliged to make in order to give his rather bizarre – but influential – conceptualization the semblance of argumentative coherence. The most illustrative example of these hardly believable logical leaps and gaps may be

---

13 As I shall stress in the following, the resonance of Herder's ideas in the Latin world was less important than within the Germanic and Slavic territories; but resonance there was, in particular in the first half of the nineteenth century with its cult of *couleur locale*. On the level of theory, Herder's ideas were an inspiration for the concepts of a cultural theorist as influential as Hippolyte Taine, who propagated the parameters of *race, milieu et moment* as determinant factors for all cultural production. And even in the twentieth century there are influences from Herderian concepts in French culture. As an example, I shall quote a passage from Guillaume Apollinaire against the backdrop of which my above polemics are formulated: "Furthermore, poets must always express a milieu, a nation; and artists, just as poets, just as philosophers, form a social estate which belongs doubtless to all humanity, but as the expression of a race, of one given environment. Art will only cease being national the day that the whole universe, living in the same climate, in houses built in the same style, speaks the same language with the same accent, that is to say never." ("The New Spirit and the Poets" [1918]. *Selected Writings*, translated by Roger Shattuck, New York: New Directions, 1971, p. 229.)

his portrait of English literature.[14] The English tradition is presented as *Germanic*, and so as the expression of a *Geist* that is parallel if not identical to that of the Germans residing on the continent. The assumption is "substantiated" by way of a brief recapitulation of the political history of the British Isles, which gives prominence to the numerous invasions by Scandinavian tribes. There is not much room for the Celtic part of the English tradition in this narrative. Yet, above all, there is no room for a capital event like the conquest of 1066. It is simply not mentioned by Herder. From that date onward, English language and culture have been a mix of Celtic, Germanic, and Latin (French) elements – the latter feature linking all subsequent English culture to the entirety of the Greco-Roman heritage and its Mesopotamian, Egyptian (etc.) antecedents.

Herder's blindness in this respect also encompasses his eulogy of Shakespeare as a Teutonic genius who supposedly gave expression to the *Volksgeist* of all Germanic tribes. Not a word is said about Shakespeare's drawing from Latin, Italian, Spanish, and Greek sources. Herder's readers are given the impression that Shakespeare's dramas mainly consisted of appearances by ghosts, witches, and other related strands apt to refute the superficiality of French rational *civilisation* in the name of a Germanic *Kultur* – whose attribute would be its being linked to dimensions of a "higher" or "deeper" truth not accessible by plain reason.

On a more general level, the argumentative weakness of Herder's tracts becomes apparent in a recurrent – and rather amazing – feature. On the one hand, the author relentlessly stresses that "authentic" culture is bound to the space and to the "race" inhabiting the space in question. If that was the case, we would have "national cultures" as diverse as the spaces on this globe (temperate, cold, hot climatic regions; coastal, maritime spaces, plains, deserts, mountains, etc., etc.); but Herder himself again and again "detects" – with a quasi-childlike joy and enthusiasm – that all these different cultures bear far-reaching commonalities if one goes back far enough in time. The "pristine" products of the different national cultures are analogous, if not identical. In congruence with the findings of emerging evolutionary biology, Herder advocates the thesis of the species' monogenesis.[15] In formulations to be found

---

14 See the two essays "Shakespear" (1773) and "Von der Ähnlichkeit der mittleren englischen und deutschen Dichtkunst"; one should also read "Auszug aus einem Briefwechsel ueber Ossian und die Lieder alter Völker" (1773); quotations are from the standard edition (*Sämmtliche Werke*, edited by Bernhard Suphan, 32 vols. Berlin: Weidmann, 1877–1909, vol. 5, pp. 159–257 and vol. 9, pp. 522–535); translations are mine.
15 The following arguments are most clearly expressed in *Auch eine Philosophie der Geschichte zur Bildung der Menschheit* (1774), in: *Sämmtliche Werke*, vol. 5, pp. 475–593, par. 7/8, 12/13 and 16/17.

some decades later in myriad texts by Romantic writers, he praises the "patriarch's tent" as the first and best model of human congregation. The "values," cultural as well as societal, that developed out of this "ground" are

> wisdom instead of science, piety instead of knowledge, the love of parents, spouses, children instead of pleasantries and debauchery. Life well-ordered, the rule by divine right of a dynasty – the model for all civil order and its institutions – in all this mankind takes the simplest, but also the most profound delight. [...] The human spirit received the first forms of wisdom and virtue with a simplicity, strength, and majesty that [...] has no equal, no equal at all in our philosophical, cold, European world. And just because we are so incapable of understanding this anymore, of feeling it, let alone taking delight in it, we mock, we deny, and we misconstrue!

And he ends his diatribe (addressing his contemporary educated readers) by apostrophizing "your philosophical deism, your aesthetic virtue [...] your universal love of all peoples" as mere foolishness.[16] – Herder does not discuss explicitly what factor vitiated this early literature of "direct" expression of the people's *Seele*; but it is evident what he had in mind (perhaps even unconsciously): it is rationality, refinement, progress – in brief: civilization – that has brought about the detrimental move away from literature as the expression of the *Volksseele*.

Herder is a (proto-)Romantic – but a naïve Romantic. He posits as "true" and "essential" what more enlightened thinkers of that age, such as Schiller, would apostrophize as a (legitimate) longing for a past that is past, which may (legitimately) be re-created by way of works of art, though under the condition that these works preserve and manifest the artificial character of the re-creation. This is the essence of Schiller's concept of the *Sentimentalisches* as opposed to the *Naives*,[17] meaning by this latter the "authentic" vestiges of pristine human culture. – It remains an open question, however, whether such a "naïve" approach to the conceptualizing of the world ever existed. It may be that mediation – in other words: the introduction of language and reflection – put an end to all such "naïveté" grounded in "immediateness" (*Unvermitteltheit*), which would thus be an attribute not of the human, but of the animal world.

I should like to make one additional point with regard to Herder's theorizing, and to the innumerable theories, up to and including postcolonialism, that are more or less direct continuators of these ideas. As already mentioned in passing, it is not without reason that concepts about literary texts and rooted-

---

[16] Par. 18/19.
[17] See *On Naïve and Sentimental Poetry* (1795).

ness first came up in a German context; nor does it seem astonishing that they were enthusiastically received in northern and eastern Europe, nor that they later found avid recipients in Latin America,[18] and in the entire (former) Third World and amongst its intellectuals. The resonance of such ideas in the strongholds of Occidental culture (France, Italy, Spain, England, in later times also in the USA) was always rather limited. The reason is a very simple one. It would be completely meaningless to claim that French (Italian, Spanish, etc.) literary culture was the expression of the *Geist* or *Seele* of tribes residing in these territories from time immemorial, for two different – but intertwined – reasons. The people living in these countries cannot be unaware that their ancestors have not been "rooted" in the soil for thousands and thousands of years; that they are rather the descendants of a somewhat wild mix of locals (Celtic), Roman conquerors (meaning: people from the Mediterranean in a very broad sense of the term), and Scandinavian conquerors of the Roman Empire (Goths, Normans). Secondly, they also cannot be unaware that their language, as well as their entire culture – and including literary texts – is to a very large extent the result not of "rootedness,"[19] but rather of transfer (*translatio imperii*,

---

[18] It is perhaps no surprise to note that – amongst others, including the most famous Brazilian novelist to date, Machado de Assis – it was Jorge Luis Borges who polemicized, imbued by irony in his typical way, against the widespread ideas of a peculiar Latin American (or even: Argentine, Mexican, Brazilian) literature, which came up in the age of Latin American "nation building": "The idea that Argentine literature must abound in differential traits and in Argentine color seems to me to be a mistake. [...] Furthermore, I don't know if it needs to be said that the idea that a literature must define itself by the differential traits of the country that produces it is a relatively new one, and the idea that writers must seek out subjects local to their country is also new and arbitrary. [...] The Argentine cult of local color is a recent European cult that nationalists should reject as a foreign import." ("The Argentine Writer and Tradition." *Selected Non-Fictions*, edited by Eliot Weinberger, translated by Esther Allen. New York: Penguin, 2000, pp. 421–427).

[19] Let me note in passing that the most important French precursor of Romanticism, Rousseau, bases his description of primordial sedentary communities, no less tainted by nostalgia than Herder's, not on the assumption of family ("blood") bonds between the members, but on the concept of contract (*contrat social*). This said, there is – as I shall briefly explain in the following – a strong influence from Herder's ideas in the two or three decades of "acute" Romanticism, in authors like Chateaubriand and Lamartine. – One has to add a special remark concerning (vernacular) literary studies as a discipline taught in the universities: this is an "invention" of the early nineteenth century. It simply did not exist previously, as literary studies treated the classical texts (Greek, Latin) only. Readers not familiar with the situation may find amazing what is, indeed, a fact: French literary studies were first established in Germany, in the newly founded, Humboldtian-style university of Bonn, by Friedrich Diez, the first professor ever appointed for the study of Romance languages and literatures (1830). It is not very difficult to imagine that literary studies at early nineteenth-century German universities were practiced along Herderian lines. And there is, indeed, one section of Post-Classical, European

going hand in hand with a *translatio studii*). In the Latin parts of Europe (including England), culture is evidently a product of the working of network-like structures, and of their constant – and finally uncontrollable – ramifications.

The difference, I would argue, from the situation in regions like the Germanic lands, eastern Europe, and those parts of the former Third World that were not totally absorbed into Western culture during the process of colonization,[20] does not consist in a difference in the situation itself; it is the *consciousness* of the situation that differs. The fact that "tribes," as well as "tribal cultures," are not something stable or "rooted," but rather the result of constant processes of exchange of genes and memes, cannot remain unknown in eras

---

literature that ideally fits the Herderian parameters, namely Medieval Literature. Consequently, modern (nineteenth-century) literary studies were in their origin almost exclusively medievalist. As Middle High German texts are to a large extent based on French models, the first literary scholars in Germany studied not only their "own," but also the Medieval French texts as well – which were largely unknown in their country of origin at that time, with the exception of troubadour lyric. This section of the French literary patrimony had been re-discovered already by François-Juste-Marie Raynouard (*Choix de poésies originales des troubadours* [1816–1821]), who was deeply influenced by Herderian concepts; his endeavors were carried on by Claude Fauriel, the first professor ever at the Sorbonne to hold a chair for "littératures étrangères" (1830). Fauriel had absorbed the basic concepts of German Romanticism as a close acquaintance of Mme de Staël, the author of the famous book *De l'Allemagne* (1810), which is seen as the first manifestation of "Romantic" ideas in the French language. Scholars like Gaston Paris, who had studied with Diez, began systematically to establish French literary studies, emulating the "German" way, that is, with an accent on medievalism. In 1835, Francisque Michel, a young scholar inspired by these new ideas, traveled to England. In the Bodleian Library he found the manuscript of the *Song of Roland* and thus "created" what has since then been the French "national" epic. Gaston Paris and his followers absorbed the Herderian ideas about "rootedness," although, as I say above, these do not make much sense in a French cultural context (this is, by the way, the reason why the very first "Herderian" medievalist in France, Jean-Charles-Léonard Simonde de Sismondi [an amateur scholar, much better known as an economist] had excluded French literature from his *De la littérature du midi de l'Europe* [1813]: it is all too obviously influenced by classical [Latin] models and thus does not fit the Herderian parameters). Herderian concepts were extremely influential up into the twentieth century and go on resonating in French literary studies. It was another decisive step, leading directly to what literary studies still are in French universities up to the present, when pupils of these medievalists transposed the concept of "national literature" into more recent periods (see Hans Ulrich Gumbrecht. "*Un souffle d'Allemagne ayant passé*: Friedrich Diez, Gaston Paris, and the Genesis of National Philologies." *Romance Philology*, no. 40, 1986/1987, pp. 1–37).

20 As for Latin America, where this total absorption did happen, the enthusiastic reception of Herderian ideas is linked to a massive revalorization of the Pre-Colombian, that is, Indian heritage. Similar to what happened in eighteenth-century Germany, but on a much more frail basis (since there is not much left from Pre-Colombian times), the rediscovery of the "autochthonous" tradition is part of the attempt at emancipation from the culture of the colonial "oppressor."

when the documentation of the past has become a routine practice. The French (Italians, Spanish) simply *know* from written evidence what their history has been, from roughly the first centuries before the Common Era onward; and they cannot deny what they and everyone else knows, however strong their longing for "rootedness" may be. In these countries, Romanticism (except for very brief periods) has always remained a mind-frame of the uncultured, the peripheral, and the non-intellectual parts of the population. In the Germanic territories, the past is known only from the age of Charlemagne onward; as for eastern Europe, the threshold of documentation lies in even later times. Since substantial written records of the past are lacking, central and eastern European nations have a tendency to *construct* a past, building their construals on the basis of their longing for certainty and stability in a world where these do not exist, where "substance" is nothing but a phantasm produced by the imagination. The political and ideological instability of many of the central and eastern European nations (and in addition: of Third World nations[21]) is, in part at least, closely linked to the fact that their historical belatedness favors attitudes concerning self-reflection that come close to a loss of reality.

There may be objections to the conceptualization of literary traditions that is implicitly hinted at above – objections that emanate from a text corpus that lies outside the temporal frame of our project, but is of particularly high importance for all (Western) literature of the more recent past, namely the nineteenth-century European novel, and especially texts we usually subsume under the heading of realism: that is, novels by Dickens, Balzac, Flaubert, Tolstoy, Fontane, to mention just a few well-known authors. Reading these novels and studying them[22] may (indeed) convey to the reader the impression

---

[21] A nation and culture as great as India first became Westernized by physical force, but later adopted Western ideals (equality, democracy) on its own volition; with certain qualifications ("people's democracy" instead of Westminster-style democracy) this description applies as well to another of the great nations and cultures in global history, China. When present-day Chinese party-officials make it their task to reassert a "Chinese identity" by fending off detrimental "Western influence," they are not aware of the extent to which they are (unconsciously) reproducing and thus falling prey to a basic concept of Western Romanticism. It remains to pray to the gods that Chinese leaders will become conscious of this constellation before they give in to the temptation to start nineteenth-century-European-style tribal wars. – Why does India seem to perform better on the stage of global politics? In contrast to China, India never knew the situation of physical predominance of one ethnic community (in China: the Han); religiously, linguistically, in terms of mores, India is a culture of myriad facets. To claim an Indian or Indic identity in terms of dichotomies ("we" vs. "the others") is much less favored by the realities than in other parts of the world, including the European nation states.

[22] Starting with my doctoral dissertation, I published a lot, and continuously, on European nineteenth-century novels and on the theoretical issues involved in the notion of realism (*Balzac und der 'Effet de réel'. Ästhetik der Wirklichkeitsdarstellung*. Amsterdam: Grüner, 1986;

of "feeling" or "sensing" the essence of "Frenchness" or of "Prussianness" – that is, of the specificity of what life in Paris or in the remote *province* was like at the times of Charles X or of Louis Philippe, or what it was like in Prussia during the era of Bismarck. Considering this mighty strand of literary realism – a tradition that has been declared obsolete many times, while it goes on flourishing, in particular in North America, but also experiences most impressive "renaissances," or even "resurrections" in Europe again and again, usually right after being declared definitively "dead" a couple of years before – is it sensible to hold that a category like "national literatures" is misconceived right from the start?

The question is evidently linked to the difference of genre, and in particular to the device of description, especially the description of places – that is, to literary topography. Balzac's famous portrayal of the *quartier latin* which culminates in the description of the *pension Vauquer* where the young Rastignac will spend his first two years in the capital and where he decides to do everything and anything to leave behind definitively such petty-bourgeois misery for the rest of his life; Flaubert's description of the city of Rouen when Emma Bovary first sees it and is fascinated by this modern "Babylon" and hence ready to behave as people in such cities do ("Cela se fait à Paris,"[23] is Léon's argument that convinces her to get on the coach in which their first sexual encounter takes place); or Fontane's description of the winter landscape on the shores of the Baltic sea, the description of which – by conveying an atmosphere of oppressive provinciality and of "nothing will ever happen here" – makes it all the more plausible that Effi Briest would succumb to the sophisticated seduction techniques of von Crampas (the first adulterous encounter takes place inside a sleigh when the Briests and a number of other people ride home after a very boring New Year's reception in a village nearby[24]) – all of these and a number of other famous descriptions seem to be inextricably linked to certain specific places which we are used to taking as

---

Zum italienischen Roman des 19. Jahrhunderts. Foscolo, Manzoni, Verga, D'Annunzio. Stuttgart: Steiner, 2002; "Das Ende von Emma Bovary." *Geschichte und Text in der Literatur Frankreichs, der Romania und der Literaturwissenschaft. Festschrift Rita Schober zum 80. Geburtstag*, edited by Hans Otto Dill, Berlin: Trafo, 2000, pp. 71–93; "Mimesis und Botschaft bei Flaubert." *Romanistisches Jahrbuch*, vol. 54, 2004, pp. 180–212; "Considérations sur *Salammbô*." *MLN*, vol. 125, 2010, pp. 731–782; "Fiacre et grenier. Quelques remarques sur *Madame Bovary* et *Effi Briest*." *La lecture insistante: autour de Jean Bollack*, edited by Christoph König and Heinz Wismann, Paris: Michel, 2011, pp. 255–284).

23 The quotes are from the *troisième partie, chapitre I*.
24 See chap. 19.

emblematic, as places concentrating the "essence" of specific national cultures in a specific period.

In response, I should first like to point out the trivial consideration that we do not have such descriptions in drama, or in poetry. In the case of drama, we typically get some information concerning time and place, but these indications almost always remain at a very elementary level. At the beginning of *Hamlet*, we are told that the castle where the action is taking place is located in Denmark; but there is nothing particularly Danish about the place or the people who live there.[25] The same holds true for the "Polish" setting of Calderón's *La vida es sueño*, or the Spanish setting of Corneille's *Cid*, to say nothing of the "Trézène" and Athens of Racine's *Phèdre*. And even if the setting is from the same period as the process of writing it down, and if the place is located in a region where the language in which the play is written is the "official" language (as is the case with Shakespeare's histories, or, in a later period, Ibsen's and Strindberg's dramas), one would not read or see these plays as instances of a specific "Britishness" or a specific "Scandinavianness."[26] – The only relevant difference between such plays and narrative texts written in the same languages is that, in one case, there is topographical description, whereas in the other there is none or close to none. In a theoretical perspective this might – at first sight – lead to the assumption that there are "national literatures" on the one hand (the novel, particularly the realist novel), and more or less trans-national or non-national literatures on the other (drama, poetry). If put in a nutshell in this way, the view just described exposes, so to speak, the

---

25 It is well known that the drama does discuss (though not very frequently) the question "what is Danish?" The most detailed answer to the question given in Shakespeare's text is, as is known just as well, that they would be heavy drinkers (I. 4. 16–18); given the present-day statistics on alcohol consumption in European countries in general, which seem to describe deeply rooted habits, one is inclined to say that if national character is based on nothing else, there is no such national character (at least not in Shakespeare's play).

26 See, on this point, once again the already mentioned polemics by Machado de Assis and Borges against the Herderian/Romantic concept of literature: "I shall [...] ask if *Hamlet*, *Othello*, *Julius Caesar* and *Romeo and Juliet* have anything to do with the history of England or the British territory, and if, nevertheless, Shakespeare is not, as well as a universal genius, an essentially English poet." ("Notícia da atual literature brasileira. Instinto de nacionalidade" [1873]. Joaquim Maria Machado de Assis. *Obra completa*. Rio de Janeiro: Nova Aguilar, 1962, vol. 3, pp. 801–809; my translation). "I think that Racine would not have begun to understand anyone who would deny him his right to the title of French poet for having sought out Greek and Latin subjects. I think Shakespeare would have been astonished if anyone had tried to limit him to English subjects, and if anyone had told him that, as an Englishman, he had no right to write *Hamlet*, with its Scandinavian subject matter, or *Macbeth*, on a Scottish theme." (Borges, "The Argentine Writer and Tradition," p. 423).

extent to which it is meaningless. Yet it must be said that what I have just formulated describes the tacit and unreflected basis of current studies in the field of literary history. The propagation of Herder's concepts was fueled by the "rise of the novel" to the status of dominant genre that has occurred since the beginning of the nineteenth century.

This brings me back to my general assumption that the concept of "national literature" is generated by the non-problematized (over-)interpretation of the bond that literary texts of any kind by necessity maintain to the extra-literary "reality" from which they originate. The primary bond is language, which is a given for any literary text. If we leave aside experiments such as Esperanto, every literary text is written in a specific language that originates from one specific community.[27] The second feature that links fictional texts to factual realities – while nurturing the illusion described above – is, indeed, topography. Since "places" (cities, mountains, lakes [think of the wonderful description of Lake Como at the beginning of Manzoni's *Promessi sposi*!]), and landscapes are "realities," a literary text that marks the fictional topography by giving it the name of an existing place is, more or less inevitably, conceived by recipients as being "organically" linked to this specific place. The more detailed the description is and the more "real" items (famous churches, well-known street-names, topographical characteristics of any kind in the case of landscape descriptions) it contains, the more the recipients are inclined to see the entire *story* as being linked to this specific place, and so as being emblematic of its specificity – that is, of its being *substantially* different from stories that could have happened in other places during the same period.

Let me come back to two famous novels mentioned above: what, in essence, is the difference between *Madame Bovary* and *Effi Briest*? There is, of course, a huge difference; Fontane's most famous novel is not just a re-writing of Flaubert's text. There is a difference in "atmosphere," as one might say. The somewhat "over-heated" and hyper-active temperament of Flaubert's heroine – culminating in her most dramatically "staged" suicide – is countered by the reserved and subdued way of talking and acting of Fontane's most prominent female figure. Even so, the basic action: a woman more or less lured into a marriage of convenience to a man she hardly knows, the incongruence of the couple's characters, needs, and desires, the relative stupidity of the (benevolent) husband, who does not realize that his wife is unhappy, the frustrated

---

[27] The intricate question of the relationship between (a specific) language and (a specific) literary text requires a frame that would far exceed the limits of this paper. The forthcoming book, from which the above deliberations are taken, contains a detailed discussion of the problem.

wife's falling prey to an experienced seducer, the gloomy ending with the heroine's premature death, the lasting incomprehension as regards the entire constellation on the mourning widower's part – all this is basically parallel. Differences in detail are more or less linked to the difference in social class. But the classes as such – petty bourgeois on the one hand, the nobility serving as high-ranking state officers on the other – are not at all specific. Consequently, it would be relatively easy to identify all the features from Fontane's text for which there is no direct equivalent in Flaubert's text in other realistic novels from the French tradition that are set in a social sphere comparable to *Effi Briest*; in particular, I would think of Balzac's *Le Lys dans la vallée*.

I would argue that the integration of extra-textual, "real" material into a literary text bestows upon recipients the *illusion* that the link is not unidirectional; that it, rather, operates in both directions. Since the action of *Madame Bovary* is set in nineteenth-century Normandy, we believe that this action is typical of the provincial France of that age. Yet seen logically, the operation just apostrophized is a reverse. In the narrative sequence mentioned above, it is not the city of Rouen that is of any importance; it is Rouen as a paradigm of the 'big city,' which is utilized to render plausible Emma's actions, which are not at all specifically French; unhappy marriages seem to be a rather universal phenomenon; the same holds true with respect to Fontane's description of the desolate Pomeranian coast; and in Balzac's *Père Goriot*, the portrait of the miserable Paris on the one hand, the splendid Paris on the other, have the function of motivating what the entire text is about: ambition ("parvenir! Parvenir à tout prix"[28]) – an impulse that is, at least according to the account in the Hebrew Bible, the most fundamental and universal characteristic of humans.

Still, doesn't the argument expounded here reduce literary texts to a collection of motifs? In some way it does indeed. The main difference from existing framings of what literary texts (and cultural products in general) are, is that my approach rejects the view that there would be *substantive* intermediate levels between what I call the material floating in the net and the actual, singular work. The latter is specific in any case: otherwise it is nothing but an instance of trivial literature, whose mark is pervasive standardization. Flaubert's text is, indeed, different from Fontane's. Yet what is questioned here is the assumption that the difference consists mainly of being a typically "French" version of the story of a woman in an unhappy marriage on the one hand, and a typically "German"/"Prussian" version on the other. The basic difference is one of individual ingenuity. All the other differences, as I argue here, regarding extra-

---

28 I quote from the edition of the text to be found in vol. 2 of the *Comédie humaine*, edited by Marcel Bouteron. Paris: Gallimard, 1971 (Bibliothèque de la Pléiade), p. 935.

textual "real" material (the reference to Catholic religious practices and officials in Flaubert, to Protestant ones in Fontane; the reference to *sous-préfets* in Flaubert, to *Landräte* in Fontane; the reference to the endlessly stretching meadows in Flaubert, to the endless sea in Fontane, etc., etc.) are necessary components of texts of this genre and from the century in question; but their specificity is irrelevant for the problem of what makes the texts works of art. This irrelevance is underpinned by the fact that readers totally unfamiliar with the "real stuff" integrated into the respective texts (people who have never traveled to Normandy, or who have never had the chance to experience the Prussian territories known as *ostelbisch*[29]) read them with great delight – and with no less delight, it seems, than people from the "national culture" from which the texts originate; this evaluation may be, I might say in parentheses, the point that differentiates works of "world literature" from all the rest of literary production.[30]

---

29 Do I need to stress that for a West German of my generation (I was born in 1952), this latter constellation did, indeed, apply for all of my readings of Fontane's novel that occurred before the reunification of Germany (1990)? Although I never experienced the regions "described" in these texts before the age of maturity, my impression as a young person (a very naïve view, as I would now say) was that the rendering of the landscape in Fontane was perfectly matched to the "realities," and that the personages and their interaction were "typically" Bismarckian-Prussian.
30 In respect of this see my "Some Remarks on World Literature." *Approaches to World Literature*, edited by Joachim Küpper, Berlin: de Gruyter, 2013, pp. 167–175.

Stephen G. Nichols
American Presidential Candidates at the Court of Charles V: How Political *Theory* Trumped Political *Theology* in Fourteenth-Century Paris

Prologue

"Populism" has been a favorite descriptor for journalists analyzing the appeal of Bernie Sanders and Donald Trump in the presidential primary campaign of 2016. But what, exactly, does the term mean in this context? Is it rigorously descriptive, or a convenient trope? Given the exigencies of media journalism, we should not be surprised to find that it suffers the kind of distortion characteristic of political races. Either it is globalized to reflect political movements in South America, Europe, North Africa, and the Middle East, or it is localized as an expression of disaffection among certain sectors of each party.[1]

There have been some valiant efforts to point out that neither Sanders nor Trump qualifies as a populist in the traditional sense of the term because they are both "working – however reluctantly – within the established order." As William Greider noted in *The Nation* last fall, "By definition, populism requires plain people in rebellion, organizing themselves to go up against the reigning powers." Such was the case of the "People's Party in the last decades of the nineteenth century, which was self-organized by scattered groups of distressed farmers." On 4 July 1892, in Omaha, Nebraska, the populists formally launched their party with a platform containing ten resolutions – of which the ninth opposed national subsidy or aid to any private corporation for any purpose, and the tenth supported the Knights of Labor's right to organize.

James B. Weaver, the presidential candidate of the People's Party in 1892, carried four states, gleaning him 22 electoral votes, thanks to over a million popular votes. The party itself took 11 seats in the US House of Representatives,

---

[1] See, for example, William Greider. "Bernie, Donald, and the Promise of Populism." *The Nation*, 21 September 2015 (www.thenation.com/article/bernie-donald-and-the-promise-of-populism. Accessed 13 February 2018), and John Cassidy. "Bernie Sanders and the New Populism." *The New Yorker*, 3 February 2016.

Note: My title refers to American presidential candidates in the 2016 primary campaign, while referencing Mark Twain's 1889 novella, *A Connecticut Yankee at King Arthur's Court.*

https://doi.org/10.1515/9783110536690-003

elected several governors, and attained a majority in the state legislatures of Kansas, Nebraska, and North Carolina.

As we know, however, historical accuracy is not a high priority for political journalism, so the "new populism" may continue to define the antiestablishment sentiment on the right that Trump has successfully exploited. And that's too bad, in a way, since it is not politics that galvanizes Trump and Sanders supporters, but hope; the hope that these candidates will remedy long-standing symptoms of social disaffection. The latter is far from novel. As Robert Pippin argued some years ago,

> postmodernism is a culture of dissatisfactions with the affirmative, normative claims essential to European modernization. [...] A culture of melancholy [and] profound skepticism [...] [led to] the experience of modernism as some kind of spiritual failure, of modernity as loss [...] [expressed by] images of death, loss, and failure, in a language of anxiety, unease, and mourning.[2]

Pippin consciously speaks of "a culture of disaffections" (in the plural) because he sees the skeptical, melancholic condition as being a recurrent trait of modernism. Like economic cycles, the culture of disaffection also waxes and wanes with periodic popular outpouring of frustration and discontent. In this, he channels Marx's dictum: "Men make their own history, but they do not make it as they please; they do not make it under self-selected circumstances, but under circumstances existing already, given and transmitted from the past."[3] Unlike Marx, however, Pippin does not perceive recurrent cycles of popular discontent as "the tradition of all dead generations weighing like a nightmare on the brains of the living."[4] He sees them rather as a natural consequence of "modern, market-based, liberal democratic societies [...] that create straightforward practical and political problems calling for corrective or progressive action."[5]

Philosophy, for Pippin, offers, as it has since Plato, a key to assessing such problems and to formulating just and effective proposals to correct them. Treatises of moral and political philosophy exist to redress disaffection within the

---

[2] Robert Pippin, *Modernism as a Philosophical Problem: on the Dissatisfactions of European High Culture*. 2nd Edition. Oxford: Blackwell, 1999, pp. xi–xii.
[3] Karl Marx. *The Eighteenth Brumaire of Louis Napoléon* (1852) ("Die Menschen machen ihre eigene Geschichte, aber sie machen sie nicht aus freien Stücken unter selbstgewählten, sondern unter unmittelbar vorhandenen, gegebenen und überlieferten Umständen." *Karl Marx/ Friedrich Engels Gesamtausgabe (MEGA)*, vol. I, 11. Berlin: Dietz, 1985, pp. 96–189, p. 96 f.)
[4] "Die Tradition aller todten Geschlechter lastet wie ein Alp auf dem Gehirne der Lebenden." (Ibid., p. 97)
[5] Pippin, *Modernism as a Philosophical Problem*, p. xiii.

social order. The problem is not the lack of a blueprint for a just society that minimizes discontent, but the ability – or desire – of the political class to adopt and implement such visions. There are precedents for such experiments in governance, however, even as far back as the Middle Ages. Perhaps no such premodern effort was as fascinating as the attempt by King Charles V of France (1364–1380) to implement social reform in his kingdom based on the precepts of Aristotle's political philosophy.

Charles V and Aristotle's *Politics*

On a deep winter's day in 1372, an unprecedented event took place in Paris at the court of King Charles V. For the first time in French history, the king filled the office of Chancellor of France by election. The chancellorship was the second most important administrative post of the kingdom, an office so crucial that French kings traditionally entrusted it only to aristocrats. But in this case Charles summoned his council – some two hundred churchmen, aristocrats, bourgeois, and others – to his residence at the Hôtel Saint-Pol for deliberation and a vote.[6]

Charles's decision to fill the office by election was so unusual that the writer of the *Grandes chroniques de France*, who recorded it, seems not to have known what to make of it.[7] While qualifying it as *notable eleccion*, "a noteworthy election," he disposed of it in a single sentence, embedded in an account of the resignation of the previous Chancellor, Cardinal Jean de Dormans, Bishop of Beauvais, and brother of the newly elected chancellor.[8]

---

6 "Le 21 février de cette année, Charles V convoqua en l'hôtel de Saint-Pol tous les membres de son conseil pour prendre part à l'élection d'un nouveau chancelier. Le mot conseil doit être pris ici dans le sens le plus large, puisque le greffier du Parlement évalue à deux cents environ le nombre des votants, prélats, barons, et autres." (Siméon Luce. "De l'élection au scrutin de deux chanceliers de France sous le règne de Charles V." *Revue historique*, vol. 16, no. 1, 1881, p. 95.)

7 "L'élection au scrutin d'un chancelier de France [...] était une nouveauté qui dut frapper vivement les contemporains." (Ibid., p. 96.)

8 "*Item*, le samedi .xxie. jour de fevrier .mccclxxi. desus dit monseigneur Jean de Dormans, Cardinal nomé de Biauvais, pour ce que il avoit esté evesque de Biauvais, lors chancellier de France, rendy au Roy les seaulx de France, et laissa l'office de chancellerie. *Et par notable elecion fist le Roy chancellier monseigneur Guillaume de Dormans chevalier, frere germain du dit cardinal de Biauvais*. Et ainsi fut le dit cardinal de Biauvais chancellier depuis que il avoit esté cardinal par l'espasse de trois ans et .iiii. mois. Car il avoit esté fait cardinal le .xxiie. jour de septembre .mccclxviii. et avoit [fol. 462r-a] tousjours esté chancellier depuis" (*Grandes chroniques de France*, BnF fr. 2813, fols. 461v-d–462r-a. Emphasis mine. All manuscript transcriptions and translations are my own, unless otherwise indicated.)

However puzzling the election of Guillaume de Dormans as chancellor may have been in 1372, it was a different matter a year later, when Guillaume suddenly died. This time, Charles made an even more startling departure from precedent. Not only did he again convene his council on 20 November 1373 for the purpose of electing a successor, but for the first time his choice fell on a commoner (*bourgeois*), Pierre d'Orgement. Of the 130 electors who attended Parlement, 105 voted in favor of confirming Pierre's appointment, while 25 voted against. The latter may reflect disapproval on the part of some nobles towards this unconventional nomination, a sentiment apparently strong enough for Charles to postpone announcing the results immediately. Although convinced of Pierre's superior qualifications (there *were* eligible aristocrats who didn't make the cut), Charles recognized that for Pierre to have the necessary authority to exercise his office, he would need a title. So he waited a month until the Christmas court convened, when he conferred a knighthood on him and then presented him as chancellor. In the words of the nineteenth-century historian, Siméon Luce, this dual infringement of consecrated procedure, "was a novelty that must have struck contemporaries vividly."[9]

That was certainly true for Nicolas de Villemer, who, as clerk of the Parlement (*greffier*), made the official record of the proceedings. His account emphasizes the steps taken by Charles to assure the confidentiality of the meeting. Each council member, Nicolas notes, had first to swear to vote for the most competent candidate (whether prelate or lay person); then came the vote, whose outcome was known only after counting the ballots (an indication that the election was not a foregone conclusion).[10] Some of the terms Nicolas uses –

---

9 "L'élection au scrutin d'un chancelier de France [...] était une nouveauté qui dut frapper vivement les contemporains." (Luce, *Revue historique*, p. 96.)

10 "*Dimanche 20. Novembre*, le Roy nostre Sire tint son grand & general conseil au Louvre, de prelats, de princes de son lignage, barons & autres nobles, des seigneurs de parlement, des requestes de son hostel, des comptes & autres conseilliers, jusqu'au nombre de six-vingt & dix personnes, ou environ, pour eslire un Chancelier de France, pource que la chancellerie vaquoit, & en general touchant, dist le Roy nostre Sire devant tous ceuz qui là estoient, tant du conseil, comme autres, que pour ceste cause avoit-il fait assembler sondit conseil, & puis fit tout aller dehors, & aprés par voie de scrutine, fit chacun de ceuz de son conseil venir à luy & par serment jurer aux Saints Evangiles de Dieu (que tous toucherent, prelaz & autres,) de luy nommer & conseiller selon leurs avis, & eslire la plus suffisante personne qu'ils sçauroient nommer, fust d'Eglise, ou autre, pour estre Chancelier de France, & furent les noms & les despositions de tous escrits par moy N[icolas] de Villemer, a ce ordonné par le Roy, & en sa presence, ou estoit avec Maistre Pierre Blanchet son secretaire tant seulement, & tout oüy & escrit, fu trouvé que Maistre Pierre d'Orgemont, paravant premier President de Parlement, nés de Laigny sur Marne, par le trop plus grand nombre des esliseus, fut nomé & esleu Chancelier de France ; c'est à sçavoir, par cent & cinq desdits esliseus : Et ce dist et publia à tous le Roy nostre Sire, & crea son Chancelier de France, ledit Maistre Pierre d'Orgemont ; lequel se excusa

e.g., *eslire*/elect, *par voie de scrutine*/vote by ballot, *suffisante personne*/most competent candidate – seem normal to us, but were radical in the context of medieval monarchy. That Nicolas uses them here attests the success of Charles V in implementing electoral reforms based on a political theory derived from Aristotle's *Politics* and *Ethics*, a work Charles commissioned the philosopher Nicole Oresme to translate into French.

For Charles, Aristotle offered an ethical, but pragmatic model of governance based on analogy with the natural world, coupled with the belief that the goal (τέλος) of the state is to assure both its autonomy and a good life for its citizens.[11] These concepts had the further advantage for Charles of propounding a model of secular governance at once compatible with Christian doctrine and still serving a large, heterogeneous population. As Aristotle says in Book II: "And not only does a city consist of a multitude of human beings, *it consists of human beings differing in kind*. A collection of persons all alike does not constitute a state."[12] More cogently still, for Charles, the ideal community must have a center, a city as a focus for beneficial governance: "for the state is essentially a form of community, and it must have a common locality; a single city occupies a single site, and the *single city belongs to its citizens in common*."[13]

Aristotle's description fits the city of Paris in 1370 quite accurately. With a diverse population of some 300,000 inhabitants drawn from all over Europe, it was the largest city in the world west of Beijing. This meant that ruling France involved first and foremost governing three separate, increasingly complex and heterogeneous sectors of the city:

1. First, there was the ever-expanding royal court, consisting of princes of the blood and aristocrats whose sumptuous *hôtels particuliers* began to occupy

---

molt humblement, & supplia au Roy qu'il vousist tenir pour excusé, & y pourvoir d'aultre, car il doutait molt, qu'il ne fust pas souffisant à cé. Et le Roy l'y respondit, que il estoit tout content, & enformé de sa souffisance ; & lors ly livra les Sceaux de France [...] Il est vray qu'en ce mesmes scrutine, fust esleu un premier President en Parlement ; mais ce ne fust pas lors publié, & pour cause, declarée le Lundy unziesme jour de Janvier ensuivant." (François Du Chesne. *Histoire des chanceliers et Gardes des sceaux de France, Distingués par les règnes de nos monarques depuis Clovis premier Roy Chrestien, jusques à Louis le Grand XIVesme du nom, heureusement Regnant*. Paris: Du Moutier, 1680, pp. 370–371. Siméon Luce quotes this passage in the *Revue historique*, pp. 96–97, but reworks the French to accord with his own philological views.)

11 Aristotle, *Politics* I.1.8 (1252b 28–36). Translated by H. Rackham. Cambridge: Harvard University Press, 1990, pp. 8/9.
12 Ibid., II.1.4 (1261a 24–25), pp. 70/71–72/73. Emphasis added.
13 Ibid., II.1.2 (1260b 40–1261a 1), pp. 68/69.

more and more space on the right bank near the king's own residences, the Louvre and Hôtel de Saint-Pol.
2. Secondly, there was a growing merchant and artisan class who carried on the growing trade in and production of goods, particularly luxury items – including illuminated manuscripts – for which Paris became renowned in the fourteenth century.
3. Thirdly, Paris had an extensive and expanding ecclesiastical domain, which included abbeys, monasteries and convents, the university and its dependencies, a vast number of churches and related institutions, as well as college foundations (such as the Collège de Navarre of which Nicole Oresme was grand master from 1356–1364).[14]

Two more historical facts help to explain King Charles's recognition of a need for secular and participatory governance: firstly, ongoing disruptions and tensions arising from the Hundred Years' War; and secondly, Charles's fraught experience – as dauphin – with the uprisings in Paris and the provinces in 1358 that nearly overthrew the Valois dynasty. In addition, Charles seems to have understood that, as the most complex urban body in Europe, Paris required a new model of governance. For example, the unprecedented increase in commerce necessitated by urban expansion generated a merchant class whose wealth – and influence with the king – often exceeded that of the nobility. In consequence, tensions between wealthy bourgeois and aristocrats were high, providing a strong incentive to make the royal council more representative of Parisian demographics.

Making the Council more inclusive, however, did not require Charles to take the extra step of allowing councilors to elect the chancellor. That he did so attests the king's concern to organize his administration according to rational and inclusive principles. The election of Guillaume de Dormans as Chancellor of France in 1372, and the even more radical election of a commoner, Pierre d'Orgement as Chancellor in 1373, must be viewed in this context. These events also illustrate Charles's concern to institute reforms based on a political theory that came with the authority of ancient wisdom (= medieval *auctoritas*).[15] There

---

[14] On the dynamic growth and history of Paris during this period, see my essay: "Paris." *Europe: A Literary History, 1348–1418*, edited by David Wallace. Oxford: Oxford University Press, 2015, vol. 1, pp. 11–42.

[15] As Oresme says in the prologue to his translation of Aristotle's *Ethics*, "Semblablement est il verité que savoir la science de politiques profite moult as sages qui ont a gouverner" ("In the same way, it is true that familiarity with political science proves invaluable to wise men whose task it is to govern"). "Prohème." Aristote, *Livres de Ethiques et politiques, translatez par Maistre Nichole Oresme*. Brussels, MS. KBR 9505–06, fol. 1c.

is no mystery as to the theory in question. Both elections are consonant with Aristotle's definition of the state (πόλις) as "a composite thing, in the same sense as any other of the things that are wholes but consist of many parts [...] for the state is a collection of citizens [...] and a citizen (πολίτης) is defined by nothing else so much as by the right to participate in judicial functions and in office."[16] More importantly for Charles's purpose, Aristotle insists that virtue and wisdom should ideally define both citizen and ruler. Aristotle insists that if virtue (ἀρετή) and wisdom (φρόνησις) must define the good ruler, so must they motivate the citizen who participates in politics.[17]

There is much truth in saying that it is impossible to become a good ruler without having been a subject. And although the goodness of a ruler and that of a subject are different, the good citizen must have the knowledge and the ability both to be ruled and to rule, and the merit of the good citizen consists in having a knowledge of the government of free men on both sides.[18]

These virtues do not simply define the aptitude for good governance citizens must possess to entitle them to hold office. They must also demonstrate these qualities as officials. By so doing, they also actualize civic virtues which ensure that the culture of governance conduces to what Aristotle calls the good life: "any state that is truly so called and is not a state merely in name must pay attention to virtue/excellence (ἀρετή)."[19] Most cogently for King Charles's reforms in the 1370s, Aristotle argues that excellence/ἀρετή is not a passive virtue, but a dynamic one that ideally underlies the behavior of elected officials, who thus demonstrate how civic virtue (πολιτική ἀρετή) can be a model for all citizens. This is roughly what Charles V means in specifying that the Chancellor of France must be a *suffisante personne*. As Aristotle puts it in the Third Book of the *Politics*: "A state is the partnership of clans and villages in full and independent life, which [...] constitutes a happy and noble life; the political fellowship must therefore be deemed to exist for the sake of *noble actions*; not merely for living in common."[20]

This passage could easily serve as an explanation of the election of the commoner, Pierre d'Orgement, to the office of Chancellor of France.[21] But be-

---

16 Aristotle, *Politics* III.1.2 (1274b 39–42), pp. 172/173.
17 Ibid., III.2.5 (1277a 16–19), pp. 188/189.
18 Ibid., III.2.9–10 (1277b 12–17), pp. 192/193.
19 Ibid., III.5.11 (1280b 7 f.), pp. 214/215.
20 The quotation continues: "Hence *those who contribute most to such fellowship have a larger part in the state than those who are their equals or superiors in freedom and birth, but not their equals in civic virtue* [πολιτική ἀρετή], *or than those who surpass them in wealth but are surpassed by them in virtue* [ἀρετή]." (Ibid., III.5.14–15 (1281a 1–9), pp. 218/219.) Emphasis added.
21 In the gloss to his translation of the passage corresponding to that quoted just above, Nicole Oresme echoes Aristotle's thought more closely than does his translation of the passage:

yond meritocracy as the criterion for political office, Aristotle argues the necessity of some form of participation in civic life for each citizen. Only when citizens acquire a moral sense of responsibility to the community can the state realize its goal of the good life. When discussing the concept of the value of a diverse citizenry within the state in *Politics* II, Aristotle reasons that individuals develop a sense of identification with the society by serving in whatever capacity fits their ability. "As the best state consists of different classes, its unity is secured by each citizen giving service to society and receiving in return benefits in proportion to his services [...]."[22]

Collective activities, such as participating in the election of officials, figure prominently among the services envisaged for the morally informed citizenry. The rationale for accepting citizens as electors – even though the election of officials "is a task for experts"[23] – is purely pragmatic. Aristotle reasons that while the multitude might not individually have sufficient virtue (ἀρετή) and practical wisdom (φρόνησις) to rule, they can be counted on for collective wisdom:

> Although each individual separately will be a worse judge than the experts, the whole of them assembled together will be better or at least as good judges, and also about some things the man who made them would not be the only nor the best judge in the case of professionals whose products also come within the knowledge of layman: to judge a house, for instance, does not belong only to the man who built it, but in fact the man who uses the house (that is the householder) will be an even better judge ...[24]

By now it must be apparent that, if initially the elections of 1372–1373 suggested a shift of authority from the king to his council, the political theory that motivates his strategy argues just the reverse. Key details of and terms used in Nicolas de Villemer's account indicate, as we will see, that Charles's decision

---

"Ce est a dire que excés ou habundance de vertu politique et pratique laquelle est vraie prudence est a preferer en cité devant liberté et devant noblece de lignage et devant richeces quant est a participer as princeys, offices, honneurs et biens publiques." ("That is to say that abundance and excess of political and practical virtue (excellence) is true wisdom and to be prized in the city above freedom, and above noble lineage, and above wealth when it comes to serving the kingdom, public offices or honors, and public works.") Albert D. Menut, "Maistre Nicole Oresme: Le Livre de Politiques d'Aristote, published from the text of the Avranches manuscript 223," *Transactions of the American Philosophical Society*, New Series, Vol. 60, No. 6 (1970), Livre III, xi, p. 132.
22 Aristotle, *Politics* II.1.5 (1261a 31), pp. 170/171. See also *Nicomachean Ethics* 1132b 33: "In the interchange of services, Justice in the form of reciprocity is the bond that maintains the association: reciprocity, that is, on the basis of proportion, not on the basis of equality."
23 Ibid., III.6.9 (1282a 8), pp. 226/227.
24 Ibid., III.6.10 (1282a 16–22), pp. 226/227.

to involve his council in important political decisions conforms to the king's determination to introduce political reform during his reign. Far from weakening the king's power, enfranchising his grand council by adapting rational principles of Aristotelian political theory provided a pragmatic, secular basis for royal authority, to buttress the more ethereal theological ones. More specifically, the chancellor elections of 1372–1373 conform to theories of good governance set forth by Aristotle, particularly in his *Politics, Nicomachean Ethics*, and *Economics*. Charles knew these works, and understood their importance for his purposes, through translations he commissioned from the fourteenth-century philosopher Nicole Oresme. But Oresme did not simply translate Aristotle, he intercalated extensive critical commentary between segments of Aristotle's text that served not only as a guide to the philosopher's thought, but also to adapt his theory to Charles's aspirations for the French monarchy.

> As for the treatise on politics, it is the science [i.e. practical knowledge theory] by which one may learn to organize and perfect kingdoms and cities, and to preserve and maintain them in good order. And to reform them when necessary. But besides these things, [political science] is valuable for and helpful in making just and useful laws, in addition to aiding in understanding, interpreting, or glossing them, as well as revising, amending, or changing them, while also helping one to know when it is time to do so, and to explain the reasons for such action.
>
> And as Aristotle shows us, this science belongs especially and principally to princes and their counselors.[25]

This passage illustrates why Oresme's glosses are an indispensable witness to the reception of Aristotle's thought in the fourteenth century. But, even more significantly, they allow us to trace the influence of his political theory on the reforms Charles V envisaged in respect to the institutions and practitioners of state governance. Fascinating as these topics may be, however, I want to pursue a less obvious consequence of the partnership between Nicole Oresme and Charles V in the nearly decade-long project of the translation and commentary of Aristotle's *Politiques, Éthiques*, and *Yconomiques*. I am referring to the seis-

---

[25] "Quant est de politiques, c'est la *science* par quoÿ l'en scet roÿaumes & citez et quelconques communitez commencier ordener et parfaire & en bon estat maintenir et garder. *Et les reformer quant mestier est*. Et avecques ce elle vault & aide a faire composer & establir laÿs humaines justes & proffitables et a les entendre & interpreter ou gloser. *Et aussi a les corriger & interpreter ou gloser*. Et aussi a les corrigier ou muer et a savoir quant temps en est et pourquoÿ & comment.
Et pour ce si comme il apparra aprés par Aristote cette *science* appartient par especial & principalement as princes & a leurs conseilliers." ("Prohème." Aristote, *Livres de Ethiques et politiques*, MS. KBR 9505–06, fol. 1b.) My emphasis.

mic shift in intellectual life, literary practices, and even to the French language which was initiated by this project.

While the radical change instituted by Charles's knowledge technology – or perhaps *politics* of knowledge might be nearer the mark – encompasses much more than translations, they are the heart of the project for at least two reasons. First of all, they legitimize it by imbuing his innovations with that most medieval of imprimaturs, *auctoritas*, authority, perceived as a mantle of classical and theological decorum. Secondly, in their guise as contemporary vernacular avatars of venerated texts, they associate the king's project with a network of texts (textnet) consisting not simply of wisdom literature whose roots burrow deep into antiquity, but also with the *active practices* of text production, citation, emulation, and language renewal cultivated by extensive interaction between the textual nodes of that network.

The glosses Oresme intercalates with his translations of Aristotle illustrate his own interaction with this network of wisdom literature. He had recourse to an exceedingly wide range of classical and theological works on which to base the commentaries. There is nothing new about the practice of citation *per se*, of course. The innovation here lies in the extent, range, and acuity of his citations. In his *Livre de Politiques d'Aristote*, for example, Oresme cites some 150 separate writers and texts, ranging from ancient Greek and Latin works to relatively contemporary treatises in Latin, Old French, and Arabic.[26] His source for these quotations, a royal library founded by Charles V, is itself a major feature of the king's politics of knowledge.

The translation project had a major impact on the French language. Oresme enriched the vernacular with a trove of philosophical and technical terms hitherto only available in Latin.[27] More significantly, he did so by actually using lexical innovation to "do" philosophy. While his translations are accurate within the medieval sense of the term, he does not hesitate to "think along" with Aristotle, so that his translations adapt Aristotle's texts to the vernacular culture and context of the 1370s. Similarly, in glossing Aristotle, Oresme recasts the philosopher's points in terms consonant with Charles's policy of instilling the essence of good governance – or at least its concepts – in his subjects.

Oresme's glosses parse Aristotle to make him relevant for contemporary political and social issues, particularly those resulting from the Hundred Years' War. By the 1370s, forty years of military expenditure had bred unrest among

---

[26] Menut, "Le Livre de Politiques d'Aristote," pp. 381–383.
[27] For a selected list of neologisms that Oresme introduced into French, see ibid., pp. 377–380.

the people. Taxation had strained the bonds of medieval social cohesion to breaking point ... and even beyond, as attested by recurrent peasant uprisings in France and England. Charles and Oresme perceived the need for just governance, and so the majority of Oresme's interventions in Book III of *Les Politiques* concern royal power (sovereignty), desirable royal attributes, nobility, what constitutes a citizen, and what constitutes a state (*cité*).[28] His comments lay particular stress on the reciprocal obligations of ruler and subjects.

Nowhere was this lesson more necessary than in the realm of economics. France was suffering an economic crisis brought about by the war, chaotic monetary policy, and harsh taxation. With Charles V's support, Oresme wrote *De moneta* ("On Money") , which is considered the most sophisticated (and revolutionary) monetary theory of the period. As Guido Hulsmann argues in *The Ethics of Money Production*, "Oresme was the first theorist to present a fully worked out ethics of money, one that shows the sheer immorality of government monopoly over currency and the adverse social effects of coinage debasement."[29] Money is not the sole possession of the state, Oresme argues, but belongs primarily to the community and to individuals.[30]

Citizenship is the best measure of reciprocity between state and individual on Oresme's reading of Aristotle. This becomes apparent in his précis of Book III of *Les Politiques*:[31] "Here begins the third book of *Politics*, in which [Aristotle] pursues his purpose and gives the definition and number of [systems of] government, and in particular of the kingdom." Of particular interest for Charles's program is the first chapter with its definitions of "citizen," "state," and the relationship of the one to the other. Now, when Oresme speaks of *citoien* "citizen," and *cité* "state," he maintains the Greek pairing of πόλις (*pólis*, city state) / πολίτης (*polítes*, citizen). He also echoes these terms in his

---

28 He also discusses the inadmissibility of women as rulers, wealth inequality, universal monarchy, Avignonese popes, the conciliar movement (for reforming Church governance), the mendicant movement, the election of bishops, how conflict between kings and/or kings and popes leads to fluidity of power, the appropriate size of a city, tyranny. See ibid., p. 375.
29 Guido Jorg Hulsman. *Ethics of Money Production*. Auburn: Ludwig Mises Institute, 2008.
30 Charles Johnson, *The De Moneta of Nicholas Oresme and English Mint Documents*. Auburn: Ludwig Mises Institute, 2005.
31 "Cj commence le tiers livre de Politiques ou quel il porsuit son entencion et met la distinccion et le nombre de policies et determine en especial de Royaume. Et contient .xxvij. chap[itres]." (V. fol. 72r of Avranches MS. 223, or fol. 77r of Brussels, KBR MS. 11201–202. For the Bibliothèque municipal d'Avranches MS. 223, fol. 72r, see: bvmm.irht.cnrs.fr/consult/consult.php?mode=visionneuse&VUE_ID=1210308&carouselThere=false&nbVignettes=4x3&reproductionId=5628&page=7&panier=false&angle=0&zoom=petit&tailleReelle=. Accessed 13 February 2018.)

use of *policies*, from Greek πολιτεία (*politeía*, cf. Latin *politia*, form of government, citizenship, administration).³²

While names may not be destiny here, they are revealing. We do not ordinarily associate terms like "citizen" or "citizenship" with medieval vernacular discourse. But when Oresme uses *citoien* to identify members of the *cité* or *policie* (πολιτεία), he evokes a very different relationship between the individual and the state than that divinely ordained model, the medieval monarchy. There, the king, haloed with authority derived from God and buttressed (at least theoretically) by the church, rules a populace of subjects, hierarchically distributed in descending order in accord with principles of political theology. In this structure, the king is two beings in one: as a man, human with a natural and corruptible body; but as a divinely anointed monarch he symbolizes the immortal body politic. As Kantorowicz noted, the king possesses a sacred and spiritual resonance: an aura, if not of divinity, then of divine agency.³³

But when we find *citoien* linked to *cité* in Oresme's French text, we face a very different kind of social contract from that of political theology. In place of the hierarchy of individual to auratic authority figure, citizenship (πολιτεία, *politia*) links the individual to a group identity, that of the *polis* or *cité*: "A citizen," Aristotle notes, is "a *partner* in a community."³⁴ Neither Charles nor Oresme can abolish medieval hierarchies, but they do propose a model that envisages citizen participation in political and community activities according to the individual's ability. In short, they adopt Aristotle's criterion of moral virtue (ἀρετή) as a secular equivalent of "nobility" as a condition for political participation and even political office, as we saw with the election of the commoner, Pierre d'Orgement as Chancellor in 1373. This is possible because Aristotle's principles of cohesion for the *polis/cité* are not imposed by divine order, but inhere as moral imperatives in the sociality of the community. "Any state that is truly so called and is not a state merely in name must pay attention to virtue (ἀρετή)," says Aristotle.³⁵

---

32 The *Oxford English Dictionary* derives the first sense of "policy" from "Middle French *policie, pollicie* government, political organization, the state (c1370), (system of) political and social organization, public administration (15th cent.), conduct, comportment (15th cent.) < post-classical Latin *politia* citizenship (late 2nd cent. in Tertullian), political organization, government (4th cent.), urbanity (15th cent.), [...] already in classical Latin (as *politīa*) as the title of Plato's *Republic* (Cicero) < ancient Greek πολιτεία citizenship, government, administration, constitution, polity, form of government < πολίτης citizen." *OED*, edited by E. S. C. Weiner and J. A. Simpson, Oxford: Clarendon Press, 1989.
33 Ernst H. Kantorowicz. *The King's Two Bodies: A Study in Medieval Political Theology*. Princeton: Princeton University Press, 1957, p. 84.
34 Aristotle, *Politics*, III.2.1 (1276b 22), pp. 186/187.
35 Ibid., III.5.11 (1280b 7 f.), pp. 214/215.

But Oresme does not simply echo Aristotle's principles for citizen franchise. His glosses constitute a running commentary on their applicability to the contemporary scene. There is a gloss to *Politics* 3, for example, where Oresme points out that Aristotle's concept of the citizen as political agent means that a citizen possesses an *inherent right* to participate in state governance. Any *citizen*, he argues, is entitled to participate in a variety of public offices, including those at the highest level. The key word here is "citizen," but it would be grossly wide of the mark to accord the term its modern connotation of universal enfranchisement succinctly voiced in the Declaration of Independence (1776 CE): "We hold these truths to be self-evident that all men are created equal [...]." Oresme parses Aristotle's political theory in ways unusual, if not revolutionary, for the fourteenth century, but universal franchise must await 1789.

Unusually for the period, however, sociopolitical hierarchy is only partially predicated on privilege. If, as he says, "lineage, birth, situation, power, or means" determine who may aspire to citizenship, they do not suffice in themselves to assure that status. On Oresme's view – and this sets his political philosophy apart from that of his time – citizenship is a right, rather than a privilege. Those with the requisite titles must earn the status of citizen by active participation – *participation de fait* is the term he uses – in some useful form of governance. In other words, for Oresme the term *citoien* denotes a form of sociopolitical agency. Citizens are those who assure that the *cité* fulfills Aristotle's definition of the *polis*: a political structure that benefits the populace as a whole. Logically, a beneficent state requires virtuous agents.

That is why Aristotle, followed by Oresme, insists that virtue (ἀρετή) define the citizen. Since nothing is more nebulous than abstract virtue, Aristotle introduces citizen-agency, with its goal of transforming abstract potential into concrete achievement, by way of translating virtue into action. At the same time, citizen-agency qua potential for action accommodates a broad range of human capacities unified by the same goal. Here is how Aristotle explains citizen-agency:

> Although the most exact definition of [each citizen's] excellence will be special to each, yet there will also be a common definition of excellence that will apply alike to all of them ... although citizens are dissimilar from one another, their business is the security of their community, and this community is the constitution, so that the goodness of a citizen must necessarily be relative to the constitution of the state.[36]

---

[36] Ibid., III.2.2 (1276b 25–32), pp. 186/187.

Turning now to the way Oresme tunes this material to accord with Charles V's reform, we see how brilliantly he glosses Aristotle's theory of the citizen agent as a secular counterpart to political theology:

> Gloss: That is to say that a citizen is someone who can be a judge himself or with others, or who can be a ruler himself or with others, or who has ways of participating in elections of rulers or judges or of taking part in public councils; for all such individuals can be rulers or judges. Item, by principality [*princey*] Aristotle often means not simply sovereign dominion [i.e. monarchy], but more broadly some public post or trust or honorable public office involving the whole community or some part thereof. *A citizen is thus someone who actually participates in one or another of these kinds of public service, or has the capability to do so, by virtue of lineage or birth, of estate, of power, or means, etc.* And the reason for this is that the *cité* is the *cité* by virtue of its being ordered according to distributive justice, which is the province of princes; and according to commutative justice, which is the province of judges; or according to [political] expediency, which is the province of counselors. And so anyone who can participate in these activities is a citizen belonging to the city and nothing else. Now some people call such citizens "bourgeois," because they can be mayors, or aldermen, or counselors, or aspire to other honorable offices.[37]

With Oresme's adaptation of citizen agency to Caroline policy we return to our starting point: the two elections for Chancellor of France in 1372–1373. Remember that the innovation took two forms: first, Charles V's recourse to *elections* by the royal council to fill the post; and, secondly, for the 1373 election, Charles's nomination of a commoner, Pierre d'Orgement. On both counts – recourse to election by the extended royal council, and the choice of a citizen candidate – these two events show Charles implementing propositions found

---

[37] "[73d] G[lose]: Ce est à dire que celuy quy est citoien quy peut ester juge sens ou /[74a] oveques autres ou quy peut ester prince sens ou oveques autre ou autres ou quy peut avoir voies en election de princes et de juges ou en conseil publiques car chascun tel participe aucunement en prince ou en jugement. *Item*, par princey Aristote entent souvent, ce semble, non pas seulement la souveraine dominacion mes generalement quelconque poste publique ou auctorité ou office publique honnorable qui resgarde toute la communité ou aucun membre de elle. *Et donques citoyen est celui quy participe de fait en aucune de telles choses ou quy est habile a ce, consideré son lignage ou nativité, son estat, sa puissance, ses possessions, etc.* Et la cause est car la cité est cité et a son estre par ordenance selon justice distributive, quy appartient mesmement as princes; et selon justice commutative; quy appartient as juges, ou selon expedient, qui appartient as conseillers. Et donques celui quy peut participer en ces operacions est citoyen en partie de cité et non autre. Et aucuns appellent telz citoiens bourgeois, car il pevent estre maires ou esquevins ou conseuls ou avoir aucunez honnorabletés autrement nommees." (Aristote, *Le livre de politiques*, MS BM Avranches, fol. 74a. bvmm.irht.cnrs.fr/consult/consult.php?mode=visionneuse&VUE_ID=1210311&carouselThere=false&nbVignettes=4x3&reproductionId=5628&page=7&panier=false&angle=0&zoom=petit&tailleReelle=%2F. Accessed 13 February 2018.)

in Oresme's translation and interpretation of Aristotle's *Politics*. At work here is nothing less than a new paradigm for governance: political theology yielding to (secular) political theory. In place of royal power located in the auratic authority of the haloed monarch, political events derive legitimacy from models based on political theory. But where do the models come from and why are they so persuasive?

While a partial answer to the first question lies in Oresme's adaptations of Aristotle's political, economic, and moral philosophy to French vernacular culture in the 1370s, the larger answer must be found in what, earlier in this chapter, I referred to as "a seismic shift in intellectual life, literary practices, and even to the French language." As the discussion of the link between Oresme's Aristotle and Charles V's political practice has demonstrated, the knowledge-politics at the root of the movement derives from a new status accorded to books and the theories they propound. That status is both institutional and practical. The institution enabling Oresme to make his commentary so authoritative was the royal library Charles founded when he came to the throne, and the massive translation project he undertook in the 1370s to transform ancient classical knowledge into contemporary French wisdom. The practical status of the political theory espoused by King Charles derives from a new technology of reading and composing books. The royal library meant that books acquired a kind of second-order status of power brokers, as media transmitting information deemed crucial for policy and conduct at court.

Sandra Richter
Cross-Cultural Inventions in Drama on the Basis of the Novel in Prose, or World Literature before World Literature: The Case of Fortunatus

In 1767 German author and critic Gotthold Ephraim Lessing launched his beautifully written polemics against French drama: he called it frightful, vain, all too rational and idealist, focused on rules and norms only. Lessing wished to ban this kind of drama from the German stage, which was still in its infancy (Lessing, of course, called it "barbarian"): indeed, during its brief period of existence, the Hamburg national theater, Lessing's theater of reference at which he himself was employed as a critic, played 70 French, 40 German, 5 Italian, and 4 English dramas, plus a Dutch text.[1] Though Lessing (like Moses Mendelssohn and Friedrich Nicolai) himself aimed to direct German theater toward the English – according to him, in retrospect Shakespeare beat Voltaire – German literature and theater history thereafter stressed the influence of French drama up to the 1760s and credited the discovery of Shakespeare on the German stage to Lessing and his contemporaries.[2] Lessing's polemic led to an unintended effect: the forgetting of the relevance of English theater and drama in the early modern German context.[3]

It goes without saying that ascriptions like these suffer from the dominance of "the national" in histories of theater and literature as well as from – so to

---

[1] J. G. Robertson. *Lessing's Dramatic Theory*. Cambridge: Cambridge University Press, 1939, pp. 44–47; G. E. Lessing. *Hamburgische Dramaturgie*, edited by Klaus L. Berghahn. Stuttgart: Reclam, 1981, pp. 622–630.
[2] On the new fascination for English drama from the 1740s, see Renata Häublein. *Die Entdeckung Shakespeares auf der deutschen Bühne des 18. Jahrhunderts: Adaptation und Wirkung der Vermittlung auf dem Theater*. Tübingen: Niemeyer, 2005 (Theatron, 46), pp. 12–27.
[3] On the early modern German Shakespeare reception (which, of course, happened through adapted Shakespeare texts without the author's name on any of the dramas), Simon Williams. *Shakespeare on the German Stage*. Vol. II: 1586–1914. Cambridge: Cambridge University Press, 1990; Anthony B. Dawson. "International Shakespeare." *The Cambridge Companion to Shakespeare on Stage*, edited by Stanley Wells and Sarah Stanton. Cambridge: Cambridge University Press, 2002, pp. 174–193, p. 176; Kareen Klein. "Paris, Romeo and Julieta: Seventeenth-Century German Shakespeare." *Shakespeare and His Collaborators over the Centuries*, edited by Pavel Drábek, Klára Kolinská and Matthew Nicholls. Newcastle upon Tyne: Cambridge Scholars Publishing, 2008, pp. 85–105.

https://doi.org/10.1515/9783110536690-004

speak – colonial perspectives, as though one culture could possibly shape another one.[4] Furthermore, in the early modern period the "national" did not even exist in the way it was understood centuries later. Yet, developing this sketch further might underline the importance of models of agency, circulation, and net structures, which are relatively new to theater and drama history but known in other areas of literary and cultural history.[5] These models can help to contest the hitherto dominant narratives and may indeed prove them wrong or half-correct. Focusing on cross-cultural inventions on stage, I will look at English-speaking drama and theater in the Holy Roman Empire – not attempting simply to replace the ascriptions to "the French" by ascriptions to "the English" but in order to explore in detail the occurrence of English drama and theater, and its overlaps with German drama and theater.

In contrast to German literary history, which claims that Shakespeare and his contemporaries were not or only little known in the Holy Roman Empire, current research has yielded insights into the activities of English wandering actors' groups in the region. In the 1590s Duke Heinrich Julius of Brunswick-Wolfenbüttel first saw English comedians in Denmark. The dramatist Thomas Sackville came to Heinrich Julius' seat, Wolfenbüttel, in 1592 in order to work at his court. The duke himself wrote plays inspired by the English and had his dramas played by the English troupes.[6] Furthermore, Jacob Ayrer, a famous Nuremberg author of the sixteenth and early seventeenth century, combined the *Meistersang* tradition with elements he found through English comedians, and adapted English dramas such as Thomas Kyd's *Spanish Tragedy* (1582–1592) into German *Knittelvers*.[7]

Among the texts that present the performances of the English wandering actors' groups – some of them expand on religious (*Der verlorene Sohn, Esther, Susanna, Daniel in der Löwengrube*), some on political topics (*The Jew of*

---

[4] Cf. Roger Lüdeke and Virginia Richter (eds.). *Theater im Aufbruch: Das europäische Theater der Frühen Neuzeit*. Tübingen: Niemeyer, 2008 (Theatron, 53).

[5] See, for instance, Michael Werner and Bénédicte Zimmermann. "Beyond Comparison: 'histoire croisée' and the challenge of reflexivity." *History and Theory*, vol. 45, 2006, pp. 30–50. On adaptations in theater and drama history see the project "DramaNet: Early Modern European Drama and the Cultural Net" funded by the European Research Council and headed by Joachim Küpper as well the corresponding project "Global Theatre Histories" funded by the German Research Foundation and headed by Christopher Balme (http://gth.hypotheses.org. Accessed 13 February 2018).

[6] Volker Meid. *Die deutsche Literatur im Zeitalter des Barock: Vom Späthumanismus zur Frühaufklärung 1570–1740*. München: Beck, 2009 (Geschichte der deutschen Literatur von den Anfängen bis zur Gegenwart, 5), p. 100.

[7] Ibid., p. 100.

Malta), present comedies, or carnival processions – at least two stand out: the Faust drama by Christopher Marlowe (debut performance 1589), and the Fortunatus drama by Thomas Dekker (debut performance 1599). They both show similar patterns of literary circulation: They are both created on the basis of German novels in prose – the *Historia von D. Johann Fausten* by Johann Spies (1587), and *Fortunatus* (1509) – which the English playwrights seem to have known through the first English translations and adaptations. Through wandering actors' companies the German novels in prose came back to the Holy Roman Empire in new dramatic versions, and re-inspired German seventeenth-century playwrights and authors to conceive of new versions of the theme – mostly in dramatic form but also in other genres. Taking the novels in prose together with the theater productions and dramatic adaptations they inspired, Faust and Fortunatus form large narrative complexes which consist of strong characters, recurring plots and scenes, and moral questions relevant to their audiences. These complexes seem to have been recognizable for centuries. Furthermore, the English troupes helped to professionalize the German stage.[8] Unlike French and Italian groups the English ones soon used the German language and excelled in popularity. They introduced entertaining forms of play such as dancing, clowning (Johan/Jan Bouset occurred already in Heinrich Julius' plays, "Stockfisch" in John Spencer's group, "Pickelhering" in Robert Reynolds' group), pantomime, and obscene allusions, more natural ways of acting and communicating with their audience in visual and oral form (music, songs) compared to contemporary theater in the Holy Roman Empire. What is more: they addressed all social classes. The shift from didactic (religious) theater that was already ongoing increased through the English troupes and helped to fund a German-speaking theater in its own right, not just as a medium of the local authorities.

Due to the fame of Christopher Marlowe and Johann Wolfgang von Goethe we are relatively well informed about the history of the Faust novel and its adaptations, but we know less about Fortunatus. I will therefore focus on Fortunatus: I shall briefly present the German novel in prose, look at Dekker's drama, examine a version of the drama used by the wandering actors' groups, and shed some light on the reception of the Fortunatus theme around 1800.

---

8 Williams (see above); George W. Brandt and Wiebe Hogendoorn. *Theatre in Europe: A documentary history: German and Dutch theatre, 1600–1848.* Cambridge: Cambridge University Press, 1993; Ralf Haekel. *Die Englischen Komödianten in Deutschland: Eine Einführung in die Ursprünge des Berufsschauspiels.* Heidelberg: Winter, 2004; Ralf Haekel. "Quellen zur Geschichte der Englischen Komödianten in Deutschland." *Jahrbuch der Deutschen Shakespeare-Gesellschaft*, 2004, pp. 180–185.

I The German Fortunatus

Conceived and written around 1490 and published anonymously in Augsburg in 1509, the German *Fortunatus* tells a family story.[9] Three generations follow in turn. The first plot is rather short: Grandfather Theodorus becomes impoverished due to his luxurious lifestyle in his Cypriot hometown of Famagusta. Most of the original German story consists of the second plot: Fortunatus, the child of fortune, leaves Famagusta in order to conserve the remainder, and perhaps restore some of the family's wealth. The family tale turns into a travel book, an adventure tale, and a detective story: Fortunatus serves the duke of Flanders and a London merchant. In London he is accused of murder.[10] The innocent young man flees into the Breton woods and encounters Fortuna, the virgin of fortune ("junkfrau gewaltig des glücks").[11] As far as her character is concerned, the novel is part of a larger pre-modern process in which the ancient goddess of fortune and fate was enthroned, incorporated into the Christian tradition, and subordinated to (Divine) providence.[12] Therefore in the German book fortune appears as a simple woman, and not threatening or evil as such.

This Christianized Fortuna offers six gifts from which Fortunatus is to choose: wisdom, abundance/riches [*Reichtum*], strength, health, beauty, and long life.[13] Astonishingly, Fortunatus decides in favour of abundance. According to the moral norms of his time – the Seven Deadly Sins and their resulting commands – he would have had to be punished, but he learns how to use and hide his gift: a small purse, a device that can produce gold at any time and in uncountable amounts. Every year, he gives 400 golden coins to a poor bride – as the Virgin of Fortune had ordered. He returns to Famagusta, marries the daughter of a duke, fathers two sons, and travels to Egypt where he is given a

---

9 Manuel Braun. *Ehe, Liebe, Freundschaft. Semantik der Vergesellschaftung im frühneuhochdeutschen Prosaroman*. Tübingen: Niemeyer, 2001.
10 John Flood. "Fortunatus in London." *Reisen und Welterfahrung in der deutschen Literatur des Mittelalters*, edited by Dietrich Huschenbett and John Margetts. Würzburg: Königshausen & Neumann, 1991, pp. 240–263.
11 *Fortunatus: Von Fortunato und seynem Seckel auch Wünschhütlein*. With a preface by Renate Noll-Wiemann. Hildesheim, New York: Olms, 1974 (Deutsche Volksbücher in Faksimiledrucken; series A, vol. 4), unpag. [Diiij verso].
12 Walter Haug. "'O Fortuna': Eine historisch-semantische Skizze zur Einführung." *Fortuna*, edited by Walter Haug and Burghart Wachinger. Tübingen: Niemeyer, 1995 (Fortuna vitrea, 1), pp. 1–22; Haekel. *Die Englischen Komödianten* (see above), pp. 160–165.
13 *Fortunatus* (see above).

wishing hat that can make him invisible, allowing him to disappear and reappear in distant locations.

The third and final plot in *Fortunatus* deals with Fortunatus' sons Ampedo and Andolosia, splitting the story into two sub-plots. Fortunatus survives into old age, which proves his moral integrity – he has shown that he can cope with a morally problematic gift. He leaves his purse and wishing hat to his sons, who compete for both. Ampedo, the lethargic one of the two, is fobbed off with a large sum of money by Andolosia, the greedy egoist. Andolosia aims for power and even greater wealth than his father had acquired. Traveling to England, he courts Agrippina, the daughter of the king, who, being an egoist herself (like her father), only wants his purse and hat. Andolosia is fooled by her, loses his gifts, is punished (horns grow on his head), manages to return to his normal form using a magic trick, wins back his gifts – and is arrested and killed by two dukes. In turn, the dukes are killed for their crime by the king, who then profits from Fortunatus' inheritance, namely the purse. The hat is lost. The story's moral is expressed in a very short final paragraph: Fortunatus should have chosen wisdom and not abundance, the text notes critically. By that, he would have enjoyed both wealth and peace amongst his offspring.

The text itself profits from the exotic it presents as well as from the fact that it admits some immorality and tests it in a fictional framework (concluded by moral remarks, of course). The result is a story of rise and fall, an allegory of fortune as well as the contrary, a dazzling amoral as well as moral tale that praises (Neostoic) moderation.[14] Ethics and wealth go together, the novel in prose concludes, as though it is opting for a double accounting – a promising message for contemporaries who, within the Christian moral framework, aimed to explore different moral horizons.

The woodcuts that illustrate the story (like other novels in prose, e.g. an Augsburg printing of *Magelone*) will, of course, have helped its dissemination. Furthermore, Hans Sachs conceived of the story in dramatic form: his *Tragedia mit 22 personen, der Fortunatus mit dem wunschseckel* [...] (1553) follows the original closely, yet also introduces new personnel such as the "ehrnholdt."[15] Sachs begins and concludes the play with moralizing remarks. Fortunatus' father is called "Fortus";[16] the king of England is replaced by the king of Cyprus.

---

14 Jan-Dirk Müller. "Die Fortuna des Fortunatus: Zur Auflösung mittelalterlicher Sinndeutung des Sinnlosen." *Fortuna*, edited by Walter Haug and Burghart Wachinger. Tübingen: Niemeyer, 1995 (Fortuna vitrea, 1), pp. 216–238.
15 Hans Sachs. "Tragedia mit 22 personen, der Fortunatus mit dem wunschseckel, und hat 5 actus." *Hans Sachs*, edited by Adalbert von Keller, vol. 12. Stuttgart: Litterarischer Verein, 1879 (Bibliothek des Litterarischen Vereins in Stuttgart, 140), p. 188.
16 Ibid., p. 189.

The novel in prose is rendered into the Nuremberg *Meistersang* verse with end-rhyme. Up to the end of the seventeenth century *Fortunatus* was translated into numerous languages, including English. The earliest English tradition to survive was published in London in 1582.

II Thomas Dekker's *Fortunatus*

When Thomas Dekker prominently took up the Fortunatus theme in his *Pleasant Comedie of Old Fortunatus*, he already knew an English translation of the novel in prose and a dramatized English version that is no longer extant.[17] Dekker (ca. 1590–1630) worked as a professional author for theater companies and was regarded as Ben Johnson's opponent.[18] Apparently, Dekker led an eventful life, in which he spent some time in the debtor's prison. His work includes speeches, pamphlets, and approximately 40 dramas that he wrote himself or in the form of collective authorship. Dekker's Fortunatus drama itself was devised for theater impresario Philip Henslowe and the Admiral's Men, revised after a performance for Queen Elizabeth on 27 December 1599, and published in the revised version in 1600.

The text was designed as a morality play, centered around a "moral parable" with a panegyrical note.[19] Indeed, compared to the German text, Dekker's version is based on allegorical poetics presented with the help of alliterations, parallelism, and tautologies: the allegory of Fortune, conceived of as a divinity, fights with the divinities Vice and Virtue. Virtue wins. Furthermore, allegorical poetics are an instrument of politics and religion that is visible through the debut performance at court. The dramatic structure also differs from the German novel in prose: Fortunatus dies early in the comedy; its focus is on the Andelocia (the new Andolosia) plot set in England, while Ampedo is almost neglected. As far as the structure is concerned, Dekker adds a "prologue at Court" (a praise of true hearts and honesty) as well as a second prologue (introducing the play as "poore Art") and an "Epilogue at Court";[20] he combines

---

17 W. L. Halsteadt. "Surviving Original Materials in Dekker's 'Old Fortunatus'." *Notes and Queries*, Jan. 17, 1942, pp. 30 f.
18 Albrecht Classen. "Die Rezeption des deutschen 'Fortunatus' in England – Thomas Dekker und seine Dramatisierung des 'Volksbuchs'." *Neohelicon*, vol. 21, no. 1, 1994, pp. 289–311.
19 Sidney R. Homan, Jr. "'Doctor Faustus', Dekker's 'Old Fortunatus' and the morality plays." *Modern Language Quarterly*, vol. 26, no. 4, 1965, pp. 497–505, 498 f.
20 Thomas Dekker. "The Pleasant Comedie of Old Fortunatus." *The Dramatic works of Thomas Dekker*, edited by Fredson Bowers. Cambridge: Cambridge University Press, 1953, The Prologue, p. 115, line 19.

prose with verse, songs, and music, and also introduces wit into the moral play: firstly, through parodic language; and secondly through the allegorical characters of "Eccho" and "Shaddow," who follow Fortunatus and Andelocia, thereby uncovering "the truth."

The story runs as follows: Poor old beggar Fortunatus meets the goddess Fortuna – an entirely different and, in fact, rather ancient and pagan Fortuna. She (as in the German book) offers the choice between "Wisedom, strength, health, beautie, long life, and riches," and calls it a "deepe Lotterie."[21] Yet, the scenery differs markedly from the German one: Fortune is surrounded by a carter, a tailor, a monk, a shepherd, nymphs, and emperors, among them Frederick Barbarossa, Sultan Bayezid, and Henry V. Fortune presents them as her "underlings."[22] She reigns through the promise of the gifts she offers and considers herself the superior worldly power – a self-presentation that deviates from the German original in which the "virgin of fortune" appears in modest form. As in the German text, Fortunatus chooses riches; he travels, plants a tree for Vice and another one for Virtue (the first bears a lot of fruit, the latter only a little), steals the wishing hat from the Turkish sultan, and suddenly dies in the course of a satyr play, already in Act II, Scene ii. His son Andelocia inherits the purse, Ampedo the hat. The majority of the comedy deals with Andelocia, who courts Agrippina, daughter of the English king Athelstane who steals his purse and hat while Andelocia turns into a beast with horns. Virtue wants to save him, provided that he eat her bitter fruits. When he regains the hat, he is sent back to England, wins back the purse and hat but is imprisoned together with his brother. Ampedo, the only virtuous character in the comedy, dies of his injuries, and Andelocia is hanged by two criminals, similar to the German version.

In the playful allegorizing that ends the text, Athelstane becomes the minion of Fortune. She advises him not to misuse her gifts: "England shall ne're be poore, if England striue, / Rather by virtue, then by wealth to thriue."[23] It is, of course, Virtue who wins the competition with Vice. The published version, which is the result of the performance at court,[24] in its asides commands Virtue to address the queen and Fortune to address her kneeling.[25] Apparently, it is the queen who presides even over the divinities. The moral play has turned into a religious and political one, not only through its performance but also

---

21 Ibid., p. 122, line 224 and p. 122, line 217.
22 Ibid., p. 121, line 174.
23 Ibid., p. 194, line 259 f.
24 Classen, "Die Rezeption" (see above), pp. 301, 307.
25 Dekker (see above), pp. 195 f., lines 308, 315.

through the way the subject is adapted to please authority: the queen who, in the doctrine of the Anglican Church of England, is its supreme head. This adaptation does not render the original more subtle; to the contrary, the outcome is simplified by the transfer into a new cultural, religious, and political context.

III The *Fortunatus* of the wandering actors' groups

When English wandering actors' groups brought Fortunatus back to the Holy Roman Empire, John Green's troupe performed the Fortunatus complex anew and at least twice: in 1608 in Graz, and in 1626 in Dresden.[26] The text, which aims to represent the Fortunatus version of the Green troupe, was printed in 1620 under the title *Comoedia von Fortunato und seinem Seckel und Wünschhütlein, darinnen erstlich drei verstorbenen Seelen als Geister, darnach die Tugend und Schande eingeführet werden* (written by an anonymous author).[27] Like most of these texts, this one too was written after the play (which itself was centered around a topic and focused on the actual performance; there are no written pre-prints of these plays).[28] The author seems to have been identified: Friedrich Menius, born 1593 or 1594 in Woldegk (Mecklenburg), a student at the University of Greifswald, later professor in Dorpat, director of a mine, and accused of heresy and bigamy.[29] Menius was the first translator of Shakespeare in Germany; impressed by Amos Comenius and Martin Opitz, he aimed to present up-to-date culture to his region.

Research has focused on the character of Fortuna and explored ways in which Dekker's and Menius' version instrumentalize the virgin/goddess.[30] Studies have assumed that Menius' text is a mere compilation from the Dekker drama and the German novel in prose (as well as of German versions of Dekker), with some refined aspects as far as style and presentation are con-

---

[26] Classen, "Die Rezeption" (see above), p. 310; Haekel, *Die Englischen Komödianten* (see above), pp. 111–113.
[27] [Friedrich Menius (?).] *Comoedia von Fortunato / seinem Seckel und / Wuenschhuetlein / Darinnen erstlich drey verstorbene Seelen als Geister / darnach die Tugend und Schwande eingefuehret werden. Spieltexte der Wanderbühne*, edited by Manfred Brauneck (Ausgaben deutscher Literatur des XV. bis XVIII. Jahrhunderts). Berlin: Walter de Gruyter, 1975, vol. II, pp. 190–267.
[28] Haekel, *Die Englischen Komödianten* (see above), pp. 100 f.
[29] Ibid., pp. 117 f.
[30] Ibid., pp. 117 f.

cerned.[31] Taking up these finding but also contesting them, I will compare the three Fortunatus versions in order to explore the ways in which wandering actors' groups and writers like Menius dealt with their texts and cultures of reference, and how these texts were compiled into new dramatic material and, thereby, transformed.

Green's and Menius' *Comoedia* can be characterized as a combination of the German novel in prose and the play by Dekker, in that it takes up most of the Dekker plot in an abridged version, and uses the German-language material and the ways the relation between characters and the whole scenery are built up in the German text. The English prologues and the epilogue are omitted, as are the "underlings" of Fortune as well as some of the allegories, the Shadow character, the songs, and the parodies of language. Music, however, seems to have been part of the play (some characters explicitly refer to music); the character Echo is kept alive as well. The story shows poor and exhausted Fortunatus in the Breton woods, mired in a witty dialogue with Echo (similar to Dekker). Yet Fortuna, who appears without her entourage, resembles the one from the German version: Fortunatus praises her as a virgin (not a divinity as in Dekker; there is no talk about a lottery or the like); she warns him not to be scared. He explains that poverty brought him into the woods, and she offers her gifts – almost in the same words as in the German novel in prose, only in the more modern language of the seventeenth century:

> Fortunate erschrück nitt / ich byn die junckfraw des glücks / und durch die einfliessung des himels und der sternen / und der planeten So ist mir verlihen sechs tugendt / [...] Das ist weyßhait / Reichtumb / Stercke / Gesundhait / Schöne und langs Leben. Da erwöle dir ains under den sechssen und bedenck dich nit lang / wann die stund des glücks zu geben ist gar nach verschynen.[32]

New characters are introduced to the play. Three ghosts (of dead souls) illustrate Fortuna's gifts, complaining about how they suffered by accepting them. Furthermore, Pickelhering plays between scenes and acts (with and without text), identifies with various characters, thereby fulfilling the role of the fool who uncovers truth through his acting, and is a reminiscence to contemporary English theater. For instance, Pickelhering shows up as Fortunatus is disappointed upon receiving the unimposing purse. The ten pieces of gold occur in both the German and English version. Yet, whereas in the German one Fortuna explains the purse, the tone of the English version alludes to the Elizabethan

---

31 *Spieltexte der Wanderbühne*, edited by Alfred Noe. Sechster Band: Kommentar zu Band I–V. Berlin, New York: Walter de Gruyter, 2007, p. 16.
32 [Menius (?)], *Comoedia von Fortunato*, p. 47.

tradition of theater. Many scenes are omitted in text of Menius and the wandering actors' group. Act Two already takes up the Sultan plot, in which Fortunatus receives the wishing hat: "der hůt ist mir lieber dann alle die klaynat so Ir. Goshen habt."[33]

In the German version Fortunatus dies from mourning his dead wife and a resulting phthisis; the new text keeps up with Dekker's allegorical tone – it is Fortune who wants revenge for the misuse of her gifts and calls for Fortunatus' death. He hands his gifts over to his sons. Act Three presents Andolosia and Ampedo but focuses on the former (like Dekker). The Agrippina plot starts immediately. Act Four sees the divinities Virtue (with a fool's cap) and Vice competing with each other and planting trees (as in the English version). The scene introduces the theft of the purse and hat by Agrippina as well as the metamorphosis of Andolosia into a beast. He is – in the German and the Dekker text – cured by eating apples from the Tree of Virtue. In Act Five, the False Doctor episode follows, in which Andolosia applies the magic of the apples on Agrippina. He wins back his purse and hat; a comical interlude (differing from the reference texts) begins in which Andolosia travels back and forth to Famagusta, and creates and gets horns. The *Comoedia* ends as it started, as a combination of the German and the Dekker text: Andolosia is killed by the dukes, Ampedo burns the wishing hat, and dies of grief. Unlike the English original, the final triumph of virtue is omitted. Yet some of the political tendency of the Dekker drama is conserved: though the actors no longer kneel in front of Queen Elizabeth, it is the English king who rules a possibly virtuous world. In the *Comoedia*, the king and Agrippina kneel in front of Fortune, and ask her for goodwill and support for the kingdom against all enemies. Fortune promises gifts and glory (expressed in the form of laurel trees). The anonymous German *Fortunatus* deviates from this, as it ends with a brief moral appeal to reason.

Clearly, the Fortunatus example shows the extent to which texts and theater "components" circulate and differ. The wandering actors' groups and/or Menius take up what they find in different contexts and present a combination into which new elements are added, resulting in a new rendering of what was found. Elements such as Pickelhering stem from the performance practice of the wandering actors' groups and seem to have pleased the audience. It may have been a credit to the English groups that they got away with their praise of English royalty. The wandering actors' groups' version is not a mere compilation, however, but an artistic piece in its own right: it is written under the

---

[33] [Menius (?)], *Comoedia von Fortunato*, p. 112.

influence of the performance – with the German novel in prose on the writer's desk.

Astonishingly enough, there is a second Fortunatus adaptation from around the same time that has largely been forgotten. The so-called *Kasseler Fortunatusdrama* shows the multiple ways in which German novels in prose traveled, thereby crossing English culture. The *Kasseler Fortunatusdrama* relies on Hans Sachs' version but carries it further (the character of Ampedo, for instance, is turned into a comical figure, an Ethiopian alludes to the miraculous, the king becomes Cypriot, etc.), and also introduces some elements of Dekker (e.g. the scene in which Andolosia appears as a doctor).[34] The text is conserved in manuscript only, and may indeed have served as a script for the stage (as remarks like "Fortus solo" and the early introduction of characters show).[35] Menius' version is not known to this playwright, who may, instead, have written in the context of English theater at the Kassel court, very likely in the decade from 1610 to 1620.[36] English troupes visited the Kassel court with its famous Ottoneum theater. Robert Browne conducted the troupe until 1607, and, until approximately 1613, various groups performed here.[37] Yet there is no exact evidence about the origin of the *Kasseler Fortunatusdrama*. It remains a small but telling enigma on the border between English and German drama. Again, adaptations like the ones discussed simplify the originals in that they moralize them. Still, the adaptations also shed some light on the production of early modern drama and theater – without which *Fortunatus* might have been entirely forgotten. Updates are a valuable cultural technique, especially on the stage, where no performance will be like another.

IV Fortunati of the 1800s

Fortunatus' story did not end here. Like ancient legends, the medieval Fortunatus narrative spread around the globe, though it seems to have been turned

---

[34] Paul Harms. *Die deutschen Fortunatus-Dramen und ein Kasseler Dichter des 17. Jahrhunderts.* Hamburg, Leipzig: Leopold Voss, 1892, p. 54.
[35] 8° Ms. theatr. 4. Landesbibliothek Kassel (http://orka.bibliothek.uni-kassel.de/viewer/image/1296566484811/133/LOG_0007. Accessed 13 February 2018.); Paul Harms, *Die deutschen Fortunatus-Dramen*; see also Heinrich Schleichert. *Landgraf Moritz der Gelehrte von Hessen-Kassel und das deutsche Theater.* Diss. Marburg 1924 (http://orka.bibliothek.uni-kassel.de/viewer/image/1422951884036/125. Accessed 13 February 2018.), pp. 55–57.
[36] Harms, *Die deutschen Fortunatus-Dramen*, pp. 89–91.
[37] Meid, *Die deutsche Literatur im Zeitalter des Barock*, pp. 330 f.

into *gesunkenes Kulturgut* in the eighteenth century when French theater and Italian opera became more popular. In Germany, there was talk of an opera called *Tragödia von des Fortunati Wunschhute und Seckel mit dem Intermedio von dem alten Proculo*, performed in Dresden in 1678.[38] Romantic authors reinvented the story and its circulation began again – yet rather in a national context. One Fortunatus event followed another. In 1802 Clemens Brentano wrote a letter to Achim von Arnim, mentioning a plan to write a new romantic version of the novel in prose. He identifies Fortunatus with Arnim, the fortune-seeking companion and airy Ariel. In 1806, Fouqué inspired Adalbert Chamisso to consider a drama called *Fortunati Glücksekel und Wunschütlein. Ein Spiel* which was published only as a fragment in 1895. Chamisso reinvents the story taking up forms typical around 1800 (such as the antiphon), and turning Andolosia into a Romantic hero: seeking his own Fortune, Andolosia struggles with his father's gifts, saves them, but renounces his beloved yet all too greedy Agrippina, whom he sends to a convent. Apparently fascinated by the Fortunatus story, Chamisso includes the motive of the purse again in his *Peter Schlemihl's wundersame Geschichte* (1814).

From 1814 to 1816, Ludwig Uhland, acquainted with Chamisso's interest in Fortunatus and, very likely, with a French version of the novel in prose,[39] conceived the narrative poem *Fortunat und seine Söhne* based on an Augsburg version of the German novel in prose. Uhland was fascinated by Fortunatus yet despised the prosaic tone of the German novel; in his poem he reflects on the literary worth of the Fortunatus topic. He stresses the harmonious end of his *Fortunat* but also the never-ending power of the empress Fortuna, who becomes almost synonymous with Providence. As though every Romantic author was aiming for his own Fortunatus version, Ludwig Tieck wrote *Fortunat. Ein Märchenlustspiel in zwei Teilen* in 1815, dedicated to the government minister Rehberg in Hanover. The latter is said to have enjoyed the play, and to have inspired the tribunal scene that frames the text. On the one hand, the plot follows the German novel in prose; on the other hand, Tieck explicitly takes up Shakespearean or Elizabethan dramatic forms such as masks and allegories, complemented by the tribunal scene in which Fortune has to defend herself. In addition to this, Tieck demonstrated some historical interest in the Fortunatus complex. He republished Menius' version of Fortunatus in his collection *Deutsches Theater* (volume II, 1817) – he was apparently able to get hold of a copy – and presented it as an anonymous German "folk play," ignoring its English

---

[38] John C. Ransmeier. "Uhland's Fortunat and the Histoire de Fortunatus et de Ses Enfans Author(s)." *PMLA*, vol. 25, no. 2, 1910, pp. 355–366, p. 357.
[39] Ibid.

theatrical context and canonizing only the text. This misunderstanding is not a forgery like James MacPherson's *Ossian*, but shows the extent to which the Romantics were interested in Fortunatus and aimed to canonize original cultural material in the German tongue. Two years later, Franz Grillparzer, himself rather a post-Romantic Austrian author, concluded this series with his *Fortunatus Wunschhütlein. Ein Lustspielplan*. In addition to this, a new Romanticist translation of Dekker was published in 1819 by the Berlin publishers Voss: *Fortunatus und seine Söhne. Eine Zauber-Tragödie*, translated by Friedrich Wilhelm Valentin Schmidt, professor of English and French and strongly influenced by the Romantic tendencies of his time. It is typical of Romanticism to canonize forerunners, and thereby to allow long-lasting historical misunderstandings. Yet Romanticism also gave back to Fortunatus (like many other texts that were rediscovered around 1800) some of the ambivalence that is characteristic of the German novel in prose.

A similar Fortunatus series occured in England. A chapbook on *The Right Pleasant and Diverting History of Fortunatus and his Two Sons* was printed in 1740 (reprinted 1752).[40] Around 1800, there were serval new Fortunati: Fascinated by Elizabethan and Jacobean plays, Charles Lamb read the collection *Old English Plays* by C. W. Dilke (1814), which also reprints Dekker's *Old Fortunatus*. In 1819 *Fortunatus and his Sons*, an adaptation of the topic that ends with the happy marriage of Andelosia and Agrippina, was performed in Covent Garden with music composed by Henry R. Bishop. William Hazlitt in his *Lectures on the Dramatic Literature of the Age of Elizabeth* (1819) praises *Old Fortunatus* as a lively and funny piece, typical of its era. Decades later, Edward Litt Laman Blanchard (1821–1889), a bohemian who wrote for the Drury Lane Theater and the *Daily Telegraph*, developed his *Little King Pippin. Harlequin Fortunatus and the magic purse and wishing hat. Grand comic Christmas Pantomime* (1875?). The story of Fortunatus is extinguished. Only his character and gifts remain. A similar version of Fortunatus had been presented in yet another adaptation at the Melbourne Opera on 27 December 1875 by Alberto Zelman (1832–1907), an Italian-born composer and since 1870 conductor of the Australian Opera Company as well as of the Melbourne "Liedertafel Harmonia," a meeting point of German emigrants during the Gold Rush era. On the Fortunatus theme, Zelman had worked together with Henry Bracy (born Samuel Thomas Dunn, 1846–1917), a Welsh tenor who specialized in comical French operas in Australia. In the English-speaking context, too, Fortunatus caught Romanticists' attention because of its miraculous content and allegorical poet-

---

40 Ibid., p. 357.

ics, as well as through the ways the narrative engages with seduction by a higher being. The Romantic reception apparently inspired then-current popular artists to transfer Fortunatus to comedy and opera; Fortunatus remained a popular subject until the end of the nineteenth century.

Conclusions

Though there are different strands of circulation in the Holy Roman Empire and in England, they cross over. Apparently, the different Fortunati result from cross-fertilization: until 1800 from cross-fertilization between Germany and England, later within the countries themselves and other literary contexts. Taking these observations together, we can see that Fortunatus has occupied an intercultural space and constituted a network of texts: as German culture is historically fragmented anyway, Fortunatus was known in deviating versions (Augsburg vs. Frankfurt). Fortunatus became floating material that spread into different genres. Character and plot migrated widely through woodcuts and the chapbook from Europe to Australia – as a European and global character, as a European and global plot. The ways in which aspects of Fortunatus have been taken up are typical of the relevant cultural context, e.g. it is typical of Dekker to introduce a concrete religious and political (Anglican) context into his play – and for Romanticism to take a step back to allegorical presentations, and introduce intimate relations such as the friendship with the minister Rehberg into the text. These updates show that it is not possible to trace all aspects of the Fortunatus stories back to their original; there are also individual inventions.

One may surely agree with ecological approaches in the world literature debate: it is mainly larger languages and popular topics such as Fortunatus that tend to survive in the history of literature, theater, and drama.[41] The fact that the Fortunatus complex was kept alive for quite a long time and was being reinvented in the Romantic period is to a large extent due to its intercultural reception, the main strand of which is English. As much as English troupes professionalized theater and drama, circulating texts like *Fortunatus* also played an important role in that shift. Fortunatus may be one of the best early modern examples of David Damrosch's claim that world literature is a "mode of circulation and reading."[42] It is typical of the early modern period that the

---

[41] Alexander Beecroft. *An Ecology of World Literature. From Antiquity to the Present Day*. London, New York: Verso, 2015, pp. 280–282.
[42] David Damrosch. *What Is World Literature?* Princeton and Oxford: Princeton University Press, 2003, p. 5. See *Companion to Comparative Literature, World Literatures, and Comparative Cultural Studies*, edited by Steven Tötösy de Zepetnek and Tutun Mukherjee. Bangalore et al.:

original text, in turn, is dissolved in this process. The value of a literary work, the concepts of authorship and *belles lettres*, were not yet invented, not to mention "world literature" as a frame of reference for contemporary texts. Yet taking into account the widespread reception of Fortunatus – the chapbook also reached the Netherlands, France, Denmark, and many other European countries – the Fortunatus complex can be viewed as European or world literature before the invention of World Literature.

This type of world literature before World Literature was genuinely inspired by its often illiterate audience; it drifted toward a poetics of perception that included all people who might be able to afford to watch a performance.[43] Its aim was to please, educate, and share a narrative complex that helped the rethinking of basic moral convictions and attitudes. English wandering actors' groups allowed their German audience to recognize the importance of a wider European cultural heritage, and profited from this themselves. Characters like Faust and Fortunatus were apparently known so well that they could compete with biblical characters. It was different with French drama and theater – as Lessing correctly notes: Firstly, the Fortunatus story as well as *Faust* is based on relatively current histories and not on Antiquity (as was the case with adaptations from the French). Secondly, the means of distribution of English early modern theater and drama went back to the pre-print era: woodcuts and wandering actors' groups (differently than the French texts, which are often based on printed books). Thirdly, the mental and literary background of these dramas was composed of morals, religion, and politics, the quarrel between religion and science, vice and virtue; the French texts move more toward issues of civic and civilized behavior, the impact of reason, and the role of religion in a developing secular world. The rich popular tradition of theater and drama, however, was moved backstage and only came into view through the rediscovery of Shakespeare in Lessing's time.

Another shift happened in the nineteenth century and around 1900, when Fortunatus seems to have been forgotten and turned into *gesunkenes Kultur-*

Foundation Books, 2013; *Approaches to World Literature*, edited by Joachim Küpper. Berlin: Akademie Verlag, 2013; Thomas O. Beebee. "Introduction: Departures, Emanations, Intersections." *German Literature as World Literature*, edited by Thomas O. Beebee, New York et al.: Bloomsbury, 2014, pp. 1–22; *Figuren des Globalen: Weltbezug und Welterzeugung in Literatur, Kunst und Medien*, edited by Christian Moser and Linda Simonis. Göttingen: V&R Unipress, 2014 (Global Poetics: Literatur- und kulturwissenschaftliche Studien zur Globalisierung, 1).

43 The democratic claim of World Literature is stressed by Caroline Levine, B. Venkat Mani. "What Counts as World Literature?" *Modern Language Quarterly*, vol. 74, no. 2, 2013, pp. 141–149.

gut.⁴⁴ The reason for this may have been the ever-changing economic conditions, morals, and mentalities as well as an increase in similar, yet different character types: there may have been too many new and specific Fortunati, also in more elaborate and contemporary outlooks. Industrialization prompted authors to produce endless series of "industry novels," with their character-type of the pre-capitalist factory owner; the professionalization of the financial market demanded novels like *L'Argent* by Émile Zola; and stories on the degeneration of merchant families (e.g. Thomas Mann's *Buddenbrooks*), and of the American Dream (e.g. F. Scott Fitzgerald's *Great Gatsby*) dominated the sphere that had been occupied by the Fortunatus complex. Building on this assumption differentiation and complexity, spatiality, context, and untranslatability come into play.⁴⁵ Fortunatus was conceived in an era that still built on an almost identical set of morals as well as on (Christian) religion. Though the character of Fortunatus and the actions in which he was involved had been depicted in differing ways, the character-type fitted in across different early modern regions and countries. In the modern world, the challenges of the new Fortunatorum as well as their beliefs, morals, and aims had drifted apart, so one character-type and one plot could not cover them all. As a consequence, the floating of the Fortunatus material was restricted to its cultural context and could not be transferred so easily. Although prediction is not the aim of studies like this one, speculation might be allowed: it may well be that through the ongoing processes of internationalization and globalization in the economic and cultural sphere, theater and drama will bring Fortunatus back one day, updated and turned into a cosmopolitical jetsetter who has substituted his magic sack for a credit card and his wishing hat for a drone.

---

44 Mariano Siskind. "The Globalization of the Novel and the Novelization of the Global: A Critique of World Literature." *Comparative Literature*, vol. 62, no. 4, 2010, pp. 336–360.
45 Emily Apter. *Against World Literature. On the Politics of Untranslatability*. London, New York: Verso, 2013.

Esther Schomacher
Sex on Stage: How Does the Audience Know? (Dovizi da Bibbiena, *La Calandra*, III.10; Shakespeare, *Henry V*, V.2)

I What does the theater do (to its audience)?

Throughout the history of European theatrical poetics the relation between the representation onstage and the audience's perception has been one of its central issues. Questions as to how the audience perceive what is happening on the theater's stage, and how this perception in turn is connected with the techniques and skills applied by the actors, haunt the whole range of theatrical discourse from antiquity onwards. Ever since Plato's and Aristotle's famously contrary opinions on this matter, the medial effects of performance have been at the heart of theatrical disputes;[1] consequently, they have been linked to basic anthropological and epistemological questions – questions, that is, concerning human ways of perception, of gaining knowledge and understanding, and especially the disruptive and/or enabling effects of representations and emotions in this process.[2]

---

[1] The debate in general is less concerned with possible objections to theatrical *texts*; since Greek antiquity it has always been the perception of theatrical representation, as well as its effects on audiences and actors, that bothers both the theater's adversaries and its apologists; see Doris Kolesch. "Theater als Sündenschule." *Theaterfeindlichkeit*, edited by Stefanie Diekmann, Christopher Wild and Gabriele Brandstetter. Munich: Fink, 2012, pp. 19–30, p. 22; Michael Connell. *The Idolatrous Eye. Iconoclasm and Theater in Early-Modern England*. New York and Oxford: Oxford University Press, 2000, p. 15.

[2] Jonas Barish sees anti-theatrical polemics as well as pro-theatrical defences from Plato and Aristotle onwards as part and parcel of more abstract epistemic and anthropological theories, especially with regard to the nexus of (physical) perception, representation and/or mediation, and knowledge. He accordingly integrates Plato's anti-theatrical, as well as Aristotle's pro-

---

Note: I would like to thank the organizers of the 2015 DramaNet conference *Poetics and Politics: Net Structures and Agencies in Early Modern Drama*, Toni Bernhart, Jaša Drnovšek, Sven Thorsten Kilian, Joachim Küpper, and Jan Mosch, for the opportunity to discuss an early version of this paper in a particularly productive and friendly atmosphere, and its participants for their inspiring comments and questions. I would also like to express my gratitude to Rudolf Behrens and his team for a productive discussion of an early draft, Jan Söffner for his untiring interest in the ideas here presented, and Stefano Gulizia for an intriguing exchange of thoughts concerning *La Calandra*.

https://doi.org/10.1515/9783110536690-005

The epistemic and anthropological dimensions of these questions touch the very basic problems of Western philosophy: How can human beings know and understand truth? How does imitation and representation (*mimesis*), or, in fact, any kind of mediation work in this process?[3] And what is the senses' role in it? Can human beings know without relying on bodily sensations and perceptions? And if all knowledge somehow depends on human sentience, does that mean feelings bring forth their own kind of understanding? Or are they merely getting in the way of the human mind's higher faculties?[4] The debate centers, therefore, on what today might be summarized as the "question of cognition and embodiment."[5]

Seen against this backdrop, it is not even surprising that for centuries philosophers, clergymen, and authors of tracts and pamphlets most carefully scrutinized what happened between actors and their audiences, and, depending on their answers to the abovementioned questions, either became the theater's sworn enemies or its avid defenders. In this age-old controversy, the "characteristic conflict" runs between the position of "a haunting acknowledgement of the potency of the theater,"[6] which – paradoxically – is usually bound up

---

theatrical position into their wider anthropological framework (Jonas Barish. *The Antitheatrical Prejudice*. Berkeley, Los Angeles and London: University of California Press, 1981, on Plato see pp. 10 f.; on Aristotle see pp. 28 f. and their *episteme* see pp. 18, 29). With regard to the Renaissance, Connell states that it is the "alteration of epistemology [...] that powerfully underlies the opposition to the transformed theatre [...]." (Connell, *The Idolatrous Eye*, p. 17).

3 As Barish notes, since Plato philosophical reflections on drama have been bound up with more general stances towards mimetic or imitational processes: "What is alleged against mimesis in general will apply to the drama with particular force." (Barish, *The Antitheatrical Prejudice*, p. 5.) For his summary of Plato's and Aristotle's contrary stances towards imitation, see ibid., p. 29. Renaissance concepts of mimesis therefore will play a part in my argument, but for the sake of clarity the discussion of relevant theories has been relegated to the footnotes.

4 Of course, a strong vein of this discourse is engaged in the ethical aspects of the senses' involvement; in particular the moral problem of pleasure derived from sensual perception is one of the most persistent and vexing in this debate. Since I will concentrate on its epistemological side, I will, unfortunately, not be able to do it justice. For a thorough discussion of this aspect of the anti-theatrical discourse, see Connell, *The Idolatrous Eye*, Chapter 1, "Theater and the Devil's Teats," p. 14–35. For a more general treatment of the problem of aesthetic pleasure in Western thought, see Joachim Küpper. "Uti and frui in Augustine and the Problem of Aesthetic Pleasure in the Western tradition (Cervantes, Kant, Marx, Freud)." *MLN*, no. 127, 2012, pp. 126–155.

5 William N. West. "Understanding in the Elizabethan Theatres." *Renaissance Drama*, no. 35, 2006, pp. 113–143, p. 126.

6 Barish, *The Antitheatrical Prejudice*, p. 5. As Stefanie Diekmann remarks, to its enemies the theater "was not *nothing*" – it was "too much" (Stefanie Diekmann. "Kein Theater für Genf. Rousseaus *Brief an d'Alembert*." *Theaterfeindlichkeit*, pp. 31–40, p. 38; my translation).

with "an all the more stinging repudiation of it"[7] on the one hand, and the claim of the theater's educational usefulness on the other hand, which is – equally paradoxically – usually linked to a belittling of its aesthetic impact.[8] The theater's opponents credit the theater with a massive (and hugely dangerous) impact on spectators' (and also actors') lives, precisely because according to their view people usually do not perceive what is referred to by the dramatic action, and instead they are directly bodily affected by the presence of the actors' bodies.[9] What is more: According to the anti-theatrical discourse, the audience will learn nothing good from attending theatrical events. With the theater's illusory presentation of characters and events, it is ill qualified to impart any form of truth.[10] The theater's supporters, in contrast, generally assume that spectators *do* follow the represented story, that they *do* understand and learn any moral and religious lessons it may impart, and that the affection of their senses – attenuated by their consciousness that what they see on stage is not happening "for real" – simply helps to make the plays' messages more impressive.[11]

---

[7] Barish, *The Antitheatrical Prejudice*, p. 5. The fact that the polemics become more acrimonious the more the theater's enemies regard it as a "strong medium" indicates an "ambivalent affective investment" on their part (Stefanie Diekmann, Christopher Wild and Gabriele Brandstetter. "Theaterfeindlichkeit. Anmerkungen zu einem unterschätzten Phänomen." *Theaterfeindlichkeit*, pp. 7–15, p. 9; my translation).
[8] Barish, *The Antitheatrical Prejudice*, p. 29.
[9] John Rainolde's anti-theatrical treatise *Th'overthrow of stage-playes* (Middleburgh, 1599, quoted here from the facsimile edition New York: Garland Publishing, 1974) raises strong objections even against morally flawless plays, because members of the audience might still be more attracted to the actors – rather than the characters they represent – especially when young men play female parts: "And what if all, who were present [...] did admire the constancie of Penelope? Could no evil affection bee therefore stirred in anie by seeing a boy play so chast a part?" (p. 111). Particularly the representation of emotions by a "stage-player" will, due to his physical presence, provoke real ones in the audience – "[...] an effeminate stage-player, while hee faineth love, [...] imprinteth wounds of love" (p. 18) – and this effect occurs, in Rainolde's view, totally independent of the represented character, or the play it appears in.
[10] According to anti-theatrical positions the illusion the theater provides will automatically taint every object of theatrical representation with "falsehood," even biblical and mystical contents. Also, a medium that consists of deceit could teach its audience nothing but deception and fraud itself. Hence, the opposition to religious drama was, if possible, even more violent than that to other dramatic forms and genres (Barish, *The Antitheatrical Prejudice*, p. 77; Connell, *The Idolatrous Eye*, p. 28–29).
[11] Thomas Heywood (1570s–1641), himself an author and playwright for the Elizabethan and Jacobean stage, claims drama to be more apt to "moove the spirits of the beholder to admiration" (p. 20) than other forms of mimetic art (such as painting or literature), and admits the theater's powerful emotional effects on its audience – "it hath power to new-mold the harts of the spectators, and fashion them to the shape of any noble and notable attempt" (p. 21) – but

It is also no surprise that pro- and anti-theatrical polemics often flared up in times of flourishing theatrical production.[12] But the same could be said vice versa: Especially in the sixteenth and seventeenth centuries, when the theater found itself at the center of reformation as well as counter-reformation cultural policy,[13] the hot-tempered debates and violent attacks on it did not necessarily

---

the cause is, according to Heywood, always the audience's enthusiasm for the impressively represented *characters*, rather than the physically present *actors*: "[...] what English blood, seeing the person of any bold Englishman presented, and doth not hugge his fame, pursuing him in his enterprise with his best wishes [...] as if the personator were the man personated?" (p. 21). Heywood claims therefore that "action was the neerest way to plant understanding in the hearts of the ignorant" (p. 27). See Thomas Heywood. "An Apology for Actors in Three Books (1612)." *Publications of the Shakespeare Society of London*, vol. 6: *Thomas Heywood: Dramatic Works*, Nendeln (Liechtenstein): Kraus Reprint LTD, 1966, without continuous pagination.

12 Barish, *The Antitheatrical Prejudice*, p. 66; see also Connell, *The Idolatrous Eye*, p. 15, for detailed examples.

13 The Protestants' and Puritans' strong scepticism (or rather: their fear, loathing, and disgust), and the more lenient position of Catholics towards the theatrical dimension of embodiment are seen in connection with the issue of their contrary answers to the question "what sort of understanding is necessary for salvation," i.e. whether liturgical practices and rituals "needed to be intellectually understood or merely corporeally performed" (West, "Understanding in the Elizabethan Theatres," p. 118). With their pro- and anti-theatrical positions, therefore, treatises also negotiated the most fundamental cultural and religious issues (Barish, *The Antitheatrical Prejudice*, p. 76), and it is no surprise that anti- and pro-theatrical controversies erupted with particular violence in countries strongly affected by the Reformation. Yet, not all Protestant writers were the theater's enemies (during the reign of Henry VIII plays were even seen as an appropriate means for promoting the Protestant cause, see Connell, *The Idolatrous Eye*, p. 21) – and not all Catholic writers were its friends, as the example of Carlo Borromeo, cardinal-archbishop of Milan in 1565–1584, demonstrates (see ibid., p. 30).

In Italy the debate was certainly less violent, and strong anti-theatrical positions are rarely found (as, by the way, is related research). Nevertheless, the theater's effects on audiences were a cause of concern, which found expression in various attempts at its purification, mostly by incorporating a restrictive view of theatrical production, especially comedy, into the genre's poetics. One striking example of Italian anti-theatricality in the shape of theatrical poetics is Pino da Cagli's *Breve considerazione intorno al componimento de la Comedia de' nostri tempi* (in: *Trattati di poetica e retorica del Cinquecento*, 4 vols., edited by Bernard Weinberg. Rome and Bari: Laterza, 1970–1974, vol. 2, p. 429–629), as Pino wanted to see theater reduced to delivering – and listening to – speeches (see Richard Andrews. *Scripts and Scenarios. The Performance of Comedy in Renaissance Italy*. Cambridge et al.: Cambridge University Press, 1993, p. 210 f.). Various Italian examples of anti-theatrical treatises, beginning with Carlo Borromeo's invectives, are published in Ferdinando Taviani. *La fascinazione del teatro*. Rome: Bulzoni, 1969, Parte Seconda: "Storia e documenti," p. 3–285. For an overview of the debate in Italy, see Claudio Bernardi. "Censura e promozione del teatro nella Controriforma." *La nascita del teatro moderno, Cinquecento–Seicento*, edited by Roberto Alonge and Guido Davico Bonino. Turin: Einaudi, 2007 (Storia del teatro moderno e contemporaneo, 1), pp. 1023–1042.

inhibit theatrical production. They also triggered, on the part of playwrights and players, a heightened self-consciousness of the "power of their medium" as well as a new awareness of theatrical "modes of representation" and the theater's "phenomenology."[14] I will suggest therefore, with Michael Connell, that early modern drama "assumed something of the character it did, not in spite of, but because of, the attack upon it."[15] Long before the anti-theatrical polemics reached the peak of their influence on theatrical practices with the famous ban on play-staging in mid-seventeenth-century England, practitioners simply could not help but take a stance vis-à-vis the diverse charges leveled against the stage.[16]

This paper will compare two plays, Dovizi da Bibbiena's *La Calandra* (1513) and Shakespeare's *Henry V* (1599), with regard to the stance they take towards this controversy: It will start out from the observation that even though neither play explicitly reflects upon the controversy's main questions, both plays provide answers to them by shaping the audience's perception in specific (and

---

14 Connell, *The Idolatrous Eye*, p. 18.
15 Ibid. The anti-theatrical polemic in some sense created and reinforced "[the theater's] power in the very act of attempting to demonize it" (ibid.). Therefore, the relation between the theater's enemies and the theater itself can be understood as "symbiotic and productive" (Diekmann, Wild, Brandstetter, "Theaterfeindlichkeit," p. 8; my translation).
16 For the ban on plays from 1642 to 1660, ordered by Parliament during the English Civil War and the Interregnum, see *English professional theatre. 1530–1660*, edited by G. W. Gladstone Wickham, H. Berry and W. Ingram. Cambridge and New York: Cambridge University Press, 2000. Even before this drastic example of the influence of the controversy on theatrical practice, playwrights negotiated its fundamental issues sometimes more, sometimes less explicitly. Ben Jonson's case is particularly apt to illustrate the often intricate relations of secret alliances and mutual fascination between attack and defence in the controversy, since Connell notes from the outset that Jonson – "in his own allegiance with humanist culture" (Connell, *The Idolatrous Eye*, p. 12) – often "seems half in agreement with [the Puritans'] critique of visual spectacle," and therefore describes his own plays as "poetry," highlighting their textuality (ibid., p. 13; see also Barish, *The Antitheatrical Prejudice*, Chapter V: "Jonson and the Loathèd Stage," p. 132–154). In various instances Jonson also insists that a true understanding of his plays is only available to readers, not to audiences (West, "Understanding in the Elizabethan Theatres," p. 120 ff.). One Shakespearean example of conscious appropriation of anti-theatrical positions within a play is, as Björn Quiring's analysis convincingly shows, *Othello* and its obsession with the emotional and physical effects of deception brought about by theatrical means (Björn Quiring. "'Men should be that they seem.' Antitheatralität in Shakespeares *Othello*." *Theaterfeindlichkeit*, pp. 73–85). Connell reads *Hamlet* in a similar vein, seeing the play's emphasis on the deceptiveness of the visual sense, and its constant concern with a possible hiatus between inward emotional state and outward appearance, as reflecting the strong iconoclastic streak of early modern anti-theatrical discourse (Connell, *The Idolatrous Eye*, p. 132 ff.).

contrary) ways, and by creating particular relationships between audience and onstage action; with this, each play also negotiates the underlying problem of cognition and embodiment.

So, contrary to the promise of its title, this paper is not – or not mainly – concerned with sex. Bluntly put, it is concerned with the question how two particular plays implement ways to make the audience know. This paper is, however, in so far concerned with sex, as these questions touching the mediality of theatrical performance seem to become particularly visible in two scenes that represent sexual relations: in Scene III.10 of Dovizi da Bibbiena's *La Calandra*, and V.2 of Shakespeare's *Henry V*. In fact, this paper will try to show that one of these scenes' main objectives is to fashion the audience's stance and perception, and, thus, to produce (or at least to highlight) precisely the kind of media effects – and the kind of knowing – that each play relies on: In the case of *La Calandra*, this paper will argue, the audience's perception is guided towards an uninvolved, detached, and superior observation of the fictional world of the play; thus, the play seems to want to highlight the fact that the audience will, firstly, know and understand something *about* this world, and that they will, secondly, know and understand its fictional character. In the case of *Henry V*, instead, the scene seems to guide the audience towards a perception and an understanding of the action that is based on their emotional and embodied taking part in it. Rather than being shown something about a closed off and therefore analyzable world of make-believe, spectators are drawn into what today's phenomenology of embodied experiences describes as "participatory sense-making."[17]

This means that within the complex field of Renaissance theories of human perception and epistemology, both plays, and in particular the two scenes upon which this paper focuses, can be identified with different, even oppositional views; views, however, which so far have not received an equal share of researchers' attention. *La Calandra* provides and requires a way of understanding on the part of the audience that has long been at the center of much of the theoretical and philosophical research on Renaissance *episteme*, and therefore seems rather familiar. It is firmly grounded in the emerging concept of knowledge as a mental representation derived from – as well as further submitted to – analysis, that is: hermeneutic and/or semantic explanation, discussion,

---

[17] Hanne De Jaegher and Ezequiel Di Paolo. "Participatory Sense-Making: An Enactive Approach to Social Cognition." *Phenomenology and the Cognitive Sciences*, no. 6, 2007, pp. 485–507, see also section V of the present essay. For an overview of related phenomenological theories see Evan Thompson and Mog Stapleton. "Making Sense of Sense-Making. Reflections on Enactive and Extended Mind Theories." *Topoi*, no. 28, 2009, 23–30.

contestation, or comparison.[18] *Henry V* and its wooing scene, on the contrary, draws on a way of understanding that for a long time Western philosophy did not regard as knowledge at all. It is only thanks to recent research in phenomenology and neuroscience on the embodied, enactive, embedded, and extended mind[19] that situated cognition has been awarded the status of being – indeed – knowledge;[20] and even more recently cultural studies have come to recognize

---

18 This strand of Renaissance – mostly Neoplatonic – accounts of the processes of knowledge-acquisition often uses the metaphor of "printing" to describe the reception of knowledge into the human brain, or the "rational soul" located there (Miranda Anderson. *The Renaissance Extended Mind*. Basingstoke: Palgrave Macmillan, 2015, quotes Bacon's [p. 82], Coeffeteau's [p. 89–90], Crooke's [p. 113], and Ficino's [p. 113] theories of the soul and its diverse parts, their locations, and abilities). The specifically human capability of gaining knowledge by reflection and learning was either conceived of as a form of remembering the "universal forms imprinted in human minds, understanding of which is filtered through sensory impressions" (ibid., p. 82), or as a process during which the brain's "substance" can "reveiue the impression of other things" (see Helkiah Crooke. *Mikrokosmographia. A Description of the Body of Man*. London, 1615, p. 455, as quoted by Anderson, *The Renaissance Extended Mind*, p. 113). Even though researchers in Germany have often taken a different angle on Renaissance *episteme* – focusing not on ways of gaining knowledge, but rather on the objects of knowledge and their processing – their findings in this case complement Anderson's examples: according to Andreas Kablitz and Gerhard Regn, who refer to earlier works by Klaus W. Hempfer, the "dominant epistemological habitus of the time" links the "constitution of knowledge" to the "interpretation of texts" (Andreas Kablitz and Gerhard Regn. "Vorwort." *Renaissance – Episteme und Agon*, edited by iid. Heidelberg: Winter, 2006, pp. 7–9, p. 7; my translations; see Klaus W. Hempfer. "Die Konstitution autonomer Vernunft von der Renaissance zur Aufklärung." *Grundlagen der politischen Kultur des Westens. Ringvorlesung an der Freien Universität Berlin*, edited by id. and Alexander Schwan. Berlin and New York: de Gruyter, 1987, pp. 95–115). Since in the Renaissance the corpus of texts is – compared to medieval times – considerably widened, this motivates the "development of a new hermeneutic consciousness" (ibid., p. 7), that is, the further contestation and discussion of knowledge, e.g. in the literary form of the dialogue (see Klaus W. Hempfer. "Probleme traditioneller Bestimmungen des Renaissancebegriffs und die epistemologische 'Wende'." *Renaissance. Diskursstrukturen und epistemologische Voraussetzungen: Literatur – Philosophie – Bildende Kunst*, edited by id. Stuttgart: Steiner, 1991, pp. 9–45).
19 Even though the four terms stress different key aspects, they all express the view that cognition is body-based and neither restricted to a closed-off and solitary brain nor entirely based on processes of mental representation, and therefore "challenge the standard model that views the body and the world as peripheral to understanding the nature of cognition." (Anderson, *The Renaissance Extended Mind*, p. viii). They are now frequently summarized as the "4E perspective" in order to emphasize their common ground (see e.g. ibid., p. viii). It would exceed the purpose of this paper to elaborate the internal differences and ongoing debates in this field: for an overview of the most important strands of research in this context see Anderson's excellent introductory chapter, "The Extended Mind," pp. 1–40.
20 See e.g.: Antonio Damasio. *Descartes' Error. Emotion, Reason and the Human Brain*. London: Vintage Books, 2006 [1994]; Mark Johnson. *The Meaning of the Body – Aesthetics of Human Understanding*. Chicago and London: University of Chicago Press, 2007; George Lakoff

the importance of concepts of embodied and extended understanding in Renaissance thought.[21] As Miranda Anderson notes: "[T]he Renaissance displays an especially marked consciousness, concern and celebration about human cognitive extendedness" and stresses the "belief that humans had porous brains and bodies" so that "external resources could play fundamental roles in their cognitive processes."[22]

The circumstance that the two different plays belong to two different cultural-political settings, and also to two different theatrical traditions each with their own, specific conditions of performance, will be seen as generally supporting the different perceptional stances, and the different ways of making the audience know, enforced by the plays. But, seen against the backdrop of their specific performative conditions, it becomes particularly clear that the plays do not simply affirm one specific mode of perception; in fact, I also intend to show how far they contest the trustworthiness of their respective perceptional stances and counterpoise them to the other way of knowing, and – to a certain extent – show their inseparability. With this, I hope to show from the example of two very specific, microscopic instances how Renaissance drama not only negotiates questions of knowledge and its relation to bodily perceptions and emotions, but also voices the related cultural anxieties – or excitement.

Even though my interest is the audience's perception and knowledge, I do not intend to analyze this with regard to a particular production of each of the

---

and Mark Johnson. *Philosophy in the Flesh – the Embodied Mind and its Challenge to Western Thought.* New York: Basic Books, 1999; P. Robbins and M. Aydede (eds.). *The Cambridge Handbook of Situated Cognition.* Cambridge and New York: Cambridge University Press, 2009; Larry Shapiro. *Embodied Cognition.* London and New York: Routledge, 2011; Zdravko Radman (ed.). *Knowing Without Thinking. Mind, Action, Cognition and the Phenomenon of the Background.* Basingstoke and New York: Palgrave Macmillan, 2012.

21 Apart from Anderson's ground-breaking study, which offers an overview of Renaissance concepts of embodied and enactive cognition, and West's analysis of the diverse notions of intellectual and corporeal understanding – and their interrelation – in Elizabethan and Jacobean theater, see also Michael Emily. "Renaissance Theories of Body, Soul and Mind." *Psyche and Soma. Physicians and Metaphysicians and the Mind-Body Problem from Antiquity to Enlightenment*, edited by John P. Wright and Paul Potter. Oxford: Clarendon Press, 2000, pp. 147–172; *Environment and Embodiment in Early Modern England*, edited by Mary Floyd-Wilson and Garrett A. Sullivan. Basingstoke: Palgrave Macmillan, 2007; with regard to Elizabethan theatrical practices and their relation to concepts of cognitive extendedness and embeddedness, see Evelyn Tribble. "Distributing Cognition in the Globe." *Shakespeare Quarterly*, no. 56, 2005, pp. 135–55 and ead. *Cognition in the Globe: Attention and Memory in Shakespeare's Theatre.* Basingstoke: Palgrave Macmillan, 2011.

22 Anderson, *The Renaissance Extended Mind*, p. ix.

plays. In comparison with Stefano Gulizia's contribution to this volume, which provides a close reading of the fascinating description Baldassare Castiglione gives of his own production of *La Calandra* in 1513 Urbino, and in particular the effects its elaborate material arrangement and the interior design of the theatrical space had on its audience, this paper is limited to a more generic approach regarding the contemporary conditions of performance. Nevertheless I would like to see it as to a certain extent complementing Gulizia's microhistorical perspective – my intention is, like Gulizia's (whose phrase I am borrowing here), to look at "what the scenes do, more than at what they mean."[23]

II (Making sense of) senseless scenes

Apart from the common motif of their representation – sex – the two scenes on which this paper focuses share another, and perhaps even more important, feature: Neither of them continues their respective play's action; they have no structural function in its intrigue. In the case of Scene III.10 of *La Calandra*, the complicated action of this exemplary *commedia erudita* remains suspended for the duration of a short *intermezzo* between two servants, which has no consequences whatsoever on the further development of the play's intricate plot, which evolves around a pair of twins. Scene V.2 of *Henry V*, known as the "wooing scene," is, from a structural point of view, equally superfluous: The main action, centering around the greatest military victory in all English history, the Battle of Agincourt, and its protagonist Henry of Monmouth, has already reached its conclusion. The French have surrendered, and Catherine de Valois, the French princess, will have to marry Henry whether she likes it or not.

It appears to be as a consequence of this senselessness, that researchers in literary, cultural, or drama studies have, in both cases, not yet come to terms with these scenes. In the case of *La Calandra*'s striking display of licentiousness on the part of the servants, scholars seem to have silently agreed to ignore it, possibly because – from a researcher's point of view – the scene causes too

---

[23] See Stefano Gulizia. "Castiglione's Green Sense of Theater." With respect to *Henry V*, I will occasionally refer to recent productions for screen and stage; unfortunately this will not be possible for *La Calandra* due to a lack of available productions. Giorgio Padoan mentions several theatrical productions of *La Calandra* in the 1970s ("Introduzione." *La Calandra: Commedia elegantissima per messer Bernardo Dovizi da Bibbiena*, edited by Giorgio Padoan. Padua: Editrice Antenore, 1985, pp. 1–34, p. 6), as does Mario Baratto. *La commedia del Cinquecento*. Vicenza: Neri Pozza, 1975, p. 14 ff., but unfortunately none of them are available on video/DVD.

few and too many problems at the same time. Its crude straightforwardness leaves little room for critical interpretation at the level of the textual surface, and at the level of structure its redundancy challenges the classical unity of action – that is: the poetical precept that the *commedie erudite* were virtually obsessed with.[24] Compared to sexual encounters in other comedies, this one is extraordinary, and also problematic, because it is casual.[25] Why the scene was even included in the play is a question that still remains to be asked. The wooing scene at the end of *Henry V* has obviously been the object of more detailed scholarly attention.[26] But, even though in this case much ink has been spilled, the purpose and function of this "minicomedy"[27] within the context of a history play that is, after all, mainly concerned with war, remains strangely obscure. Today the main branch of criticism reads it as basically a chauvinistic and/or nationalistic humiliation of the French princess and, by extension, the French people, as well as a crude (and somewhat superfluous) affirmation of the king's male and/or English identity.[28]

---

24 For the emergence of the Italian *commedia erudita* as a conscious imitation/emulation of the classical Roman comedy, and its faithful reliance on the classical poetical unities, see D. Radcliff Umstead. *The Birth of Modern Comedy in Renaissance Italy*. Chicago and London: University of Chicago Press, 1969.

25 It is not unusual for early Italian comedies to include sex between their pairs of young lovers. In other examples of early comedies, however, like Ariosto's *La Lena* and *I Suppositi*, and – of course – Machiavelli's *La Mandragola*, these encounters always happen offstage and are then reported to other characters as well as to the audience via the classical technique of teichoscopy. More importantly, in other comedies sex is always crucial to the respective play's plot, as its happy ending routinely legitimizes the lovers' pre-existing relationship.

26 Or rather, as Goldman put it, it looks back on "a long tradition of solemn critical disapproval" (Michael Goldman. *The Energies of Drama*. Princeton: Princeton University Press, 1972, p. 72).

27 Donald Hedrick. "Advantage, Affect, History, *Henry V*." *PMLA*, no. 118, 2003, pp. 470–487, p. 470.

28 See e.g.: Karen Newman. "Englishing the Other: 'Le tiers exclu' and Shakespeare's *Henry V*." *Fashioning Femininity and English Renaissance Drama*, edited by ead. Chicago: University of Chicago Press, 1991, pp. 95–108; Helen Ostovich. "'Teach You Our Princess English?' Equivocal Translation of the French in *Henry V*." *Gender Rhetorics: Postures of Dominance and Submission in History*, edited by Richard C. Trexler. Binghamton: Center for Medieval and Early Renaissance Studies, 1994 (Medieval and Renaissance Text and Studies), pp. 147–161; Philip Seargeant. "Ideologies of English in Shakespeare's *Henry V*." *Language and Literature*, no. 18, 2009, pp. 25–44; Grace Tiffany. "Being English Through Speaking English: Shakespeare and Early Modern Anti-Gallicism." *Word and Rite: The Bible and Ceremony in Selected Shakesperean Works*, edited by Beatrice Batson. Newcastle-upon-Tyne: Cambridge Scholars Publishing, 2010, and Alison Walls. "French Speech as Dramatic Action in Shakespeare's *Henry V*." *Language and Literature*, no. 22, 2013, pp. 119–131. Apart from the sometimes obvious anachronisms of this perspective, the simple historical fact that the Tudor monarchs descended in a direct line from the historical Catherine of Valois (and her second husband Owen Tudor) provides the

I will argue here that it is in these senseless scenes that each of the plays shapes and fashions the perception of the audience. That is, whatever the plays presuppose the theater can do is exacerbated in these scenes: the senseless scenes may be senseless only with respect to the plays' plots – in performance, this paper will show, their sense coincides with their effect on the audience's perception. It is no coincidence, then, if both in *La Calandra* and in *Henry V* the senseless scenes are also the most *sensual*.[29] If, as I will argue here, it is the purpose of both scenes to shape the spectators' experiences, it is no surprise that the scenes intensify the experiencing.[30]

III *La Calandra*: who knows what?

Dovizi da Bibbiena's early play, staged for the first time in 1513 as part of a series of court festivities in Urbino,[31] is not only one of the most successful Italian comedies of the sixteenth century,[32] it is also one of the most complicated. Luckily, the details of the several amorous *intrecci* – mistaken identities, sexual crossdressing, and adultery included – are not of great importance for this paper's argument. At the center of the comic confusion is a motif obviously

---

most convincing argument against this interpretation. Stephanie Downes. "French Feeling: Language, Sex and Identity in *Henry V*." *Shakespeare and Emotions. Inheritances, Enactments, Legacies*, edited by Robert S. White. Basingstoke and New York: Palgrave Macmillan, 2015, pp. 59–68, instead reads the scene as an example of complex, non-pejorative, and ambivalent negotiations of "emotional expression and cross-linguistic communication" (ibid., p. 66). I will refer to her observations further on.

29 Thanks are due, and gladly given, to Stephen Nichols (Baltimore), who brought this connection between senselessness and sensuality in both scenes to my attention.

30 For the further development of my argument it is essential to view both plays as dramatic works intended for performance (that is: not intended for silent scholarly reading), and in agreement with much of the recent research on English Renaissance drama I will assume that performance constitutes much of their meaning and artistic potential.

31 Apart from Stefano Gulizia's contribution to this volume, see A. Fontes-Baratto. "Les fêtes à Urbin en 1513 et la *Calandria* de Bernardo D. da Bibbiena." *Les écrivains et le pouvoir en Italie à l'époque de la Renaissance (serie II)*, edited by André Rochon. Paris: Université de la Sorbonne Nouvelle, 1974, pp. 45–80; Franco Ruffini. "Analisi contestuale della *Calandria* nella rappresentazione urbinate del 1513." *Biblioteca teatrale*, nos. 15/16, 1978, 70–139, and *Commedia e festa nel Rinascimento. La* Calandria *alla corte di Urbino*. Bologna: Il Mulino, 1986.

32 Pamela D. Stewart. "A Play on Doubles. The *Calandria* Play." *Modern Language Studies*, no. 14, 1984, pp. 22–32, p. 22; Stefano Gulizia. "Spatial traffic. Cognitive ecologies of Bibbiena's *Calandra*." *Studi rinascimentali*, no. 9, 2011, pp. 115–127, p. 117; but mostly G. L. Moncallero. "La fortuna della *Calandria* nel Cinquecento." *Aevum*, no. 42, 1968, pp. 100–103.

taken over from Plautus' *Menaechmi*,[33] namely a pair of twins, Lidio and Santilla, who were separated as infants and who have each independently come to Rome to look for their respective sibling, only to find themselves involved in intertwined love stories in the course of which they each take on their sibling's identity and gender: Lidio falls in love with the rich lady Fulvia; in order to deceive her husband Calandro ("lo sciocco per antonomasia"[34] and the predestined victim of the comic *beffa*), he goes to their rendezvous dressed as a woman, which then causes the betrayed husband – of all people! – to fall in love with him. In the meantime Santilla (or "Lidio femina," as stage directions call her) faces a most inconvenient marriage proposal: her master Petrillo, who does not know her true gender, wants her to marry his daughter. This complicated situation brings forth a whole range of confusing coincidences and false identifications, a number of which are mediated by a charlatan sorcerer named Ruffo, who pretends to be able to change a person's gender, only to be surprised at what he sees as his own success. Needless to say, it all ends well – in the way Italian comedies sometimes end well: the twins meet, and eventually recognize, each other, they revert back to their true identities and genders, they each find a conveniently rich spouse, and Lidio, though guilty, is saved from the accusation of adultery.

Research has successfully shown that *La Calandra* is – maybe more than any other play belonging to the *commedia erudita* tradition – based on a strict division of the theatrical space into two distinct compartments, each of which is, for the duration of the play's intrigue, inhabited by a specific group of characters who are only aware of a limited part of the play's intrafictional reality.[35] Pamela Stewart has convincingly described the effects this has on the characters: two neatly separated groups form around the two twins;[36] the members of each group only know one twin's background story and this shapes their actions as well as their perception of the unfolding events. With the comic confusion in full swing, characters repeatedly express their own lack of understanding of what is going on around them.[37] Little by little the members of the two groups do get into contact with members of the other group, and this

---

[33] See Padoan, "Introduzione," p. 158.
[34] Pamela D. Stewart. "Il testo teatrale e la questione del doppio destinatario: l'esempio della *Calandria*." *Quaderni d'italianistica*, no. 1, 1980, pp. 15–29, p. 17.
[35] Ibid., p. 16 f. Note especially the diagram showing the distribution of knowledge between the characters of the play on p. 17.
[36] Ibid., p. 16.
[37] See Fessenio in IV.6 or Samia in V.1. I will refer to the play's text according to the edition by Padoan; references in brackets are to this edition.

eventually leads to their acknowledgement of the respective other half of the play's reality, and, finally, to the reunion of the twins and the solution of the various *intrecci*. Essentially, though, even the obligatory *lieto fine* is based on this division of knowledge, and on its effect of excluding some characters from the whole truth even at the play's conclusion.[38] That is, the twins' luck and fortune builds on the fact that neither Lidio's future father-in-law, nor Fulvia's stupid husband, nor their future spouses will ever be aware of the whole truth.[39] This division of knowledge is implemented and reflected, according to Giulio Ferroni's reading, by the comedy's initial "compartizione economica dello spazio" and its overcoming as the comedy unwinds.[40] The characters' limitation of knowledge is mirrored by their spatial confinement: the members of the two groups initially inhabit two separate areas of the stage, with Fulvia's and Calandro's house as the center of one, and Petrillo's house at the center of the other, and their growing recognition is strongly linked to the dissolution of this spatial segregation.[41]

Ultimately, the division of the theatrical space in *La Calandra* and the division of knowledge among its characters appear congruent, to the extent that the different areas of action can be identified as spaces of knowledge: the play not only displays the limitations of the characters' insight into the play's action as limits upon spatial movement and overview, but also highlights the fact that a certain point of view on the comical events is – literally – caused by the observer's *perspective* and therefore coincides with a certain physical position in space.[42] As Stefano Gulizia rightly notes, in *La Calandra* insight depends directly on "spatial traffic," that is: physical position and movement in space.[43]

---

[38] Giulio Ferroni. "I due gemelli greci a Roma: il doppio e la scena nella *Calandria* del Bibbiena." *Studi romani*, no. 28, 1980, 23–33, p. 32.
[39] "[...] essi non conoscono e non vengono mai a conoscere né l'una né l'altra parte della verità, [...]." Stewart, "Il testo teatrale," p. 17; see Ferroni, "I due gemelli," p. 32.
[40] Ibid.
[41] Lidio and Santilla "[...] si impadroniscono dello spazio della scena romana come spazio del radoppiamento [...]." (ibid., p. 31). As is typical of this genre, this doubling of the twins' action-space is in turn confirmed by a doubling of their economic wealth, see ibid., p. 32; with regard to the complementarity of spatial and economic possibilities of action in the *commedia erudita*, see Rudolf Behrens and Esther Schomacher. "Semantische Subversionen städtischen und häuslichen Raums in der Komödie des Cinquecento." *Raum-Erkundungen. Einblicke und Ausblicke*, edited by Elisabeth Tiller and Christoph Mayer. Heidelberg: Winter, 2011, pp. 89–124, p. 113–117.
[42] Stewart sees this as part of the play's "giuoco fra i vari destinatari e le varie prospettive dalle quali questi consideranno gli avvenimenti," see Stewart, "Il testo teatrale," p. 15.
[43] Gulizia, "Spatial Traffic," p. 127.

For the play's spectators this direct link between spatial position or movement and knowledge has strong – and not wholly unpleasant – implications. To them, the coincidence of spatial position and availability of knowledge applies in a particular way: in *La Calandra* it is the audience alone who find themselves in the position of observing the action onstage from the outside. Therefore, the spectators – "divinely amused and omniscient"[44] – are able to identify the limitations of each character's individual perspectives on what happens, as well as to integrate the characters' limited knowledge into the bigger picture of the play's entire action.[45] If other *commedie erudite* incorporate the position of strategic overview into their cast of characters – usually in the shape of a savvy servant who pulls the strings of the comic *intrecci*[46] – mirroring, as it were, the audience's overview from inside the fictional world, *La Calandra*, quite uniquely and remarkably, does not. As Stewart remarks laconically: "It would be difficult to find a scene which does not presuppose a difference in the levels of information between characters and audience."[47] As I will try to show, in Scene III.10 this is taken to the extreme: here the space of the theater is strictly hierarchized into several spaces, which in turn coincide with different areas of knowledge *about* the action. At the same time the knowledge of the audience is extended to a heightened awareness of the fictional quality of the performance.

Within the context of the play the servants' amorous tête-a-tête is introduced by a little soliloquy by the *serva* Samia, in the course of which she expresses her support and sympathy for her mistress Fulvia, who had, in a previous scene, abandoned all sense of propriety and gone off, dressed as a man, to see her lover Lidio. Samia declares without much further ado that she will now do the same and see her lover Lusco, and promptly disappears into Fulvia's house, locking the door. Shortly afterwards another servant, Fessenio, arrives and requires access to the very same house. What is happening in III.10,

---

44 "olimpicamente divertito e onnisciente", Stewart, "Il testo teatrale," p. 16.
45 "Durante tutto lo svolgimento della commedia nessuno dei personaggi riesce a capire interamente quello che sta accadendo: soltanto il pubblico è al corrente di tutta la verità." (Ibid.)
46 The best-known example of this would be the character of Ligurio in Niccolò Machiavelli's *La Mandragola*, see Angela Guidotti. "Una perfetta macchina drammaturgica: La *Mandragola*." *Il modello e la trasgressione: commedie del primo '500*, edited by ead. Rome: Bulzoni, 1983, pp. 61–101.
47 "Sarebbe difficile trovare una scena che non presupponga un diverso livello di informazione fra personaggi e spettatori." (Stewart, "Il testo teatrale," p. 16) In *La Calandra*, spectators are aware of both of the twins' true identities and genders and their tactics of cross-dressing from the "Argumento" onwards (s. *La Calandra*, p. 65–66); they would also be the only ones to comprehend the real causes of Ruffo's supposed magic.

then, is as simple as it is graphic: two servants (Samia and Lusco) have sex inside the house of Samia's mistress, while another servant (Fessenio) tries to enter the house from the outside. The short dialogue of the scene links the servant's desire to enter the house to what is going on inside it: On finding the entrance locked, Fessenio, on the outside, gives instructions as how to open it. Samia, on the inside – obviously giving an excuse for not opening the door – keeps telling him that she is trying to unlock the door but failing because the key does not work. After a while, with Fessenio on the outside getting more and more impatient, the door opens and the action resumes its vertiginous pace. An audience, though, informed of Samia's intentions and therefore in the know about what is happening behind the closed door, will unmistakeably decode her descriptions of the action indoors – such as "putting the key in the lock" ("metter la chiave nella toppa," III.10.167), "shaking" or "rattling" the key ("Scuoto quant'io posso," III.10.177), or "oiling" it ("ho tutta unta la chiave," III.10.179) – as unequivocal, and actually rather coarse metaphors for the servants' erotic encounter.

In this way, the difference in knowledge on the part of the audience and the characters involved (especially Fessenio) becomes the very foundation of the scene's lewd comicalness: The fact that the audience know better what is going on behind the closed door than Fessenio in front of the door does, is the reason why the audience can (correctly) interpret Samia's comments from the inside as bawdy metaphors, while, as the audience also observes, Fessenio (wrongly) takes them literally. If the play is – in its very structure – based on the audience's advantage of information, here this theatrical ploy is played out to its fullest comic potential, and, as such, is brought to the fore: the audience is obviously not only supposed to chuckle about Samia's and Lucio's cleverly concealed rendezvous, but also about Fessenio's total ignorance and naïveté, and the striking, comical contrast between the character's limited insight and their own unlimited knowledge regarding the theatrical world.

According to Stewart it takes the final solution of the comic *intrecci* to bring at least some of the characters level with the audience. After the twins' proper identification, Stewart sees Lidio and Santilla, their servants, and Fulvia in the same position of complete understanding that the audience has occupied all along.[48] A closer look at Scene III.10 reveals this to be only partly true: the scene, it seems, not only emphasizes and visualizes the segregation of the theatrical spaces and the different levels of knowledge distributed among characters and spectators – its outright farcical character also highlights its fictiona-

---

[48] Stewart, "Il testo teatrale," p. 18.

lity. After all, through all its sexual hilariousness the scene is positively exhibiting its own status of make-believe. The graphic bawdiness of Samia's metaphors seems to have been designed for the purpose of reminding the audience of the fact that nothing is *really* going on behind the painted door of the set design, and that this world, about which they know everything there is to know, is indeed a fictional one.[49] The play therefore confirms the classical concept of theatrical mimesis as a semiotic structure, which brackets the action in an as-if-dimension:[50] here, theatrical representation clearly refers to something that is not really there, and requires the audience's ability to decode its signs. At the same time it is based, it seems, not so much on the idea of a Coleridgean "suspension of disbelief," but rather on a particularly heightened and continued disbelief – that is: on the "recognition of fiction as fiction," which not only adds yet another amusing, reflexive level of meaning to the theatrical event, but also allows for "insight purged of illusions."[51] The sex on stage evidences in this case that, on the audience's part, the play presumes – and generates –

---

[49] The sex on stage in this case is obviously one of the instances where "the form winks at the content" and therefore becomes more visible as such (Bert O. States, *Great Reckonings in Little Rooms. On the Phenomenology of Theater.* Berkeley et al.: University of California Press, 1985, p. 32.

[50] Even though this is not the place to discuss Platonic and Aristotelian concepts of mimesis in general – and theatrical mimesis in particular – it is probably safe to say that both assume mimetic representation to refer to, or "stand for," that which it represents: Plato's critique of mimesis in *Politeia*, Book 10, is based on the "distance" he sees between representation and the eternal true ideas (see Joachim Küpper. "Mimesis und Fiktion in Literatur, Bildender Kunst und Musik." *Zeitschrift für Ästhetik und allgemeine Kunstwissenschaft*, vol. 53, no. 2, 2008, pp. 169–190, p. 169, n. 2), but Plato nevertheless sees one as – ineptly or wrongly – referring to the other (see Arbogast Schmitt. "Mimesis bei Aristoteles und in den Poetikkommentaren der Renaissance." *Mimesis und Simulation*, edited by Andreas Kablitz and Gerhard Neumann. Freiburg: Rombach, 1998, pp. 17–53, p. 27). According to Aristotle it is thanks to the referential structure that mimesis may be useful in processes of learning: theatrical and poetical mimesis can teach the characteristics of a person (be he/she fictional or historical), because it shows his/her actions in so far as they express this particular character (ibid., p. 37), and are understandable as its signs. As Schmitt demonstrates, Renaissance commentaries on Aristotelian poetics tend to shift the focus of the semiosis of theatrical representation towards the "natura ipsa" of world and humankind (see ibid. 45), that is: "good" representation is understood as a metonymic or metaphoric encryption of commonly human traits, vices, and actions. On the question of mimesis in connection with the "as-if"-dimension of fiction – which remains strangely unreflected in Aristotle – with respect to Augustine's *Soliloquia*, see Küpper, "Mimesis und Fiktion," p. 172 f. On the 'sign-structure' of representation see ibid., p. 175, n. 17.

[51] Rudolf Behrens. "Die Vorstellung des Eros. Imagination und Liebesgenese in der Literatur von Früher Neuzeit bis Romantik (Ficino, Du Plaisir, Marivaux, Foscolo)." *Liebessemantik. Frühneuzeitliche Darstellungen von Liebe in Italien und Frankreich*, edited by Kirsten Dickhaut. Wiesbaden: Harrassowitz, 2014, pp. 93–131, p. 100; my translation.

a twofold knowledge about the representation on stage: a knowledge *about* the theatrical fiction that is superior to the perspectives of the fictional characters, and a reflective knowledge *about* its fictionality. And so, even as the play reaches the *lieto fine* with all its enlightening moments of recognition, its audience will still know more than its characters.

Even though it is beyond the purpose and reach of this paper to elaborate on the cultural-political meaning of the play as a theatrical reflection of the Medicean conquest of Roman space in their ascent to the papacy,[52] or on its Boccaccian filiation,[53] the very existence of both of these undeniable dimensions of its meaning may further enhance my point: watching the intricate play *and* following its political-allegorical as well as its intertextual references appears to be a pursuit focused very much on (self-)reflexive intellectual gratification.

Needless to say, this does not deny that the audience's phenomenal experience may not at the same time be characterized by a feeling of "togetherness" brought forth by the collective quality of the theatrical event,[54] which may have even been enforced by their communal understanding of the play's semiotic sub-strata – by them all 'getting the joke.' Their understanding of the play itself, however, is a markedly representational knowledge with the fictional world as its object.[55]

---

[52] R. L. Martinez. "Etruria Triumphant in Rome: Fables of the Medici Rule and Bibbiena's *Calandra*." *Renaissance Drama*, no. 37, 2010, pp. 69–98, see also Ferroni, "I due gemelli," p. 33.
[53] On Boccaccio's *Decameron* as pre- and/or subtext of the play, which has not only obviously influenced its content and the development of its characters but is present even on the linguistic / stylistic level of the comedy, see, with many references to further studies on this subject, Padoan, "Introduzione," p. 18 ff.
[54] Gulizia, "Spatial Traffic," p. 118.
[55] With the drastic difference of social status between audience and characters in mind, I would go so far as to argue that the audience's "togetherness" depends to a great extent on their "apartness" from the play's characters: the audience form a community in so far as the characters constitute its "other" (see, with a slightly different focus, Gulizia, "Spatial Traffic," p. 118). Significantly, the play's surprisingly persistent preoccupation with physical experience, corporeality, and sensory perception, as has been compellingly described by Gulizia, is observable mostly in characters that clearly belong to the lower social classes (servants), or are marked by their lack of intellect (Calandro). Other characters use allusions to corporeality mostly for cruel mockery and ridicule, as in the whole sequence of Calandro's supposed transportation in a chest.

IV *Henry V*: everybody knows

Of course, in the scene of "royal romance"[56] at the end of the "warlike Harry['s]" (Prologue 5) military campaign, no one actually has sex on stage. Yet, motivated (if at all) by the scene's obvious and outspoken preoccupation with the issue of dynastic continuity, sex is continually evoked, alluded to, or hinted at.[57]

The history play, written somewhere in spring / early summer of 1599 as the third part of Shakespeare's so called "Henriad," continues the dynastic tale of its prequels by staging the military accomplishments of the second Lancastrian king. Not only does the rebellious prince Hal, who in the two parts of *Henry IV* was seen running wild in the taverns of Eastcheap, complete his transformation into a charismatic, yet sometimes cruel and cold-hearted leader. He also declares war on France under the pretence of a genealogical claim to the French throne, crosses the channel with a small army, conquers Harfleur, and virtually annihilates the French army in the famous Battle of Agincourt. This then gives him the right to claim the French princess's hand in marriage as well as a large number of dukedoms and the position of heir to the French throne. During the negotiations following his victory Henry declares the Princess to be his "capital demand" (V.2.95), and the French King Charles VI is in no position to object. Henry doesn't need to woo her. And yet he does.

It is almost annoyingly simple to describe what happens on stage: Henry sends his noble counsellors off to negotiate once more with the French king and his entourage, asks that Princess Catherine will be left behind with him, and then talks quite a lot. Her answers to his rhetorical endeavors consist mostly of "I cannot tell vat is dat," "I cannot tell," or "I don't know dat" (V.2.173; 189; 204). At some point Henry speaks equally basic French, a little later they kiss, and at that very moment (thanks to Shakespeare's impeccable sense of timing) King Charles and the whole group of French and English nobles return.

---

56 William Shakespeare. *Henry V*, edited by Gary Taylor, Oxford: Oxford University Press, 1982 (The Oxford Shakespeare), p. 28. References in brackets are to this edition.
57 V.2.198–202; V.2.205–208; with regard to the play's continued reference to the problem of dynastic continuity as well as questions of male fertility and sexual prowess, see Rebecca Ann Bach. "Tennis Balls: *Henry V* and Testicular Masculinity, or, According to the *OED*, Shakespeare Doesn't Have Any Balls." *Renaissance Drama*, 30, 2001, 3–24. During the reign of Elizabeth I these matters evidently had a specific biopolitical background; see Marie Axton. *The Queen's Two Bodies: Drama and the Elizabethan Succession*. London: Royal Historical Society, 1977, 112 f.

Complications arise, however, when it comes to describing *how* it happens. They start with Shakespeare's refutation of each and every one of the idealistic models of behavior Renaissance culture offered for this topical situation of courtship. From the outset Henry refers to the most elementary stereotypes of Renaissance discourses of love in their courtly, Petrarchist, and Neoplatonic varieties, only to refuse to follow any of their playbooks.[58] And if the king's behavior frustrates expectations, then the princess's does, too. Instead of gracefully accepting the royal offer of marriage, her short evasive answers tease and stall Henry, who – for once in the entire play – seems to be completely out of his depth until, at long last, he does something he is charmingly incapable of: speaking French. In most productions this is the moment when the ice finally begins to melt.[59] From this point onwards, Henry and Catherine start sharing a tone of playful self-deprecation.[60] The complications continue, because little by little the colloquy turns into what I will call – for want of a better (or more historically correct) term – a flirt.

---

[58] As far as I am aware, this has not been noted before. For an overview of the plural Renaissance concepts of love and their connected discourses I refer to Dickhaut, *Liebessemantik*; Klaus Hempfer. "Die Pluralisierung des erotischen Diskurses in der europäischen Lyrik des 16. und beginnenden 17. Jahrhunderts (Ariost, Ronsard, Shakespeare, Opitz)." *Germanisch-Romanische Monatsschrift*, 38, 1988, pp. 251–264; *Amor sacro e profano. Modelle und Modellierungen der Liebe in Literatur und Malerei der italienischen Renaissance*, edited by Jörn Steigerwald. Wiesbaden: Harrassowitz, 2012, and id. *Amors Renaissance. Modellierungen himmlischer und irdischer Liebe in der Literatur des Cinquecento*, Wiesbaden: Harrassowitz, 2014; with a particular focus on Shakespeare, see Jill Line. *Shakespeare and the Ideal of Love*. Rochester: Inner Tradition, 2004; *Souls with Longing. Representations of Honor and Love in Shakespeare*, edited by Bernard J. Dobski and Dustin A. Gish. Lanham: Lexington Books, 2011; and Stanley Wells. *Shakespeare, Sex & Love*. Oxford: Oxford University Press, 2010. On the ironic details of this refusal of Renaissance discourses of love, in so far as they constitute contemporary knowledge *about* love, as well as its consequences for the play's contesting of Renaissance concepts of subjectivity, see E. Schomacher. "How to Rule, How to War, How to Love – and How to Act: Shakespeare's *Henriad* and Skills." Forthcoming.

[59] See e.g. Dominic Dromgoole's production for Shakespeare's Globe, available on DVD as *Shakespeare's Globe Henry V*, Season 2012, Globe on Screen, 2012; the wooing scene starts at about 02:21:00 of the play. The same holds for Kenneth Branagh's film production *Henry V*, Renaissance Films PLC, 1989. A different – and, to my view, not entirely convincing – interpretation was developed in Thea Sharrock's production *Henry V, The Hollow Crown, Part 3*, BBC, 2012, where Henry's attempt at speaking French (as well as most of the scene's bawdiness) was cut.

[60] See *Henry V*, V.2.179–185 or V.2.210–211; the change of mood is also reflected in the fact that from this part of the scene onwards Catherine is addressed as someone Henry is willing to let into his sphere of political power (see "England is thine, Ireland is thine, France is thine, and Henry Plantagenet is thine," V.2.230–231; or "We are the makers of manners," V.2.262), and is taken seriously as a political force herself ("queen of all," V.2.235).

Critics have never ceased to point out that from a logical point of view this flirtatiousness is highly unconvincing:[61] in addition to the much discussed language barrier, and the blatant political motivation of their marriage, Henry and his army have just done away with several members of Catherine's family. Actors and directors, however, feel that Shakespeare provided "the simplest answer" to the scene's apparent incongruity with the rest of the play, that is, the premise "that the two characters do literally in the course of one brief interview fall in love."[62] Also, the multiple logical impediments to the characters' romantic attachment do not prevent audiences from enjoying the scene.[63] Still today, audiences simply do not seem to watch whatever is happening between the king and the princess from a logical point of view.

I will try to show here that the reason why they do not so is because the scene, in a way, does not allow them to. In fact, I will try to show that the scene works so well on stage precisely because it succeeds in involving the audience on a physical-emotional level; it purposely, and skillfully, makes them share its flirtatious mood, rather than analyse its preconditions. It aims at a "corporeal grasp of something that eludes cognitive understanding."[64] That way, the audience do not think of the reasons why King Henry V and Princess Catherine of Valois should or should not fall in love. Instead, they just fall in love with them.[65] And I aim also to show that, in this case (as opposed to *La Calandra*), it is precisely this emotional sharing and taking part, as a form of non-referential and embodied knowledge, that the play as a whole requires and implements. Much like in *La Calandra*, then, the senseless, yet sensual scene is where the play's presuppositions concerning the audience's perceptive stance become most obvious and their implementation is taken to the extreme.

---

[61] So much so that Hedrick even proposes to read the scene against its own text, in an admirable attempt to defend it against critical disapproval (see Hedrick, "Advantage, Affect, History," p. 470; p. 478–480).

[62] Kenneth Branagh. "Henry V." *Players of Shakespeare 2. Further Essays in Shakespearean Performance by Players with the Royal Shakespeare Company*, edited by Russell Jackson and Robert Smallwood. Cambridge et al.: Cambridge University Press, 1988, pp. 93–105, p. 104.

[63] In Gary Taylor's words, "in the theatre'" the scene is still "irresistible" (*Henry V*, p. 71); according to Michael Goldman any critical assessment of the scene should take this into account as a consciously produced theatrical effect: "The theatrical weight of the wooing scene in *Henry V* […] must be calculated on the assumption that the actor playing the King will try to generate the most pleasure allowed him by the lines and the events of the scene." (Goldman, *The Energies of Drama*, p. 8).

[64] West, "Understanding in the Elizabethan Theatres," p. 125.

[65] The intense reactions of the audience throughout the scene are perceivable even on the published DVD of Dominic Dromgoole's production of *Henry V*.

I will suggest that the scene achieves the effect of drawing spectators into its emotional dynamics by using a combination of several scenographic and performative techniques; over the next few pages I will take a closer look at two of them. Sex does, in one way or another, play an important part in both: The first of these techniques consists of the pervasive presence, actually a kind of *crescendo*, of what Stanley Wells has dubbed "accumulatively lewd wordplay."[66] And the second one I would like to describe as an accentuation of the embodied aspects of acting, that is: an accentuation of the fact that what actors do is not just pretending.

The lewd wordplay, in this case, works in a similar way as in other Shakespearean scenes of sexual banter in comedies such as *Much Ado About Nothing*, *As You Like It*, *Love's Labour's Lost*, or *The Twelfth Night*, that is, by alluding to erotic and/or sexual connotations of words, figures of speech, or metaphors, while at the same time keeping their denotative meaning in play. In this way the sexual undertone is only ever insinuated or implied, and often remains intriguingly doubtful; its very perceptibility as such depends on the context – and the hearer. Whether a specific figure of speech is understood as a "bawdy quibble"[67] strongly depends on whether there are others around it that are, and on the hearers' accumulating receptiveness to them.[68] In these other cases of Shakespearean badinage, however, the allusions are usually addressed to another of the play's characters.

As Stephen Greenblatt has stressed, in these dialogues of "erotically charged sparring" language is "perfectly embodied";[69] He argues that the dialogues function as a theatrical transformation of the "erotic heat" or "friction"[70] that medical theories of Early Modernity assumed was necessary not only for conception and procreation, but also for the formation of the foetus's gender, and hence that they allow room for the characters' formation and acknowledgement of their own (sexual) identities.[71] Characters do not express an

---

66 Wells, *Shakespeare, Sex & Love*, p. 93.
67 Ibid., p. 148.
68 Stanley Wells rightly notes in this regard that "Shakespeare's language is polyphonic; rather as, in listening to music played on a keyboard, our ears may pick out a note of a melody while subordinating its harmonies in our consciousness, so in a passage of Shakespearean verse, though we may subconsciously acknowledge the possibility of a sexual undertone, that sense forms only a small part of our apprehension of what is said." (Ibid., p. 9)
69 Stephen Greenblatt. "Fiction and Friction." *Shakespearean Negotiations. The Circulation of Social Energy in Renaissance England*. Berkeley: University of California Press, 1988, pp. 66–93, p. 89.
70 Ibid., p. 85.
71 Greenblatt sees the erotic wordplay in Shakespeare's plays as a theatrical appropriation of contemporary theories of procreation, and their concept of erotic heat: just as medical treatises

"inward" emotional state – or even an individuality – that somehow existed prior to, and independently of, this "sparring." Instead they enact and share emotion with and through their bawdy exchanges.[72]

In the wooing scene of *Henry V*, though, the French princess does not speak English well enough to join in the game. This time the only possible addressee of the bawdiness is the audience – an audience, moreover, who have been prepared for this by the "English lesson" Catherine receives from her nurse in Scene III.4, where mispronounced English vocabulary ("gown," "foot") drifts over into French obscenities.[73] It seems, therefore, the effects of the scene's erotic "dallying with words"[74] are aimed at the spectators: again, its bawdiness does not so much express something the spectators have to decode in order to know something about the scene or its characters, but rather brings forth a specific mood that the audience is invited to share.[75] They are drawn towards a participatory mode of knowing, or being in sync with the characters, rather than interpreting them. Therefore, Henry's bawdiness deserves closer attention.

Examples abound, and they grow more and more drastic and explicit as the scene goes on, so that most modern productions avoid playing up to the many double-entendres:[76] they range from Henry's insistent pleas that Catherine might "take" or "have" – rather than choose, accept, or simply marry –

---

argue that "[...] the generative power of nature centers on fruitful, pleasurable chafing" (ibid., p. 88), Shakespearean drama in particular turns this – in its verbalized form – into a means of the generation of characters and their individuality.

72 "[A]t moments [Shakespeare's] plays seem to imply that erotic friction *originates* in the wantonness of language [...]" (ibid., p. 89).

73 "Foot" in the Princess's ears obviously sounds similar to the French *foutre*, "gown," mispronounced by her nurse as "cown," is associated with the French *con*, cfr. III.4.46–51.

74 Greenblatt, "Fiction and Friction," p. 90.

75 The scene's use of language therefore provides an example of what Jan Söffner describes as "organic and tool-like infusion of language into a certain feel (*Gespür*) and action" (see Jan Söffner. *Partizipation. Metapher, Mimesis, Musik – und die Kunst, Texte bewohnbar zu machen*. Paderborn: Fink, 2014, p. 55; my translation). Greenblatt comes closest to observing this aspect of Shakespearean language, and in particular his "erotic sparring," in acknowledging that Shakespearean drama not only "uses" the "erotic power" of friction, but also "returns it with interest, as it were, to the audience" (Greenblatt, "Fiction and Friction," p. 88).

76 One reason for this may be that, for a modern audience at least, they sometimes border on "groan-jokes," those jokes "so obvious that the hearer may even feel a kind of comic resentment at being expected to find [them] funny" (Wells, *Shakespeare, Sex & Love*, p. 90). Luckily though, for my purposes, Dominic Dromgoole's celebrated version for Shakespeare's Globe, London, in 2012 showed the scene with much of its sexual imagery intact, and I will occasionally refer to this production's way of staging it.

him,[77] to his jesting assertion that, if only methods of wooing were more suitable to his talents ("if I could win a Lady at leap frog"), he should "quickly leap into a wife" (V.2.138–139).[78] Further examples of sexual wordplay include Henry's anticipation of Catherine's mocking comments about "those parts in me that you love with your heart" (V.2.194), or even – as a kind of reverse wordplay – his curiously coy translation of the French "baiser" as "to kiss" (V.2.255).

Their cumulative effect can probably be best described by comparing it to the perception of a rhythm or a melody: not only does it cause an interplay of what Husserl calls "retention" and "protention";[79] that is, something like a reverberation of what has just been said, and its opposite, an anticipation of what will be said,[80] which works on a physical, embodied level, bringing about a phenomenal presence of what is past and what is anticipated.[81] The "accu-

---

[77] For "take" see most prominently V.2.162–164: "If thou would have such a one, take me; and take me, take a soldier; take a soldier, take a king." For his uses of "have," see V.2.225; 236–237. With regard to other Shakespearean examples of the use of "take" in the sense of "have sexual intercourse with," see Wells, *Shakespeare, Sex & Love*, p. 151.

[78] In Dromgoole's production Jamie Parker as Henry sophisticatedly plays up to this sexual pun by turning it into a Freudian slip *avant la lettre*: he shows Henry react to his own line as if he realized its bawdy innuendo only after saying it; see *Shakespeare's Globe Henry V*, 02:28:00. This also goes to show that in performance sexual puns – even if spoken by a male character – need not appear chauvinistic.

[79] Edmund Husserl. *Texte zur Phänomenologie des inneren Zeitbewusstseins*, edited by Rudolf Bernet. Hamburg: Meiner, 1985; see Francisco J. Varela. "The Specious Present: A Neurophenomonology of Time Consciousness." *Naturalizing Phenomenology*, edited by Jean Petitot. Stanford: Stanford University Press, 1999, pp. 266–314.

[80] As Merleau-Ponty beautifully explained, the "perceptual field [...] draws along in its wake its own horizon of retentions, and bites into the future with its protentions." (Maurice Merleau-Ponty. *Phenomenology of Perception*. London et al.: Routledge, 1962, p. 416).

[81] Bernhard Waldenfels's precise analysis of the connection of rhythm, perception, and embodiment has proved very enlightening in this regard: Bernhard Waldenfels. "Zeitverschiebung. Motive einer Phänomenologie der Zeiterfahrung." *Zeit und Text. Philosophische, kulturanthropologische, literarhistorische und linguistische Beiträge*, edited by Andreas Kablitz, Wulf Oesterreicher and Rainer Warning. Munich: Fink, 2003, pp. 33–45, where he describes rhythm as belonging to those *Bewegungsgestalten* ("figures of movement") that are "neither purely physical nor purely psychological"; their formation (*Gestaltbildung*), he states, takes place "between things and body and transgresses both" ("spielt sich zwischen Dingen und Leib ab und greift auf beide über [...]." p. 40; my translation). Much like the accumulating bawdiness, in rhythm the single elements are not identical but become identified as our experience keeps "coming back to them" (ibid., p. 40; my translation). For the importance of rhythm for the interpretation and performance of emotion in Shakespearean plays (though without reference to its perception by an audience), see Peter Groves. "'My Heart Dances:' Performing Emotion through Shakespeare's Rhythms." *Shakespeare and Emotions. Inheritances, Enactments, Legacies*, edited by R. S. White. Basingstoke et al.: Palgrave Macmillan, 2015, pp. 83–94.

mulatively lewd wordplay" also actively involves the listeners – in this case: the audience – in the process of perception: they cannot passively receive it, because it only exists as long as their own perception creates it and takes part in it. The first technique, therefore, causes a kind of transgression of the stage's boundaries on the audience's part: the spectators become part of the performance in so far as their active, embodied reception and complementation, as it were, becomes an integral constituent of the scene's emotional dynamics.

With the second technique the further blurring of the differences between theatrical representation on stage and the world of the audience in front of the stage originates in the stage business itself: when Henry and Catherine kiss at the end of their private conversation, the audience bears witness to a performance that is clearly not only make-believe. The stage kiss belongs to – and is probably the one of most intense examples of – a whole range of actions on stage that contest the classical paradigm of mimesis. As Renaissance drama – and Shakespeare in particular – was well aware: stage business that relies on the actors' bodies questions the supposed separation and the referential structure between the as-if-world of theatrical fiction and its "signified," the "real" or phenomenal world, but also the one between actor and character:[82] An apple eaten on a stage is gone from the "real world," and is digested not by a fictional character;[83] dances or fencing duels cannot be played on stage unless the actors are apt dancers or fencers in "real life." As Hamlet despairingly attests: tears shed on stage are not just a character's tears.[84] And there simply is no way for actors to "represent" a kiss, except by really kissing. Significantly, the wooing scene culminates in a moment in which the action on stage is as real as actions in front of it.[85]

---

[82] The boundaries and separations between make-believe and "real life" were perceived as (dangerously) permeable and precarious, as is shown by the anti-theatrical writers' fears of the effects of acting on the actors, but also by a number of medieval and early modern theater legends (see with respect to the first, Laura Levine. *Men in Women's Clothing. Anti-Theatricality and Effeminization, 1579–1642*, Cambridge: Cambridge University Press, 1994; with respect to the urban legends of the theater see Jody Enders. *Death by Drama and other Medieval Urban Legends*, Chicago: University of Chicago Press, 2005).

[83] See ibid., p. 5.

[84] I am, of course, referring to the famous Hecuba Soliloquy in II.2. of Shakespeare's *Hamlet*, especially Hamlet's attributing the tears to the actor (First Player), rather than the character: "What's Hecuba to him, or he to Hecuba, | That he should weep for her?" See the scene's reading with regard to the First Player's embodiment of emotion in John H. Astington. *Actors and Acting in Shakespeare's Time. The Art of Stage Playing*, Cambridge et al.: Cambridge University Press, 2010, p. 17.

[85] It ends, as Enders puts it, with a moment that provokes questions about "where theatre ends and life begins" (see Enders, *Death by Drama*, p. 2). On the inseparability of representational mimesis and the dimension of embodiment in drama, see with respect to modern drama

With this, the scene blurs even the most basic distinctions of theatrical representation – the one between audience and actors –, and dissolves the most elementary division of theatrical space – the one between auditorium and stage.[86] With the audiences' embodied participation and the actors' embodied performing, theirs is the non-representational knowledge of a "shared space."[87]

In this way the history play also aims at a mode of perception that tends to fade-out the issue of its fictionality. Of course, the play does fictionalize the historical events and characters it shows; it obviously appropriates them – sometimes rather approximately – and it explicitly points to the fact that what the audience see on stage is *not* identical with what really happened during the historical Henry V's war in France.[88] For the audience's emotional and physical taking-part, though, the difference between fiction and reality does not count for much: under the condition that the audience do contribute to the performance and work with the actors, the theater becomes the appropriate space of "bringing forth" the "warlike Harry, like himself" (Prologue 5).

Erika Fischer-Lichte. "Was verkörpert der Körper des Schauspielers?" *Performativität und Medialität*, edited by Sybille Krämer. Munich: Fink, 2004, pp. 141–162, and "Verkörperung/Embodiment. Zum Wandel einer alten theaterwissenschaftlichen in eine neue kulturwissenschaftliche Kategorie." *Verkörperung*, edited by ead., Christian Horn and Matthias Warstat. Tübingen et al.: Francke, 2001, pp. 11–25.

86 West, "Understanding in the Elizabethan Theatres," p. 134 f.

87 The concept of "shared space" has been developed in phenomenological and cognitive research on gestures (see Matthew Ratcliffe. "The Structure of Interpersonal Experience." *The Phenomenology of Embodied Subjectivity*, edited by Rasmus Thybo Jensen and Dermot Morgan. Cham et al.: Springer, 2013, pp. 221–238); for an example of its usefulness in the description of aisthetic experiences see Esther Schomacher and Jan Söffner. "Warum es mit Repräsentationsformen nicht getan sein kann. Sieben Thesen zum Enactive Criticism." *Repräsentationsformen von Wissen. Beiträge zum XXVI. Forum Junge Romanistik in Bochum (26.–29. Mai 2010)*, edited by Eva Siebenborn, Annika Nickenig and Judith Kittler. Munich: Meidenbauer, 2011, pp. 125–149, p. 132. As with the concept of "second-person interaction" developed by Shaun Gallagher and Dan Zahavi (see *The Phenomenological Mind. An Introduction to Philosophy of Mind and Cognitive Sciences*. London et al.: Routledge, 2008, p. 176), the emphasis is on an understanding independent of conscious analysis or "identification"; Gallagher's and Zahavi's concept refers to this kind of understanding with respect to other people's actions and feelings (that is, it is focused on the "problem of other minds", p. 184 ff.); whereas this is the attempt to describe a similar understanding with respect to works of literature, independent of a conscious construction of meaning or identification with the characters. For further elaboration see Söffner, *Partizipation*, chapter 1.4 "Sprache als Fertigkeit," pp. 68–79.

88 See Taylor's summary of the instances where Shakespeare departs from the historical sources and chronicles of his time, *Henry V*, p. 31 f. The play's Epilogue explicitly reminds the audience that its "bending author"'s (Epilogue 2) depiction of "mighty men" (Epilogue 3) was "mangling by starts the full course of their glory." (Epilogue 4).

V Bodies, minds, and stages

"The space of the stage and perception belong together,"[89] Ulrike Haß summarizes the observation that stage architecture and design, and the practices of performance connected with them, reflect a culture's concepts concerning human perception. As it turns out, though, this is not so easily done, when in the culture in question several, sometimes contrary concepts concerning human perception are in circulation, and the issue of how human beings perceive, learn, and know is itself the cause of much disconcertment, but also excitement or even exhilaration. And Renaissance culture is, as Miranda Anderson has pointed out, such a case.

This means: Even if both plays – and particularly their senseless and sensual scenes – enforce, or implement, a certain way for the audience to know and understand, they do not simply affirm this knowledge; especially when they are seen in the context of their specific conditions of performance and their different stage architecture, it is obvious that they also (at least subliminally) contest it by counterpoising it to its respective other. If both plays can be said to reflect Renaissance concepts of human understanding, they also reflect their contrariety.

La Calandra's highlighting of the audience's referential, detached, visual-analytical "knowing-that" is obviously enabled – and even supplemented – by the conditions of performance provided by Italian court festivities (of which the performance of *commedie erudite* was a standard ingredient from the late fifteenth century on):[90] The Serlian picture-stage with its elaborate, perspectivally constructed design showing an idealized version of the city where the comedy is set, the spectators seated in a closed-off auditorium, usually at some distance from its proscenium, in strict hierarchical order with the person of highest social rank sitting vis-à-vis the vanishing point of the said set design, the very marked difference of status between the aristocratic members of the audience and the characters on stage – all of this seems to second the perceptional observations developed from the striking example of III.10:[91] the setting

---

[89] Ulrike Haß. *Das Drama des Sehens*. Munich: Fink, 2006, p. 15; my translation.

[90] Cesare Molinari. "Scenografia e spettacolo nelle poetiche del Cinquecento." *Il Veltro*, vol. 8, no. 6, 1964, pp. 885–902; Giovanni Attolini. *Teatro e spettacolo nel Rinascimento*. Rome et al.: Laterza, 1988, p. 42 ff.

[91] See the collection of theories concerning theatrical architecture and stage design provided by Ferruccio Marotti. *Storia documentaria del teatro italiano. Lo spettacolo dall'Umanesimo al Manierismo. Teoria e tecnica*. Milan: Feltrinelli, 1974, as well as Pierre Francastel. *Guardare il teatro*. Bologna: Il Mulino, 1987; on the audience's position and perception in Italian Renaissance drama, see Cesare Molinari. "Les rapports entre la scène et les spectateurs." *Le lieu théâtral à la Renaissance*, edited by Jean Jacquot. Paris: Centre National de la Recherche Scien-

contributes to providing the audience with "a complete view of the action from a masterful distance,"[92] and in doing so shapes the audience's experience in accordance with emerging contemporary concepts of intellectual understanding and knowing, that is: humanism's growing epistemological confidence in visual perception and its mathematical/geometrical foundation,[93] the privilege given to the visual sense as the one closely linked to the higher mental faculties of reason, and the (possibly even more growing) confidence in human capacities to learn and understand by deciphering, semiotic analysis, and reflection.[94]

But yet, not only does the play itself contain elements that contradict this preference for visual-referential knowledge by displaying its vulnerability to deceit.[95] More importantly the strict congruity of point of view and knowledge itself stresses the fact that, ultimately, any point of view, and therefore any understanding – even the audience's – is coincident with a physical, corporeal position; that is, the spectators' distanced, analytical, apparently non-corporeal understanding as such also hinges on a specific placement of their bodies within

---

tifique, 1968, pp. 61–71, and "Gli spettatori e lo spazio scenico nel teatro del Cinquecento." *Bolletino del Centro Internazionale di Studi di Architettura Andrea Palladio*, no. 16, 1974, pp. 145–154.

92 Curiously, William West's synopsis of everything the Elizabethan theater is *not* provides a perfect description of the audience's position in Italian Renaissance drama, see West, "Understanding in the Elizabethan Theatres," p. 136.

93 With the (re)discovery of linear perspective, the visual sense is – on the one hand – revalued as a mainly rational-mechanical device, even if – on the other hand – the very understanding of its functioning allows for the creation of enhanced illusionistic effects for the human eye (see Frank Büttner. "Rationalisierung der Mimesis. Anfänge der konstruierten Perspektive bei Brunelleschi und Alberti." *Mimesis und Simulation*, pp. 55–87, p. 63 ff. and p. 75). Connell particularly emphasizes the ambivalence in much of this epistemological reassessment of the human senses: "At issue was where the eye could legitimately be directed" (Connell, *The Idolatrous Eye*, p. 33).

94 See e.g. Connell's account of the "epistemological dialectic of image and word" (ibid., p. 5) in Renaissance England, in his Chapter 2: "Word Against Image: The Context of Iconoclasm," pp. 36–51. Connell repeatedly stresses the importance of a widespread printing culture as the medial-technological basis for this epistemological shift, as typography made "exact, unvarying texts possible and lent thereby an increased confidence to the 'word-in-space'." (Ibid., p. 29)

95 Most misunderstandings throughout the multi-layered intrigue of the play are, ultimately, optical illusions, while – especially during the virtuosic scenes of sexual cross- and un-cross-dressing, of replacement of one twin by the other – it is often only the sense of touch, that is, the direct physical contact, that eventually proves the truth; see e.g. *La Calandra*, IV.2 or V.2. See in a similar vein the section 'Touching and Wearing' in Gulizia, "Spatial Traffic," p. 119–121.

the theatrical architecture. The audience's understanding seems disembodied, because it is based on their bodies' distance from the action onstage. In this way, their taking part in the experience of the court festivity and their sharing of courtly habits appear as a basic condition for them to be in the right position and develop the right perceptional stance towards the play.[96] The audience's referential, semiotic understanding of the play, therefore, is by no means bodiless.

To come back to the comedy's senseless scene once more: Even as it exacerbates the audience's intellectual knowledge about the play's fictional world, its motive does emphasize, perhaps in a comically ironic way, the presence of bodies. After all, the scene is about sex.

In the case of *Henry V* the contestation of the audience's knowledge – this time their embodied, embedded understanding – can be traced in the play itself. Even if *Henry V* does, from its famous Prologue onwards, explicitly aim at the physical and emotional collaboration of the audience, it does so in a way that emphasizes the inseparability of embodied and intellectual understanding, and thereby constantly undercuts the modern distinction between mind and body.

Of course, the typical octagonal Elizabethan theaters – with their roofless center, where spectators paid one penny to watch the plays standing up, exposed to the elements, but in touching distance of the low and rather bare stage[97] – "are arranged to resist" the "imaginary distance and control" associated with the picture stage.[98] In *Henry V* Shakespeare seems to have gone out of his way to highlight the participatory effects of this very setting as early as the Prologue: when the Prologue ironically and self-consciously reminds the audience that the theatrical venue (the "unworthy scaffold," "cock-pit," or "wooden O," Prologue 10; 11; 13) and the actors ("flat unraisèd spirits," Prologue 9) are the company's most reliable assets,[99] he also alludes to the fact

---

[96] In much the same way as Gulizia concludes from his close reading of the play's performance in Urbino within the context of elaborate *intermezzi*, the audience's attitude towards the play may be orientated less towards their "social domination," but rather towards the exploration of their "social skills"; see Gulizia, "Green Sense," in this volume.

[97] See Andrew Gurr. *The Shakespearean Stage, 1574–1642*. Cambridge: Cambridge University Press, 1992; Henry S. Turner. *The English Renaissance Stage: Geometry, Poetics and the Practical Spatial Arts, 1580–1630*. Oxford: Oxford University Press, 2006.

[98] West, "Understanding in the Elizabethan Theatres," p. 136.

[99] With theatrical practice in mind, I assume that the Prologue is not – as it has sometimes been read (as e.g. in Melissa D. Aaron. "The Globe and *Henry V* as business document." *Studies in English Literature 1500–1900*, no. 40, 2000, 277–292) – sincerely apologetic. As Gary Taylor put it: "In practical terms, the modesty of the Chorus implies considerable confidence: in the theater, one apologizes only for one's most reliable effects, while expressing the greatest pos-

that, if indeed the theater makes them take part in the performance, this is not the fault of its "physical limitations,"[100] but actually their achievement.[101]

What is more: The Prologue, as well as several of the Chorus's other speeches, explicitly enjoin the audience to contribute to the project of "bring[ing] forth | so great an object" (Prologue 10 f.), turning the performance into a collective effort of actors and spectators.[102] The recurring grammatical imperatives, however, consistently fuse what today would be seen as mental and physical efforts: "Let us [...] | on your imaginary forces work," the Prologue requests, only to invoke an active, equally physical employment of "thoughts" on the spectators' part: "Piece out our imperfections with your thoughts: | Into a thousand parts divide one man, | and make imaginary puissance." (Prologue 23–25), "'tis your thoughts that now must deck our kings" (Prologue 28); later on the Chorus exhorts the audience: "Work, work your thoughts" (III.0.25), and "eke out our performance with your mind." (III.0.35). The performance, it appears, is an effort that involves the audience's mental *and* physical faculties to the point where they become indistinguishable – "thoughts" can be "worked," "piece out," and "deck kings," imagination can provide "puissance," and a "mind" can "eke out."

---

sible confidence about anything wobbly." (*Henry V*, p. 56). For the interesting history of different critical readings of the Chorus, see Lawrence Danson. "*Henry V*: King, Chorus, and Critics." *Shakespeare Quarterly*, no. 34, 1983, pp. 27–43.

100 Goldman, *The Energies of Drama*, p. 59.

101 William West's brilliant description of this effect of Elizabethan stage architecture deserves to be quoted at length: "While the Elizabethan theater had no 'fourth wall' in the sense that the phrase came to have in the nineteenth century [...], it would be more accurate to say that the Elizabethan stage also lacked second and third walls (because it was on a thrust) and that the first wall was really a wall – not an imaginary barrier only [...]. Or perhaps it would be better to say that the Elizabethan theater *did* have a fourth wall, but one that encircled and included its audience. [...] [E]arly modern plays show the theater's whole circle, embracing both stage and pit, as set apart from the world outside it. Audience and actors have distinct parts, but are mutually permeable." (West, "Understanding in the Elizabethan Theatres," p. 133.)

102 Dennis Kezar. "Shakespeare's guilt trip in *Henry V*." *Modern Language Quarterly*, no. 61, 2000, pp. 431–461, p. 435 f. even sees this as similar to religious ritual. Goldman, *The Energies of Drama*, p. 58 ff., emphasizes the analogies between Henry's speeches to his army and the Chorus's speeches to the audience: "All but one of the half-dozen famous speeches of the play have in common a concern for encouraging their hearers to make some kind of demanding effort, whether of action, feeling or imagination." According to Goldman it is therefore no surprise if "the Chorus sounds very much like the King" (p. 59). This, however, puts the spectators in a situation very similar to the actors playing the soldiers. To further underscore this aspect of common effort and the audience's sharing in the performance, in Dromgoole's production the king's speeches are mostly spoken directly to the audience, who in these scenes are addressed as Henry's army, courtiers, etc.; see the most intense example, in Jamie Parker's version of "Once more upon the breach" (III.1.), at 00:47:35 of Dromgoole's production.

With this, *Henry V* builds on Renaissance concepts of fluid, porous bodies, on notions of bodily receptiveness to others' feelings through the movement of "humors" and "passions" between bodies and their immediate environment, on notions of the "infectiousness" of moods, psychophysiological states, or feelings – as well as their status as a participatory kind of knowledge in its own right.[103] But it also negotiates circulating theories about the social, physical, and embodied foundations of human cognition,[104] that is: about the inseparability and interdependence of cognition and embodiment.

And to return once more to the play's senseless scene: For all its dependence on the audience's physical-emotional participation, the wooing scene also needs their semiotic understanding. Researchers noticed long ago that *Henry V* is one of Shakespeare's most multilingual plays,[105] and the English

---

[103] As Anderson demonstrates with regard to a wide range of Renaissance writers, within the framework of Galenic anthropology world, body, and mind are mutually permeable; physical action and body states are perceived as interrelated with thought and imagination (see Anderson's summary, *The Renaissance Extended Mind*, p. 114 f.); West accordingly observes that "[...] certainly the sense [...] that thought might happen in detachment from physicality is a notion that is emergent rather than dominant in the period [...]" (West, "Understanding in the Elizabethan Theatres," p. 138).

[104] On Renaissance theories of "humors" and "passions" as conceptualizing complex interrelations and interdependences between mind and body (rather than a clean-cut dualism), see especially: Noga Arikha. *Passions and tempers: a history of the humours*. New York: Ecco, 2007; Katherine Parks. "The Organic Soul." *The Cambridge History of Renaissance Philosophy*, edited by Charles B. Schmitt. Cambridge: Cambridge University Press, 1988, pp. 464–484; *Reading the Early Modern Passions: Essays in the Cultural History of Emotion*, edited by Katherine Rowe, Gail Kern Paster and Mary Floyd-Wilson, Philadelphia: University of Pensylvania Press, 2004; Ulinka Rublack. "Fluxes: The Early Modern Body and the Emotions." *History Workshop Journal*, no. 53, 2002, pp. 1–16; with a special focus on Shakespearean works in this context see Ina Habermann. "Breathing Stones – Shakespeare and the Theatre of the Passions." *Shakespeare-Jahrbuch*, no. 140, 2004, pp. 11–27; David Hillman. "*Homo Clausus* at the Theater: Closing Bodies and Opening Theaters in Early Modern England." *Rematerializing Shakespeare: Authority and Representation on the Early Modern English Stage*, edited by Bryan Reynolds and William N. West, New York: Palgrave Macmillan, 2006, pp. 161–185; Arthur F. Kinney. *Shakespeare and Cognition: Aristotle's Legacy and Shakespearean Drama*. New York: Routledge, 2006; Gail Kern Paster, *Humoring the Body. Emotions and the Shakespearean Stage*. Chicago et al.: University of Chicago Press, 2004; *Shakespeare and the Culture of Emotion*, edited by Richard Meek (*Shakespeare*, no. 8, 2012, special issue); Gesa Stedman. "'The Noblest Comment on the Human Heart': Shakespeare and the Theories of Emotion." *Shakespeare-Jahrbuch*, no. 140, 2004, pp. 115–129; *Shakespeare and Emotions. Inheritances, Enactments, Legacies*, edited by Robert S. White, Mark Houlahan and Katrina O'Loughlin. New York: Palgrave Macmillan, 2015.

[105] Jean-Christophe Meyer. "The Ironies of Babel in Shakespeare's *Henry V*." *Representing France and the French on the Early Modern English Stage*, edited by id. Plainsboro: Associated Universities Press, 2008, pp. 127–142.

king's wooing of the French princess makes linguistic difficulties one of the scene's central problems.[106] Focusing entirely on the subject of national identity and difference (indicated by the lack of understanding) between the *characters*, researchers have noticed to a much lesser degree that – in order for the scene to work in an early modern playhouse – its *London audience* must have been expected to be capable of following the French dialogues, and, at least on a basic level, of translating back and forth between English and French. Otherwise the many jokes of linguistic interferences, or the humor of Henry's helpless attempts at speaking French, would have been lost.[107] The audience's sharing in the flirtatious mood, therefore, is interrelated with their representational, semiotic interpretation of linguistic signs.

VI *As-if* or not *as-if*?
Theatrical answers to cultural questions

This paper concerns two plays written in different languages, in different countries, belonging to different theatrical traditions and different genres, one at the beginning of the sixteenth century, one at its end. Still, as this paper set out to explore, apparently neither can avoid dealing with the same aisthetic and epistemic questions and concerns touching the theater; and even though neither provides explicit answers to those questions, they both do address them – particularly in their otherwise senseless scenes – by shaping the audience's perception, experience, and ultimately the ways of making the audience know and understand the action on stage. If dramatic production is necessarily located within the wider cultural net that surrounds and involves the theater, the aim of the paper has been to unravel some of its threads in the direction of circulating notions, and the connected anxieties and/or hopes, regarding human knowledge and sentience. In Early Modernity these issues seem to have found a particularly suitable outlet in the discourse surrounding the theater and its effects, whether it took the shape of an increased intellectual interest in poetics, or of an irreconcilable public controversy.

At first sight both plays seem to show no inclination for risk avoidance within the context of theatrical-epistemic debates. On the contrary, *La Calandra* and *Henry V* positively confirm the theater's enemies' most dreadful suspicions, undermining at the same time the strategies of its defenders: In addition

---

106 Downes, "French Feeling," p. 61.
107 Ibid., p. 59; p. 63.

to the occasional lewdness of the play's texts, *La Calandra* exhibits a self-conscious fictionality of the theatrical world which, as anti-theatrical writers see it, as such not only enters into an unholy competition with God's creation, but also demonstrates its own "falsehood," frivolity, and intentional deceit. And even though it might seem that the perceptional stance it requires from – and enhances in – its audience, with its emphasis on the audience's intellectual understanding, was quite close to the one pictured by the theater's defenders – by no stretch of the imagination does *La Calandra* provide the kind of edifying moral tale the apologists usually referred to in order to prove the theater's usefulness. And while the King's heroic deeds in *Henry V* would indeed offer a lesson for audiences much to the taste of the theater's defenders – as Thomas Heywood's *Apology for Actors* actually confirms[108] – Shakespeare's play explicitly does not aim at the audience's intellectual deciphering of a possible symbolic meaning, but exhorts the audiences' involvement on an emotional and physical level, and voluntarily sets out to affect them – just as the theater's enemies feared.

Yet, as a second glance reveals, the plays' implicit answers to the epistemic questions underlying the debate prove less purely provocative, but rather, in a complex way, conciliatory. Whereas the Renaissance theatrical discourse only allows for definite, clear-cut positions regarding the epistemic value of the stage – *either* it is perceived as a fictitious, as-if representation, and then audiences can learn from it by looking through the theatrical medium at its mediated message, *or* it is perceived as the immediate presence of sensual stimuli, whose representational, as-if dimension (its message) tends to be disregarded due to their inescapable corporeal infectiousness and attraction, and hence audiences can learn nothing – theatrical production itself obviously experiments with transitions and interstices: it can revalue embodied experience and interaction in the theater as a form of understanding, and extend the possibility of detached intellectual understanding to encompass its own mediality, but it can also obviously negotiate the interrelatedness, and interdependence of cognition and embodiment. With this, it brings the Renaissance's epistemic disconcertment, as it were, up against the theatrical debates' narrow trenches of *as-if* or not *as-if*.

---

[108] "What English prince, should hee behold the true portrature of that famous King Edward the Third, foraging France, [...] and would not bee suddenly inflam'd with so royal a spectacle, being made apt and fit for the like atchievement. So of Henry the Fift; [...]." (Heywood, "An Apology," p. 21).

Stefano Gulizia
Castiglione's 'Green' Sense of Theater

> It is impossible to imagine the Neoplatonist, elitist Castiglione recommending that a courtier, or his friend the emperor Charles V, learn the minutiae of keeping account and receipt books. It would be hard to keep one's *sprezzatura* while toiling over balance sheets.[1]

So wrote Jacob Soll, in 2009, brilliantly recasting Peter Burke's previous discussion of chivalric and courtly values in Castiglione's *Book of the Courtier* within a new history of knowledge and politics. There are several things to notice about this quotation. First, Soll suggests that the vast information system that lies at the very center of the rise of the modern state was actually indebted to humanist pedagogy in two ways – that is, through the instrumental legacy of measurement developed by the *ars mercatoria*, and through the antiquarian ideals of learning related to the use of historical scholarship and paperwork – rather than to be seen as a complete departure from earlier conceptions of the legal archive, both in terms of scale and as an aesthetic object. Second, even though royal business was larger and infinitely more complex than its Quattrocento predecessors, none of its instruments, old and new, were self-evident in their use. The type of double-entry bookkeeping favored by Tuscan merchants, for instance, or Luca Pacioli's insistence that inventorying should be kept in real time, needed to be articulated, as Soll has shown, by a new class of interpreters and instructors. Thus, these practices also needed a community of scholars and consumers already aware of their importance, and capital assessment, in turn, had a function in creating a larger public in which people's interests and undertakings switched from manufacture to use and meaning.

My question in this chapter is: how can we best describe the managerial dimension of Castiglione in his time and space? To answer that question, I take Castiglione's unusual engagement as a stage-manager to be a representative instance of theatrical networks and public-making in early modern Italy. The event took place in the ducal palace of Urbino on the last Sunday of carnival, on 6 February 1513, and involved a production of Bernardo Dovizi da Bibbiena's successful comedy *Calandra*. The degree to which that performance is able to stand as an adequate description of an early, coalescing phase of trade, distance, and sociability in European drama as a whole depends not

---

[1] Jacob Soll. *The Information Master: Jean-Baptiste Colbert's Secret State Intelligence System.* Ann Arbor: The University of Michigan Press, 2009, p. 54.

https://doi.org/10.1515/9783110536690-006

necessarily on the play's documented capacity to outstrip many competitors, but rather, I submit, on its meta-reflection on staging. The *Calandra* is not a theatricalized essay on authorial responses and rewritings, but it does focus, in its insistence on touching and wearing, on the detachability of theatrical wardrobe (at least in Scenes 1.2 and 4.2).[2] You might perhaps want to imagine Castiglione as being especially keen to exploit such engineering of the senses in his role as theatrical director and being aware of how that playtext was a slice taken from a larger, networked organism of public-making across a range of intellectual and artistic activities. Indeed, what he had to say to his friend Dovizi, who was a frequent guest in his conversations (both real and fictional), could neatly find its counterpoint in the Roman production of the Plautine comedy *Poenulus* (*The Little Carthaginian*), also of 1513, which fell to the credit of a famous stage-manager, Tommaso Inghirami, known as Phaedra because of his iconic reprise of a classical figure and his proclivities for cross-dressing. In what follows I am not aiming to reconstruct the literary echo or the archival trail of these parallel festivals; in either case, a dossier could be easily assembled.[3] I focus, instead, on one specific document: the letter that Castiglione addressed to Bishop Ludovico Canossa (1475–1532), reminiscing with instructive details upon the making of *Calandra* in Urbino, and ruminating on the emotional aftermath of the night.

At least since Alessandro d'Ancona's seminal study *Origini del teatro italiano* (*Origins of the Italian theater*), of 1891, Castiglione's letter has been rightly celebrated as a primer on the early fabric of Renaissance entertainment in Italy by a distinguished observer. In this line of scholarship the celebratory aspects have eventually overwhelmed the epistemological ones. My approach here differs in part because I am more interested in Castiglione's entrepreneurial awareness than in his courtly ideology, and in part because I am persuaded that by attending to what is often frankly instrumental in the Canossa letter a host of historical actors would emerge – people, that is to say, other than courtiers and patrons. In other words, Castiglione the 'project manager' functions

---

[2] On the materiality of theatrical memory see Peter Stallybrass. "Hauntings: The Materiality of Memory on the Renaissance Stage." *Generation and Degeneration: Tropes of Reproduction in Literature and History from Antiquity through Early Modern Europe*, edited by Valeria Finucci and Kevin Brownlee. Durham: Duke University Press, 2001, pp. 287–316. Here and below, I cite *Calandra* from Giorgio Padoan's critical edition: *La Calandra: Commedia elegantissima per messer Bernardo Dovizi da Bibbiena*. Padua: Antenore, 1985, p. 204.

[3] See Fabrizio Cruciani. "Le feste per Isabella d'Este Gonzaga a Roma nel 1514–1515." *Teatro e storia*, vol. 2, 1987, pp. 167–188, and Laura Giannetti Ruggiero. "When Male Characters Pass as Women: Theatrical Play and Social Practice in the Italian Renaissance." *Sixteenth Century Journal*, vol. 36, 2005, pp. 743–760.

as a discursive gateway to skills, audiences, networks, and the style of their imagined movement; such itinerancy, in turn, complements the study of early drama in the way that paying attention to sound and vagrancy has completed the picture offered by traditional histories of print based only on sales at the bookstalls.[4] Likewise, in what follows I am not trying to find faults in Soll's reconstruction of modern expertise, but only to point out how Castiglione's association with the mechanics of theater puts significant pressure on his recasting as a spiteful, aloof humanist. There is a genuine concern for 'media effects' in the letter:[5] what works and what does not; things that are immediately bankable, and those that are not. There is also a considerable amount of *sprezzatura*, I would further argue, in supervising a scribbled memorandum intended for the painters and woodcutters employed in Urbino. And a sense of hurry, of scurrying servants as on the Roman stage, and of the play itself as a bounded object, is a shared experience for a broad range of theatergoers, from pimps to the pope.

Since my focus is both limited and local (though my goals are quite broad, and related to Esther Schomacher's discussion of cognition and embodiment in this volume), I will not attempt to emulate Ronald Martinez's take on the rising fortunes of literary Tuscan in Dovizi's *Calandra*, which I have discussed elsewhere.[6] Nor will I follow some of the recent work on Castiglione by scholars such as Jennifer Webb, Olga Zorzi Pugliese, and W. R. Albury – Webb in relation to Federico da Montefeltro's *studiolo* and its spatial self-policing, which she sees, after Stephen Campbell and Foucault, as an integrated system where visibility is a trap; Zorzi Pugliese in light of Castiglione's praise of architecture's durability as a trope able to overcome time; and Albury across a wide reclamation of medicine and statecraft, especially Ottaviano Fregoso's argument that courtier-physicians ought to cure diseased states of corrupt leaders.[7] Each of them has produced impressive historical scholarship, all of it aiming to speak more or less to the same assimilation of aesthetic construction and theatrical

---

4 See Rosa Salzberg. *Ephemeral City: Cheap Print and Urban Culture in Renaissance Venice*. Manchester: Manchester University Press, 2014.

5 For a suggestive analysis of 'media effects' and the meaning of 'senseless scenes' see Esther Schomacher, "Sex on Stage: How Does the Audience Know?" in this volume.

6 See Stefano Gulizia. "Spatial Traffic: Cognitive Ecologies of Bibbiena's *Calandra*." *Studi rinascimentali*, vol. 9, 2011, pp. 115–127.

7 See Jennifer D. Webb. "All is not fun and games: Conversation, play, and surveillance at the Montefeltro court in Urbino." *Renaissance Studies*, vol. 26, 2011, pp. 417–440; Olga Zorzi Pugliese. "Unity and Multiplicity: Castiglione's Views on Architecture in the *Cortegiano*." *Mitteilungen des Kunsthistorischen Institutes in Florenz*, vol. 54, 2012, pp. 257–266; and W. R. Albury, *Castiglione's Allegory: Veiled Policy in The Book of the Courtier*. Farnham: Ashgate, 2014.

display that I am questioning. They read the *Book of the Courtier* against the background of the synesthetic and perspectival reduction of the ideal city-state that it proposes ("non un palazzo, ma una città in forma de palazzo esser pareva,") ("not a palace, but a city in the shape of a palace"), Urbino's skyline being, of course, the palace.[8]

To be sure, Castiglione's 1513 staging of *Calandra* contributes to the ideological dimensions of this culture, but my approach differs from theirs because I intend to look at what the play does more than at what it means. Indeed, my interest depends on the idea that its core knowledge and geographical compass are indeterminate, that it orchestrates interest communities that would be hard to describe as publics, and that its performance relies on the capacity to elicit, gather, and anchor a variety of sensorial and cognitive responses. Thus far, the dominant mode of theatrical analysis with regard to early Italian texts has been a notion similar to *historia* described by Michael Baxandall in his groundbreaking *Painting and Experience*, which quite against the artisanal training of its main spokesmen, including Leon Battista Alberti, relegates bodies and instrumentality to their mere materiality, and privileges instead elite membership and the mainstreaming of the humanist gaze.[9] As a challenge to Baxandall's argument for the way theatrical things necessarily fashion urban images and identity, we can add Castiglione's stage-setting as a compelling case for the social agency of things themselves and for the 'greening' of entities like the earliest and improvised playhouses. At the same time, a mode of analysis centered on corporeal rather than intellectual comprehension is well suited to the study of Castiglione's management as something truly worldly.

The idea of 'green' theater derives from Bruce R. Smith, who emphasizes that a study that attends to the materiality of the theatrical evidence – including curtains and sixteenth-century furnishing owned by people of certain means in which the color green appears to have been prominent – must also acknowledge "the embodiedness of the investigator in the face of that evidence."[10]

Although explicitly modeled after features of Shakespeare's art, such historical phenomenology captures a vast array of forms that is of great interest beyond Elizabethan culture: apart from the situatedness of what is known,

---

[8] See Baldassare Castiglione. *Il libro del Cortegiano*, edited by Giulio Preti, Turin: Einaudi, 1965, p. 12.
[9] For Baxandall's approach, see Patricia Lee Rubin. *Images and Identity in Fifteenth-Century Florence*. New Haven: Yale University Press, 2007.
[10] Bruce R. Smith. *The Key of Green: Passion and Perception in Renaissance Culture*. Chicago: Chicago University Press, 2009, p. 8.

which remains a central issue in early Italian playtexts, the comedic plots in the age of Ariosto, Dovizi, and Machiavelli remind us that Galenic medicine made the thinking subject absolutely dependent on seeing, hearing, touching, tasting, and smelling. Furthermore, Plautine or Boccaccian tricks such as those adapted by Dovizi da Bibbiena were always more likely to prioritize or engage strongly with physicality. Finally, to the extent that the *commedia erudita* facilitated a reuse of Roman materials in England, the anthropological pluralism and self-reflexiveness of a play like *Calandra* is directly answerable to the emergence of an international comedy of errors through a process of circulation of various spin-offs that are alternatively textual, oral, and artifactual.[11] As a result, taking a cue from Smith's concerns with 'thinking' color, Castiglione's letter is not 'green' simply in analogy with familiar tropes of environmental criticism, but because it left an archival record in the wake of the creation of a social space of conversation.

My argument identifies a political and managerial dimension of Castiglione's staging of *Calandra* not with its investments in the landedness of the Urbino court in early modernity, which was already conventional as an articulation in its own rights, but with its engagement with the bodily groundedness of theatergoing, calibrated through noise and a neighbor's response. The political dimension of the play, I suggest, is bound up with its ability to cultivate sensorial practices. *Calandra*'s artistic effects, once we disentangle ourselves from its permutations of various bits of action, work generally to expand the experience of laughter through absorption and intense physical subjugation to the stage. Ideas and practices are not, of course, entirely separable, but in this case Castiglione's handling of the comedy, its material reiteration and imagined publicity, is part of a larger process of action, democratization, and association that tries to authenticate and open bodies for the theater. That is why the entrepreneurial intervention of an author whose ideology has been routinely characterized in traditional Platonic-moralist terms needs to be understood as a vehicle of social skills, not social dominance. What Castiglione experienced and then advocated was a spectator's idea of theater rather than an original directorial view.

It also needs to be pointed out that the writing and first performance of *Calandra* in 1513 and in Urbino are not points of absolute origination since Bernardo Dovizi da Bibbiena was already adapting material which itself had a 'Roman' life in the theater and which, in turn, would come to represent, almost

---

11 See Tiffany Stern. "Watching as Reading: The Audience and Written Text in Shakespeare's Playhouse." *How to Do Things with Shakespeare: New Approaches, New Essays*, edited by Laurie Maguire. Oxford: Blackwell, 2008, pp. 136–159.

as if by design, the perfection of Rome's revival in various aspects of contemporary artistic life. From the moment of its inception onwards, dissemination, revision, and response had been an integral part of the dialogized meaning of *Calandra*.[12] On the one hand, the record of Castiglione's brilliant orchestration could stand as a fountainhead, but he is also a link in the chain of 'mailing' a play from Rome to Urbino, and later from Urbino to Venice in the 1520s, on the other hand.[13] Rootlessness and not a sense of here and now is what emerges from these transactions, even though with early modern drama it is hard to resist the temptation to lock a play's plot within the specific political conditions of the court or city-state in which it is embedded – physically or fictionally.

In fact, Dovizi's text finds its path into stage and publication in such a way as to emphasize its similarities with two culturally and linguistically adjacent playtexts: the Spanish *Celestina*, which was first appropriated by the Ciceronian circles in Rome,[14] and Ariosto's *Negromante* (*The Necromancer*), whose topical representation of medical charlatanism pushes the vestigial Jewishness of the protagonist to different levels of verisimilitude, according to the different audiences it summons in its successive rewritings.[15] *Calandra* too is part of this migratory impulse. In this discussion, I want to consider not only playwright, players, playgoers, and Castiglione as a stage director, but also the social agency of the props and costumes that traveled along with the movement of texts and scenarios – the torches, vases, and Trojan tapestries explicitly recalled in the letter to Bishop Canossa.

I will come to the social life of props, but first I want to imagine the first moment in the performance of Dovizi's play in Urbino in which, according to Castiglione's intensely self-regarding reconstruction, things fall under the spell of a green disguise. The moment that I have in mind is in the third paragraph of the Canossa letter. Castiglione has just re-emerged from the initial and cumbersome epistolary address and reminded his friend of a marine elegy sent along with the mail. He then excuses himself for not expanding on the play,

---

[12] On the vexed question of Castiglione's proem, see the discussion of my "Spatial Traffic: Cognitive Ecologies of Bibbiena's *Calandra*." *Studi rinascimentali*, vol. 9, 2011, pp. 115–127; pp. 124 f.

[13] For a discussion of theatergrams in movement, see *Transnational Exchange in Early Modern Theater*, edited by Robert Henke and Eric Nicholson. Farnham: Ashgate, 2008.

[14] See José Luis Canet. "La Celestina y el mundo intelectual de su época." *Cinco siglos de Celestina: Aportaciones interpretativas*, edited by Rafael Beltrán and José Luis Canet. Valencia: Universitat de Valencia, 1997, pp. 43–61.

[15] See Giuseppe Coluccia. *L'esperienza teatrale di Ludovico Ariosto*. Lecce: Manni, 2001, pp. 162–166.

trusting that the recipient of his notes would have already consulted a range of witnesses to the performance at the time of writing. At this juncture, Castiglione describes the scene of *Calandra*. Here acoustic and watery signals adjust their mutual orientation frequently. The resulting impression is at once thick and fleeting, insinuating yet superimposed. Until the gaze moves upward:

> Al cielo della sala erano attaccati pallottoni grandissimi di verdura: tanto che quasi coprivano la volta; dalla quale ancora pendeano fili di ferro per quelli fori delle rose che sono in detta volta: e questi fili tenevano dui ordini di candelabri da un capo all'altro della sala, che erano tredici lettere, perché tanti sono li fori.
>
> From the roof of the hall hung giant balls of greenery, to the point of almost taking over the vault of the room, from which were also lowered iron strings through the holes of the rose windows that are over there: and these strings held two layers of chandeliers from one side of the hall to the other – thirteen in all, like the rose windows.[16]

The passage tells us something important and easily overlooked about the kind of stage created for *Calandra* in Urbino. The location is a richly decorated hall, vaulted and with interlocked rose windows, which is made to function as an occasional playhouse mostly on the strength of intermixing the voices of human actors with a field of foliage, flowers, and fruit, along with sleek chandelier lights and Latin inscriptions framed in light blue. The process of transformation in the room – at least, within the textual selection I have chosen to cite – starts with the most distinctive feature in the ensemble: giant balls of greenery and garlands. Floral arrangements on such grand scale were not found *in situ* in Federico da Montefeltro's palace at any given time; they neither helped establish a 'country house' ideology, nor did they necessarily foster the court's wealth. If anything, part of their task was to give an expressive voice to the artisanal dimension of the playing company itself, by forcing it to move among shadows and lights, and by suggesting differences in scale between two sets of images offered to the viewers. Staging *Calandra* under spheres of decorative moss ensures that Castiglione's green is simultaneously something one sees from without, and within which one sees.

Repeatedly, Castiglione's letter invites the viewer's eye to move from one side to the other of the woven narrative, as if in a palimpsest. The greenery hung from the roof is a neat complement to the flower-and-ivy borders of a Renaissance tapestry, as well as of a richly decorated printed edition. By implicit design, the *Calandra* production in Urbino accentuated Arachne's equiv-

---

[16] Castiglione's letter was included, without its concluding part, in the anthology *Delle lettere facete et piacevoli di diversi grandi huomini et chiari ingegni* [...], edited by Dionigi Atanagi. Venice: Zaltieri, 1561. Translation mine.

ocal art rather than the lurking of Ovid's more turbulent chaos. It is possible to read in the tamed wilderness above the wood planks of the theater the equivalent of the play's investment in comic business. They are both logofugal: they flee from words. And they emphatically contradict the interpretation of *habitus* as a style of behavior as opposed to as a philosophical precondition of embodiment.[17]

In the late fifteenth-century Italian tradition of courtly entertainment the green matrix, as telescoped and re-envisioned by Leonardo da Vinci, already functioned within a larger theatrical context, both as the gentlemanly induction to a feast and as a self-justifying wit produced by advances in technology. I am not referring here to the painter's many sketches of machines – some of which are almost indistinguishable from Brunelleschi's own machinery, like the moving heaven-machine used in the Florentine staging of sacred representations, and some of which, like the 'noise generator' in the manuscript *Arundel 263*, are straightforward devices to bring thunder, wind, and rain to the popular theater – but rather to the comparatively lesser-known work that Leonardo left in a room of the Sforza Castle in Milan known as the *Sala delle Asse* during the 1490s [fig. 1]. A testing ground for his experiments, this *Sala* was fitted with a painted forest canopy and images of tree trunks lining the wall; its purpose may have been a simple extension of Leonardo's idea of offering to his wealthy patron a knightly automaton, based on a grandiose hydraulic conception.[18] Still, in this example a green ceiling as contrived as in the Urbino celebrations functioned as a threshold, showing the cunning intelligence of *techne* and its green offsprings and subtexts.

It may be useful, at this point, to add some reflections on how the Renaissance idea of green, not only as established symbol of youth or the pastoral mode, was developed in relationship with the bookselling culture in which wanderers and rogues thrived. Such a development would reach a point of maturity with Shakespeare, and specifically in *The Winter's Tale*, where the appearances of the color green become a running commentary on the career of Robert Greene the balladeer and on the suspicious mischief that, along with criminal dexterity, accompanied his itinerant selling of pamphlets and roman-

---

[17] For the first interpretation, see Peter Burke. *The Fortunes of the Courtier: The European Reception of Castiglione's Cortegiano*. Philadelphia: University of Pennsylvania Press, 1995, p. 29, who notes how the sociologist Pierre Bourdieu followed the medieval translators of Aristotle; a new discussion in Evelyn Tribble. "Distributing Cognition in the Globe." *Shakespeare Quarterly*, vol. 56, 2005, pp. 135–155.
[18] See E. R. Truitt. *Medieval Robots: Mechanism, Magic, Nature, and Art*. Philadelphia: University of Pennsylvania Press, 2015.

Fig. 1: Leonardo da Vinci's wall and ceiling painting in *Salla delle Asse* (detail) from ca. 1498, tempera on plaster.

ces. Even in Castiglione's own days, however, subsuming the stage-scenery under a dome of artificial green means reminding the audience of how literary metamorphosis should always try to outperform roguery and its subset of texts and trinkets in order to enact itself – and of how, in order to study the early stages of literary circulation as an emerging industry, one needs to pay attention to the cultural power of robbery and tactics of stealing. The 'wanderings' of a play such as *Calandra* do not seem to threaten the social unity of Urbino, but Castiglione needs to signal the role performed by the songs he introduced into the spectacle in order to encourage actual unity, while promoting his unusual managerial tasks to wide courtly attention.

Castiglione in Urbino is a man who is never able to go public, someone who feels the need to feign that an outburst of anger occurred while dealing with the master woodcutters and the singing personnel, musicians, and dancers summoned to Urbino for the festival.[19] But his intimate correspondent in

---

[19] "[...] chi avea da combattere e con pittori e con maestri di legnami [...]." ("[...] he who had to fight both with painters and woodcutters [...].") *Calandra*, p. 207.

the Lucanian town of Tricarico must have known, upon receiving news of the 1513 *Calandra*, that Castiglione's letter spoke to his deep pride in handling personally and directly the stage workers and their requests, seeing in particular that the eccentric mythological performances surrounding the play – which, though technically separated from text and plot, were a customary benchmark in evaluating the success of an event such as a carnival – were executed to everyone's satisfaction. As a whole, in fact, the letter to Canossa provides a brilliant argument for seeing the political force of early theater not as the emergence of a supposed bourgeois subjectivity, with the usual corollary of considering a courtier's engagement in fields like *feast* or *drama* as a challenge to social rivals and upwardly mobile persons through imitation of their social betters, but simply as a prospect for people from different walks of life to take their concerted action into the real world. There is more at play in Castiglione's management of Dovizi's drama than a wily *sprezzatura* ostensibly trying to swallow a hard province of mechanical entertainment and information: the groups of workers that he moves around as the show's director express the necessary relationship between publicity and personhood. Likewise, once we account for the basic fact that a perfect courtier must always hide or dissimulate his innermost thoughts, the robust role that Castiglione played among 'actors,' including giving them a new prologue to act since the old, authorial one arrived too late in Urbino to be used,[20] is communal and describes a middle ground in the theater-making practices between publishing, playing, and playgoing.

Possibly, and attractive though it is, the construction of Castiglione the joiner and theatrical entrepreneur is just a fiction, not a system, of a piece with the active creation of authority and accessibility in the *Book of the Courtier*. It is tempting, however, to discover effects of that ideal commonwealth of skill and publicity I have been describing in his discussion of stage management. Within the Canossa letter, to be sure, a most promising place to do so is the ample treatment of the songs, dances, and masquerades interspersed in *Calandra*, which occupies the central paragraphs of Castiglione's dispatch and takes up almost half its space. While there is no space here to tackle adequately the representative publicity of these musical *intermezzi*,[21] the premise of my interpretation is that these artifacts were on the move (sometimes expensively so, being in themselves bulky and with oscillating degrees of precision), and

---

[20] See *Calandra*, p. 205.
[21] See at least Nino Pirrotta. *Li due Orfei, da Poliziano a Monteverdi*. Turin: Einaudi, 1975; and Anthony M. Cummings. *The Politicized Muse: Music for Medici Festivals, 1512–1537*. Princeton: Princeton University Press, 1992.

therefore should be understood primarily as material objects in market conditions.

By slightly downplaying the musical dimension of these artifactual components of the 1513 *Calandra* in Urbino – which, in fairness, is hardly at the forefront of Castiglione's own interests – we can also understand how the chosen *intermezzi* operated a potentially transitional exchange across the social spectrum: a manufacturing or constructing public (artisanal to a lesser or greater extent, often organized in structures resembling medieval guilds),[22] a normative public (mostly concomitant with humanists at court and their elite guests), and a consuming public (overlapping with, yet not exhausting, the 'crowd' of playgoers, and open to significant disagreements on how anyone ought to interact with an isolated bodily exploit).

This view introduces some important changes to our established narratives of sixteenth-century courtly entertainment. First, none of the performers cited by Castiglione could ever count on scripted movements of such perfection as to ensure a fully beautiful execution: the writer's hyperbolic emphasis on how each *moresca* dancer, even if impeded by the torch he had to carry, as in Juno's allegorical retinue, pushed his art to 'every possible limit' only underlines the reality of failure looming large over their presentation. Second, the *intermezzi*, which could easily be mistaken as a 'closed' form of association because of their mythical iconology,[23] effectively catered to heterogeneous interest groups – perhaps not cohesive enough to claim the Habermasian requirements of equality and parity, but with impressive potential for strangers or foreigners to 'buy in' and share the interests of local theater-focus groups. Finally, Castiglione's letter actually narrowed, rather than widened, the gulf between aristocratic audiences and *virtuosi*; one might observe, as well, that its insistence on seemingly mundane details such as the fish scales on the costumes of the acting crew, or the bright and motley-colored apparel of the parrot impersonators, instead of the finer points of Ovidian exegesis, encouraged a more open and egalitarian form of discussion.

Reorienting appreciation for the lavish *intermezzi* of 1513 away from courtly ideology and toward skilled contributions, trade, and sociability, means having Castiglione interact with the apprentice system of theatrical troupes and its 'amateurs.' In addition, his casting for *Calandra* comments on a delicate moment in early Italian drama when things became 'matters of concern' (and no

---

[22] On the mechanics of early Italian companies of drama, see Ludovico Zorzi. *L'attore, la commedia, il drammaturgo*. Turin: Einaudi, 1990, pp. 31–33.
[23] A useful treatment of urban rituals and parades is Samuel Kinser. "Presentation and Representation: Carnival at Nuremberg, 1450–1550." *Representations*, vol. 13, 1986, pp. 1–41.

longer 'matters of fact'). The tendency up to now has been to see Castiglione as a purveyor of asymmetrical discourses of power and information; on that basis alone, it would be logical to assume that in his job as stage-manager he had also adopted a top-down approach. And yet the Canossa letter clearly asserts that the emotions of bystanders and playgoers were swayed and seized across the hall, that a premium was placed on understanding as a precondition of the cognitive ecology peculiar to playhouses, and that, in effect, even the triumphalist, Medicean device was contradicted by the plot's circling back to scenes of raw corporeal wit and sexual innuendo. In 1513, the viewer of *Calandra* did not access the play all at once, but had to move backwards and forwards, as well as sequentially around the walls – from ornamental tapestries to balls of greenery. In short, Castiglione's 'green' sense of theater preserved what in Habermas's parlance is the idea of "social intercourse."[24]

A more nuanced description of the Urbino festival, it seems to me, is one in which the celebration of status or rank is replaced by an argument on how a shared 'tact' (combined with theatrical 'touch') was progessively seen as befitting equals. There is a neglected hint in Castiglione's letter that Dovizi's play had a social life even before playbooks and scripts were distributed, that is, that it was an agent capable of making a difference in the interregional system of newsmongering and that its meaning was more urgent than just an invitation to urban courtiers to bask in the ersatz recreation of a prized cultural good from Tuscany. This hint is Castiglione's repeated conviction that his bishop friend must have kept himself informed on the progress of *Calandra* through the itinerancy of its own echo. In the pragmatics of the letter, a virtual readership is conjured up by virtue of the very act of its address. In this light, Castiglione's hailing of a specific theater 'public' – a community of means already 'in the know' that needs no rehearsing of the obvious, as the letter declares – provisionally constitutes and generates an audience, instrinsically, by apostrophizing it. The writer's strategy compares interestingly with those *subjunctive-creative* addresses studied by Michael Warner as many examples of a *world-making* enterprise, although in Castiglione's case the play's true publicity does not depend on its spatiality as much as on the engineering of its *sensorium*,[25] which gains strength, to a certain extent, from the very variety of people in attendance and their bemusement.

---

[24] Jürgen Habermas, *The Structural Transformation of the Public Sphere: An Inquiry into a Category of Bourgeois Society*. Translated by Thomas Burger. Cambridge, MA: MIT Press, 1991, p. 36.

[25] See Michael Warner. *Publics and Counterpublics*. New York: Zone Books, 2002.

As a professional project manager, Castiglione had to avail himself of both social and rhetorical notions of the wider public. What his recipient is invited to consider while reading the letter, namely *Calandra*'s power of exertion in the court of public opinion in Italy, also has an anticipatory effect on the behavior of the actual public that would read the published version of the letter. This is far from a private exchange among intellectual snobs. Grievances with the working class operating the stage of the festival are not the only notation entrusted with relevance by Castiglione. Many readers have expanded on the passage in his letter to Canossa that describes the setting of the stage from the point of view of Medicean promotion, either by arguing that Calandro's ambiguous pedigree looks back at Ficinian mysteries, or by observing how mutually advantageous was a triumphalist semantics based on Roman restoration,[26] but few critics, if any, came to terms with the fact that this information is framed by a praise of the state workers of Urbino, who did miracles with the schedule of their assignment. What strains belief, Castiglione says, is that four months turned out to be sufficient for Urbino's public hands to erect an arch with faux-reliefs.[27] At this point, the printed tradition of Castiglione's letter reads the variant *operai* for *opere* ('blue collars' for 'works'), making the sounds of physical labor on the theatrical space curiously distorted, ventriloquised almost, as though piped in from somewhere else. Nor is Castiglione's marveling an isolated feature. His monitoring of the theatrical space is further nuanced by an archaeology of gender, sustained by a realization that, judging from available circumstantial evidence at the 1513 celebrations in Urbino, child actors put their older, professional counterparts to shame, and that nothing inspires like the wonder of watching 'tiny oldies' achieving with stage gestures the Greek gravity of Menander.[28]

Workers and kids have not gained any significant space in the history of early Italian drama. But it was their adjoining forces that impressed Castiglione the most: at any rate, more than the emblazoned Latin, the hangings of silk, or the excellent finishing of many stage props. Presumably, our lack of responsiveness derives from a historiography whose goal is to claim through the theatrical object an elevated status concurrently reinforced by the primacy of the eye over other senses in aesthetic considerations of public festivals, by the

---

[26] See Luciano Bottoni. *La messinscena del Rinascimento: "Calandra," una commedia per il papato*. Milan: Angeli, 2005, pp. 57–100; and Ronald L. Martinez. "Etruria Triumphant in Rome: Fables of Medici Rule and Bibbiena's *Calandra*." *Renaissance Drama*, vol. 37, 2010, pp. 69–98.
[27] See *Calandra*, p. 204.
[28] See ibid., p. 205.

Fig. 2: A woodcut from Girolamo Parabosco's *Il Pellegrino* (*The Pilgrim*), 1552.

humanist training of all the historical actors involved in the staging of play-texts, and by an increasing importance of perspectival design. In these accounts, the real pursuit of this fusion of research tools is an underlying intimation of philosophical detachment. Scaffolded platforms and greenwood, however, punctuated a performative execution in which the qualities and valences of green cognition are hardly exhausted by the strategic display of a city stage reserved for the elite. Castiglione's letter, in fact, should remind us of how frequently overlooked are urban communities of artisans and the share that they took in the rituals and commissions of early modern theatrical companies and brigades, effectively blurring boundaries rather than facilitating social ascent.

We lack convincing or definitive documentary evidence on the 1513 carnival in Urbino, but the 'grounding' of *Calandra*'s audiences is vividly presented by Castiglione himself when he remarks on the seating arrangements as if in a moat, with a watery landscape receding and alternating with the roof of a castle-keep. In support of the way Castiglione 'greened' Dovizi's play as its director, one might cite a relatively well-known woodcut from the comedy *Il Pellegrino* (*The Pilgrim*) written by Girolamo Parabosco (1524–1577), as republished by Gabriel Giolito's Venetian firm in 1552 [fig. 2]. At first glance, Parabosco's thick grid on stage looks like the anchoring of a full, mathematical eradication of local differences. In truth, its Serlian conquest or measurement, that is, the violent subduing of the space of representation into perspectival imperatives, proceeds hand in hand with what in Robert Weimann's terms is the separation between *locus* and *platea* – with a player walking in great strides to gain an intersecting center-stage, which is situated midway, acoustically and environmentally no less than visually, between false doors and tapestries at the back, and a standing, stalking public in front.[29]

The effect of the green stuff in Castiglione's reduction of *Calandra* is first or foremost a material witness. Yet fewer critics have taken the 'materialism' of floral arrangements incumbent on the stage sets of 1513 literally in order to chart the implications for both the play and its manager of changing theories of ecological cognition and the senses that it involves.[30] Taken together, the consistency, color, and even smell of the large balls of greenery account for the multiple traces of time embedded in theatrical things. In his letter to Ludovico Canossa, Castiglione's preoccupation is with material inventories and a shifting mnemonic economy encompassing environment, audience, players, and playtexts. Similar is Luchino Visconti's design for Carlo Goldoni's *L'impresario delle Smirne* (*The Impresario from Smyrna*), which was performed in Venice in 1957 and in which a massive curtain synchronically encapsulated and bridged a system of medieval, neighboring *continuum* into new states of the action. So it is with Visconti's giant curtain as with Castiglione's 'moat' imagery or, in this particular case, with the great Elizabethan scenes of gravedigging: remembering is like moving simultaneously back and forth in time, and the traces of past interaction are never completely erased.[31] Unfortunately, this branch of theatrical investigation has been overwhelmingly empiricist, and within a predominantly Italian tradition of inquiry only a few readers have promoted the image of learned comedy and revivalist drama as a palimpsest of material traces, or an assemblage of real-world features, excavating 'green' as a natural, semi-natural, and wholly artificial substance. In this chapter, using a celebrated letter in a slightly unusual manner, I have tried to demonstrate that Castiglione had keen interests in cognitive distribution, in managing information, and in the consequences of distance and deferral, not only in the banal sense that it took a certain number of months for a troupe to stage or 'mail' a *Calandra* from Rome to Urbino, for instance, but precisely because the resulting time lag enabled a Latourian network of inscription, calibrated at key nodes of such theatrical traveling.

---

29 On the double projections of theatrical space, see Robert Weimann. *Author's Pen and Actor's Voice: Playing and Writing in Shakespeare's Theatre*. Cambridge: Cambridge University Press, 2000.
30 See Henry S. Turner. "*King Lear* Without: The Heath." *Renaissance Drama*, vol. 28, 1997, p. 177.
31 See Jonathan Gil Harris. *Untimely Matter in the Time of Shakespeare*. Philadelphia: University of Pennsylvania Press, 2009.

More intimate – and greener still – are the circumstances in which Castiglione realized the powerful pull of song and music as a site of mediation between the smaller and larger communities of his court, and, more specifically, in which he discovered the importance of well-executed *intermezzi* for his overall conception of the 1513 carnival in Urbino. Given how potent and physical is his reconstruction of the events on behalf of his bishop friend, and how very concrete, sensory, and thoroughly textured is the imaginary recasting of his staging of *Calandra*, it is remarkable that the letter has received scant attention as a leverage to localize the discrete publics or interest groups that made up the theatrical polity in the early modern period. In my reconstruction, onlookers are often palpably present, in a phenomenological sense, crammed together into the theater, and what has traditionally appeared as the secure, unassailable, and privately controlled space of a humanist-courtier could be entered and willingly invaded by sound. As a result, the permeability of human agency across physical environments and of Renaissance spaces in general, which has been the object of growing interest in recent years,[32] might bring a new awareness to the study of drama and its historical networks.

Another criterion would be to compare these findings to two among the most crucial communicative functions that, according to the *Book of the Courtier*, ambassadors and envoys performed in their serving duties: secrecy and management. To the extent that the Boccaccian theater-machine of Bernardo Dovizi functioned in essence as a *lingua franca* across different Italian states, then its green execution in Urbino could stand as a figure of complete legibility and unmediated knowledge – an acoustic or visual circuit linking one stage to the next. At the same time, in analogy with the other automatic machines and counterfeit voices described in Castiglione's treatise,[33] and perhaps, even better, with the logic of Leonardo's breaching of the inside-out in the *Sala delle Asse* in Milan, to green a *Calandra* was to create an artificial chirping sound. Castiglione's hard-won acquaintance with the paradox that a writer's secrets were best protected by divulging them – indirectly or directly controlling the means of their printed dissemination – made him uniquely positioned to enjoy

---

[32] See Elizabeth S. Cohen, and Thomas V. Cohen. "Open and shut: The social meanings of the Cinquecento Roman house." *Studies in the Decorative Arts*, vol. 9, 2002, pp. 61–84; Flora Dennis. "Sound and domestic space in early modern Italy." *Studies in the Decorative Arts*, vol. 16, 2009, pp. 7–19; and Kate Colleran. "*Scampanata* at the widows' windows: A case-study of sound and ritual insult in Cinquecento Florence." *Urban History*, vol. 36, 2009, pp. 359–378.
[33] See Jessica Wolfe. *Humanism, Machinery, and Renaissance Literature*. Cambridge: Cambridge University Press, 2004.

the privilege that by taking on his public task as a project manager he both expanded and eradicated what was most individuated and unreproducible about the private self.

Bernhard Huss
Luigi Groto's *Adriana*: A Laboratory Experiment on Literary Genre

English translation by Martin Bleisteiner

The present paper examines Luigi Groto's tragedy *Adriana*, with occasional references to the author's dramatic oeuvre in general, and to his second tragedy *Dalida* in particular. An analysis of the *Adriana*'s poetics reveals that two different generic templates were superimposed in the play's composition: implementing a poetic program which will be illuminated in the following pages, Groto transferred Petrarchan lyricism to the genre of tragedy. The issue we are dealing with thus pertains to two thematic fields at the same time, namely the *Poetics of Early Modern Drama*, and the *History of Genres / Cross-fertilization between Genres*. If we subsequently focus our attention on the *Adriana*, this is only due to constraints of space: as it were, Groto's dramatic oeuvre as a whole could well be called a large-scale laboratory experiment on literary genre. Given its sheer volume, however, – it consists of the published plays *Dalida* (1572), *Il pentimento amoroso* (1576), *Adriana* (1578), *Emilia* (1579), *Il tesoro* (1580), *Calisto* (1582), *Alteria* (1584), and the "dramma sacro" *Isac* (first printed in 1586, but premiered as early as 1558[1]), while other works remained unpublished and were consequently lost, among them several tragedies[2] – a more comprehensive survey will have to be deferred to another occasion.

Unlike today, Luigi Groto – often called "Cieco d'Adria" in reference to his blindness – was an extremely well-known literary figure during his lifetime. A quote from Ben Jonson's *Volpone* illustrates Groto's popularity quite succinctly: when the eponymous protagonist claims that, "The poet | as old in time as Plato and as knowing | Says that your highest female grace is silence," Lady Would-Be replies: "Which o' your poets? Petrarch? Or Tasso? Or Dante? | Guarini? Ariosto? Aretine? | Cieco di Hadria? I have read them all" (3.4.76–81).[3] The fact that Groto ranks among the most illustrious exponents of early modern Italian literature in this passage shows that he has rightly been called a "weit

---

[1] See Marzia Pieri. "Il 'laboratorio' provinciale di Luigi Groto." *Rivista italiana di drammaturgia*, vol. 4, 1979, pp. 3–355, p. 5, incl. n. 8.
[2] Groto's own references to unpublished plays in various prefaces and letters indicate that he was working on a *Ginevra*, an *Isabella*, a *Progne*, and a *Mirra* in 1560/1561 and 1572; see Pieri, "Il 'laboratorio'," p. 18, n. 30.
[3] See Ben Jonson. *Four Comedies*, edited by Helen Ostovich. London: Longman, 1997.

https://doi.org/10.1515/9783110536690-007

ins 17. Jahrhundert hinein [...] in ganz Europa berühmte[r] Mann" ("a famous man, till the seventeenth century well-known everywhere in Europe").[4] Groto (1541–1585),[5] a prolific author despite his physical affliction, was far more than a simple man of letters from the provinces: public authorities commissioned a series of political speeches from him; he penned numerous letters, which were edited at the beginning of the seventeenth century in three anthologies; he composed (lost) dialogues as well as commentaries on scholarly texts on topics as diverse as astronomy, geology, and agriculture; he revised Ariosto's *Cinque canti* and Boccaccio's *Decameron*, and supplied a commentary to those works. Yet from today's perspective, his place in literary history was ultimately secured by his substantial *Rime*[6] and his plays, which received considerable attention in his time.[7]

---

4 Andrea Mott-Petavrakis. *Studien zum lyrischen Werk Luigi Grotos. Interpretation und literarhistorische Einordnung seiner Rime* (Hamburger Romanistische Dissertationen 23). Hamburg: Romanisches Seminar der Universität Hamburg, 1992, p. 9. For a brief history of the reception of Groto's œuvre during and after his lifetime, see Françoise Decroisette. "'Pleurez mes yeux!' Le tragique autoréférentiel de Luigi Groto, l'Aveugle d'Adria (1541–1585)." *Cahiers d'Études Italiennes*, vol. 19, 2014, pp. 165–184, pp. 165–167; see ibid. 182–184 for a basic overview of Renaissance and modern editions, a list of early modern translations of the *Pentimento amoroso* and the *Emilia* into French, and a selection of the most pertinent recent research. All translations are mine.

5 Giovanni Benvenuti. *Il Cieco di Adria. Vita ed opere di Luigi Groto*. Sala Bolognese: Forni, 1984 provides a biographical outline and a short characterization of Groto's works in his brief study. For further biographical sketches and additional information on Groto's social background, see Franco Rizzi. "Le socialità profonde: La famiglia di Luigi Groto Il Cieco d'Adria." *Luigi Groto e il suo tempo (1541–1585)*. Vol. 1: *Atti del convegno di studi, Adria, 27–29 aprile 1984*, edited by Giorgio Brunello and Antonio Lodo. Rovigo: Minelliana, 1987, pp. 23–60; Mott-Petavrakis. *Studien zum Werk Grotos*, pp. 9–13; Valentina Gallo. "Groto (Grotto), Luigi (detto il Cieco d'Adria)." *Dizionario Biografico degli Italiani*, Rome: Istituto della Enciclopedia Italiani, vol. 60, 2003, pp. 21–24. An early biography by Francesco Bocchi. *Luigi Groto (Il Cieco d'Adria), nato 8 settembre 1541 – morto 13 dicembre 1585). Il suo tempo, la sua vita e le sue opere*. Adria: Eredi Guarnieri, 1886 has not been completely superseded by more recent research; among other things, it supplies a catalogue of editions from 1586 to 1886 (pp. 93–104) which is still very useful.

6 For a more detailed discussion and further reading, see Bernhard Huss. "Luigi Grotos *Rime*: Manierismen als implizite Metapoesie." *Manierismus. Interdisziplinäre Studien zu einem ästhetischen Stiltyp zwischen formalem Experiment und historischer Signifikanz*, edited by Bernhard Huss and Christian Wehr. Heidelberg: Winter, 2014 (*GRM*, Supplement 56), pp. 71–92 and Bernhard Huss. "Figura auctoris und Selbstreferenz des poetischen Diskurses bei Luigi Groto." *Germanisch-Romanische Monatsschrift*, vol. 64, no. 4, 2014, pp. 407–427. (Italian version forthcoming in the proceedings of the conference "IV Col·loqui internacional Mimesi: Metaficció – Renaixement & Barroc," Universitat de Barcelona, 3–4 October 2013, edited by Josep Solervicens and Antoni Lluís Moll).

7 Contrary to what the cliché of Cinquecento "closet drama" might suggest, most of the plays mentioned above were actually performed on stage; on the dates of individual performances,

Publications on Groto's dramatic oeuvre are few and far between; one notable exception is the *Adriana*, which Ariani's modern edition has reinterpreted and made accessible.[8] However, subsequent research has mainly focused on the question of whether Shakespeare had access to Groto's play and whether he used it as a source for his *Romeo and Juliet*.[9] This reticence on the part of researchers stands in marked contrast to the response Groto's plays elicited

---

see Luciana Zampolli. "'Una scena di perpetua durevolezza': le projet théâtral de Luigi Groto, l'aveugle d'Hadria." *Théâtre de cour, théâtre de ville, théâtre de rue. Actes du Colloque International, 26–28 novembre 1998*, edited by Robert Horville, Olinda Kleiman and Godeleine Logez. Lille: Université de Lille 3, 2001, pp. 93–104, p. 94, incl. n. 4–11; Barbara Spaggiari. "La presenza di Luigi Groto in Shakespeare e negli autori elisabettiani." *Italique*, vol. 12, 2009, pp. 173–198, p. 189 f., n. 12; on the two tragedies *Adriana* and *Dalida* in particular, see Pieri, "Il 'laboratorio'," p. 23, n. 39, as well as Giulietta Bazoli. "Groto e Shakespeare: un confronto possibile?" *Quaderni Veneti*, vol. 39, 2004, pp. 7–27, p. 26, n. 64 on the *Adriana*.

8 Besides Ariani's edition of the *Adriana* with the accompanying introduction and commentary (Luigi Groto. "Adriana." *Il teatro italiano II: La tragedia del Cinquecento 1*, edited by Marco Ariani. Turin: Einaudi, 1977, pp. 281–424), see also the important chapter on the *Adriana* as a prime example of Mannerist tragedy in Marco Ariani. "Il Manierismo e la dissoluzione della struttura tragica." *Tra classicismo e manierismo. Il teatro tragico del Cinquecento*, Florence: Olschki 1974 (Accademia Toscana di Scienze e Lettere "La Colombaria," Studi 31), pp. 179–230, pp. 212–230. For further information on the *Adriana*, especially on its Petrarchan stylemes, which I discuss in more detail below, see Bernhard Huss. "Petrarkismus und Tragödie." *Der Petrarkismus – ein europäischer Gründungsmythos*, edited by id. and Michael Bernsen. Göttingen: V&R unipress, 2011 (Gründungsmythen Europas in Literatur, Musik und Kunst 4), pp. 225–257, pp. 240–244.

9 Giancarlo Cavazzini. "Dall'*Adriana* a *Romeo and Juliet*: problemi di un rapporto." *Luigi Groto e il suo tempo (1541–1585)*. Vol. 1: *Atti del convegno di studi, Adria, 27–29 aprile 1984*, Rovigo: Minelliana, 1987, pp. 337–353 and Bazoli. "Groto e Shakespeare" are only two fairly recent examples of studies that focus on the Shakespearean angle. Given the overall scarcity of research on Groto, the fact that this question has been revisited time and again over the course of far more than a century means that valuable resources have been diverted from more pressing issues; Michele Biancale. *La tragedia italiana nel Cinquecento*. Rome: Tip. Capitolina D. Battarelli, 1901 is an exemplary case in point: concerning the *Adriana*, his chapter on Groto (pp. 223–247) confines itself to a handful of fairly vacuous condemnations of the play, with all other references to the text being about the possibility of Shakespeare using it as a source (the general tendency, expressed on several occasions, is that it is quite unthinkable for a genius of Shakespeare's stature to have adopted anything from an inferior author like Groto). For the most thoughtful observation known to me in regard to this issue, see Gabriele Baldini. "Teatro classico italiano e teatro elisabettiano." *Atti del Convegno sul Tema: Il teatro classico italiano nel '500 (Roma, 9–12 febbraio 1969)*, Rome: Accademia Nazionale dei Lincei, 1971, (Accademia Nazionale dei Lincei, Quaderno 138), pp. 149–159, p. 153, who draws attention to the presence of the famous nightingale in the lovers' parting scene in Shakespeare's version which can already be found in Groto's play. Strangely enough, this crucial detail has been overlooked by researchers time and again.

among his contemporaries: public reception was lively indeed, at least as far as the dissemination of plays in print was concerned,[10] and both of his tragedies went through multiple re-editions throughout the late sixteenth and early seventeenth centuries.[11]

Groto is an exceptional phenomenon among the playwrights of his time. Like many of his peers, he was a member of several academies – namely the *Addormentati* of Rovigo, the *Pastori frattegiani*, and the *Illustrati* of Adria, a society which he himself had founded.[12] Unlike most of his fellow writers (another notable exception would be Giambattista Giraldi Cinzio in Ferrara), Groto personally supervised stage productions of his plays: the author simultaneously served as dramaturg and director. Groto also appeared on stage as an actor in productions of *Isac* and *Emilia*, and the 1584/85 season saw him perform the title role in Orsatto Giustinian's production of Sophocles' *King Oedipus*, the much-noticed opening premiere of the Teatro Olimpico in Vicenza.[13] Groto's plays were performed in various public settings in Adria: *Isac* was staged in the church of Santa Maria della Tomba, *Dalida* in the Loggia of the Palazzo Civico (and later in Verona), *Il pentimento amoroso* in the Palazzo Pretorio (later in the Palazzo Civico), and *Adriana* in the Loggia of the Palazzo Civico as well as later in Venice.[14] Groto also had a stationary theater built in Adria, presumably out of wood, in which the premiere of his comedy *Emilia* took place on 1 March 1579.[15]

In a word, Groto was a true "man of the theater."[16] Arguably, this is even more true of him than of his more famous colleague from Ferrara: Groto con-

---

10 On the early publication history of Groto's plays, see the synopsis in Zampolli, "'Una scena di perpetua durevolezza'," pp. 103 f.
11 Groto, "Adriana," pp. 282 and 284 list a total of ten editions of the *Adriana* before 1626; so does Pieri, "Il 'laboratorio'," p. 23, n. 39, who also gives a total of eight editions for the *Dalida* up until 1646.
12 Decroisette, "'Pleurez mes yeux!'," p. 168.
13 See Groto, "Adriana," p. 281.
14 Additional information is once again to be found in the publications listed in notes 6 and 10. For further details on all plays, see also the thorough references in the annotations to Pieri. "Il 'laboratorio'," as well as the summary in Decroisette, "'Pleurez mes yeux!'," p. 168.
15 Ibid., pp. 168 f.
16 See Pieri, "Il 'laboratorio'," p. 4: "Per questo egli è uno dei pochi scrittori cinquecenteschi che, privo dei vincoli e della protezione di una corte, curi lo spettacolo in ogni sua fase, dalla stesura del testo all'allestimento e talvolta alla interpretazione, e che metta in scena pressoché tutti i suoi componimenti, instaurando un rapporto non episodico con un pubblico socialmente composito." On the similarity between Groto and Cinzio in terms of their unusually comprehensive dramaturgical involvement, see also Birgit Ulmer. "Tragödientheorie als Wirkungsästhetik in Giambattista Giraldi Cinzios *Orbecche* und *Altile*." *Renaissancetheater. Italien und die europäische Rezeption / Teatro del Rinascimento. Italia e la ricezione europea*, edited by Rolf Lohse. Tübingen: Narr, 2007, pp. 193–213, p. 209.

sciously experimented with any and all available dramatic genres, which were considered distinct in Renaissance theoretical discourse and whose boundaries were subject to extensive scholarly discussion.[17] While *Dalida* and *Adriana* represent the genre of tragedy, Groto also explored pastoral drama with *Calisto* and *Il pentimento amoroso*, comedy with *Emilia*, *Il tesoro*, and *Alteria*, and biblical drama with his *Isac*. In the preface to the *Emilia* (amidst numerous ostentatious gestures of humility), the author himself raises the claim that what sets him apart from his fellow playwrights is the fact that he has not only accomplished the notoriously difficult feat of being an established writer of both tragedies and comedies, but that he is also the only writer to have succeeded in the pastoral genre as well: "E tanto più temerario si scoprirebbe il mio ardire, che havendo io già dato fuori il pentimento amoroso, nuova favola pastorale, parrebbe ch'io presumessi d'abbracciar non pur una ò due, ma tutte & tre insieme queste Sceniche, & si diverse professioni."[18]

By exploring the full spectrum of genres that the Secondo Cinquecento had at its disposal, Groto puts the productive potentials of the three major dramatic registers to the test: his experiments involve tragedy, comedy, and pastoral drama. Groto is uncompromising in the way in which he investigates the extent and the limits of each genre; the *Emilia*, for example, can be regarded as a comedy with an affinity for tragedy.[19] To call Groto's approach experimental, however, does not imply consent to the notion of experimentalism that Rolf Lohse has fairly recently sought to attribute to Renaissance Italian drama:[20] for Lohse, the term experiment implies the creation of "something new" that eludes previous norms and breaks away from existing models. Too one-dimensional to be applicable to the Renaissance and rather unreflecting at that, this idea of what constitutes an experiment is ultimately the result of

---

[17] For a detailed discussion of the contemporary theoretical distinction between tragedy and comedy, see Paola Mastrocola. *L'idea del tragico. Teorie della tragedia nel Cinquecento*, Soveria Mannelli: Rubbettino, 1998 (Iride 18), pp. 71–116.

[18] Luigi Groto. *La Emilia, comedia nova di Luigi Groto Cieco di Hadria. Recitata in Hadria, il dì primo di Marzo. MDLXXIX*, Venezia, Francesco Ziletti, 1579, fol. a4ᵛ (and f., n.p.). See also Luciana Zampolli. "La réflexion théâtrale de Luigi Groto: de la critique des codes à l'autoreprésentation." *Le théâtre réfléchi. Poétiques théâtrales italiennes des Intronati à Pasolini*, edited by Françoise Decroisette. Saint-Denis: Presses Universitaires de Vincennes, 2000, pp. 29–49, p. 39; Decroisette, "'Pleurez mes yeux!'," p. 169.

[19] See Salvatore Di Maria. "Groto's *Emilia*: Fiction Meets Reality." *The Poetics of Imitation in the Italian Theatre of the Renaissance*. Toronto, Buffalo and London: University of Toronto Press, 2013, pp. 84–104, esp. pp. 96 f., 104 (where, however, the aspect of genre history remains somewhat underdeveloped in favor of content-related observations).

[20] See Rolf Lohse. "Sperimentalismo nel dramma del Cinquecento." *Renaissancetheater*, edited by id., pp. 215–229, esp. pp. 215–218, 227 f.

inappropriate progressivism. Groto is an exponent of Renaissance Mannerism who, in his "provincial laboratory" (as Pieri so memorably put it in 1979), subjects the individual ingredients provided by the literary repertoire of his day to an experimental "stress test" in order to investigate their ability to react and amalgamate with each other. Not only do Groto's literary experiments have a strong impact on his literary practice in terms of *inventio*, *dispositio*, and *elocutio*, triggering a process of radical refunctionalization – his works also reflect upon the tenets of contemporary normative poetology, which Groto explores in what could perhaps be called selective "test assemblages." What will prove to be the case for the tragedies is also strikingly true for the *Rime*, where Groto stretches the normative precepts of orthodox Bembism to the utmost: Petrarchan diction and Petrarchan topics are subjected to antithetical and oxymoronic hyperbole until they reach breaking point. Manifesting itself in relentless experimentalism, Mannerism's tendency to carry the subdivision and differentiation of lyric formulae to the extreme reveals the possibilities *and* the limitations of the set of rules governing the literary system.[21] Generally speaking, the functionality of the various generic categories is investigated by Groto *in actu*, an activity that includes an examination of each individual genre's capability to cope with infiltration by "alien" elements (e.g. by the epigrammatic tradition that finds its way into lyric Petrarchism in the vernacular). In poetry, Groto's linguistic-stylistic radicalization is a reflexive response to the exigencies of Bembist literary doctrine, whose precepts are pushed to the very limit of their applicability. The norms prescribed by the prevalent system are thus renegotiated and strained to the point where it becomes questionable how long and in which direction the "official" literary code can still be developed.

The direct connection to late-Renaissance Mannerism is evident. The Secondo Cinquecento's propensity to experiment with literary forms – especially when faced with the considerable regulatory burden imposed by contemporary poetology – is directly linked to the Renaissance "philologization" of the engagement with literature, to the ever-increasing awareness of the problems that afflicted early modern discourses on literary theory.[22] The acting out of Mannerist idiosyncrasies in the literary text, and an experimentalism that has sometimes been interpreted as a provocation are thus by no means mere symptoms of a subjectivist and individualistic *distancing* from rules. To be sure, there have been attempts to establish such an antagonistic stance as a constituent

---

[21] For a detailed discussion, see Huss. "Luigi Grotos *Rime*."
[22] See Aldo Scaglione. "Cinquecento Mannerism and the Uses of Petrarch." *Medieval and Renaissance Studies*, vol. 5, edited by Osborne Bennett Hardison. Chapel Hill: University of North Carolina Press, 1971, pp. 122–155, p. 134.

feature of Mannerism,[23] and a pronounced hostility towards rules also ties in nicely with Lohse's thesis of progressivism in regard to literary experimentation. Yet authors produce their literary Mannerisms against the backdrop of a body of theory that aims at an aesthetic fixation in terms of literary production and textual composition. This normative body is reflected in their works, which gain metapoetical significance in turn – the critical tension between the text itself and the conditions that enable it is a central component of the experiments taking place in Groto's "laboratorio provinciale" ("provincial laboratory").

The strain placed on literary parameters and methods of textualization by such an experimentalist approach potentially entails the risk of a disintegration of normative precepts.[24] This is not to say, however, that a Mannerist like Groto is pursuing a complete break with the rules,[25] a unilinear struggle against the norm,[26] a kind of anti-normative "escape." Rather than that, his goal is to subject the formal framework within which he operates to a final test of its resilience.[27] This is the reason for his "ambiguo rapporto di fedeltà-trasgressione rispetto ai modelli" ("ambiguous relation of fidelity-transgression

---

23 See for example Wylie Sypher. *Rinascimento, manierismo, barocco*. Padua: Marsilio, 1968, p. 146 (and passim).
24 See Gustav René Hocke. "Manier und Manie in der europäischen Kunst." *Merkur*, vol. 10, 1956, pp. 535–558, pp. 556 f.; Sypher, *Rinascimento*, p. 131.
25 Cf. Scaglione. "Cinquecento Mannerism," p. 127, who posits that a "restiveness toward the 'rules' as guidelines to be surpassed and violated" is a characteristic trait of Mannerism as a whole.
26 For such a notion of Mannerism, see Gustav René Hocke. *Manierismus in der Literatur. Sprach-Alchimie und Esoterische Kombinationskunst. Beiträge zur Vergleichenden Europäischen Literaturgeschichte*, Hamburg: Rowohlt, 1959, p. 239 (Mannerism always constitutes an "Aufstand gegen Regelzwang"); Arnold Hauser. *Der Manierismus. Die Krise der Renaissance und der Ursprung der modernen Kunst*, Munich: Beck, 1964, p. 25 (and passim); Tibor Klaniczay. "La lotta antiaristotelica dei teorici del manierismo." *Tiziano e il manierismo europeo*, edited by Rodolfo Pallucchini. Florence: Olschki, 1978 (Civiltà Veneziana, Saggi 24), pp. 367–387.
27 On poetological stress tests, as well as on the negotiation of the normative framework in Mannerism and its significance for literary theory, see also Amedeo Quondam. *La parola nel labirinto. Società e scrittura del Manierismo a Napoli*, Bari: Laterza, 1975, pp. 1–22; Gerhard Regn. "Barock und Manierismus. Italianistische Anmerkungen zur Unvermeidbarkeit einer problemlastigen Begriffsdifferenzierung." *Europäische Barockrezeption*, edited by Klaus Garber. Wiesbaden: Harrassowitz, 1991 (Wolfenbütteler Arbeiten zur Barockforschung 20.2), vol. 2, pp. 879–897; and James Mirollo. "The Mannered and the Mannerist in Late Renaissance Literature." *The Meaning of Mannerism*, edited by Franklin W. Robinson and Stephen G. Nichols. Hanover: University Press of New England, 1972, pp. 7–24, pp. 16–18 (who evaluates Mannerism as a "parasitic" and "parodistic" literary current straining against High Renaissance rules of art).

to the models"),[28] and this is the explanation for the apparent paradox that Hauser has attributed to Mannerism in general, namely that (according to Hauser) it implies a "lotta continua contro il formalismo e contro quello che si potrebbe definire il 'feticismo' dell'arte" ("a continuous fight against formalism and against what could be defined as 'fetishism' of art") on the one hand, while being "un'arte formalistica" ("a formalistic art") on the other, "feticistica, affettata, estranea all'indole del soggetto creatore" ("fetishist, affected, alien to the genius of the creative subject").[29] The relationship between Groto's experiment and the repertoire of tradition-bound methods that it draws upon is highly complex: what is being created in the author's alembic is not something *new* in the sense of unilinear progression – as it were, his experimental set-up is designed to put the existing ingredients under pressure in order to produce hitherto unknown alloys, compounds, and distillates.

Cinquecento tragedy is particularly well suited to this type of experimentation, as Fabio Ruggirello quite rightly points out: "Il teatro tragico, destinato a diventare nel Seicento una delle espressioni più significative di un'estetica incentrata sul ruolo del fruitore, nel Cinquecento si presta ad essere territorio di intraprendenti sperimentazioni." ("The tragic theater, destined to become, in the seventeenth century, one of the most significant expressions of an aesthetics focused on the role of the recipient, in the sixteenth century proves to be a territory of eager experimentation.")[30] In Groto's particular case, and especially in regard to the stylistic layout of the *Adriana*, the production of tragic texts indeed proves to be "una fucina di elaborate esperienze formali" ("a forge of elaborate formal experiences").[31]

The *Adriana* is designed as a tragedy of compassion. The evocation of what Aristotle has termed ἔλεος, in Italian the affect of *pietà*, is the play's main

---

28 Edoardo Taddeo. *Il manierismo letterario e i lirici veneziani del tardo Cinquecento*. Rome: Bulzoni (Biblioteca di Cultura 56), 1974, p. 60.
29 Arnold Hauser. "L'alienazione, chiave del manierismo." *Problemi del manierismo*, edited by Amedeo Quondam. Naples: Guida, 1975, pp. 157–175, p. 171.
30 Fabio Ruggirello. "L''occulta virtù' del testo. Deissi ed ostensione nel teatro tragico cinquecentesco." *Italica*, vol. 83, no. 2, 2006, pp. 216–237, p. 216. The approach of Oster is not at all helpful in this context. Her not always independent study fails to substantiate the tentative thesis contained in its title "Klassizismus als Experiment": nowhere does it achieve a conclusive explication of the nexus between "classicism" and "experiment" (a nexus which, I would argue, can hardly be fully understood without taking Mannerism into account), see Angela Oster. "Klassizismus als Experiment. Tragödie und Theater(un)kultur im Kontext der italienischen Renaissance (mit einem Ausblick auf die französische Klassik)." *Ethos und Form der Tragödie. Für Maria Moog-Grünewald zum 65. Geburtstag*, edited by Niklas Bender, Max Grosse and Steffen Schneider. Heidelberg: Winter, 2014 (*GRM*, Supplement 60), pp. 85–136.
31 Pieri, "Il 'laboratorio'," p. 23.

concern. Compared to the *Poetics* itself, but also to interpretations of Aristotle that were widespread in the Italian Renaissance,[32] this approach must appear somewhat reductive and one-sided. In fact, the *Adriana* is the direct result of an experiment in which one of the fundamental tenets of Aristotelian poetology is split up and replaced by a dichotomy: Groto's project detaches the twin affects of ἔλεος and φόβος.[33] Having created an experimental diptych in the pastoral domain (*Calisto* as a somewhat risqué piece reminiscent of satyr plays, *Il pentimento amoroso* as a nod towards comedy),[34] Groto proceeds to write out another antithesis in the field of tragedy. The preeminent tragedies of the Cinquecento (such as Giraldi's *Orbecche* and Speroni's *Canace*) maintain a certain distance to the tragedies of classical antiquity as a matter of principle,[35] but Groto increases this distance considerably by embarking upon "due spericolate avventure formali significativamente lanciate in opposte direzioni" ("two audacious formal adventures, significantly launched in opposite directions").[36] Contemporary theory held that the affects of *compassione* and *spavento* belonged together, even though a distinction between *tragedia affettuosa* (παθητική) and *tragedia accostumata* (ἠθική) was maintained with an eye on Aristotle's *Poetics* (Chapter 18).[37] Groto, on the other hand, separates ἔλεος and φόβος, assigning them individually to a tragic diptych consisting of the *Adriana* as a tragedy of *compassione* and the *Dalida* as a tragedy of horror. Clearly, this is no unconditional affirmation of Aristotelian doctrine.[38] What

---

[32] See Brigitte Kappl. *Die* Poetik *des Aristoteles in der Dichtungstheorie des Cinquecento*. Berlin and New York: de Gruyter, 2006 (Untersuchungen zur antiken Literatur und Geschichte 83), who offers some fundamental reflections regarding this issue.

[33] For a more detailed discussion, see Bernhard Huss. "Luigi Grotos tragisches Diptychon aus Mitleid und Schrecken: *La Adriana* und *La Dalida*." Archiv für das Studium der neueren Sprachen und Literaturen, vol. 252, no. 1, 2015, pp. 83–104.

[34] See Pieri, "Il 'laboratorio'," pp. 16 f., and the overarching argument that is made there.

[35] On this issue, see Marco Ariani. "La trasgressione e l'ordine. L'*Orbecche* di G. B. Giraldi Cinthio e la fondazione del linguaggio tragico cinquecentesco." *La Rassegna della Letteratura Italiana*, vol. 83, 1979, pp. 117–180, p. 117.

[36] Pieri, "Il 'laboratorio'," p. 17, who is not referring to the opposition between "compassion" and "horror" here, but rather to the generic templates of Senecan tragedy vs. pathetic love tragedy (ibid. 17 f.). Herrick 1965 noticed the dichotomy between the two plays even earlier: the *Adriana* is subsumed under the category of sentimental-pathetic "Gothic and Romantic Tragedies," whereas the *Dalida* is discussed in the chapter "More Blood" (i.e., in the context of the tragedies of horror that followed in the wake of the *Orbecche*).

[37] See Nicolò Rossi. "Discorsi intorno alla tragedia." *Trattati di poetica e retorica del Cinquecento*, edited by Bernard Weinberg. Bari: Laterza, 1974, vol. 4, pp. 59–120, pp. 117 f.

[38] On Groto's dissociation from basic parameters of the classicist norm, see Zampolli, "La réflexion théâtrale," pp. 30–37.

we encounter here is exactly the same Mannerist attitude that I have already demonstrated in the context of the *Rime*: Groto seizes every opportunity a certain (sub)genre provides in terms of representation and effect. Differing radically from the rational and moderate plays in the tradition of Trissino's *Sofonisba* with their attempt to functionalize an "Aristotelian" form for the domestication of passions,[39] Giraldi's *Orbecche* inaugurates the poetics of the tragedy of horror in exemplary fashion for the Renaissance.[40] Once the tragedy of horror and the tragedy of compassion have become identifiable as distinct subgenres, Groto promptly puts their respective potentials to the test.[41]

The *Adriana* is frequently considered a "typical" Mannerist tragedy – if not *the* Mannerist tragedy – of the Cinquecento.[42] In the *Adriana*, the pathetic love story that forms the basis of the "Romeo and Juliet" paradigm (gleaned from the Romeo-e-Giulietta novellas by Luigi Da Porto and Matteo Bandello) is relocated to the ancient city of Adria. Adria is under siege: the city is surrounded by King Mezenzio's Latian army, a state of affairs that has a very unfortunate impact on the budding romance that has developed between his son, Latino, and Adriana, the daughter of Adria's king, Atrio. Meeting secretly in the besieged city, the lovers carry on their amorous involvement even after Latino accidentally kills Adriana's brother in combat without realizing the identity of his adversary. With the death of Adriana's brother, the political situation has become highly volatile. To remedy the dangerous lack of a successor, Adriana's parents arrange her marriage to the heir to the Sabine throne. Adriana sees

---

[39] See Marzia Pieri. *La nascita del teatro moderno in Italia tra XV e XVI secolo*. Turin: Bollati Boringhieri, 1989, pp. 137 f.

[40] For a basic discussion of this issue, see Maraike Di Domenica. "Manierismus vs. Aristotelismus. Zur ästhetischen Subversion regulativer Prinzipien in den Horror-Tragödien der italienischen Renaissance." *Manierismus. Interdiziplinäre Studien zu einem ästhetischen Stiltyp zwischen formalem Experiment und historischer Signifikanz*, edited by Bernhard Huss and Christian Wehr. Heidelberg: Winter, 2014 (*GRM*, Supplement 56), pp. 93–111. On Giraldi's groundbreaking role, see Marco Ariani. "L'*Orbecche* di G. B. Giraldi e la poetica dell'orrore." *La Rassegna della Letteratura Italiana*, vol. 75, 1971, pp. 432–450; Marco Ariani. "Ragione e furore nella tragedia di G. B. Giraldi Cinthio." *Tra classicismo e manierismo. Il teatro tragico del Cinquecento*, Florence: Olschki, 1974 (Accademia Toscana di Scienze e Lettere "La Colombaria," Studi 31), pp. 115–178; Ariani. "La trasgressione."

[41] *Nota bene*: these subgenres can only be defined on a typological scale, i.e. in terms of a certain predominance of compassion over horror, or vice versa. They cannot be distinguished in the sense of a mutually exclusive presence of each of the two affects.

[42] For a statement to this effect, see for example Cavazzini, "Dall'*Adriana* a *Romeo and Juliet*," p. 345: "Con la stesura dell'*Adriana*, Luigi Groto ci fornisce il reperto più consapevole e tragico di tutta la drammaturgia del Cinquecento, presentandoci la tragedia manierista nella sua forma più matura"; see also ibid., p. 348.

only one way out: She follows the seemingly helpful advice of a magician, who offers to concoct a powerful potion that will leave her unconscious for several hours. Once presumed dead, so the plan goes, she will escape from the city after her "funeral" to live happily ever after – in secrecy, to be sure, but reunited with Latino. Adriana swallows the narcotic. According to plan, she is thought dead by all and sundry and promptly laid in her grave. Contrary to the magician's scheme, however, Latino is left uninformed about what is really going on: he arrives at Adriana's grave convinced that she is indeed dead. Confronted with the "corpse" of his beloved, Latino poisons himself in desperation. Yet shortly before he dies, Adriana awakes – when Latino succumbs to the poison after a last intimate dialogue between the two lovers, Adriana stabs herself to death next to Latino's lifeless body. In the end, the city of Adria is destroyed by a flood deliberately caused by Latino's father. This all-encompassing cataclysm bridges the chasm that separates the play's temporally remote setting from the present, a move for which the prologue has prepared the audience from the very outset: ultimately, the Adria of Groto's contemporaries represents nothing more than the pitiful remains of former glory; the tragedy's action has given the audience a glimpse of the last days and hours of the present city's mighty predecessor.

My claim that the *Adriana* constitutes a "tragedy of compassion" is substantiated as early as in the first lines of the separate prologue[43] preceding the play:

[1] Se mai tragedia agli occhi vostri offerta,
     indi pietoso umor per forza trasse,
     propizi spettatori, questa, ch'oggi
     viene a farvi di sé dolente mostra,
[5] può trar dal petto vostro e da le ciglia
     un'Etna di sospiri, e un mar di pianto.
     Tra per l'autor ch'a voi la ordisce, e trama,
     pien d'ogni oscuro, e tragico accidente,
     che chiusi avendo in nube eterna gli occhi,
[10] meraviglia non è, s'eterna pioggia
     di lacrime ne sparge, e altrui le move;
     e per color che 'n lei vanno introdotti,
     i piú fedeli, e piú infelici amanti,
     che trafigesse mai lo stral d'amore,

---

[43] In deploying such a prologue, Groto follows the example of Giraldi's *Orbecche*; on the poetological significance of this self-positioning, see Zampolli, "La réflexion théâtrale," pp. 30–32.

[15] anzi d'amor non già, ma stral di morte;
e alfin per la città, dove s'adempie
la mestissima istoria.[44]

Metapoetical statements right at the beginning of the text proclaim the emotional effect that the *Adriana* is designed to achieve: more than any other play, so the text itself declares, this is a tragedy capable of evoking "pietoso umor," that is, tears of compassion (line 2) – in fact, as the hyperbole in line 6 informs us, the anticipated result is nothing short of a "Mount Etna of sighs" and a "sea of tears." Conflating the fictional world with metapoetical aspects and with the self-fashioning of the empirical author – a move typical of Groto[45] – the text claims that the eternal "rain of tears" ("eterna pioggia | di lacrime," 10 f.) to be created is in no small part due to the eternal clouding of its author's eyesight. The intention of the play is thus made quite obvious: its goal is the evocation of one of the two Aristotelian affects, namely compassion (*pietà*, ἔλεος – significantly, horror is omitted). This feeling of compassion is not to be engendered by a particularly brutal plot, as would be typical for a tragedy of horror along the lines of Giraldi Cinzio's *Orbecche*, but rather by the sentimentalist presentation of a "mestissima istoria" (17), a "singularly sad story." The play's action is so singularly sad because the protagonists' love story takes such a singularly unhappy course – as it were, the two lovers are the most unhappy couple ever, "i piú fedeli, e piú infelici amanti, | che trafigesse mai lo stral d'amore" (13 f.).[46] For one thing is certain: this is a love story with a

---

[44] "[1] If ever a tragedy presented to your eyes | by force extracted pitiful liquids from them, | then, well-disposed spectators, this one which | comes today to present itself to you painfully, | [5] is able to extract from your chest and from your eyelids | a Mount Etna of sighs and a sea of tears: | This might be due to the author who creates and weaves it for you, | full of all sorts of dark and tragic incidents, | and who has his eyes closed in an eternal cloud, | [10] so that it is no wonder if he sheds | an eternal rain of tears and causes it in others; | it might also be due to those who are introduced in the play, | the most faithful and most unhappy lovers | ever transfixed by the arrow of love, | [15] no, not the arrow of love but rather the arrow of death; | finally it might be due to the town where the singularly sad story | fulfills itself."

[45] For a detailed discussion, see Huss, "Grotos tragisches Diptychon;" see also Zampolli, "La réflexion théâtrale," pp. 30, 38, 40–42; Luciana Zampolli. "Les voyages du témoin: le 'destinataire privilégié' de *L'istoria novellamente ritrovata di due nobili amanti* (1524) di Luigi Da Porto à *La Adriana* di Luigi Groto (1578)." *Les traces du spectateur. Italie, XVIIe et XVIIIe siècles*, edited by Françoise Decroisette. Saint-Denis: Presses Universitaires de Vincennes, 2006, pp. 63–82, p. 72 incl. n. 29.

[46] The play's lachrymose love plot can be traced back all the way to the novelistic basis on which Groto constructs his tragedy of compassion. Matteo Bandello's version of the story (Seconda parte, Novella IX of the 1554 collection) significantly carries the title "La *sfortunata morte di dui infelicissimi amanti* che l'uno di veleno e l'altro di dolore morirono, con varii accidenti" (italics added), thereby gesturing towards the "tragic" ending appropriate to a som-

fatal ending; the prologue leaves no doubt about that, when it informs us that this is the type of story in which the arrow of love ("lo stral d'amore," 14) turns into an arrow of death ("stral di morte," 15).

At this point, in addition to having recognized the play's references to the sombre novellas of Da Porto and Bandello, the knowledgeable audience of the Cinquecento may well have guessed at the stylistic and generic register that would subsequently be deployed in the staging of this "singularly sad story."[47] After all, the coupling of sighs and tears ("sospiri," "pianto"), the antithesis of "amore" ("love") and "morte" ("death"), the image of the "stral d'amore" ("arrow of love"), and the linking of "stral" ("arrow") and "morte" ("death") were devices only too familiar to theatergoers and readers from Francesco Petrarca's omnipresent *Canzoniere (Rerum vulgarium fragmenta)*.[48] As the sty-

---

bre novelistic love plot. Both Da Porto's and Bandello's novellas repeatedly and explicitly state that both texts feature a plot conducive to the evocation of *pietà* (Luigi Da Porto. *Giulietta e Romeo novella storica. Aggiuntavi la novella di Matteo Bandello su lo stesso argomento, il poemetto di Clizia Veronese, ed altre antiche poesie, col corredo d'illustrazioni storiche e bibliografiche*, edited by Alessandro Torri. Pisa: Nistri, 1831, p. 46: "la misera e pietosa morte di questi amanti"; Matteo Bandello. "Novella IX: La sfortunata morte di dui infelicissimi amanti che l'uno di veleno e l'altro di dolore morirono, con varii accidenti." *La seconda parte de le novelle*, edited by Delmo Maestri. Alessandria: Edizioni dell'Orso, 1993 [Contributi e Proposte 6], pp. 58–85, p. 58: "un pietoso caso e infortunio grandissimo," ibid., p. 84: "il pietoso caso degli sfortunati amanti"). Yet both novellas share more with the *Adriana* than just the affective charge that becomes visible in the recurring theme of compassion and pain revolving around the amorous fortunes of the protagonists: the strong emotional involvement of Adriana's parents, who attempt to secure their daughter's consent to an unwanted marriage with threats and openly displayed anger only to mourn her excessively once she is dead, can be encountered both in the novellas *and* in the *Adriana*. It is evident that the *Adriana* is a transgeneric derivate based on features of the novella, namely its bias towards *pietà* and its specific approach to the modeling of affects and to the structuring of the plot (in both genres, the implementation of these aspects into language is achieved via the deployment of Petrarchan formulae; see also the following note for additional details).

47 Groto's text is not alone in drawing on lyrical Petrarchism, as I will go on to show. The two novellas also avail themselves of Petrarchan elements, albeit to a lesser degree. Both Da Porto and Bandello deploy the Petrarchan repertoire in various passages of their novellas, especially in the context of Romeo and Giulietta's amorous affects. In Bandello's version, the closing speeches that Romeo addresses to the allegedly dead Giulietta (Bandello, "Novella IX," p. 82) and that Giulietta addresses to the well and truly dead Romeo (ibid., p. 84) are particularly striking in that they amass an oxymoronic series of Petrarchan antitheses such as *gioia–dolore*, *allegrezza–dolore*, *dolce–amaro*, *vivo–morto*, and *vivere–morire*. From a poetological vantage point, and in light of literary predecessors such as Speroni's *Canace*, the amalgamation of Petrarchism and tragedy (a more detailed discussion will follow promptly) must clearly have suggested itself to Groto when he accessed his novelistic hypotexts.

48 Concerning "sospiri" and "pianto," cf. *RVF* 207.96 ("pianto, sospiri e morte"), 332.45 ("i sospiri e 'l pianto"; ibid. at line 46 also the conjunction of "tears" and "rain," "pioggia") –

lemes of the *Canzoniere* are so prominently displayed in Groto's works, it is hardly surprising, in light of the sixteenth century's penchant for "literary programs," that the same repertoire is also present in the poetry of the very originator of "orthodox" High Renaissance Petrarchism, that is, in Pietro Bembo's *Rime*.⁴⁹ The prologue bears out the assumption that the love story between Adriana and Latino is not only aimed at the evocation of ἔλεος, but that it follows an essentially Petrarchan configuration: while the text emphasizes that the depicted pair of lovers is ideally suited to inspire feelings of compassion in the audience ("Questo pensier [...] | de' movervi a pietà di questi amanti, | che però per se stessi anco pòn farlo" – "This thought [...] | must move you to feel compassion with these lovers, | who, however, are able to cause this effect by themselves, too," lines 48–50), the situation of the protagonists is simultaneously referred to with the term "sweet yoke" ("Anzi fu dolce il giogo ..."; what follows is an explicit enumeration of parallel cases from literary history, such as Pyramus and Thisbe or Hero and Leander). The "sweet yoke" is, of course, a textbook example of the ever-popular Petrarchan motif of the pains of love. Indeed, we encounter it right at the beginning of one of Petrarch's most famous sonnets: "L'aura celeste che 'n quel verde lauro | spira, ov'Amor ferì nel fianco Apollo, | et a me pose un dolce giogo al collo" ("The heavenly breeze which breathes in that green laurel, | where Love wounded Apollo in the side | and put a sweek yoke on my neck"; *RVF* 197.1–3). As we can see, Groto's text clearly marks its Petrarchan references. The poetic agenda that the text outlines here could be summed up as follows: in order to turn tragedy into an efficient vehicle for the Aristotelian affect of compassion, the *Adriana* relies on a Petrarchan formula in the portrayal of its central and originally novelistic plot element, namely the young couple's amorous relationship.⁵⁰ What we are dealing with

---

Groto's turn of phrase in l. 6 is aimed at a *superatio* of the Petrarchan affects of mourning. Regarding the antithetical junction of "amore" and "morte," cf. *RVF* 39.2, 40.1, 212.11, 266.5 f., 270.106, 274.2, 307.4. For the "stral d'amore," cf. *RVF* 87.11, 151.8, 216.7, 241.4; for the "stral di morte," cf. *RVF* 296.8. Salvatore Di Maria. *The Italian Tragedy in the Renaissance. Cultural Realities and Theatrical Innovations*, Lewisburg, PA: Bucknell UP and London: Associated UP, 2002, p. 45 f. suggests that the deployment of Petrarchan diction could have triggered an "effect of recognition" in the audience, thereby reinforcing a particular attitude towards the play – a very interesting thought that we cannot pursue here in any further depth. See Francesco Petrarca. *Canzoniere*, edited by Marco Santagata. Milan: Mondadori, 1996.

49 For "sospiri" and "pianto," cf. *Rime* 17.23; for "amore" vs. "morte," *Rime* 114.13 f., 142.207, 148.1 f.; for "stral d'amore," *Rime* 13.1 f., 82.8, 99.6 f., *Stanze* 7.6 ("lo stral d'Amor").

50 A brief remark in Pieri, "Il 'laboratorio'," p. 21 indicates a certain awareness of this strategy, although this line of thought unfortunately remains unexplored – as Pieri argues, Groto deploys "un intreccio novellistico assai compassionevole, che gli permette di metter a frutto le sue risorse di petrarchista consumato" in the *Adriana*.

here is thus an experiment on genre: the lyrical register suitable for the depiction of the pains of love, familiar from the works of Petrarch and Bembo, infiltrates a tragedy that is ultimately derived from the tradition of the novella, and which is specifically designed to evoke *pietà*.[51] As we shall see, this program is implemented all through the text. In an expositional dialogue with her nursemaid (1.1), Adriana herself describes the hitherto unknown experience of love with the help of a chain of oxymoronic concepts, whose Petrarchan origins are so evident as to make lengthy explanatory enumerations superfluous:

> Fu il mio male un piacer senza allegrezza,
> un voler, che si stringe, ancor che punga.
> Un pensier, che si nutre, ancor che ancida.
> [65] Un affanno che 'l ciel dà per riposo.

---

51 At this juncture, we cannot elaborate in any more detail on the fact that Groto also implants references to several other genres into tragedy (see for example Zampolli, "Les voyages du témoin," 69). The references to *topoi* from the epic domain that Groto has integrated into the play (for example: comprehensive reports on the martial goings-on outside the city walls [1.2], Adriana's first encounter with Latino in the mode of teichoscopy [1.1], the "Aeneid-like" names of Mezenzio and his son Latino), as well as from the field of *romanzo* and *poema eroico* (for example: the disguise that leads to the death of Adriana's brother at the hands of Latino, who is unaware of his adversary's identity and has no intention of killing his beloved's kin [1.3, 2.2]), lend the events of the love plot an air of romance that is far removed from the "mood" of a sombre tragedy of horror in the tradition of Seneca, a model that Groto radicalizes in the *Dalida*. Latino's killing of Adriana's brother offers the perfect occasion to showcase Groto's genre-transgressing technique of montage: Groto derives the overall motif from said Romeo-and-Juliet novellas, but he rebuilds it by drawing on the *topos* of a martial duel with a disguised or unrecognized adversary, a staple feature of romance and epic. In Da Porto's and Bandello's versions, Romeo kills T(h)e(o)baldo Cappelletti, Giulietta's cousin. Da Porto has the killing take place in the fierce melee of a street fight, and explains it by Romeo's furious anger (Da Porto. *Giulietta e Romeo*, p. 27: "vinto dall'ira [...] di un sol colpo in terra morto lo distese," an event which the narrator classifies as "omicidio"). Bandello, on the other hand, moves towards an exoneration of Romeo in ethical terms: here, Romeo's behavior in the encounter with Adriana's relative is conciliatory at first – only after being provoked and attacked does he join the fatal scuffle (the narrator's version matches Romeo's own account, given when the latter is already fatally poisoned and placed in the family vault of the Cappelletti, next to Tebaldo's corpse [Bandello. "Novella IX," pp. 67 f., 82 f.]). In Groto's version, the killing finally takes place in complete ignorance of the victim's identity, in accordance with the familiar pattern of epic and romance. Latino's bloody deed leaves him ethically untainted, as befits a protagonist in a tragedy of compassion (however, this set-up is far less compatible with the Aristotelian concept of the tragic protagonist as someone who is neither completely good nor completely bad). Precisely because the *Adriana* is a tragedy of compassion and not a tragedy of horror, Groto has good reason not to make use of the gruesome motif of placing an only apparently dead Adriana next to her relative's putrefying corpse, a fate that befalls Giulietta in Bandello's version.

> Un ben supremo, fonte d'ogni male.
> Un male estremo, d'ogni ben radice.
> Una piaga mortal, che mi fec'io.
> Un laccio d'or dov'io stessa m'avvinsi.
> [70] Un velen grato ch'io bevei per gli occhi.
> Giunto un finire, e un cominciar di vita.
> Una febre, che 'l gelo, e 'l caldo mesce.
> Un fel piú dolce assai, che mele o manna.
> Un bel foco, che strugge, e non risolve.
> [75] Un giogo insopportabile, e leggero.
> Una pena felice, un dolor caro.
> Una morte immortal piena di vita.
> Un inferno, che sembra il paradiso.[52]

Yet the incorporation of Petrarchan registers into a tragedy of compassion is not the result of an ingenious proto-baroque *bizzarria*, of a poetic *capriccio* – rather than that, Groto's experiment constitutes an intensified reaction to normative poetological tendencies (this conforms precisely to the poetics of Groto's *Rime*, whose pointed Mannerisms likewise attempt to make full use of the leeway that the Bembesque set of rules for lyric diction provides[53]). The origin of these normative tendencies is twofold, as I will briefly show: they derive both from poetological Aristotelianism and from Pietro Bembo's attempt to cast Petrarch as the stylistic epitome of poetical language.[54]

In Aristotle's famous definition in the sixth chapter of the *Poetics* (1449b), ἡδυσμένος λόγος is listed as one of the basic characteristics of tragedy. Modern German translations of the *Poetics* differ in their interpretation of this passage. Manfred Fuhrmann translates ἡδυσμένῳ λόγῳ as "in anziehend geformter Sprache" ("written in an appealing style"),[55] whereas Arbogast Schmitt renders it as "in kunstgemäß geformter Sprache" ("written in artful diction").[56] The

---

52 "My malady was a pleasure without joy, | a willing which is grasped even though it stings, | a thought that one nurtures even though it kills, | [65] a labour which heaven donates for relief, | the highest good, fountain of all evil, | the most extreme evil, root of all good, | a lethal wound, inflicted on me by myself, | a loop of gold by which I have enchained myself, [70] a pleasant poison which I drank with my eyes, | the end and the beginning of life bound together, | a fever that mixes ice and heat, | a bile much sweeter than honey or manna, | a beautiful fire which destroys but does not dissolve, | [75] a yoke, unbearable and light, | a happy torment, a dear pain, | an immortal death full of life, | a hell which seems to be paradise."
53 For further details, see Huss, "Luigi Grotos *Rime*."
54 For a more detailed discussion of this problem, see Huss, "Petrarkismus und Tragödie."
55 Aristotle. *Poetik*, translated and edited by Manfred Fuhrmann. Stuttgart: Reclam, 1994, p. 19.
56 Aristotle. *Poetik*, translated and edited by Arbogast Schmitt. Berlin: Akademie Verlag, 2008 (Aristoteles: Werke in deutscher Übersetzung, 5), p. 9.

fact that each of the two translations highlights a different aesthetic aspect – reception vs. production – is indicative of the need to interpret the Aristotelian dictum regarding the style appropriate to tragedy. The Cinquecento responded to this need in its exegesis of Aristotle, in its stylistic debates, and in its theory of tragedy. In keeping with Alessandro de' Pazzi's Latin translation of the *Poetics* (1536),[57] commentators frequently render ἡδυσμένῳ λόγῳ as "sermone suavi."[58] Within the poetological frame of reference of the Renaissance,[59] this translation effectively points away from the noble and elevated literary register, gesturing instead towards what could be termed a "lyrical" style appropriate to a medium – or perhaps even lower – register.[60] The feature "sweet and lyrical" is detached from its ties to specific segments of tragic syntax, and projected onto the language of tragedy as a whole. The early commentary by Maggi and Lombardi is a case in point: both interpreters are fully aware of the fact that Aristotle's treatment of tragedy is characterized by segmentation and differentiation as far as the deployment of various media and the corresponding usage of appropriate language are concerned. Yet the *suavitas* of tragedy is a given for Maggi and Lombardi – even outside the choral passages that constitute "lyrical parts" in the narrower sense. The use of *rhythmus* and *har-*

---

57 The decisive passage is quoted in Bernard Weinberg. *A History of Literary Criticism in the Italian Renaissance*, 2 Vols., Chicago: The University of Chicago Press, 1961 (Midway Reprints: 1974), vol. 1, p. 372 ("sermone suavi"). Pazzi's desire to do justice to the etymological roots of ἡδυσμένος in ἡδύς ('sweet,' 'pleasant') is evident here. In 1498, Giorgio Valla still rendered the passage as "iucunda oratione," although he follows this with a definition of the appropriate diction for tragedy via the attributes "suavis" and "oblectabilis" (quoted at length ibid.).
58 See for example Francesco Robortello. *In librum Aristotelis De arte poetica explicationes. Paraphrasis in librum Horatii, qui vulgo De arte poetica ad Pisones inscribitur.* Munich: Fink, 1968 (Florence: Torrentino, 1548) (Poetiken des Cinquecento 8), pp. 52, 55; Vincenzo Maggi and Bartolomeo Lombardi. *In Aristotelis librum* De poetica *communes explanationes.* Munich: Fink 1969 (Venezia: Vincenzo Valgrisio, 1550) (Poetiken des Cinquecento 4), pp. 96 f., 99 f.; Antonio Riccoboni. *Poetica Aristotelis latine conversa.* Munich: Fink 1970 (Padua: Paulus Meietus, 1587) (Poetiken des Cinquecento 22), pp. 7 (translation), 29 f. (paraphrase, the passage is rendered as: "suavi sermone, qui fiat suavis, & iucundus"). This interpretation also finds its way into more general poetological discussions of the Cinquecento; see for example Antonio Sebastiano Minturno. *L'arte poetica*. Munich: Fink 1971 (s.l.: Valvassori, 1564) (Poetiken des Cinquecento 6), p. 74: "la qual si fà con soave parlare."
59 For Aristotle himself, ἡδυσμένος λόγος has nothing to do with the categories of a multilayered poetics of style. The amalgamation of his particular turn of phrase with such categories is a phenomenon that is typical of the Renaissance reception of Aristotle, where the establishment of intricate connections between Aristotelian theorems and traditional notions of stylistic decorum is standard procedure.
60 See Hermann Lindner. "Mittlerer Stil." *Historisches Wörterbuch der Rhetorik* 5, Tübingen: Max Niemeyer, 2001, pp. 1366–1372 and "Schlichter Stil." Ibid., vol. 8, 2007, pp. 502–509.

monia in the spoken verses of tragedy (for Maggi and Lombardi: its specific properties in regard to language and metre) is sufficient to create *suavitas*, and the spoken passages of tragedy thus qualify as *carmen* in their own right.[61] By contemporary standards, however, this ubiquitous *suavitas* can be interpreted as a typically lyrical characteristic.

A strong current in the Cinquecento's exegesis of Aristotle, which in turn played a key role for the literary practice of Italian Renaissance tragedy,[62] thus attaches a stylistic label to tragedy which – despite the best efforts of commen-

---

61 In this context, see Maggi/Lombardi. *In Aristotelis librum*, p. 99 ("At primum quid sibi per SUAVEM SERMONEM velit, declarat, quod scilicet numerum, & harmoniam, & melos habet. per numerum autem, atque harmoniam, metrum: per melos vero, chori cantus intelligit. Et quoniam sermonis suavis sunt plures species, ideo subiungit, quomodo species illae in diversis Tragoediae partibus reperiantur, quasdam absolvi metro dicens: hoc est in aliqua Tragoediae parte sermonis suavitas est, metri tantum causa, ubi chorus non canit: quaedam vero pars suavem sermonem habet, quoniam accedit cantus"). For Maggi and Lombardi, *metrum* is the result of the deployment of *numerus* and *harmonia*, and this linguistic-metrical configuration is what justifies the equation of *sermo suavis* and *carmen* in the first place: "carmen [...] sermonem suavem esse apertum est" (ibid., p. 96). The term *carmen* is somewhat narrower in scope, however, in that *sermo suavis* also includes the "melic" choral parts: "nam etsi carmen sermo suavis sit, non tamen quivis suavis sermo carmen tantum est: cum praeter carmen interdum contineat & melos" (ibid., p. 99). *Suavitas* is thus ubiquitous in tragedy.

62 Attempts by Rolf Lohse. "Lizenz zum Fingieren. Dichterische Freiheit und Zeitgeschichte in der italienischen Tragödie des 16. Jahrhunderts." *Fiktionen des Faktischen in der Renaissance*, edited by Ulrike Schneider and Anita Traninger. Stuttgart: Steiner, 2010 (Text und Kontext 32), pp. 211–232, pp. 212, 216 (and passim), and Enrica Zanin. "Pourquoi la tragédie finit mal? Analyse des dénouements dans quelques tragédies de la première modernité." *Cahiers d'Études Italiennes*, vol. 19, 2014, pp. 45–59, to relativize the significance of poetological Aristotelianism for the production of tragedies in the Cinquecento have to be rejected as unfounded. Both authors employ a tendentially monolithic notion of Aristotelianism which pushes the plural positionings that characterize sixteenth-century discussions of literary theory into the background, acting as if Renaissance Aristotelianism and 'pre-Aristotelian' (a catchphrase which usually covers late antiquity, the Middle Ages, and parts of the quattrocento) theoretical discourses were mutually exclusive to a large extent. Yet it is quite clear that Renaissance Aristotelianism represents a multi-layered, fragile, often contradictory, and non-coherent 'system,' the lofty claims of Aristotelians in regard to genre classification notwithstanding. A superficial look at theoretical reflexion in the Cinquecento is more than sufficient to show that literary practice stands in an unusually close relationship to historic theory formation in this particular historical context (Giraldi Cinzio's theoretical texts and their relationship to his tragedies are a case in point; the same holds true for Speroni's theoretical deliberations and his *Canace*). My statements above are intended to demonstrate that a play like the *Adriana* can only be explained appropriately if its relationship to the theoretical discourse it so strongly reflects is taken into account. It goes without saying that friction and ruptures between historic literary theory and literary practice do exist – they are not a valid counterargument in this context, however.

tators to do justice to Aristotle's phrasing – is actually far better suited to lyric poetry, at least from the perspective of contemporaries well-versed in the poetology of stylistic stratification. This means that a productive correlation between the genre of tragedy on the one hand, and the stylized lyricism of Petrarchan provenance on the other, begins to emerge – a theoretical potential that Groto will indeed put into practice.

From a different angle, Pietro Bembo's theoretical deliberations further contribute to this interaction. In conformity with the treatise *De compositione verborum* (Περὶ συνθέσεως ὀνομάτων) by Dionysius of Halicarnassus,[63] Bembo's *Prose della volgar lingua* (1525) proclaims as stylistic ideal a balanced blend of "gravità" ("gravity") and "piacevolezza" ("amenity," "pleasantness").[64] In the second book of the *Prose*, "gravità" and "piacevolezza" are treated as stylistic effects devoid of semantic and content-related implications. From Chapter 9 on, Bembo provides an in-depth explanation of how both "gravità" and "piacevolezza" are created via the deliberate deployment of "suono" ("sound"), "numero" ("rhythm"), and "variazione" ("variation"): they are the combined result of appropriate sound effects, the author's usage of rhythm and rhyme, and a technique of skillful variation. When it comes to striking the perfect stylistic balance in verse, Bembo's normative role model is Francesco Petrarca, whereas Giovanni Boccaccio serves an analogous function in the domain of prose. In the context of tragedy, this has a rather noteworthy effect: the very author whom Bembo casts as the model for stylistically elevated tragedy composed in verse – Petrarch – is decidedly *not* an author of *gravitas*, as would befit the *stylus gravis* which alone is suitable for tragedy according to traditional notions of stylistic decorum.[65] This issue is connected to a fundamental problem that haunts Bembism's relationship to "elevated" topics. Even though Bembo pushes the traditional doctrine of three stylistic levels as far into the background as possible, he nonetheless establishes a distinction right

---

63 See Claudia Berra. "L'idea di stile dagli *Asolani* alle *Prose*." Prose della volgar lingua *di Pietro Bembo*, edited by Silvia Morgana, Mario Piotti and Massimo Prada. Milan: Cisalpino, 2000 (Quaderni di Acme 46), pp. 277–302, pp. 284–290; see also Rosa Casapullo. "I termini della critica e della retorica nel II libro delle *Prose*." Ibid., pp. 393–408, p. 397 and passim.
64 See Pietro Bembo. *Prose della volgar lingua. L'editio princeps del 1525 riscontrata con l'autografo Vaticano latino 3210*, edited by Claudio Vela. Bologna: CLUEB, 2001, esp. Book 2 (passim), as well as passages from Book 1, such as ibid., p. 44 (Chapter 1.18).
65 For a concise overview, see Bernhard Huss. "Gattung/Gattungstheorie." *Der Neue Pauly. Enzyklopädie der Antike*, vol. 14: *Rezeptions- und Wissenschaftsgeschichte*, edited by Manfred Landfester. Stuttgart and Weimar: Metzler, 2000, cols. 87–95, and "Literaturtheorie." *Der Neue Pauly. Supplemente 9: Renaissance-Humanismus. Lexikon zur Antikerezeption*, edited by Manfred Landfester. Stuttgart and Weimar: Metzler, 2014, cols. 558–566.

at the beginning of the second book between (a) "materia grande" ("grand subject-matter"), to be represented with words ("voci") which qualify as "gravi, alte, sonanti, apparenti, luminose" ("grave, high, sounding, effulgent, radiant"); (b) "(materia) mezzana" ("intermediate subject-matter"), with "voci mezzane e temperate" ("intermediate, temperate words"); and (c) "(materia) bassa e volgare" ("low and vulgar [subject-matter]"), with "(voci) lievi, piane, dimesse, popolari, chete" ("light, humble, simple, popular, calm [words]").[66] Although the Prose painstakingly avoids any content-dependent restrictions on the poetic choice of language from that point on, Bembo is nonetheless forced to link the lexis of three stylistic levels to the semantics of three corresponding levels of subject matter in the passage above. What is more, Bembo lacks an author capable of serving as a role model for elevated topics (where Bembo compares Virgil and Petrarch, both appear as representatives of a "middling" style),[67] and he keeps his distance from serious, elevated, difficult topics in poetry as a matter of principle, preferring balanced and "middling" topics instead.[68]

Concerning the tragedy of the Cinquecento, this leads to the conclusion that, while the doctrine of different stylistic levels and their corresponding subject matter is still in force, no author capable of acting as an adequate model for the elevated genre of tragedy can be named for the Italian language. Without offering any explicit commentary, Bembo places Petrarch in this vacant position by setting him up as the prototype for *all* poetry in verse, and thus also as the prototype for tragedy *per se*.[69] Combined with the fact that commen-

---

66 Bembo. *Editio princeps*, pp. 61 f. (Chapter 2.4.13).
67 Carlo Dionisotti's commentary on the deliberations in Chapter 1.18 of the *Prose* is thus highly apposite: "al Virgilio delle *Georgiche*, non dell'*Eneide*, corrisponde il Petrarca delle *Rime*" (Pietro Bembo. *Prose della volgar lingua, Gli Asolani, Rime*, edited by Carlo Dionisotti. Milan: TEA, 1989, p. 121, n. 5).
68 Dante, of whom the text says "sarebbe stato più lodevole, che egli di meno alta e di meno ampia materia posto si fosse a scrivere, et quella sempre nel suo mediocre stato avesse scrivendo contenuta" (Bembo. *Editio princeps*, p. 103, Chapter 2.20.17), clearly serves as a negative example in comparison to Petrarch, and also to Boccaccio; see Bernhard Huss. "'Esse ex eruditis, qui res in Francisco, verba in Dante desiderent.' Francesco Petrarca in den Dante-Kommentaren des Cinquecento." *Questo leggiadrissimo poeta! Autoritätskonstitution im rinascimentalen Lyrik-Kommentar*, edited by Gerhard Regn. Münster: LIT, 2004 (Pluralisierung & Autorität 6), pp. 155–187, pp. 159–161.
69 The fact that this raised a major problem for tragedy as a whole has hardly ever been noticed with any degree of clarity; in addition to Huss, "Petrarkismus und Tragödie," however, see also Michael Nerlich. "Zur Sonderstellung der italienischen Bühnendichtung im 16. und 17. Jahrhundert." *Romanische Forschungen*, vol. 79, 1967, pp. 62–94, esp. 82–91 and the conclusion: "Letzten Endes scheitert das Drama in Italien an der zu starken Tradition: der zwangsläufig seit Petrarca entwickelte dichterische Führungsstil kann sich zwar noch das Epos erobern,

taries on Aristotle's *Poetics* defined the style of tragedy as *sermo suavis*, the transfer of Petrarch's poetical authority to tragedy via the implementation of a *stile dolce e soave* could now appear to be warranted by Aristotelian tradition. Such a transfer, however, depends on the Bembistic postulate that Petrarchan stylemes and their semantic implications are clearly distinguishable, free from content-related ballast, and thus transferable without problems to more humble or more elevated subject matter.

That is by no means the case: stylistic Petrarchisms are always fraught with the semantic connotation of a painful, self-referential contemplation of emotional sensitivities. In spite of this, Groto performs their transfer into tragedy with considerable emphasis. In a similar vein to Sperone Speroni's *Canace*, equally experimental and much discussed at the time, Groto avails himself of his chosen stylistic means via an expansion of the melic-Petrarchan line of tradition. Like the *Canace*, the *Adriana* is characterized in stylistic terms by a strong influx of wholly unmasked Petrarchisms. From within their poetic register and completely unfettered by the stylistic "heaviness" that the poetology of the tragic demands to satisfy its desire for *gravitas* and *magniloquentia*, the *Adriana*'s Petrarchan stylemes are free to exert their influence on the staging of the ἔλεος-evoking amorous setbacks that befall the unfortunate couple – a pair of lovers who, as we should keep in mind, are *only* of interest due to the pains of love they experience, and not because they are, say, the *dramatis personae* of a moral exemplum, or the victims of a spectacular fall from an exalted position in the social hierarchy. It is only fitting that the pains of love be expressed in antitheses clearly modeled on the Petrarchan/Petrarchist pattern that I have already discussed in the examples above.

This is where the difficulties arise: the massive deployment of Petrarchan stylemes can and does impede the evolution of the tragic plot. I shall illustrate this problem with two distinctive examples, the first of which is taken from the first scene of the first act. Adriana has just confessed her love for Latino to her nursemaid, only to be advised to desist from pursuing the relationship for a whole variety of reasons. This is Adriana's riposte:

> O sventurata me. Che dunque faccio,
> quinci frenata da' consigli tuoi,
> [400] quindi spronata dal crudel tiranno,
> ch'è amaro, ed è da noi chiamato Amore?
> Perderò dunque la vita, e la fama?
> Lascerò dunque il mio amator, piú caro

---

scheitert aber bei dem Versuch, sich auch der *tragedia* zu bemächtigen und verhindert somit auch deren (gelungene) Herausbildung" (p. 94).

>   a me, che l'onor mio, che la mia vita?
> [405] Per cui solo son io cara a me stessa?
>   Trarrò l'amante mio dunque in periglio?
>   Lascerommi morir priva di lui?
>   Porrò la mia nutrice in questa nave?
>   Porrò, per salvar lei, me sola in mare?
> [410] Tradisco il padre mio donde ebbi il sangue?
>   Lascio il mio sposo, da cui spero il seme?
>   Darò la morte a chi mi die' la vita?
>   Torrò me dunque a chi mi dà se stesso?
>   Sprezzo chi meco ebbe commune il ventre?
> [415] Lascio che meco avrà commune il letto?
>   Sprezzo colei, da le cui viscere esco?
>   Lascio colui, nel cui cuor vivo impressa?
>   Tradirò il mio paese, dove nacqui?
>   Lascerò il mio signor, nel cui cor vivo?
> [420] Ahimè, che questi eserciti fan guerra
>   minor d'intorno a queste belle mura,
>   che al cor mio intorno i miei vari pensieri.
>   Ma io (per dirti il ver), cara nutrice,
>   non volea, che cosí mi consigliassi.
> [425] Ben consigliata esser volea del modo,
>   che può darmi ottenuto il mio desire.[70]

Adriana's reply, saturated with Petrarchisms and buckling under the load of a Mannerist quota of antithetical and oxymoronic stylemes, unfolds the emotional state of indecision from its beginning to line 419 (that is, for the duration of more than 20 lines), a condition that she refers to as "i miei vari pensieri" (line 422) towards the end of that passage in a gesture towards the Petrarchan

---

[70] "Alas! Unhappy me! What shall I do then, | here bridled by your counsel, | [400] there spurred by the cruel tyrant | who is bitter [amaro] and whom we call Love [Amore]? | Shall I thus lose my life and my renown? | Will I thus abandon my lover, dearer to me | than my honor, than my life? | [405] My lover, who alone makes me appreciate myself? | Will I thus put him at risk? | Will I agree to die without him? | Will I put my nurse in this boat? | Will I put out to sea alone, in order to save her? | [410] Shall I betray my father who has donated my blood to me? | | Shall I quit my bridegroom whose seed I hope to attain? | Will I give death to the one person who gave me life? | Will I take myself away from the one who gives himself to me? | Shall I despise him who shared the womb with me? | [415] Should I abandon the one who will share the bed with me? | Can I disdain the one from whose viscera I came to life? | Could I leave the one in whose heart impressed I live? | Will I betray my country where I was born? | Will I abandon my lord in whose heart I live? | [420] Alas, these armies make less war | around these beautiful walls | than make my various thoughts around my heart. | But to tell the truth, my dear nurse, | I would not have wished that sort of a counsel from you. | [425] I had wished advice about the best way | to obtain what I desire."

contrariety of affect. What we encounter up to this line is "Petrarchan stasis" of the type that Andreas Kablitz has succinctly described in reference to Torquato Tasso's *Il re Torrismondo*: "Petrarcas lyrische Sprache ist wesentlich Affektrepräsentation, sie ist damit auch wesentlich monologische Rede, und diese Eigenart bleibt nicht ohne Folgen für die Struktur des auf der Bühne geführten Gesprächs. Personenrede ist hier zu erheblichen Teilen Selbstdarstellung, eine gar nicht enden wollende Exposition von Befindlichkeiten, in denen das Geschehen selbst seine Wirkung wie seine Bedeutsamkeit erst zu gewinnen scheint."[71] The effusion of lyrical paradigms is briskly cut short by Adriana's last four lines. The nursemaid's counsel (developed over exactly 147 lines) and Adriana's own subsequent deliberations are declared null and void, which causes the plot to relapse: as it were, around 180 lines brimming with Petrarchisms have added nothing to the syntagmatic development of the tragedy; nothing has "happened" except on the level of language.

Time, too, seems to come to a standstill on many occasions in this tragedy, especially when the protagonists are discussing the love they feel for each other. My second example is taken from the dialogue between Adriana and Latino in the third scene of Act Two – Latino has just given voice to his conviction that separation will eventually prove inevitable for the lovers. Adriana replies:

> E s'io star non potea non dirò un giorno,
> ma un'ora pur senza vedervi, or, come
> tanto da voi starò spazio lontana?
> E se pensando al partir vostro solo,
> [85] tanto ho dolor, che fia quando partiate?
> Che fia quando poi siate al fin partito?
> Ogni dí mi parrà maggior d'un anno.
> Il sol zoppo, il ciel orbo, il giorno notte,
> la notte inferno, l'aria tenebrosa.
> [90] Amare l'acque, e vedova la terra.
> Saran le luci mie prive di luce,
> dove entrerà, per non uscirne, il pianto.
> Dond'uscirà, per non entrarvi, il sonno.

---

71 Andreas Kablitz. "Tragischer Fall und verborgene Wahrheit. Torquato Tassos *Re Torrismondo*." *Tragödie. Idee und Transformation*, edited by Hellmut Flashar. Stuttgart and Leipzig: Teubner, 1997 (Colloquium Rauricum 5), pp. 84–109, pp. 95 f. ("Petrarch's lyrical diction is essentially a representation of affects; it is, therefore, also essentially monologic diction, and this peculiarity has certain consequences for the structure of the dialogue to be staged in the scene. Here the direct discourse of the characters is largely self-representation, an infinite exposition of inner states on which the effect and significance to the dramatic action are based.")

>   Con voi verrà il cor mio, resterà il seno.
> [95] Alfin né morta resterò, né viva.
>   Non morta, sentirò pur troppo affanno.
>   Non viva, lungi da la vita mia.
>   Ite veste, ite gioie, ite catene.[72]

Adriana's response is characterized by emotional stasis. The paradigmatic accumulation and variation of antithetical images is no longer even capable (as in the previous example) of expressing a true wavering between conflicting options, a necessity of coming to a decision, a "Hamlet-like" situation – it merely strings endless pairs of opposites together, expressing the single theme of the pains of love over and over again. Whereas tragedy can "typically" be expected to promote the syntagmatic development of its plot, narrative momentum is suspended here to allow for a variation of elements that ultimately derive from the exact same conceptual paradigm. As a result, the paradigmatic renders the syntagmatic inoperative – a process that calls to mind the "typical" plot of comedy as Rainer Warning so impressively described it.[73] The achieved effect is miles away from levity or comical failure, however. Quite to the contrary, the apparatus of repetition supplied by the *Rerum vulgarium fragmenta* relentlessly perpetuates a situation of suffering without the least hope of rescue.

Endlessly repeating the literary paradigms of painful love, this poetic-cum-tragic elegism runs the risk of dismantling the very principles of Aristotelian poetology:[74] "Luigi Groto, coerentemente con la sua definizione di poetica conte-

---

[72] "And if I have not been able to live an hour, let alone a day | without seeing you, how could I now | exist so far away from you? | And if I suffer so much just imagining | [85] your departure, what will happen if you depart in fact? | What will happen if you finally will have departed? | Each day will seem to me longer than a whole year: | the sun limping, the heaven blind, the day night, | the night hell, the air dark, | [90] bitter the waters, widowed the earth. | My eyes will be bereft of daylight, | where weeping will enter and not leave anymore, | which sleep will leave and not enter any more. | My heart will go with you, my breast will remain. | [95] In the end I will not be dead, nor alive, | not dead, even though I will feel far too much pain, | not alive, even though far away from my life. | Leave me, robes, leave me, joy, leave me, chains!"

[73] See Rainer Warning. "Elemente einer Pragmasemiotik der Komödie." *Das Komische*, edited by Wolfgang Preisendanz and Rainer Warning. Munich: Fink, 1976 (Poetik und Hermeneutik, 7), pp. 279–333.

[74] Groto's *Adriana* would thus conform to what Marco Ariani has postulated as a basic trait of Mannerist tragedy: the temporal and spatial coordinates of a syntagmatically organized plot structure dissolve, and discourse takes on a life of its own through the constant repetition of lyric/melic elements; see esp. Ariani. "Il Manierismo," p. 182 (on Speroni's *Canace*: "dissolve ogni chiarezza di dibattito etico-ideologico in un cantabile continuato," "una specie di *dissoluzione melica della situazione tragica*," italics in the original), pp. 184, 187 (again on the *Canace*: "il liquefarsi della situazione agìta in un raziocinare melico arguto ma immotivato ideologica-

nuta nel prologo tesa a dissolvere in via definitiva la precettistica aristotelica, costruisce una tragedia assolutamente eterogenea, non solo per la consapevole frantumazione delle unità spazio-temporali, ma anche e soprattutto per la ossessiva ricerca formale di un linguaggio che diventa esso stesso il centro propulsore del ritmo scenico."[75] The stringency of discursive reasoning, the argumentative order of replies, the motivated – that is, the "probable" and "necessary" – progression of the plot are all severely curtailed.[76] As it were, the plot's substance disappears under a thick layer of lyrical diction,[77] while the massive presence of linguistic Petrarchisms and their extensive deployment and conceptual intensification, which the text almost seems to relish, ultimately erode the cohesion of the tragic action. As we have seen, the tragedy of tears indulges in the broad exposition of a world of thought firmly grounded in a Petrarchan substrate. Another clear example of this is the monologue in which Latino seeks to justify his unintentional killing of Adriana's brother (2.2): riddled with antitheses, fraught with a multitude of concepts, and demonstratively drawing on the stylistic repertoire of Petrarchan love poetry, this block of text is a monolithic 349 lines long, completely uninterrupted by any reply on the part of Adriana. Here, the advancement of the tragic plot clearly takes second place behind the unfolding of Petrarchan language. With its overwhelming mass of text, running to almost 140 tightly printed pages, the play is unable to make good on the demand of plausibility raised by Aristotelian doctrine.

A rather curious impression emerges: retardation of the plot coincides with an overexpansion of the unity of time.[78] The imprecise temporal markers that

---

mente"), p. 215 (on the *Adriana*: "la *dissoluzione spazio-temporale* del genere tragico," italics in the original).
75 Cavazzini, "Dall'*Adriana* a Romeo and Juliet," p. 347.
76 See Nicola Mangini, "Il teatro veneto al tempo della controriforma." *Luigi Groto*, edited by Brunello and Lodo, pp. 119–137, pp. 123 f.
77 See Ariani, "Il Manierismo," pp. 204, 216.
78 On top of this, the Aristotelian notion of unity of time is overtly thwarted by Groto himself: the prologue claims (lines 78–90) that the supposed author found the "istoria" concerning the two protagonists "scritta in duri marmi," along with a note containing the charge to put this history into writing. According to the prologue, the task given included permission for the tragic *dispositio* of events, authorization for the necessary overstretching of the unity of time, as well as an anticipatory justification of the un-classical usage of a tragic prologue. The result is of course the play itself, whose plot is available to the reader in the form of the text, or to the audience in the form of a performance on stage. In a clear case of metalepsis, Adriana herself voices this future task for an "author" at the end of the play's *azione*, that is, in the depths of antiquity: it is her wish to have her own unhappy love story chiselled "in duri marmi" so as to motivate "qualche autor, mosso a pietà, negli anni | avvenir" to bring it up to date with the help of drama and theater: "la riduca in forma, ch'ella | possa rappresentarsi a' fidi amanti" (5.8.59–69); see also 5.8.114–117, where the Mago assures that he will pass on this

the text provides make it difficult to determine the exact duration of the main plot – a minimum of two days and two nights, perhaps even an additional day, has been suggested[79] – and unity of place is obscured by a copious mass of language suffused with Mannerisms.[80] Given the absolute centrality of the amorous misfortune around which the play's Petrarchism revolves, a centrality which relegates the workings of the plot to a position of secondary importance compared to the comprehensive discussion of affects, the construction of a properly Aristotelian story arc with a tangible tragic transgression (ἁμαρτία) at its center turns into an impossibility. Permanently busy discussing their emotions, the characters do not so much transgress – they simply misunderstand each other. A misunderstanding is the cause of lethal catastrophe; death by technical failure casts its shadow ahead over the lovers' final conversation. The audience's lachrymosity that results (or at least, the lachrymosity that the text is explicitly trying to evoke) is tantamount to a comprehensive feeling of ἔλεος; if any kind of tragic catharsis is to be found here at all, we ought to be fully aware of the pronounced distance from "orthodox" Aristotelianism that results from the almost complete absence of tragic horror.[81]

---

assignment of textualization to the unknown future author (on this metalepsis, see Zampolli 2000, pp. 33 f.; Zampolli 2006, pp. 70 f., 73 f.). Here, Luigi Groto receives the cue to write his story from the very characters populating the plot that he himself has invented. This "strange loop" amounts to a flagrant breach of contemporary notions regarding Aristotelian plausibility.
79 See Bazoli, "Groto e Shakespeare," pp. 23 f., incl. n. 60.
80 Hence the erroneous conclusion in Marvin T. Herrick. *Italian Tragedy in the Renaissance*. Urbana, IL: The University of Illinois Press, 1965, p. 215: "The last act of *Hadriana* is somewhat unusual among neoclassical Italian tragedies because in it the scene changes several times between the city of Adria and the enemy camp." Contrary to what Herrick believes, Latino does not move back and forth between his encampment and the city of Adria in the fifth act. Unity of place is in fact maintained, although the Petrarchan deluge makes this feature of the text somewhat difficult to discern.
81 Zampolli, "La réflexion théâtrale," p. 33, diagnoses an elimination of Aristotelian catharsis at the end of the *Adriana*, although the issue is not elaborated in any depth. Decroisette, "'Pleurez mes yeux!'," p. 177 draws a connection between the *Adriana* and Lorenzo Giacomini's medically and physiologically founded concept of catharsis (see "De la purgazione de la tragedia." *Trattati di poetica e retorica del Cinquecento*, edited by Bernard Weinberg. Bari: Laterza, 1972, vol. 3, pp. 345–371) – yet the two Aristotelian affects are once again conceptualized jointly and discussed alongside a further range of "purged" emotions in Giacomini; see esp. p. 362: "E quindi si convince l'error di coloro che giudican la compassione riguardare altri, il timore noi stessi, dicendo Aristotile il timore esser verso i simili a noi, cioè verso le persone tragiche a le quali veggiamo soprastare gravissimi mali, che caduti dànno spavento e compassione a noi, i quali temendo o compassionando ci purghino da affetti o più tosto da appassionamenti e 'concetti tali,' cioè di tristezza, di sospetto, di sollecitudine, di affanni, di desperazione, et insomma di tutto lo stuolo degli affetti dogliosi simili o congiunti a la compassione et al timore."

Yet Groto finds a use for Petrarchan stasis which goes beyond a portrayal of the trials and tribulations that this "mestissima istoria" holds in store in matters of love: the mournful stasis in terms of plot development overflows into a mourning for the state of the world as a whole.[82] Framed by the prologue and the closing scene, the permanent lamentation that is woven into the fabric of the play's language is transformed into a deep cosmological pessimism that no longer confines itself to the love-related suffering of individual characters, but encompasses misery on a far grander scale. The lament of the individual expands and turns into a lament for a "doomed mankind," as the text makes clear on the penultimate page: "Non lacrimate, donne, il vostro male, | tutta piangete a un tempo la cittate, | ché 'n danno universale | si disdicon le lacrime private" ("Do not beweep, women, your misfortune, | rather bewail the town, all together! | For in the face of universal disaster | private tears are inappropriate"; 5.9.90–93).

Arguably, the calculated exploitation of the semantic potential inherent in a tragedy interwoven with Petrarchan elements is what makes the *Adriana* so compelling. The play aligns itself with its "horrible sister" *Dalida* in that any "learning effect" the plays may cause can only consist in an all-encompassing *meditatio mortis*, far removed from the ideologies that govern the behavior of the characters in the fictional world. The affective reward for this *meditatio* is a form of ἔλεος far exceeding a mere reaction to character-related aspects of the plot, or a certain emotional response elicited by the tragic characters. It is rooted in the grim acknowledgement of the inevitable vulnerability of human existence. In each and every one of the countless manifestations of the *conditio humana*, misery steadily renews itself – at best, there are gradual differences. Personal suffering is only a tiny element in the big picture of Groto's tragic arrangement: the demise of the two protagonists is but a remote echo of the far greater demise of the city of Adria, which Latino's father brings about with a gratuitous act of revenge scantily motivated by a dream vision (5.9.29–33). Adria and its surroundings will fall victim to deliberate inundation – all characters in the fictional world will drown in the approaching flood shortly after the curtain has fallen,[83] and the ancient city of Adria will be destroyed.[84] The

---

[82] And not just for the deplorable state of the city of Adria, as Zampolli, "Les voyages du témoin," p. 75 would have us believe.

[83] The muffled roaring of the flood is already audible as the action draws to a close: "Udite già il rumor che a noi s'appressa, | qual di molte moline accolto suono, | o come di celeste orribil tuono" (5.9.103–105).

[84] On the "αἴτιον [...] del tutto ribaltato, in quanto della città di Adria non si canta l'origine e l'edificazione, ma la sua distruzione," and on the play's fixation on catastrophe that is thereby revealed, see Marco Ariani. "Introduzione." *Il teatro italiano* II: *La tragedia del Cinquecento*, edited by Marco Ariani. Turin: Einaudi, 1977, vol. 1, pp. VII–LXXX, p. L. On the expansion of

city's demise is in turn only a miniscule scene from the dismal panorama that showcases the utter futility of human existence. This quasi-existentialist structure acts as the indispensable sounding board for the lovers' lament, giving it relevance in the first place.[85] Unmotivated and unfathomable disaster in combination with inescapable "danno universale" ("universal damage") are the constituent parts of such darkness, a darkness in which disaster never ends.[86] Ultimately, *this* is the counterpart to the perpetual paradigmatic variation of tragic diction in the *Adriana*: the deeper, "ideological" purpose of disabling the syntagmatic structure lies in an all-encompassing pessimism that only ever expects to encounter the immutability of ubiquitous disaster.

Both the play's love plot and its "cosmic" perspective, its overall outlook on a world described as a fundamentally tragic place, are deeply marked by the resigned declaration of inescapable contingency. This declaration is behind the death of the pair of lovers, just as it motivates Adria's utterly senseless destruction, which flies in the face of the war objectives of both sides. Groto inscribes this extreme variety of a tragic worldview into the space made available by the fragmentation, modification, and partial suspension of Aristotelian norms. So black is this worldview, so impenetrable the darkness of its pessimism, that any attempt to tap into the genre's powers to exemplify issues of moral philosophy is simply out of the question, no matter how customary such an activity may have been with Groto's contemporaries. If anything, this feeling of pessimism is enhanced even further by the explicit connection that the play establishes to the stale and gloomy present of its Adriatic audience.[87] The *Adriana* quite literally leaves no way out – considering the scope of its tragic program, the reaction of its addressees may well be panic and claustrophobia. If an audience can feel locked into a black cage, Groto accomplishes this with his extraordinary blend of sheer tragic impact and a Petrarchan-cum-lyrical proclamation of pain in the everlasting night.[88] Only the infiltration of tragedy

---

the theme of suffering from the protagonists themselves to a collective level, see Zampolli, "Les voyages du témoin," p. 75.

85 In this context, Cavazzini, "Dall'*Adriana* a *Romeo and Juliet*," p. 345 places particular emphasis on the role of the dark, devastated, and catastrophic landscape bereft of meaning which the text evokes as the surroundings of its immediate setting.

86 The play ends with the words: "Sol mai non giunge un mal, giungono molti, | sempre in drapel raccolti. | Per poco mai fortuna non comincia | a perseguire un misero. Ella il preme, | e mentre ei piange, in tanto | gli apparecchia cagion di novo pianto" (5.9.127–132).

87 On the historical situatedness of Groto's plays (including a "somber" comedy such as the *Emilia*), see Di Maria, "Groto's *Emilia*," esp. pp. 88 f.

88 At least in regard to Groto's two tragedies, this "ideological darkness" raises the question of whether Zampolli, "'Una scena di perpetua durevolezza'," esp. pp. 98–100 is correct in assuming that Groto's dramatic project is intended as an "educational program" for the city of

with a persistent lamentation cast in the stylized language of Petrarchism has made it possible to plunge the genre into such utter darkness. Groto's experiments with the generic repertoire that he finds at his disposal may not have produced anything completely new – what they accomplished, however, is an undreamed-of expansion of what can be considered radically tragic, above and beyond the confines of orthodox Aristotelianism.

Adria with a "pedagogic function," or whether this postulation is the result of an uncritical acceptance of Groto's own (strategic) invocation of the contemporary *topos* of *miscere utile dulci* (Horace, *Ars poetica* 343 f.). Ultimately, what is at stake here is the fundamental and unresolved problem of how the hopelessness of the tragic perspective on the world relates to the lives of its addressees and to the reactions that it provokes.

Cristina Savettieri
The Agency of Errors:
Hamartia and its (Mis)interpretations
in the Italian Cinquecento

In this article, I would like to address the concept of error and its relationship with agency in a twofold way: first, I shall explore some interpretations of Aristotle's concept of *hamartia*[1] as reworked by the first scholars and intellectuals to deal with the *Poetics* as translators, commentators, theoreticians, and playwrights in the context of sixteenth-century Italy.[2] On a second level, a theo-

---

1 Aristotle refers to *hamartia* in Chapter 13 of the *Poetics* (1453a 7–10), which is devoted to plot-construction, as follows: "Since, then, the structure of the finest tragedy should be complex, not simple, and, moreover, should portray fearful and pitiful events (for this is the distinctive feature of this type of mimesis), it is to begin with clear that: (a) good men should not be shown passing from prosperity to affliction, for this is neither fearful nor pitiful but repulsive; (b) wicked men should not be shown passing from affliction to prosperity, for this is the most untragic of all possible cases and is entirely defective (it is neither moving nor pitiful nor fearful); (c) the extremely evil man should not fall from prosperity to affliction, for such a plot-structure might move us, but would not arouse pity or fear, since pity is felt towards one whose affliction is undeserved, fear towards one who is like ourselves (so what happens in such a case will be neither pitiful nor fearful). We are left, then, with the figure who falls between these types. Such a man is one who is not preeminent in virtue and justice, and one who falls into affliction not because of evil and wickedness, but because of a certain fallibility (*hamartia*). He will belong to the class of those who enjoy great esteem and prosperity, such as Oedipus, Thyestes, and outstanding men from such families." I am quoting from the translation by Stephen Halliwell. *The Poetics of Aristotle. Translation and Commentary.* London: Duckworth, 1987, p. 44.
2 My article will not tackle Aristotelianism as a general cultural phenomenon of the Italian literary and philosophical culture of the Renaissance, since I am mainly interested in the seminal shaping of the theoretical discourse on tragedy, which does not coincide exclusively with re-elaborations of the *Poetics*, while certainly overlapping with an Aristotelian core. Bibliography on the circulation and reception of the *Poetics* includes: Bernard Weinberg. *A History of Literary Criticism in the Italian Renaissance.* Chicago: Chicago University Press, 1961, vol. 1, pp. 349–423; Martin Lowry. "Aristotle's Poetics and the Rise of Vernacular Literary Theory." *Viator*, no. 25, 1994, pp. 411–425; Daniel Javitch. "The assimilation of Aristotle's *Poetics* in Sixteenth Century Italy." *The Cambridge History of Literary Criticism*, edited by Glyn Norton. Cambridge: Cambridge University Press, 1999, vol. 3, pp. 53–65; Brigitte Kappl. *Die Poetik des Aristoteles in der Dichtungstheorie des Cinquecento.* Berlin/New York: de Gruyter, 2006; Enrica Zanin. "Les commentaires modernes de la *Poétique* d'Aristote." *Études littéraires*, vol. 43, no. 2, 2012, pp. 55–83. The impact of the *Poetics* on early modern genre theory has been analyzed by, among others, Daniel Javitch. "The Emergence of Poetic Genre Theory in the Sixteenth Century." *Modern Language Quarterly*, vol. 59, no. 2, 1998, 139–169. The relationship between

https://doi.org/10.1515/9783110536690-008

retical one – perhaps a meta-theoretical one – I shall try to tackle "error" as a fundamental occurrence within processes of cultural circulation, one that can engender momentous movements and displacements and, thus, define long-term arrangements within a specific discursive field. By analyzing some of the unstable answers Renaissance scholars provided to the questions "What is an error? When and how does it engender catastrophic consequences? Who is the person who errs? To what extent do errors result from agency?", I would like to claim that this intense scholarly debate revolving around the notion of "error" still resonates in some features of the modern discussion on tragedy and the tragic.[3] Despite being grounded upon interpretative mistakes, cultural syncretism, and hybridizations, and even intellectual rivalry and agonism, and thus apparently being incomprehensible outside the historical context in which it took place, this body of theory and criticism established the discussion on tragedy as a plural and unstable form of thinking. I would like to argue that the structural instability of this discursive field, made up of theoretical views inconsistent with each other and, in some cases, inconsistent *per se*, is the condition of possibility of the polymorphic modern debate on tragedy, which interestingly, despite being highly fragmented if not pulverized, is one of the very few areas of literary theory and criticism still haunted by normative impetuses:[4] a field of extensive relativism and legislative fantasies at once, in which the "anything goes" of postmodern approaches to tragedy coexists with a fierce tendency to reassess definitions, to enforce categories and boundaries, and ultimately to seek the ungraspable Grail of the essence of the tragic.

The concept of error is, among the many whose circulation was promoted by the refashioning of the *Poetics*,[5] one of the most prolific in terms of the

---

the circulation of the *Poetics* and early modern theories of tragedy has been reassessed by, among others, Paola Mastrocola. *L'idea del tragico. Teorie della tragedia nel Cinquecento*. Soveria Mannelli: Rubbettino, 1998; Timothy Reiss. "Renaissance Theatre and the Theory of Tragedy". *The Cambridge History of Literary Criticism*, vol. 3, pp. 231–247.

3 Similarly, Michael Lurie, one of the few scholars who has been committed to bridging the gap between the early modern and the modern reception of tragedy, claims that the early modern discussions on tragedy "not only have shaped both the entire reception history of ancient drama and the history of dramatic theory in Europe, but have also deeply influenced all subsequent critical approaches and responses to Greek tragedy." See Lurie. "Facing up to Tragedy. Toward an Intellectual History of Sophocles in Europe from Camerarius to Nietzsche." *A Companion to Sophocles*, edited by Kirk Ormand. Oxford: Blackwell, 2012, p. 440–60, at p. 441.

4 See Halliwell, *The* Poetics *of Aristotle*, p. 123: "the theory and criticism of tragedy is one area where vestiges of an older didacticism can still be traced, usually taking the form of a quest for the 'essence' of tragedy and a resolve narrowly to delimit its sphere."

5 Renaissance interpretations of *hamartia* have been analyzed deeply in Michael Lurie. *Die Suche nach der Schuld. Sophokles'* Oedipus Rex, *Aristoteles'* Poetik *und das Tragödienverständ-*

diverse interpretations it still produces. Scholarship on *hamartia* has developed massively in the last forty years,[6] and even outside the field of Aristotelian studies issues relating to the responsibility of the tragic hero have always been highly divisive. Disputes on the tragic quality of given literary works have often revolved around the extent to which an agent can be considered responsible for the misfortunes he undergoes. It is a gray zone, in which the limits of human agency and of its unmasterable outcomes are at stake, and as such it engenders clashing responses.

In analyzing some specific interpretations of *hamartia*, I do not aim to measure the distance between the Renaissance refashioning of the concept and its original meaning. That is a critical exercise that has already been accomplished, as in Brigitte Kappl's in-depth inquiry on the early modern Italian reception of the *Poetics*, which gives me the chance to point out what I do *not* aim to do. Kappl claims that relevant modern scholarship has failed to understand the critical work of Renaissance theoreticians and commentators outside the paradigm based on some keywords: *Moralisierung, Rhetorisierung, Systematisierung,* and *Rationalisierung*.[7] The aim of her study, in fact, is to acknowledge the extent to which this body of theory and criticism laid the foundation of modern literary theory beyond the threshold of the nineteenth century, supposedly marked, as Peter Szondi famously claimed, by a shift from normative to speculative poetics.[8] While fully agreeing on the need to overcome the narrative based on the opposition between heteronomous pre-modern norms and aesthetically autonomous modern concepts, I believe that the distance separating the *Poetics* from its first early modern readers should not be overshadowed: they indeed departed from Aristotle, not just because of moral concerns, but above all because they were committed to a massive process of cultural *translatio* and reinvention, in which the foundation of a modern theatrical practice

---

nis der Neuzeit. Berlin: de Gruyter, 2004; Kappl, *Die Poetik des Aristoteles*, pp. 226–266; Rolf Lohse. *Renaissancedrama und humanistische Poetik in Italien*. Munich: Wilhelm Fink, 2015, pp. 183–87.

6 See, among others, Thomas C. W. Stinton. "*Hamartia* in Aristotle and Greek Tragedy." *Classical Quarterly*, vol. 25, 1975, pp. 221–54; Martha C. Nussbaum. "Tragedy and Self-sufficiency: Plato and Aristotle on Fear and Pity." *Essays on Aristotle's* Poetics, edited by Amélie O. Rorty. Princeton: Princeton University Press, 1992, pp. 261–290; Nancy Sherman. "*Hamartia* and Virtue." *Essays on Aristotle's* Poetics, pp. 177–196. A history of the interpretation of *hamartia* can be found in Lurie, *Die Suche nach der Schuld*, pp. 79–91 and 278–386.

7 See Kappl, *Die Poetik des Aristoteles*, p. 2.

8 Peter Szondi. *Poetik und Geschichtsphilosophie II: Von der normativen zur spekulativen Gattungspoetik*. Frankfurt: Suhrkamp, 1974.

and ultimately of a modern critical discourse on poetic genres was at stake.⁹ The approach to this fascinating and unprecedented process should, then, go beyond either appreciation or belittlement of how close it came to Aristotle.¹⁰ In a sense, I take it for granted that these re-readings *are* misinterpretations of the Aristotelian concept: even when they are not thorough misinterpretations, they do diverge from their major *Auctor* as much because of their zealous orthodoxy as due to their bold independence. In other words, I am not specifically interested in singling out the interpreters who best grasped Aristotle's intentions between the lines; rather, I am interested in the conceptual instabilities that such readings embody and in the fluid theoretical space they open up.

My first example includes the writings – an apology and three lectures – that the playwright Sperone Speroni wrote in defense of his tragedy *Canace*, published in 1546, yet already read and known in 1542 in Padua within the Accademia degli Infiammati. The tragedy was harshly criticized in an anonymous *Giuditio* circulated right after the composition of the work and later published in 1550, the author of which has been identified as Giovan Battista Giraldi Cinzio, the first playwright to restore tragedy to the stage.¹¹ *Canace* is

---

9 See, for instance, the case of Giraldi Cinzio, a theoretician and playwright himself who, in his *Discorso intorno al comporre delle commedie e delle tragedie*, distorts Aristotelian concepts not only because of his didactic aims and Christian background, but also due to his need to justify his own dramatic practice. See Daniel Javitch. "Introduction to Giovan Battista Giraldi Cinthio's *Discourse or Letter on the Composition of Comedies and Tragedies*." *Renaissance Drama*, vol. 39, 2011, 197–206. In general, Javitch stresses how it was the production of modern tragedies that stirred theoreticians to discuss the genre, and not the other way around. See Javitch. "On the Rise of Genre-Specific Poetics in the Sixteenth Century." *Making Sense of Aristotle. Essays in Poetics*, edited by Øivind Andersen and John Haarberg. London: Duckworth, 2001, pp. 127–44 (p. 133). See also Salvatore Di Maria. *The Italian Tragedy in the Renaissance. Cultural Realities and Theatrical Innovations*. Lewisburg: Bucknell University Press, 2002.
10 See Terence Cave. "The Afterlife of the Poetics." *Making Sense of Aristotle*, p. 200: "In practical terms, we can certainly say that some readings of the Poetics – for example, certain of the interpretations advanced by neo-Aristotelian theorists of the early modern period – are 'wrong', in the sense that they are incompatible with the linguistic, cultural and intellectual world which Aristotle and his treatise belonged. [...] Yet a certain unease begins to creep in at the point where we find earlier interpretations being dismissed on the assumption that scholarship, like technology, gets better and better all the time. [...] It follows that one should at least let the reception history of the *Poetics* have its full and independent value, rather than congratulating its approximations to what current scholarship regards as correct while deploring or mocking its aberrations and deformations."
11 It was Christina Roaf who attributed the *Giuditio* to Giovan Battista Giraldi Cinzio in the article "A sixteenth-century 'Anonimo': the author of the *Giuditio sopra la tragedia di Canace et Macareo*." *Italian Studies*, vol. 14, 1959, 49–74. She then edited a book collecting the tragedy, the *Giuditio*, and the apology and three lectures that Speroni gave in Padua to respond to the harsh criticism of the anonymous writer: Sperone Speroni and Giambattista Giraldi Cinzio.

based on an epistle in Ovid's *Heroides* (XI), and represents the disastrous outcomes of the incestuous love between Canace and her brother Macareo (Macareus in Ovid), Aeolus' children, who fell in love with each other, compelled by Venus. The goddess was seeking revenge on Aeolus himself for the tempest he provoked against her son Aeneas leaving Troy after the sack of the city. When their father finds out about the incest, Canace is forced to kill herself; Macareo in turn commits suicide and their newborn child is left to die.[12]

The *Giuditio*, written in the form of a dialogue, tackles, among others, the issue of the moral quality of *Canace*'s protagonists and, hence, of their atrocious moral error, with a clear reference to Chapter 13 of the *Poetics*. As Daniel Javitch points out, it is in the *Giuditio* that we find for the first time *persone mezzane*, that is middling characters, as a necessary requirement for tragic plots to arouse pity and fear.[13] While, on the one hand, this sounds like a precise retrieval of one of the *Poetics*' non-negotiable tenets, on the other, through the example of Orestes discussed by the anonymous critic, this quite soon proves to be a "creative" recovery: Orestes is middling to the extent that he is, at the same time, evil for having killed his wicked mother Clytemnestra, and virtuous for avenging his father Agamemnon. In other words, his being average results from both the extremes – virtue and wickedness – he covers.[14] Accordingly, Speroni's incestuous siblings are here considered definitely wicked and hence inappropriate tragic agents unable to arouse pity and fear, in that their deeds are classified as a voluntary crime and not as an error originating from ignorance. Complying with the didactic interpretation of catharsis

---

Canace e scritti in sua difesa – Scritti contro la Canace, edited by Christina Roaf. Bologna: Commissione per i testi di lingua, 1982. Javitch disputes this attribution in "On the Rise of Genre-Specific Poetics," p. 136 f.

12 On Speroni's *Canace* see Christina Roaf. "Retorica e poetica nella *Canace*." *Sperone Speroni*. Padua: Editoriale Programma, 1989, pp. 169–191; Richard A. McCabe. *Incest, Drama and Nature's Law*. Cambridge: Cambridge University Press, 1993, pp. 101–106; Maria Maslanka Soro. "Il mito di Eolo e il problema del tragico nella tragedia *Canace* di Sperone Speroni." *Rivista di letteratura italiana*, vol. 28, no. 3, 2010, pp. 35–44; Lohse, *Renaissancedrama und humanistische Poetik*, pp. 329–36. The play has been translated into English by Elio Brancaforte, Toronto: Centre for Reformation and Renaissance Studies, 2013.

13 See Javitch, "On the Rise of Genre-Specific Poetics," p. 138.

14 See Speroni/Cinzio. *Canace*, p. 101: "Né sono scelerati Oreste e Elettra, ma persone mezzane, cioè che sono tra il buono e il reo, e perciò (come dice Aristotile) atte alla compassione. Paiono bene scelerati per la morte della madre, ma sono buoni in far vendetta del padre." ("Nor are Orestes and Electra wicked, rather they are middling characters, who dwell between the good and the evil, and therefore, as Aristotle claims, they are suited to fostering compassion. They look wicked with regard to the death of their mother, but they are good in that they avenge their father." My translation).

that Cinzio elaborates in his *Discorso intorno al comporre delle commedie e delle tragedie* (published in 1554, but written in 1543),[15] such a plot cannot supply viewers with a palatable moral truth, since an evil action perpetrated willingly does not translate into any virtuous instruction.

> Perché simili favole, quanto a' costumi, i quali sono di grandissima considerazione nelle Tragedie, sono pessime, e perciò da non essere ammesse nel cospetto de' popoli, ad esempio della vita de' quali si ritrovaro le Tragedie da' più saggi poeti, come avete da Platone e da Aristotile e dalle stesse Tragedie che tuttavia si leggono.[16]

Moralism and didacticism prevail over moral reasoning: the circumstances under which the agency of the characters occurs are disregarded, and no case is made for the external compulsion they undergo, which could make such severe blame at least disputable. However, the starkness of the censure signals a sense of critical uneasiness in dealing with a case of reversal in which, in fact, no recognizable error occurs, except the failure to oppose dooming, insurmountable forces.

The apology in defense of *Canace* and the relevant lectures Speroni delivered in Padua follow, as Christina Roaf has stressed, a convoluted line of reasoning.[17] First, the argument relating to the wickedness of the characters is simply reversed: not only are Canace and Macareo considered the best middling characters to be found in a tragedy, but they are also justified by their age and their kind of error, which is a pitiful one in that it results from love:

> Ma quai persone potea trovare il mio amico, la cui fortuna di felice in infelice tornata, tanto in sé ritenesse di quel terrifico e miserando che alla tragedia è richiesta, quanto già n'ebbero gli infortuni di Canace e di Macareo? E ecco che, perché meglio due tali affetti si commovessero, non contento il poeta che i due fratelli fosser mezzo tra buoni e rei [...] volle imitarli il poeta nella età lor giovenile, nella quale è men vergogna il fallire, e la compassione è maggiore. E volle insieme che quello errore che fu cagion della lor miseria, fosse errore amoroso, con esso il quale [...] rade volte adiviene che da pietade si discompagni.[18]

---

15 See G. B. Giraldi Cinzio. *Discorsi intorno al comporre*, edited by Susanna Villari. Messina: Centro Interdipartimentale di Studi Umanistici, 2002. An English translation of the *Discorso* by Daniel Javitch has appeared in *Renaissance Drama*, vol. 39, 2011, pp. 207–255.
16 Speroni/Cinzio, *Canace*, p. 111. ("Plots like this, with respect to their mores – which are of very great importance in tragedies – are the worst and therefore are not to be admitted to the view of the people; tragedies were invented by the wisest poets to instruct their lives by examples, as you learn from Plato and from Aristotle and from those same tragedies which are still read." My translation).
17 See her "Introduction" to the edition mentioned above.
18 Speroni/Cinzio, *Canace*, p. 191. ("But what persons could my fellow find, whose reversed fortune held as much of that terror and pity tragedy requires as the misfortunes of Canace and Macareo had? Hence, in order to arouse those two emotions, the poet not only made them

This tautological statement, which restores the term "error" instead of "crime," moves toward the apology of immoral love, a legitimate theme for literary works such as the Fourth Giornata of Boccaccio's *Decamerone*, which tackles tragic stories of transgression.[19] A significant inconsistency arises here: Canace and Macareo are claimed to be middling and as such as complying with Aristotle's criteria, but at the same time their error is considered immoral, the only reason to admit it in a tragedy being the examples provided by major literary works in which immoral love is considered able to arouse pity. Instead of keeping to his first point and demonstrating to what extent the siblings meet the standard of the middling character, Speroni embraces a different apologetic strategy, which discards moral concerns and concentrates on the emotional effects (public mourning at funerals) that tragic immoral love can engender. While apparently trying to hold to Aristotle, Speroni bypasses the relationship between the moral quality of the characters and the need for fear and pity to be elicited, and subordinates the former to the latter.

In the first lecture in defense of his *Canace*, Speroni seems keen to display once again Aristotelian orthodoxy by quoting and paraphrasing Vincenzo Maggi's comment on chapter 13 of the *Poetics*:

> Se adonque il terrore e la compassione nasce dalla similitudine che è tra l'uomo che patisce alcun male e colui che lo vede patire, perché vedendo io alcuno che a me sia simile oppresso da qualche infortunio, pensando io che sopra di me possi medesimamente cadere, son mosso a terrore e pietà di tal fatto; e avendosi la tragedia a rappresentare alla moltitudine, la quale è d'uomini posti tra buoni e malvaggi, però facea bisogno che le persone tragiche fossero mezane, acciò che la somiglianza che era tra esse e il populo del teatro avesse a nascer la compassione e il terrore che la tragedia propone.[20]

---

middling but imitated them in their youth, in which errors are less shameful and pity is greater. And he decided also that the error causing their misfortune should be an error of love, which rarely is not accompanied by pity." My translation).

19 Ibid., p. 192: "Mai il Boccaccio, in quella quarta giornata che tutta è tragica, non fa morire uno innamorato che con le lagrime di tutto 'l popolo del suo paese non l'accompagni alla sepoltura: e pur ne muoiono alcuni da' cui amori malamente fu violata or la ubidienza paterna or la familiarità del signore, or l'amistà degli eguali, or la ragione delle genti, e or la fede de' collegati." ("In the fourth Giornata, which is entirely tragic, never has Boccaccio made a lover die without the sorrow of all the people of his town accompanying him to the burial: yet the loves of those who die violated the obedience towards the fathers, the familiarity of the lord, the friendship of the peers, the common sense of the people, and the trust of the allies." My translation).

20 Ibid., p. 211. ("If then terror and commiseration arise from the similarity existing between the man who suffers some evil and the one who sees him suffer [for if I see one who is like myself oppressed by some misfortune and if I think that this could fall upon me in the same way, I am moved to terror and pity of such an event] and since tragedy is to be presented to the multitude, which is made up of men placed in an intermediate position between the good

Given this theoretical premise, the line of reasoning turns baffling. While Speroni appropriately starts setting out an argument on the circumstances under which the incest occurs, that is, an external compulsion whose responsibility lies with Venus,[21] he develops further the legitimacy of incestuous love, permitted among ancient peoples as natural and prohibited only by specific laws in given contexts.[22] Rather than reflecting on the disempowerment that, according to the plot he provided, undermines the characters' agency, Speroni persists in defending the legitimacy of incest by means of a bizarre comparison with the gods' habits. If one turns back to the tragedy, the motive of the unjust external compulsion exerted by Venus on Canace and Macareo is indeed emphasized,[23] and so there would be room to argue against the inherent wickedness of the siblings. Nonetheless, Speroni shifts the focus towards the difference between sins of incontinence and those caused by boldness and disregard of the laws, and thus he implicitly reassesses the nature of the siblings' error:

> Io dico, Signori, che si debbe fare differenza grande fra coloro che peccano per forza d'amor soverchio e tirati da grandissimo affetto, e quelli che per presunzione e temerità e per dispregio delle leggi commettino simili eccessi.[24]

Instead of entering the gray zone of the characters' agency and discussing the conundrum of the external compulsion, Speroni resorts to Dante's literary

---

and the wicked, it was therefore necessary that the tragic characters had to be middling, so that from the similarity between them and the people in the audience there might arise compassion and terror." My translation).

21 See ibid., p. 213: "Dice Deiopea che i suoi figliuoli non meritano morte dal padre perché essi hanno per forza commesso quello che i dei fanno per voluntà in cielo. [...] E come sforzati siano incorsi in questo errore, è da sé chiaro e dalle parole molte volte dette in molte parti della tragedia, cioè che Venere, per prender vendetta di Eolo dell'ingiuria fatta da lui ad Enea suo figliuolo, aveva loro indotto e fatto forza a peccare." ("Deiopea says that her children do not deserve the death from their father because they committed, under compulsion, what the gods in heaven do by choice. [...] And how they were forced to fault is clear in itself and in the words frequently repeated in many parts of the tragedy – that is, that Venus, wishing to take revenge on Aeolus for his abuse done to her son Aeneas, had misled and forced them to sin." My translation).

22 See ibid., p. 215: "Nel vero non è dalla natura vietato la congionzion del fratello e della sorella, ma dalle leggi e non già da tutte" ("Indeed laws, and not even all, forbid the sexual union between brother and sister, while nature does not." My translation).

23 The old servant as well as Macareo himself and his mother Deiopeia refer to the insurmountable power of Venus by using metaphors signifying coercion and passivity.

24 Speroni/Cinzio. *Canace*, p. 218. ("I believe, gentlemen, that one should mark a sharp distinction between those who fault because of the power of an excessive love and stirred by a great passion and those who commit such excesses because of their boldness and audacity and contempt of the laws." My translation).

authority to ennoble his work and neutralize any criticism against the moral quality of his characters, who would be comparable to the lovers of *Inferno* V.²⁵ Eventually, then, by means of the reference to incontinence, a key Aristotelian concept that marks a fundamental distinction within the moral geography of Dante's *Inferno*, Speroni can turn back to the *Poetics*, reaffirm his orthodoxy by quoting the passage of Chapter 13 on *hamartia*, and relocate Canace and Macareo under the label of middling characters committing human errors:

> Per queste ragioni gli errori de gli amanti non sono sceleratezze, ma si debbano chiamar umani, perché l'uomo ama come ragionevole e perciò umanamente pecca; e se così è che l'error de gli inamorati sia umano, adonque noi semo nella particola di Aristotele dove dice che persone tragiche sono quelle che *non per dedecus et pravitatem sed humano quodam errore in infelicitatem lapsi sunt*.²⁶

In a way, incontinence would be a good solution for reading *Canace* in the light of the requirements of the *Poetics* as illustrated in Maggi's comment, but it does not apply to what happens in the tragedy, where the protagonists are in fact doomed to fall in love with each other, unless one gives an interpretation of Venus' intervention as an allegory of the power of love and the human inability to control passions. This would be an interesting ex-post self-reading by Speroni, which, however, is not allowed by the tragedy itself, since the motifs of vengeance and external compulsion, rather than incontinence and lack of self-command, re-emerge throughout the work as justification of the incest.

This complex layering of different arguments is overturned by a sudden interpretative twist, which engages Speroni in demonstrating that even evil agents can arouse pity and consequently suit tragic plots. This means that, even if Canace and Macareo, as incestuous lovers, were considered wicked, this would not prevent their story from being the subject of a good tragedy. As frequently happens when commentaries on the *Poetics* depart from its theoretical framework, Speroni claims that Aristotle was wrong in prescribing middling characters as a requirement for tragedy to arouse pity, and suggests that the

---

25 Ibid., p. 225: "S'inamorò donque Francesca di Paolo perché Amore non perdona amare a nullo amato ma vuole e sforza che chi è amato riami." ("So Francesca fell in love with Paolo because Love does not pardon anyone loved from loving in return but wants and forces the beloved to love in turn." My translation).
26 Ibid., p. 228. ("For these reasons, lovers' errors are not crimes and should be deemed human, because the human being loves as a reasonable creature and hence faults as human; and if it is true that lovers' error is human, then we fall in the scope of that paragraph in which Aristotle says that tragic characters are those who *non per dedecus et pravitatem sed humano quodam errore in infelicitatem lapsi sunt*." My translation).

ancient tragedians mastered the tragic art much better than the philosopher did. Within Speroni's apologetic writings, this is the point that most sharpens the clash between theoretical demands and literary practices.

Let me briefly recapitulate the elements collected up to this point: according to their defender, Canace and Macareo are middling, their love being, however, immoral. Incest, in any case, is a legitimate theme for tragic plots, and furthermore it is also socially acceptable, given that many cultures allow it. Canace and Macareo, moreover, are incontinent and, thus, as the sinners punished in the first zone of Dante's *Inferno*, they are not evil – they have just been unable to dominate their passions. Consequently, they fall within the theoretical spectrum outlined in the *Poetics*. This standpoint proves to be unsteady, as it is suddenly overcome by the argument defending the appropriateness of evil agents within literary works. It is not Speroni's tragedy that does not comply with the rule of the middling character: it is the rule itself that has no correspondence with the ancient tragic corpus. Beside the bold claim of independence from theoretical constraints, what is striking is the abrupt change in the argumentation, which ends up spanning one extreme to the other.

What follows is not consistently linked to this new stance – evil agents can be tragic – because Speroni argues that the harsh remarks against his work depend on the identification of Canace and Macareo as tragic characters, which would prove to be an incorrect assumption. For also the ghost of the siblings' child, l'Ombra, could awake pity and hence act as the tragic character of the drama.[27] What does this new twist have to do with the idea, set out just beforehand, that wicked persons can arouse pity? Of course, there is no logical connection between these two arguments, and the lack of logic at this point of the lectures makes Speroni's defense sound desperate. Following this new line of reasoning, he claims that also Deiopeia, the siblings' mother, could be eligible as a tragic character, in that she mourns pitifully the death of her children. Not content with this hypothesis, Speroni closes his lecture by reversing his position once again and singling out Aeolus as the real tragic figure in the tragedy.

One could simply argue that not only is Speroni a poor apologist, but this hectic gathering of opposite justifications implicitly also expresses his uneasiness in defending his own work as much as his critical blindness in reading it.

---

[27] Ibid., p. 240: "io non so perché non si potesse più tosto dire che questa compassione avesse a cadere sopra l'Ombra, poiché dalle sue proprie parole si po' traggerne miglior argomento che non ha fatto costui" ("I don't know why it could not rather be argued that this pity should be directed toward the Ombra, since from his words a better case can be made than the one [the anonymous critic] made." My translation).

If we were to observe from above, looking down on the conceptual schema underlying his arguments, we would see a fluid space devoid of a center, within which critical discourse turns nomadic – as the triple identification of the tragic character shows – and drifts in different directions, while concepts and cultural references multiply and overlap to the extent that Aristotle is at the same time recognized as the authority providing the perfect tragic pattern, and dismissed as a restrictive theoretician unable to master tragedy. Rules and transgression coexist in an unstable, undecidable set, which fails to grasp the crucial question the tragedy raises: What is the error of Canace and Macareo? What is an error committed under an external compulsion?

Between the composition of the *Canace* in 1542 and the apologetic lectures delivered by Speroni in 1558, new Latin commentaries on the *Poetics*, such as those by Robortello or Maggi, raised the benchmark of Aristotelian scholarship, while expanding the theoretical discussion on *hamartia* and, consequently, the floating of unstable concepts relating to it. In his remarks on Chapter 13 of the treatise, Robortello refers quite aptly to the third book of the *Nicomachean Ethics* (1–5) in order to explain *hamartia* under the light of involuntary deeds committed *di'agnoian*, that is, through ignorance (*per imprudentiam*), an interpretation much praised by modern scholars.[28] Yet, when dealing with the relationship between the error through ignorance and the requirement of the middling character, the scholar has to admit that this pattern applies only to a few tragedies of the ancient corpus or, better, only to *Oedipus the King*.[29] Indeed, Robortello claims, one can find in ancient tragedies virtuous characters who suffer undeserved harms. This is the case of Hercules, Electra, and even Orestes, whose stories would be repulsive according to Aristotle's conceptual framework.[30]

---

28 See Francesco Robortello. *In librum Aristotelis de arte poetica explicationes*. Munich: Wilhelm Fink, 1968, pp. 129–33. On Robortello's commentary see Weinberg, *A History of Literary Criticism*, pp. 388–399. The most complete survey of Robortello's analysis of *hamartia* is in Lurie, *Die Suche nach der Schuld*. See also Kappl, *Die Poetik des Aristoteles*, pp. 230–33.
29 See Robortello, *In librum Aristotelis explicationes*, p. 133: "Non debent igitur omnes veterum tragoediae perpendi hoc examine, aut redigi ad hanc normam; nam praeter actionem, personamque Oedipodis, qualem expressit Sophocles, nescio, an aliam reperias apud ullum ex veteribus." ("Hence, not all the tragedies of the ancients should undergo this scrutiny, or be composed according to this criterion; in fact, beside Oedipus' action and character, as Sophocles gave shape to them, I do not know whether you could find another tragedy [of this kind] in any of the ancients." My translation).
30 See Ibid., p. 133: "Quod si redigas ad hanc normam Aristotelis, erit nefarium scelus, id est μιαρὸν, Electram bonam immerentem infelicem esse, et incommoda pati tam magna." ("For if you conformed to this rule by Aristotle, it would be repulsive – that is μιαρὸν – that Electra, who is good, is unhappy without deserving it, and endures such great misfortunes.")

Rather than exploring the moral features of this alternative plot, Robortello departs from the question, and sets about explaining why, notwithstanding the scarcity of tragedies complying with the requirement of the middling character combined with the error *per imprudentiam*, Aristotle concentrated almost exclusively on this rather rare plot. In the following paragraph, the commentator turns back again to the requirement of the middling character, which seems a necessary tenet in order to prevent human beings from being disgusted by misfortunes that hit virtuous agents, and from feeling alienated from the gods, who would be supposed to disregard human destinies:

> Atque sic patet, noluisse Aristotelem omnino bonum virum concedere in actione tragica; sed aliquid tamen detraxisse ab ea persona, quam mediam constituebat inter bonum et malum. [...] Nam malus commiserationem non excitat, si infelix fuerit, tantum abest, ut excitet terrorem et metum. Bonus commiserationem quidem excitat, si quid adversi patiatur; at non terrorem, sed potius μιαρὸν. Ac sicuti terror inducit in animos religionem, obstringitque eos magis cultu quodam, ac pietate erga deos, quorum potentia extimescunt; sic τὸ μιαρὸν animos abalienat prorsus a Diis, qui quasi mortalia negligant, probitatemque hominum non intueantur, foveantque eos, qui virtute fuerint praediti, malis multis bonos viros conflictari permittant; ex qua re indignatio gravis oritur in animis hominum in Deos ipsos et opinio ipsos securum (ut ille ait) agere aevum, ac ociose dormitare in regendis mortalibus, maximum enim providentiae Deorum signum esse iudicant homines, si viros bonos praemiis afficiant, improbos autem ulciscantur, maleque perdant.[31]

An inconsistency marks this paragraph: while on the one hand Robortello explains why undeserved misfortunes potentially undermine religious devotion and nurture a feeling of alienation from the gods, on the other he does not connect this remark with the abovementioned reassessment of the requirement of the middling character, which, according to him, would suit only *Oedipus the King*. What happens, then, in the majority of the tragic corpus that, accord-

---

[31] Ibid., p. 134. ("Thus it is evident that Aristotle did not want to allow an entirely good character into the tragic action, but took something away from that person whom he established as middling between good and evil. [...] In fact, the evil person does not arouse pity, whenever unfortunate, not to mention arousing horror and fear. The virtuous person does arouse pity, if he or she suffers a misfortune; but [this case does not provoke] fear, rather repulsion. And fear elicits a sense of reverence in [human] souls and binds them with a certain worship and devotion towards the gods, whose power they are afraid of. Accordingly, repulsion alienates [human] souls from the gods, who would allow good men to undergo great harms, as if they neglected mortal matters and did not care about men's virtue and [did not] support the virtuous. And hence a grave indignation against the gods themselves originates in human souls, and the idea even arises that they live a safe life and are idly sleepy in ruling human things; in fact, men consider it to be the highest sign of divine providence when gods reward virtuous men and punish and badly destroy the evil." My translation).

ing to Robortello himself, encompasses stories of good characters suffering undeserved misfortunes? Where will one relocate their error? If Electra and Hercules are virtuous, either their stories are repulsive – and this is not the case, as Robortello points out – or there is, in his line of reasoning, a conceptual blank that fails to tackle this alternative configuration and urges a rethinking of the bond that connects errors and agency. What follows is even more remarkable: instead of developing further the example of a tragedy that revolves around a virtuous agent without eliciting repulsion, Robortello refers to Ajax as the character who, disdaining the gods, deserves their punishment. It is not simply an odd and crudely moralistic interpretation of Sophocles' *Ajax*: it contradicts at once both the requirement of the middling person – no blasphemer could be deemed middling – and the interpretation of *hamartia* as error *per imprudentiam*, since a direct link seems to connect Ajax's blasphemy with the punishment Athena inflicts upon him.[32]

A double movement occurs in Robortello's remarks on Chapter 13: on the one hand, he attempts to explore different plot configurations beside the Aristotelian; on the other, a sense of uneasiness and theoretical anxiety prevents him from inquiring how the agency of a virtuous character can engender errors, or to what extent a tragic plot can be developed in the absence of errors or human fallacy.

Even though in Robortello's commentary no room is left for such an inquiry, the hypothesis of a tragic plot revolving around a virtuous agent who suffers a drastic reversal of fortune was widely discussed in the Italian Renaissance. Late antique and medieval scholarship that allowed an interpretation of tragedy as a lament upon undeserved misfortunes striking virtuous persons was still influential and, as some scholars claim, affected the circulation and interpretation of Aristotelian concepts.[33] What is striking is that theoreticians with radically different ideological and religious backgrounds converge on this alternative pattern. In Antonio Minturno's theoretical dialogue *De poeta*, published in 1559, a case is made for the death of Christ, the most innocent of men, to be considered a tragedy:

---

32 See ibid., p. 134: "Sic scilicet discimus, omnes deorum contemptores, atque obtrectatores male mulctari a Diis, pellique in amentiam." ("Thus, with no doubts we learn that all despisers and detractors of the gods are punished by the gods and driven to madness." My translation).
33 See Enrica Zanin. *Les fins tragiques. Poétique et éthique du dénouement dans la tragédie de la première modernité (Italie, France, Espagne, Allemagne)*. Geneva: Droz, 2014, pp. 109–122; Lohse, *Renaissancedrama und humanistische Poetik*. On tragedy as a lament in late antique and medieval theoretical writings see Henry Ansgar Kelly. *Ideas and Forms of Tragedy from Aristotle to the Middle Ages*. Cambridge: Cambridge University Press, 1993.

> Mors enim illa salutaris, quam Christus, ut vitam mortalibus restitueret, non invitus, at libenter sane oppetivit, non esset profecto tragice deploranda, si minus in Theatrum afferri deberent quae viro probo accidissent, ac ferenda indigne potius, quam miseranda esse viderentur.[34]

The role of *hamartia* as well as of agency is drastically neutralized, while the goodness of the character and the violence of his reversal become central.[35] A catholic bishop participating in the Council of Trent, Minturno provided an influential theoretical ground for martyr tragedy, as Pierre Corneille points out in his *Examen de Polyeucte*.[36]

In his monumental vernacular translation of and commentary on the *Poetics*, published in Vienna in 1570, Lodovico Castelvetro, sentenced to death as a heretic and hence having fled from Italy,[37] claims that the plot of the virtuous undergoing misfortunes best suits the eliciting of pity and fear:

> Io non posso comprendere come la persona di santissima vita, trapassando da felicità a miseria, non generi spavento e compassione, e molto maggiori ancora che non fa la mezzana. Conciosia cosa che coloro li quali menano una vita così santa, come generalmente fa la moltitudine popolare, prendano maggiore spavento e più si sgomentino veggendo la persona migliore di loro patire, che non farebbono se vedessono uno simile a loro, dubitando che a loro non incontri simile disavventura; e si presenta loro davanti alla

---

[34] Antonio Sebastiano Minturno. *De Poeta* [1559]. Munich: Wilhelm Fink, 1970, p. 182. ("That saving death of Christ, which he willingly and freely sought in order to restore life to mortals, should certainly not be deplored as tragic, even if events striking the just man were to be brought on stage and seemed to be endured ignominiously rather than deserving pity." My translation). See also p. 183: "De Christo autem Servatore eodemque Deo nostro ac Domino, an tragoedia confici possit, qui fecit, ipse viderit. Mihi vero videtur genus illud mortis tam acerbum fuisse, ac tam inhumanum, ut quisque praeclarum illi ipsi et gloriosum, nobis autem fuerit salutareque in summam tamen miserationem adducat."

[35] It is worth noting that Minturno mantains a medieval framework, according to which tragedy is the genre that expresses the instability of all human matters (p. 179): "ut videmus non esse rebus prospere fluentibus fidendum, nihil infra esse tam diuturnum tamque stabile, quod caducum non sit et mortale, nihil tam firmum ac validum, quod demum nequeat everti, nihil tam felix, quod miserum, nihil ita summum, quod infimum effici non possit." ("We see that all things occurring happily should not be trusted, that among them there is nothing so lasting and steady that it is not transitory and mortal, nothing so firm and solid that it cannot be eventually overthrown, nothing so happy and outstanding that it cannot become miserable and of lowest grade." My translation).

[36] See Kappl, *Die Poetik des Aristoteles*, p. 249; Zanin, *Les fins tragiques*, pp. 171–180.

[37] See Ludovico Castelvetro. *Letterati e grammatici nella crisi religiosa del Cinquecento*, edited by Massimo Firpo and Guido Mongini. Florence: Olschki, 2008, in particular Cesare Vasoli's chapter "Ludovico Castelvetro e la fortuna cinquecentesca della *Poetica* di Aristotele," pp. 1–24. On Castelvetro's translation and commentary see Weinberg, *A History of Literary Criticism*, vol. 1, pp. 302–311.

mente l'argomento evangelico: "Se queste cose sono avenute in legno verde, quanto maggiormente averranno in secco?". E a cui s'avrà compassione, se non s'ha compassione all'uomo santissimo caduto in miseria? Certo niuno. Adunque la persona di singolare santità trapassando da felicità a miseria non era da rifiutare perché non potesse generare spavento e compassione. Ma dice Aristotele che non genera né spavento né compassione, ma sdegno contro Dio, il che è cosa abominevole. E io dico che non seguita, posto che sia vero che simile trapassamento di simile persona generi sdegno contro Dio, che non generi ancora spavento e compassione; né lo sdegno contro Dio annulla lo spavento e la compassione, sì come quando una persona mezzana riceve danno ingiustamente da alcuno prendiamo sdegno contra il dannificante ingiustamente, e non per tanto siamo senza spavento e senza compassione per l'accidente avenuto senza sua colpa al dannificato.[38]

Overturning Robortello's argument, Castelvetro argues that such a configuration would in any case be repulsive, since common people still believe in God's justice and care in human matters. In a very subtle and oblique way, Castelvetro questions the connection between undeserved misfortunes striking eminent characters and the feeling of indignation against God that this plot could elicit: by referring to the *communis opinio*, his reasoning eschews the discussion of the moral boundaries of tragedy's subject matter, while it contents itself with exploring the mentality and beliefs of a hypothetical common audience. In

---

38 Ludovico Castelvetro. *Poetica di Aristotele vulgarizzata e sposta.* 2 vols., edited by Werther Romani. Bari: Laterza, 1978, pp. 361–362: "I am unable to understand why the fall of a man of very holy life from happiness to misery should not arouse pity and fear; why it should not, in fact, arouse greater pity and fear than the fall of a man of ordinary virtue, for those whose lives are not of holiness comparable to his, as the lives of common people generally are not, are more terrified and dismayed by the sufferings of one better than themselves than by those of one of their own kind. The experience of such a fall would fill them with the fear that they may well be visited by a similar misfortune, bringing before their minds the Gospel text (Luke 23:31), 'For if they do these things in a green tree, what should be done in the dry?' And who shall be pitied if not the saintly man who falls into misfortune? For if we are moved to pity by those who suffer unjustly, who deserves misfortune less than a man of most saintly life? None assuredly, and the representation of a supremely saintly man falling from happiness to misery should not therefore have been rejected as incapable of moving audiences to pity and fear. Yet Aristotle asserts that the fall of such a man does not fill us with pity and fear but with indignation against God, which is a blasphemous state of mind. To which I reply that if we are filled with indignation against God it does not follow that we are not also filled with pity and fear. The indignation does not extinguish the pity and fear. When, for example, a person of ordinary virtue is unjustly injured by someone, we feel indignation against the latter, but do not for that reason fail to be moved to pity and fear by the undeserved suffering of the injured man." Translation taken from Andrew Bongiorno. *Castelvetro on the Art of Poetry. An Abridged Translation of Lodovico Castelvetro's* Poetica d'Aristotele Vulgarizzata et Sposta. New York: Binghamton, 1984, p. 162. With reference to this passage, interestingly Enrica Zanin claims that Castelvetro makes room for tragedy as a genre tackling ambiguous or even immoral cases. See Zanin, "Les commentaires modernes de la *Poétique* d'Aristote," p. 80.

other words, Castelvetro does not contest the potential immorality of the reversal hitting a virtuous character on the basis of God's inherent justness, but rather on the basis of what common people believe and imagine.[39] A tragedy can indeed develop without apparent errors and clear retribution mechanisms.

Up to the last part of the century, moralistic interpretations of *hamartia* multiply along with its reductive reassessment: both delimit a fragmented theoretical space where retribution in the form of a seminal poetic justice cohabits with innocent suffering, the control of passions, and an idea of agency as detached from will and intentions. In a treatise published in 1586, some thirty years after Speroni's lectures, Giason Denores, a former student of philosophy in Padua, recalls the quarrel about *Canace* and proposes again some of the arguments Speroni himself elaborated, such as the comparison between the siblings and Paolo and Francesca in Dante's *Inferno*, along with incontinence as the error in which their tragic fate originated.[40] The theoretical framework of Denores's treatise is, in a way, even more fluid than Speroni's: the requirement of the middling character falls together with an unequivocal moralistic scheme requiring punishment as retribution for sins and evil deeds, while the scope of the concept of error widens to the point that it includes ignorance, incontinence, impatience, rage, and fear, which could engender inadvertency, vengeance, and excesses of love and hate:

> Tra buone e cattive poi sono quelle altre le quali, per qualche errore umano d'ignoranza, d'incontinenzia, di intoleranzia, di temenza, d'ira, commettono alcuna volta casi atrocis-

---

[39] Castelvetro uses expressions such as "assolve nella sua mente Iddio da ogni peccato" ("in his mind absolves God from all guilt"), "s'imagina" ("imagines"), "s'induce a credere" ("leads himself to believe").

[40] Giason Denores. *Discorso intorno a que' principii, cause et accrescimenti che la comedia, la tragedia et il poema eroico ricevono dalla filosofia morale e civile e da' governatori delle republiche; onde si raccoglie la diffinizione e distinzione della poesia nelle predette tre sue parti e la descrizione particolare di ciascheduna* [1586]. *Trattati di poetica e retorica del Cinquecento*, 4 vols., edited by Bernard Weinberg. Bari: Laterza, 1970–1974, vol. 3, p. 387: "Non è in tutto cattiva Canace e Macareo, perché hanno peccato per incontinenza. Non è in tutto cattiva Francesca appresso Dante." ("Canace and Macareo are not entirely wicked, since they have sinned because of incontinence. Francesca is not entirely wicked according to Dante." My translation). A few lines below, Denores continues as follows: "Questo avertimento di Aristotele se avessero molto ben inteso e considerato coloro che hanno ripresa la tragedia del signor Sperone, non sarebbono stati tanto arditi nel ragionar così copiosamente delle persone mezzane e scelerate che intravengono nelle tragedie." ("If those who have criticized the tragedy of master Sperone had fully understood and weighed this prescription by Aristotle, they would have never been so bold in discussing so copiously the middling and the wicked characters who appear in tragedies." My translation). On Denores's treatise see Weinberg, *A History of Literary Criticism*, vol. 1, pp. 621–26.

simi, come per inavertenza, per vendetta delle ingiurie ricevute, per odio, per inimicizie, per amore o per qualche altra cagione somigliante. [...] atrocità commesse per un certo errore umano intende Aristotele tutte quelle che fanno gli uomini per ignoranza, per impeto e per furor di odio, di lussuria, di vendetta, di timore, le quali passioni sono a noi communi naturalmente con gli altri animali senza ragione, e si dicono commesse per un certo errore umano.[41]

Even virtuous agents are allowed in tragic plots, in that their resilience against suffering, which does not result from errors, demonstrates their moral excellence. The polymorphic character of this all-encompassing passage is all but exceptional, and seems to embody and crystallize the typical instability marking the whole field of discourses on tragedy in the Italian Cinquecento: similar or even analogous concepts generate opposite interpretations, and different sources overlap in an attempt to grasp the opacities of human errors and suffering as shaped by the *Poetics*.

A clear-cut watershed supposedly split the history of tragedy and tragic theories into two stories inconsistent with each other: the first, running up to the second half of the eighteenth century, tends to be characterized as one haunted by strict poetic norms and suffocating moralistic concerns that affected the production as much as the reception of literary works; the second, whose beginning coincides with the birth of aesthetic autonomy and a drastic philosophical turn, allegedly dismissed old-fashioned prescriptive poetic theories, rooted in wrong, heteronomous interpretations of classical sources. While scholars in modern literature either tend to neglect early modern theoretical writings on tragedy as erratic and unoriginal views, or else commit to amending their distortions and freeing tragedy from a thick web of heteronomous interpretative habits, scholars in classics and of the early modern period are concerned with pinpointing the errors that the modern philosophical drift has engendered, leaving our cultural furniture unable to comprehend ancient and early modern tragic works.[42]

---

41 Denores, *Discorso*, p. 385: "Between the good and the wicked are those others who, because of a certain human error caused by ignorance, incontinence, impatience, fear, or rage, commit atrocious deeds, such as for inadvertency, revenge for insults received, hatred, hostility, love, or for some similar reasons. [...] By atrocities committed because of a certain human error Aristotle means all those that men perpetrate because of ignorance, impulse, and outburst of hatred, lust, revenge, and fear, all passions that we humans share with other animals with no intellect, and which are said to be performed because of a certain human error." My translation. See Kappl, *Die Poetik des Aristoteles*, p. 254.
42 Two recent examples are William Marx. *Le tombeau d'Œdipe: Pour une tragédie sans tragique*. Paris: Minuit, 2012; Blair Hoxby. *What was Tragedy? Theory and the Early Modern Canon*. Oxford: Oxford University Press, 2015, pp. 3–56.

Yet, our contemporary theory in ruin, as Terry Eagleton termed it,[43] would be inconceivable without the conflicting energies that allowed a prismatic expansion of the *Poetics* in the Renaissance and the foundation of a polymorphic theoretical space. The quest for the essence of the tragic, which is indeed a typical modern phenomenon, only apparently replaced early modern moral didacticism, for new forms of post-religious heteronomy, expressed in radical or conservative ideologies, still haunt the battlefield of the tragic. The unprecedented and unsystematic body of theory that developed in the sixteenth century scattered its conceptual materials through different cultural contexts and epochs, with long-term effects. Two of its main strands, respectively emphasizing individual responsibility and innocent suffering, still occupy the deepest layers of the modern debate. Issues relating to the moral and emotional responses to literary works or the literary elaboration of human agency did not simply fade out at the turn of the nineteenth century. In his *Vorlesungen über die Ästhetik*, for instance, Hegel tackles the issue of innocent suffering with a strongly prescriptive stance, which very much reprises old arguments about the indignation it engenders in the spectator: "Ein unvernünftiger Zwang aber, eine Schuldlosigkeit des Leidens müßte statt sittlicher Beruhigung nur Indignation in der Seele des Zuschauers hervorbringen."[44]

Innocence, responsibility, and empathy, albeit interspersed with metaphysical radicalism, are indeed principal concerns in the brave new world of the dead-and-still-alive tragedy, a field in which critical gestures of exclusion, bounding, and prescription[45] coexist with a rhizomatic body of monadic theoretical discourses and narratives. The genre that has given aesthetic shape to the oscillations of human imperfection, vulnerability, and suffering is the subject of a most divided history, which developed across the centuries in disparate cultural contexts thanks to errors, hybrids, and misappropriations, and

---

43 See Terry Eagleton. *Sweet Violence. The Idea of the Tragic*. Oxford: Blackwell, 2002.
44 George Wilhelm Friedrich Hegel. *Vorlesungen über die Ästhetik*, edited by Eva Moldenhauer and Karl Markus Michel. Frankfurt: Suhrkamp, 1970, vol. 3, p. 548. ("An irrational compulsion and innocent suffering would inevitably produce in the soul of the spectator mere indignation instead of ethical peace and satisfaction." Translation taken from Hegel. *Aesthetics: Lectures on Fine Art*, translated by Thomas Malcolm Knox, Oxford: Oxford University Press, 1975, vol. 2, p. 1216.) It is in this context that Hegel categorically bars innocent heroes from tragedy: "Solch einem Heros könnte man nichts Schlimmeres nachsagen, als daß er unschuldig gehandelt habe. Es ist die Ehre der großen Charaktere, schuldig zu sein" (p. 546). ("No worse insult could be given to such a hero than to say that he had acted innocently. It is the honour of these great characters to be culpable" p. 1215).
45 A good example of this kind is George Steiner's essay "A Note on Absolute Tragedy." *Journal of Literature and Theology*, vol. 4, no. 2, 1990, pp. 147–156.

still, strangely, has been haunted by an overpowering fear of those errors so vital to its expansion. Apparently inconclusive and centrifugal discussions on *hamartia* in the Renaissance are indeed a synecdoche of the whole history of tragedy. Nothing resembles the theory of tragedy more closely than its own history.

Stephanie Bung
Playful Institutions: Social and Textual Practices in Early Spanish Academies

When the members of the very young Académie Française acted officially for the first time ever, that is, as representatives of a chartered corporation, they immediately overstepped the boundaries of their self-defined jurisdiction: they broke their own rules by taking sides in the context of the famous *Querelle du Cid*. In 1637 they published their statement *Les sentiments de l'académie française sur la tragi-comédie du Cid*, which led Corneille to make some significant changes to his play. Looking back, these changes and *Les Sentiments de l'académie* represent the beginning of the *doctrine classique*, the most fundamental doctrine of poetics in seventeenth-century France. But Corneille was not a member of the academy and he had not asked for his successful play to be judged. The academy intervened anyway, even though their statutes only allowed for judging the work of members.[1] Interestingly enough, this act of 'misbehaving' – from the viewpoint of the academic rules – was followed by an act of recognition by the authorities: a few months after the outbreak of the *Querelle du Cid*, the Parlement de Paris acknowledged the Académie Française as an established corporation within the realm of Louis XIII.[2] This recognition is arguably even more interesting than the well known fact that it was of course the cardinal de Richelieu who forced the academy to intervene in this struggle. The members of the oldest and most powerful corporation of France acknowledged the institutional status of the academy, and in doing so they acknowledged the public relevance, and a certain autonomy, of 'academic concerns.'

As scholars have shown within the last two decades,[3] the *Querelle du Cid* is a fine example of the transformation European academies had to go through when they first became chartered literary institutions. However, the picture of those transformations is far from complete. In order to grasp its complexity, it

---

[1] See article XLV of the academy's statutes (www.academie-francaise.fr/linstitution/statuts-et-reglements. Accessed 13 February 2018).
[2] See ibid.: "Lettres patentes pour l'établissement de l'Académie française, signées du roi Louis XIII en janvier 1635, *enregistrées au Parlement le 10 juillet 1637.*" (My italics.)
[3] See in particular: Jean-Marc Civardi, *La querelle du Cid (1637–1638). Édition critique intégrale.* Paris: Champion, 2004; Christian Jouhaud, *Les pouvoirs de la littérature: Histoire d'un paradoxe.* Paris: Gallimard, 2000; Hélène Merlin. *Public et littérature en France au XVIIe siècle.* Paris: Les belles lettres, 1994; Hélène Merlin-Kajman. *L'excentricité académique: littérature, institution, société.* Paris: Les belles lettres, 2001.

https://doi.org/10.1515/9783110536690-009

is worth looking at another example of academies by moving from seventeenth-century France to Golden Age Spain, where the shaping of the academic idea into an acknowledgeable corporation was even more complicated. There is no continuity between what is called *academia* in Spain before and after the foundation of the royal academy that was modeled after the Académie Française in 1713.[4] We actually know very little about Spanish academies that precede the Real Academia Española (RAE). In some cases – for example a certain academy of Madrid that is famous for being mentioned in Lope de Vega's *Arte Nuevo*[5] – we have no means to tell if the gatherings in question were more than a rhetorical device.[6] In other cases, even when there is better documentation of social and textual practices, the institutional nature of these practices is at least very questionable. But how can we learn more about the institutional side of cultural networking in early modern Europe if the meaning of what is called *academy*, *academia*, or *académie* differs from one country to another, and – at least on the Iberian peninsula – even within the boundaries of one country? These questions constitute the heuristic frame of this paper on the first Spanish academies, and it is within this frame that we can begin to understand the different transformations of a literary institution called 'academy' in early mod-

---

[4] See Christine Bierbach. "Todos maestros, todos discípulos: Spanische Akademien vor 1700." *Europäische Sozietätsbewegung und demokratische Tradition: Die europäischen Akademien der Frühen Neuzeit zwischen Frührenaissance und Spätaufklärung*, 2 vols., edited by Karl Garber and Heinz Wismann, vol. 1. Tübingen: Niemeyer, 1996, pp. 513–533, p. 518. This article, although written two decades ago, is still one of the most thoughtful and relevant studies about academies in Golden Age Spain.

[5] When Lope de Vega published his famous *Arte nuevo de hacer comedias en este tiempo* (1609), one of the most influential poetics in Spanish literature, he addressed the members of "the valiant academy of Madrid." Comparing this place to the academies of ancient Greece and Rome, he begins his *Arte nuevo* as if it were an open letter to an authority on poetics; an ironic open letter, of course, since this is how Lope defends himself against the 'academic' rules of Aristotle. There have been attempts to identify this particular academy (see most recently Jesús Cañas Murillo. "Corte y academias literarias en la España de Felipe IV." *Anuario de Estudias Filológicos*, vol. 35, 2012, pp. 5–26, here: pp. 8–10), but we still do not know much about its existence. There may in fact have been many so-called academies in Madrid in the early seventeenth century, but there are no statutes, no programs, nor any act of institution that would allow us to be certain about this one.

[6] As is possibly the case in Lope's *Arte Nuevo* (see Karl Vossler. *Lope de Vega und sein Zeitalter*. Munich: Biederstein, 1947, p. 121; Hans Ulrich Gumbrecht. *'Eine' Geschichte der spanischen Literatur*, Frankfurt: Suhrkamp, 1990, vol. 1, p. 378). Lope would not have been the only author to invent an academy, as can be seen from the list of *academias ficticias*, established by José Sánchez (see *Academias literarias del Siglo de Oro español*. Madrid: Gredos, 1961, pp. 167–193). Sánchez' compilation of Golden Age academies is still very valuable, mainly because of his extensive quotations from manuscripts that would otherwise be difficult to find.

ern Europe as well as the complexity of the task. In order to grasp the latter, it is necessary to address at least the main difficulties – terminology, documentation, and territory – that we encounter by searching for these institutions within the boundaries of seventeenth-century Spain. By doing so, this paper is conceived as preliminary, yet necessary work to prepare the ground on which one may pursue the investigation of European academies in the future.

1 Terminology: Permanent and non-permanent *academias*

As we can see in the dictionary of Covarrubias from 1611, the Spanish word *academia* had by then already been adopted for contemporary practices. However, by referring to the ancient world and describing the place and the practice of Plato's school, the dictionary still locates the academic idea within the understanding of a glorious past linked closely to the age of Greek philosophy itself. Whilst this idea may be *imitated* in the present, it is not *replaced* by something worthy of a description for its own sake.

> Academia, Fue un lugar de recreación, y una floresta que distava de Athenis, mil passos dicha assi de Academo Heroa; y por aver nacido en este lugar Platon, y enseñado en el, con gran concurrencia de oyentes, sus discipulos se llamaron Academicos, y oy dia la escuela o la casa, donde su juntan algunos buenos ingenios a conferir, toma este nombre, y le da a los concurrentes.[7]

However, the real problem of terminology can be found a little later, in the dictionary of the RAE of 1726 known as *Diccionario de autoridades*. Here, the classic definition of Plato's *academia* is followed by two different meanings. The first one sounds comforting, since it is very 'close to home,' that is, to our modern understanding of the term: "[Academia] Es tambien la Junta ò Congreso de personas eruditas, que se dedican a el estudio de las buenas letras, y a tratar y conferir lo que conduce a su mayor ilustración, como lo executan las

---

[7] *Tesoro de la lengua castellana o española compuesto por el licenciado Don Sebastian Cobarrubias Orozco* [...]. Madrid: Sanchez, 1611. ("*Academia* was a place of recreation and a forest a thousand paces from Athens, which was called Academo Heroa; and because Plato had been born in this place and had taught a great number of listeners there, his students called themselves academics, and nowadays the school or the house where some good minds congregate to debate takes this name and extends it to the participants." My translation).

Academias de Italia, España, Francia y Portugal, [...]."⁸ This is the meaning we have in mind when we think of the Académie Française for example, or the Real Academia Española itself. But this meaning is followed by another one which, for us, is less obvious: "[Academias] Latamente se llaman assí las Juntas literarias, ò Certamenes que ordinariamente se hacen para celebrar alguna acción grande, [...] o para exercitarse los ingenios que la componen, y casi siempre son de Poesia sobre diferentes assuntos. [...]"⁹

These two definitions, as well as the gap between them, are highly significant.¹⁰ What matters here is the difference between permanent and non-permanent, between institution and occasion. On the one hand we think of an academy whose members meet on a regular basis; on the other hand we must imagine an event, like a celebration or a poetry contest, or a poetry contest within a celebration. The problem is to differentiate between these two meanings, especially within a document that only refers to some *academia* without further details. This brings us to the second difficulty in the study of early modern academies in Golden Age Spain: documentation.

---

8 *Diccionario de la lengua castellana*. Madrid: del Hierro, 1726 (www.rae.es/recursos/diccionarios/diccionarios-anteriores-1726–1996/diccionario-de-autoridades. Accessed 13 February 2018). ("Equally, an assembly or meeting of erudite persons who are dedicated to the study of literature, and discuss that which can further its excellence, as it is practiced by the academies of Italy, Spain, France, or Portugal." My translation).
9 Ibid. ("In a broader sense, this is also the name of literary assemblies or contests, which usually serve to celebrate some momentous event [...] or to exercise the participants' wits, and almost always consist of poetry on various subjects." My translation). This definition seems to be applied only to the plural of *academia*, which is interesting for it already points to the non-permanent structure of those gatherings.
10 Recent studies of Golden Age academies seldom fail to mention this discrepancy (see Pasqual Mas i Usó. *Academias y justas literarias en la Valencia barroca: Teoria y prática de una convención*. Kassel: Reichenberger, 1996, pp. 1–4; José María Ferri Coll. *La poesía de la Academia de los Nocturnos*. Alicante: Publicaciones de la Universidad de Alicante, 2001, p. 57), but they rarely take it into consideration when thinking about paradigmatic issues. Helmut C. Jacobs, without going into further details, for his *explananda* are mainly the Spanish academies of the eighteenth century, compares the first type of academy to literary *salons*, which is an interesting idea which should be taken into account in future explorations (see Helmut C. Jacobs. *Organisation und Institutionalisierung der Künste und Wissenschaften: Die Akademiegründungen der spanischen Aufklärung in der Tradition der europäischen Akademiebewegung*. Frankfurt: Vervuert, 1996, p. 19).

2 Documentation: The playfulness of statutes

Since they are supposed to testify to a specific *event*, non-permanent *academias* are often quite well documented.[11] However, the textual and social practices that can be found here are more likely to evolve from the medieval tradition of tournaments and jousts, even if the field of *armas* is replaced by the field of *letras*. As for the more permanent gatherings based on statutes and regularity, they are on the contrary very poorly documented. At this point, and since the latter statement may come as a surprise, it is very important to be clear about our understanding of 'documentation,' which differs from that employed by earlier studies of academies in Golden Age Spain. There is no doubt about the existence of permanent academies before 1700, because, as Jacobs has already pointed out, their impact on the literary texts of this period is remarkable.[12] It does, however, make a difference whether the name of an academy is just mentioned once or twice in a book or in a letter, whether fictional or even semi-fictional masterpieces are supposed to draw the portrait of an academy, or whether there are actual documents that can be classed as the textual 'output' of an academy (mainly handwritten *actas*). Our understanding of 'documentation' covers only the latter case. Thus, our study necessarily differs from the studies mentioned above that do not make this discrimination between sources, and therefore consider significantly more academies to be 'documented' than we do. These attempted inventories and surveys are not necessarily obsolete, and they give very useful hints to what may lead to an interesting case study in the future. But, since our study aims for the adoption of a systematic approach within this field of research, we shall accordingly concentrate on cases that can already be traced back to *actas*, statutes, or at least to a specific audience.

The most famous example of *personas eruditas* who met on a regular basis is the Academia de los Nocturnos.[13] This academy was founded in Valencia in

---

11 One of the most famous cases is La Academia del Buen Retiro, a celebration for Felipe IV that took place in 1637. As Sánchez states, there are at least two manuscripts that contain the program of this occasional academy, which can be consulted in the National Libraries of Madrid and Paris (see Sánchez, *Academias literarias*, pp. 134–154; Sánchez himself quotes extensively from these manuscripts).
12 See Jacobs, *Organisation und Institutionalisierung der Künste und Wissenschaften*, p. 23.
13 That this is the most famous case is clear from the significant bibliography dealing with this academy, including not only various scholarly articles, but also modern editions of the *actas* such as: *Cancionero de los Nocturnos de Valencia*, 2 vols., edited by Pedro Salvá Mallén. Valencia: Ferrer de Orga, 1872; *Cancionero de los Nocturnos de Valencia*. Segunda parte, edited by Francisco Martí Grajales. Valencia: Vives y Mora, 1906; *La Navidad de los Nocturnos en 1591*, edited by Arturo Zabala. Valencia: Castalia, 1946; *Actas de la Academia de los Nocturnos*,

1591 and existed until 1594. At least in comparison to tournaments and jousts it can clearly be characterized as a permanent gathering. The manuscript begins with a set of rules, the "Instituciones de la academia de los nocturnos." Most of the items of this text – not to mention its entire form – seem to conform to our idea of a modern academy. The following passage is often supposed to present this impression, which is why we quote it at full length:

> II. Ítem, ordenamos que la Academia se [h]aya de çelebrar en las casas del Ille. don Bernardo Cathalán, nuestro muy caro y muy amado Académico, el qual [h]aya de ser y sea presidente de [e]lla, prestándole desde agora la obedencia que en semejante caso se requiere.
>
> III. Ítem, ordenamos que todos los académicos [h]ayan de tomar el nombre conforme al de la Academia.
>
> IV. Ítem, ordenamos que todos los académicos se junten un día cada semana, que será el miércoles, y que de una semana para otra esté nombrado un lector, el qual sea obligado a leer una licción de aquello que se le encomendare, de la qual resulte a los oyentes muchas erudición y doctrina, y que a los demás académicos les repartan los trabajos conforme sus ingenios y que sea repartición a voluntad del señor Presidente y con el parecer y acuerdo del lector que entonces fuere.
>
> V. Ítem, ordenamos para el buen govierno de la Academia que el señor Presidente [h]aya de nombrar un Consiliario con el qual consulte todas las cosas que huvieren de hazer: assí de repartir los sujetos, como de recibir académicos, como de otras qualesquier cosas tocantes a la Academia. Y que el Consiliario se le dé silla al lado del señor Presidente y al lector, ni más ni menos, pero con condición que la vez que el Consiliario lea no [h]aya de haver más de dos sillos.
>
> VI. Ítem, ordenamos que se [h]aya de elegir un secretario, el qual tenga obligación de escrevir en el libro de la Academia todas las obras que en ella se hizieren, assí en prosa como en verso, las quales se [h]ayan de escrivir en la casa donde se tiene la Academia y no en otra parte, porque no salga el libro de poder del Sor. Presidente.[14]

---

5 vols., edited by José Luis Canet, Evangelina Rodríguez and Josep Lluís Sirera. Valencia: Edicions Alfons el Magnànim, 1988–2000.

14 Quoted in: Pasqual Mas i Usó. *Academias valencianas del barroco: Descripción y diccionario de poetas*. Kassel: Reichenberger, 1999, pp. 60–61. ("II. Further we decree that the Academy is to be hosted at the houses of the illustrious don Bernardo Cathalán, our most beloved Academician, who is to be the Academy's president, by giving him from now on the obedience that is required in such cases. III. Further we decree that all academicians have to take a name compatible with the name of the Academy. IV. Further we decree that all academicians meet once a week, which will be on Wednesdays, and that each week there shall be nominated a lecturer who will be obliged to read a lesson of what is advisable and instructive; and that the work will be distributed to the other academicians according to their spirit and capability, which has to be approved by both the president and the lecturer in charge. V. Further we decree that in order to provide for a good government of the Academy, the president shall nominate a councillor with whom he is to consult about everything that has to be done, such as the distribution of the subjects, the reception of academicians, and other things regarding

What exactly makes these statutes seem so familiar to a modern reader? The Academia de los Nocturnos has a president (item II), Bernardo Cathalán, whose house is where the sessions take place. The academy consists of regular meetings (item IV) which are dedicated to intellectual work ("erudición y doctrina"). The president appoints a councillor (item V) and the members of the academy elect a secretary (item VI). The task of the secretary consists in documenting the 'output' of this academy: He is supposed to write down any piece of work that has been performed within the walls of Bernardo Cathalán's house during the meetings. What we have here is what we expect from an academy, that is, written proof not only of its existence and its set of rules, but also of the literary practices that took place within its meetings. Thus, if the Academia de los Nocturnos is a famous case today, the reason for this fame may stem not only from the fact that it is one of the earliest Spanish academies, but also from the specific quantity and quality of its documentation. It is tempting to consider this academy as a model, as a paradigmatic case even, because from our understanding of an institution it looks familiar.[15] But we should be aware that this may be a teleological way of thinking, especially since *los Nocturnos* are likely to be the *only* case that provides us with this kind and this amount of information. What seems to be a paradigm for this particular period may very well be the exception, and the following example tends to corroborate this hypothesis, although, at first sight, it is very close to the documentation of the *Nocturnos*.

The manuscript in question bears the inscription "Pítima contra la Ociosidad."[16] This title – which can be translated as "remedy for idleness" – states

---

the Academy; and that the councillor shall be seated next to the president and to the lecturer, no more nor less, but with the reservation that when the councillor reads there will be no more than two seats. VI. Further we decree that there is to be elected a secretary, whose obligation will be to inscribe into the book of the Academy every work that has been conceived within its walls, both in prose and in verse, which has to be written in the house where the Academy takes place and not at other places, in order to keep the mastery of the book in the hands of the president." My translation).

15 See Bierbach, *Spanische Akademien vor 1700*, p. 534: "Während die Nocturnos zweifellos den Prototyp der literarischen Akademien Spaniens verkörpern [...]."; A. L. Prieto de Pauly. "El modelo italiano en la formación de las academias literarias españolas del primer barroco: Los 'Nocturnos' como paradigma." *Relaciones culturales entre Italia y España*, edited by E. Giménez, J. A. Ríos and E. Rubio. Alicante: Publicaciones de la Universidad de Alicante, 1995, p. 133–148.

16 The manuscript can be found here: bdh-rd.bne.es/viewer.vm?id=0000100085&page=1. Accessed 13 February 2018. The text has been partly published by Sánchez, *Academias literarias*, p. 253–258, as well as in: *Linajes de Aragón: Revista quincenal ilustrada*, vol. 3, no. 20, 1912, pp. 357–363. It is nevertheless important to have a look at the first five folios of the manuscript to get an idea of its significant material quality.

the self-given aim of the academy, the members of which gathered in the house of Don Gaspar Galcerán de Pinós y Castro, Conde de Guimerá, in June 1608. As is explained on the first pages of the book, there was a specific reason for these gatherings:

> La ociosidad, madre de los vicios, enemiga de la virtud, madrastra de los buenos, encuentro y hazar [sic] de los honestos, padrastro de los recogidos, es la que roe, consume y devora los entendimientos aplicados a lo bueno [...]. Y así todos unánimes y conformes fueron de parecer que se pusiese en ejecución lo propuesto, acordando que dicha junta y congregación se intitulase Pítima Contra la Ociosidad, pues era acudir con remedios saludables al daño que en estas soledades podía hacer.[17]

If the members of *la Pítima* came together in order to resist the dangerous charms of idleness,[18] they also adhered to a set of rules that bears a remarkable resemblance to the statutes of *los Nocturnos*. Both manuscripts begin with a list of paragraphs (*las instituciones*), framing the academic practice the way chartered institutions still do today. In both cases, the members appoint a president, a councillor, and a secretary, the members are given fictional names to enhance the sense of belonging to the academy,[19] and both manuscripts serve to put the 'outcome' of the academician's work into writing. However, where *los Nocturnos* content themselves with thirteen items, the members of *la Pítima* have sixty-three paragraphs that cover nine entire pages of the manuscript. This 'flooding' of the start of the manuscript is actually the noteworthy part of this observation: The appearance of the items on pages two to nine tells us something about how they were conceived. The first ten items form two columns, each column being written on a single page (pages five and six, the recto and verso of one folio). Items 11 to 35 constitute four columns, but this

---

17 Quoted in: Sánchez, *Academias literarias*, pp. 252–253. ("Idleness, mother of the vicious, enemy of virtue, evil stepmother of the good, antagonist of the honest, evil stepfather of the decent, is what gnaws away, consumes, and engulfs the spirit that is dedicated to the good. [...] And so everybody agreed that what had been suggested should be realized, that was to name the company in question *Pítima Contra la Ociosidad* and to find some beneficial cure against the damage that could be done in this solitude." My translation).
18 This passage, constructed on the Renaissance topos of idleness, points to the classical culture of this academy. On the Renaissance topos of idleness see Virginia Krause. *Idle Pursuits: Literature and Oisiveté in the French Renaissance*. Newark: University of Delaware Press, 2003.
19 The 'academic names' are one of the reasons why these Spanish academies are so often linked to Italian academies of the sixteenth century, where this onomastic tradition originates. However, the link between Italy and Spain remains to be explored, at least in a more systematic way than has been done so far. Hence, in this particular study we try not to put too much weight on the Italian connection.

time there are two columns per page (pages seven and eight, the recto and verso of two folios). Item 35 overlaps onto page nine where there is also a short concluding note and the signature of the host, the count of Guimerá. The remaining twenty-eight items now go 'backwards,' being inserted into the free space left by the second column of the statutes (page six) and on pages two to four, where items 45 to 63 fill the space left free next to the preliminary discourse.[20]

What does this disposition of the *instituciones* tell us? The original set of rules obviously comprised only thirty-five paragraphs, since the signature of the count closes the matter. Then something happened that made the members of *la Pítima* feel that they needed some more statutes. But why? The content of items 36 to 63 does not explain anything, and they do not seem to be indispensable either. On the contrary, they seem to have been added for the sheer pleasure of invention, or even for the pleasure of *writing* those statutes, since some of them are rather redundant. The flooding of the manuscript also reveals a certain dynamism, the acceleration of a process that got out of hand. Those *instituciones* undeniably have a playful character, as if inventing the rules for some sort of game eventually *became* the game. The members of *la Pítima*, at least to judge from their manuscript, invented more and more rules that consisted in describing a social practice called *academia*. This brings to mind the meta-game of Urbino that Baldassare Castiglione portrayed in his famous *Libro del cortegiano*.[21] Of course, the noblemen and -women who (allegedly) gathered in the chambers of the duchess of Urbino in the early years of the sixteenth century described and discussed the rules for being the perfect courtier (as opposed to the perfect academician); they also met only three days in a row, whereas *la Pítima* seems to have been active for about six months. Still, there is a resemblance that is at least as convincing as the resemblance the manuscript bears to the book of *los Nocturnos*. As Christine Bierbach has already pointed out,[22] just like Elisabetta Gonzaga, the duchess of Urbino, and her lady-in-waiting, Emilia Pia, the central figures of *la Pítima* are noblewomen, the countess of Guimerá and her mother, the countess of Eril. This

---

[20] This is why the consultation of the manuscript cannot be supplanted by consultation of the published version of the statutes (see note 17).
[21] See Baldassarre Castiglione. *Il Cortegiano*, edited by Amadeo Quondam. Milan: Mondadori, 2002. Of course there are really two 'meta-games' in the *Cortegiano*; the actual game of the courtier ("il più bel gioco che fare si potesse," ibid., p. 28), and the game that led to finding this game ("la scelta del gioco," ibid., p. 19–28). The *instituciones* of *la Pítima* can be read as an allusion to each of them; they are a preliminary act as well as a code of practice.
[22] Bierbach, *Spanische Akademien vor 1700*, p. 535.

aristocratic environment[23] differs from the more urban milieu of *los Nocturnos*, and may perhaps account for the impression of playfulness that arises from the manuscript: Castiglione invented the notion of *sprezzatura* for a kind of relaxed behavior that suits noblemen and -women who would never let themselves be mistaken for scholars.[24] So even when we look at the academy that is – from the viewpoint of documentation – closest to the academy of Valencia, we are obliged to state important differences; indeed, important enough to question the paradigmatic status of the Academia de los Nocturnos mentioned above. And yet they have one last quality in common which brings us to the final issue that a discussion of Golden Age Spanish academies should raise: since the estates of the Guimerá are located near Zaragoza, the gatherings of *la Pítima* as well as the meetings of *los Nocturnos* took place in the eastern territories of Spain, under the crown of Aragón.

---

23 Don Gaspar Galcerón de Pinós y Castro, Conde de Guimerá belongs to the higher aristocracy. His grandmother for example, Doña Luisa de Borja, Duquesa de Villahermosa, was a grandee's daughter, born into the famous house of Borja and married into the house of Aragón. His grandmother and his wife Doña Isabel Inès de Eril are both portrayed by Diego Ignacio Parada in his work about *Escritoras y Eruditas Españolas* (Madrid: Manuel Minuesa, 1881, pp. 184–186 and p. 212–213). For Parada it is Doña Isabel Inès de Eril who has to be accounted responsible for the foundation of *la Pítima*, even though the Conde de Guimerá was himself a man of culture ("distinguido escritor, erudito y anticuario," ibid., p. 212) and close to Vincencio Juan de Lastanosa.

24 One may argue that the *actas* of *los Nocturnos* also reveal a 'playful' character as they have a tendency to mockery (see José María Ferri Coll. "Burlas y chanzas en las academias literarias del Siglo de Oro: Los *Nocturnos* de Valencia." *Actas del XIII Congreso de la Asociación Internacional de Hispanistas*, 4 vols., edited by Carlos Alvar and Florencio Sevilla. Madrid: Castalia, 2000, vol. 1, pp. 327–335), but this is the rough tone of satire, more likely to be encountered in a masculine environment. This is actually the main difference between the two circles, because, as has been shown by José María Ferri Coll ("El *Libro* de la Academia de los Nocturnos." *Anales de literatura española*, no. 20, 2008, pp. 189–210), the community of *los Nocturnos* consists of both noblemen *and* commoners, but there is no woman among them. They seem closer to the Italian author Stefano Guazzo than to Castiglione. In his famous book *La conversazione civile* (1574), Guazzo pictures an ideal of academic brotherhood that is independent of female influence.

3 Territory: Aragonese *académicos* and *caballeros*

It may be no coincidence that academies – in the sense of permanent gatherings – are better documented for the Aragonese than for the Castilian area.[25] The problem that must be addressed here is the political tension between those territories. At the beginning of the seventeenth century, the cities of Aragón were eager to defend themselves against the loss of independence on both the political and the cultural level. Significantly, the constitution they wanted to defend was one in which Aragón was almost entirely governed by traditional urban corporations. To illustrate how this context may well have motivated the founding of academies, we will examine one last example, which refers to an academy in Zaragoza and was written by the poet and playwright Lupercio Leonardo de Argensola.

Among literary historians, "los discursos de Argensola" – like "las institucíones de la Academia de los Nocturnos" – are famous for allegedly providing a paradigm of the ideal, that is the humanist, Spanish academy. Although the humanist idea of the perfect brotherhood of learned people certainly does inform the whole text, this paradigmatic status is – once again – questionable. First of all, Argensola is clearly addressing an audience that demands diplomatic skills. He is speaking to the members of a group called *academia* in order to convince them of their civil duties and responsibilities. In doing so, he claims that history is the key concept of self-respect and – as we would say today – of 'cultural identity':

> E ignorar uno las historias de su tierra y de sus mayores es ignorancia, tan culpable como no haberse visto jamás al espejo, ni saber en su imaginación qué manera de rostro tiene, y aun peor, porque es como ignorar los dedos de sus manos, y los miembros de que consta su cuerpo."[26]

---

[25] Obviously, it seems perfectly possible that this is (also) due to its close relationship with Italy. However, since it is precisely the link between Italian and Spanish academies that needs to be explored eventually, we should not jump to conclusions yet. All we know for sure at present is that there are three early cases of permanent Spanish academies whose *actas* have been preserved; and that all three cases – the *academias* of Valencia, Zaragoza, as depicted above, and Huesca (see Sánchez, *Academias literarias*, p. 261–266) – relate to the territories belonging to the "crown of Aragón." In addition to these *actas*, there is the famous case of Argensola's *discorsos* written for "an academy of Zaragoza" that will be discussed now.

[26] Quoted in: Sánchez, *Academias literarias*, p. 239–240. ("And to ignore the history of one's territory and ancestors is ignorance, as blameworthy as if you had never seen yourself in the mirror, or as if you could not even imagine what your face looks like, or even worse, because it would be like ignoring the fingers of your hands and the parts of your body." My translation).

For Argensola, history should be at the centre of this academy's activity; he even considers it the matrix of knowledge: "[...] pero la historia, con afabilidad y dulzura, de todos toma lo mejor, y es, por decirlo brevemente, un diversorio donde todas la ciencias y las artes reposan; enseña sin cansancio (como dije que lo hacía esta junta), hace que en pocos años vivamos muchos años [...]."[27] The last sentence puts history on a par with philosophy, or at least echoes Seneca, who claims in *De brevitate vitae* that the only way to have a long life is to pass time with philosophy. Still, it is history, not philosophy, that seems to be more likely to capture the audience's attention. It is like a *mise en abîme* of the whole idea of *academia*, or at least of this particular academy. So who are the men whom the author of this speech is addressing? Whilst there is no way of knowing for sure, there is enough evidence to make the following assumption:

Argensola seems to be addressing a group of young, perhaps hot-blooded noblemen, who are not so much interested in philosophy as in politics. Talking about history can be considered an attempt to 'meet halfway,' nobility being inextricably linked to the history of one's own family and territory. At one point, Argensola even addresses his audience directly by calling them *caballeros*: "Considerando yo que los más de vuesas mercedes son caballeros aficionados al ejercicio militar y que para este fin hay en esta ciudad fundada la antigua y nobilísima cofradía de San Jorge ..."[28]

The mention of the fraternity of Saint George, an actual chivalric fraternity apparently founded in 1505,[29] is very interesting. The members of this fraternity consider themselves to be not only noblemen, but knights; one of their most important activities is the organization of tournaments and jousts. But what is even more important for our purposes is that in 1591 this *cofradía* had been fighting alongside the Aragonese rebels in the context of what is known as the *Alteraciónes de Aragón*. These *alteraciónes* can be understood as a mini-Fronde at the end of which Felipe II took away a number of privileges (*Fueros del*

---

27 Ibid., p. 240. ("[...] but history, with affability and sweetness, takes the best of everything; to put it briefly: it is a reservoir for arts and sciences; it teaches without exhaustion [as I said that it is done in this assembly], its effect is that in only a few years we live many years [...]"; my translation).

28 Ibid., p. 240. ("When I come to think of the fact that most of you honorable gentlemen are knights who are enthusiastic about military exercises, and that to this end there has been founded, in this town, the venerable and most noble fraternity of Saint George ..."; my translation).

29 The abovementioned Cofradía de San Jorge is the predecessor of an existing fraternity called the Real Maestranza de Caballeria de Zaragoza (see www.rmcz.com/historia1.htm. Accessed 13 February 2018).

Reino) from the kingdom of Aragón and its towns. When the Aragonese rebels had lost the battle and Felipe II granted forgiveness, he excluded from this act of generosity numerous members of the Cofradía de caballeros de San Jorge.[30]

We do not know exactly when Argensola wrote his *discursos*, but they are only a couple of years away from the *Alteraciónes de Aragón*.[31] The idea of an "academia de Zaragoza" at a time when the Cofradía was still enfeebled by the royal disapproval could be perceived – from the authorities' point of view – as a threat. To temper this threat, Argensola not only advises his pupils not to publish any poetry that might comment on the political situation in Aragón,[32] but also draws a 'counter-picture' of their gatherings that is taken from the humanist idea of an academy. The problem is to reconcile this picture with the self-perception of his audience, that is of the *académicos* who are actually mainly *caballeros*. The whole text is very thoughtfully constructed, and the sugarcoating of philosophy by calling it history is just one example of this. Argensola has to convince the members of a more chivalric than scholarly assembly that it would be better to leave the field of *armas* in order to defend

---

30 See ibid.
31 Argensola as well as his brother Bartolomé Leonardo de Argensola were very aware of the rebellion, as we can see from the fact that both of them wrote about it (see Lupercio Leonardo de Argensola. *Informacion de los sucesos del Reino de Aragón en los años de 1590 y 1591*. Madrid: Imprenta real, 1808; Bartolomé Leonardo de Argensola. *Alteraciones populares de Zaragoza año 1591*, edited by Gregorio Colás Latorre. Zaragoza: Institución Fernando el Católico, 1996).
32 "[...] Jamás han faltado delatores y malsines: de esta verdad tenemos experiencia, porque los señores Virrey y Justicia de Aragón, mal informado, hablaban de esta junta aplicándole ciertos versos y libelos, y que aquí se censuraba el gobierno público. Quisieron saber de mí la verdad; y como tiene tanta fuerza, no solamente perdieron esta opinión, pero alabando lo que aquí se hace, creen que la república tiene en vuesas mercedes defensores de virtud y maestros que, con su ejemplo, enseñarán a cada cual a contenarse dentro de sus límites." Quoted in: Sánchez, *Academias literarias*, p. 241. ("There are always traitors and maleficent people: we know this from experience, because the viceroy and the chief judge of Aragón, misinformed, spoke of this assembly, to whom they ascribed certain verses and pamphlets in which the government is criticized. They asked me for the truth; and since the truth has so much power, not only do they not think this any more, but, praising what is done here, they believe that you are virtuous defenders of the commonwealth, and that what is taught here ensures that everyone is content and stays in his place." My translation).
What Argensola probably had in mind here are the *pasquines* of 1591, which he does not want the literary output of this academy to be (mis)taken for. On the *pasquines* of 1591 see: Paloma Bravo. "El Pasquín: Condiciones de escritura, diffusión y recepción en la Revuelta Aragonesa de 1591." *L'écrit dans l'Espagne du siècle d'or: pratiques et représentations*, edited by Pedro M. Cátedra, Maria Luisa López-Vidriero and Agustin Redondo. Salamanca: Publications de la Sorbonne/Ediciones de la Universidad de Salamanca, 1999, pp. 33–42.

their Aragonese identity on the field of *letras*. This is why the humanist idea of an academy impregnates the whole speech, even if Argensola cannot put too much emphasis on the Italian model: "En Italia ha habido y hay Academias famosas; más ¿para qué buscamos ejemplos extranjeros?"[33]

Thus the author claims that, when it comes to *academias famosas*, there is a Spanish tradition you can draw on. But why is this tradition so hard for us to grasp? This question brings us back to the terminological problem mentioned at the beginning of this paper: evidently Argensola can rely on the Spanish meaning of *academia* in the sense of a non-permanent gathering where the idea of a medieval, chivalric contest is still alive. His audience is likely to respond to this meaning rather than to the humanist model that can be found in Italy. Torn between poetics and politics, between *armas* and *letras*, this particular academy leans clearly towards the former, even if the author of the *discursos* strongly recommends the latter. For an academy closely linked to a corporation that has fallen from grace – the Cofradía de caballeros de San Jorge –, it is important that its institutional character, where the humanist model is fused with the Spanish tradition of jousts and tournaments, should spring from intellectual concerns.

4 Conclusion

Having examined three important cases of well documented early Spanish academies – in the sense of permanent gatherings – we can make the following assumption: there is no paradigm, no 'ideal academy' in Golden Age Spain, let alone a wide range of humanist academies imitating the Italian model. This is what the attempted inventories of Sánchez and King as well as more recently established surveys of early Spanish academies do not allow us to see, for they are focused on continuity. The presumption of continuity is built on a model of development where the academies of Renaissance Italy form the starting point, and the chartered corporation of the RAE, conceived on the basis of the French model, is considered the end point. This is what makes the *actas* of La Academia de los Nocturnos look like a paradigmatic case that proves continuity. The problem with this approach is that it may take for granted what needs to be thoroughly examined.

---

[33] Quoted in: Sánchez, *Academias literarias*, p. 240. ("In Italy they had and still have famous Academies; but why search for foreign examples?" My translation).

Early Spanish academies are cultural knots, where different, sometimes even antagonistic elements are tied together: noblemen and scholars, permanent and occasional gatherings, medieval and humanist traditions, and last but not least poetics and politics. Still, it is important to keep in mind that we have to look carefully at the social and textual practices linked to those 'knots.' We do not yet know much about their institutional nature, and even the existence of rules and statutes does not automatically transform them into literary corporations, as we can see from the playful character of La Pítima contra la Ociosidad as well as from how Lupercio de Argensola's diplomatic skills are required to address the members of an academy in Zaragoza. Does this mean that these social and textual practices are not a valuable contribution to our understanding of the institutional development of early European academies? Actually they are, even though they demand careful consideration: On the one hand, they do not lead directly to what we think we know, that is literary academies being authorities in poetic concerns. On the other hand, the diversity of these cases does not equal arbitrariness. There has to be a model – the statutes of *los Nocturnos* and *la Pítima* are too alike not to share some kind of predecessor –, and this model is likely to derive from Italy. However, this virtual Italian model is probably not a homogeneous phenomenon either. There is a big difference between Castiglione's rules for the ideal courtier and Stefano Guazzo's reflections on civil conversation to begin with, let alone between the actual academies in Siena, Florence, or Casale, for instance. And in Spain as well as in other countries, those Italian books and rules and playful institutions tend to blend with traditions that go back to the Middle Ages, eventually leading to a manifold landscape of social and textual practices. To study those landscapes in Spain, France, Germany, and even in Italy is not an obsolete task, for it allows us to know more about the early modern European cultural net of which academies like these are an essential part.

Franz Gratl
The Role of Music in Folk Drama: An Investigation Based on Tyrolean Sources

1 Introduction

A brief overview of the secondary literature dealing with folk drama reveals a significant lack of interest in musical aspects. On the part of theater and literary scholars, it is primarily the functional aspects of music, if any, that are taken into consideration. On the part of musicologists, music in folk drama has played a marginal role in research, something that can be said about theater music in general. In the article "Schauspielmusik" (stage music) in the most important German music encyclopedia, *Die Musik in Geschichte und Gegenwart*, Detlef Altenburg states: "Demgegenüber gilt in der deutschen Musikwissenschaft Schauspielmusik weithin als unergiebiges Randphänomen der Musikgeschichte."[1] There are some exceptions: Medieval folk drama, especially liturgical and mystery plays, have attracted music scholars from the nineteenth century to the present. Another example of a quite well-investigated tradition is Viennese folk plays of the nineteenth century. The article "Volkstheater" in the *Österreichisches Musiklexikon*,[2] for example, is almost completely focused on Vienna. As a special field that cannot be appropriately described as "folk play," but which was a major source of influence, Jesuit drama also attracted interest quite early.[3]

---

[1] Detlef Altenburg and Lorenz Jensen. "Schauspielmusik." *Die Musik in Geschichte und Gegenwart*, 2nd ed., Sachteil, vol. 8. Kassel et al.: Bärenreiter, 1998, pp. 1035–1049, p. 1035. Translation: "In comparison to that [to the state of research regarding stage music in Renaissance and Baroque France, Italy, and Spain], German musicology has considered stage music as an unrewarding, marginal phenomenon."
[2] Otto G. Schindler and Rudolf Flotzinger. "Volkstheater." *Österreichisches Musiklexikon*, vol. 5. Wien: Verlag der Österreichischen Akademie der Wissenschaften, 2006, pp. 2556–2558.
[3] See Johannes Müller. *Das Jesuitendrama in den Ländern deutscher Zunge: Vom Anfang (1555) bis zum Hochbarock (1665)*. Augsburg: B. Filser, 1930 (Schriften zur deutschen Literatur, vol. 7/8). Relevant for the Tyrol: Ellen Hastaba. "'Jesuitenspiele' in Innsbruck (1562–1773)." *Musikgeschichte Tirols*, edited by Kurt Drexel and Monika Fink. Innsbruck: Universitätsverlag Wagner, 2004 (Schlern-Schriften, vol. 322), vol. II, pp. 375–413; inspired by the Jesuit tradition, the Benedictines too cultivated school plays, e.g. in the Gymnasium of Meran, run by the monks of Marienberg; see Franz Gratl. "Musik zu Innsbrucker und Meraner Schulspielen: Quellen aus dem Benediktinerstift Marienberg (Südtirol) in Konkordanz zu den gedruckten Periochen." *Der frühe Buchdruck in der Region: Neue Kommunikationswege in Tirol und seinen Nachbarländern: Beiträge der wissenschaftlichen Tagung in der Bibliothek des Tiroler Landesmuseums Ferdinandeum am 23. und 24. Oktober 2014 anläßlich der Ausstellung „Druckfrisch:*

From pioneers such as the writers Ignaz Vinzenz Zingerle and Ludwig von Hörmann onwards,[4] Tyrolean folk drama of the sixteenth to nineteenth century, which will be the focus of this paper, has been collected and researched. The research and publications of the historian and ethnologist Anton Dörrer[5] are of crucial importance; the leading figures of more recent scientific research on folk drama are Eugen Thurnher, Ekkehard Schönwiese, and Ellen Hastaba.[6] The substantial publications of these authors can be taken as a valuable guide to research and a tool to locate the sources; Ellen Hastaba has published a complete list of relevant sources preserved in the Tiroler Landesmuseum Ferdinandeum.[7] Neither Zingerle and Hörmann, nor Dörrer paid much attention to musical aspects; the same can be said of Schönwiese and Hastaba, though the latter at least stresses the importance of musical *intermezzi* in folk drama and mentions some significant sources from the Upper Inn Valley.

Apart from the fact that none of these scholars was a musicologist or had a special interest in music, this neglect can also be explained by the nature of the sources. Usually, folk drama is preserved in the form of handwritten scripts intended for practical use by the performers. The use of music is indicated in different ways, which will be discussed later in this paper. The scripts are not musical sources as such. If genuine musical sources were used in performance, which would mean that notated music would have been played from (presumably handwritten) musical parts, they evidently have not been preserved together with the scripts. In the case of the Tiroler Landesmuseum Ferdinandeum, the scripts, as written sources, would have been integrated into the museum library, while the score and parts would have been transferred to the music collection. The biggest problem is the lack of musical sources, if we compare the situation to the scripts. Some recent findings shed a new light on this issue.

Der Innsbrucker Wagner-Verlag und der Buchdruck in Tirol", edited by Roland Sila. Innsbruck: Universitätsverlag Wagner, 2016 (Schlern-Schriften, 366), pp. 283–302.

[4] Both Zingerle and Hörmann dealt with folk drama in connection with their investigations of Tyrolean rural life and folk customs. Many scripts preserved in the library of the Tiroler Landesmuseum Ferdinandeum Innsbruck came from Hörmann's private collection.

[5] Dörrer published an impressive corpus of articles dealing with folk drama.

[6] Eugen Thurnher. *Tiroler Drama und Tiroler Theater*. Innsbruck et al.: Tyrolia, 1969; Ekkehard Schönwiese. *Das Volksschauspiel im nördlichen Tirol. Renaissance und Barock*. Wien: Verlag der Österreichischen Akademie der Wissenschaften, 1975 (Theatergeschichte Österreichs, vol. II: Tirol, no. 3); Ellen Hastaba. *Das Volksschauspiel im Oberinntal*. Diss. Innsbruck, 1986.

[7] Ellen Hastaba. "Theater in Tirol. Spielbelege in der Bibliothek des Tiroler Landesmuseums Ferdinandeum." *Veröffentlichungen des Tiroler Landesmuseums Ferdinandeum*, vols. 75/76, 1995/1996, pp. 233–343.

But let us return to some questions that have already been touched upon: If music was part of a performance of folk drama, what kind of music was it? Was it written down, or perhaps just improvised? Was it real "folk music," in analogy to folk drama? Was it newly composed or pre-existing music? What was the functional role of music in folk drama?

One can imagine that, given that folk drama is a vast and varied field, the answers cannot be generalized, but it seems useful to start with the last point, the functional role. Theater music is, above all, functional music: It is usually applied to mark and to accompany specific moments in drama – the overall beginning, the end, the beginning and end of the several acts, entries and exits of actors, and so on. But it can also be used to elevate crucial scenes by the way in which spoken words are replaced by sung words. The influence of opera and Jesuit drama can be illustrated by the introduction of a completely musical prologue, and operatic influence further by the insertion of musical *intermezzi*.

2 Indications concerning music in non-musical sources

In the following, I will present some characteristic examples to show how music is indicated in the sources for folk plays from the region.

2.1 The Joseph Play of Axams (1677/78), TLMF Bibliothek FB 32070

In this manuscript, which was written by "Joseph Maurer, und Hanns Dollinger, beede der Zeit wonhafft zu Axambs" (i.e. living in Axams, a village some 15 kilometers west of Innsbruck) about 1677/78, music is frequently indicated, but not further specified. "Mussica" accompanies the exit of actors and the end of scenes. The standard formula for the indication of music is: "Mussica / [e.g. Joseph] trit ab". This information recurs very frequently; therefore it can be assumed that the music was short and merely functional, perhaps even improvised. The script contains no information about the performers or the scoring of the music, which must have been instrumental music because we have no sung texts. Not even the comprehensive and extensive list of persons acting in the Joseph play of Axams, which is attached to the manuscript, mentions musicians.

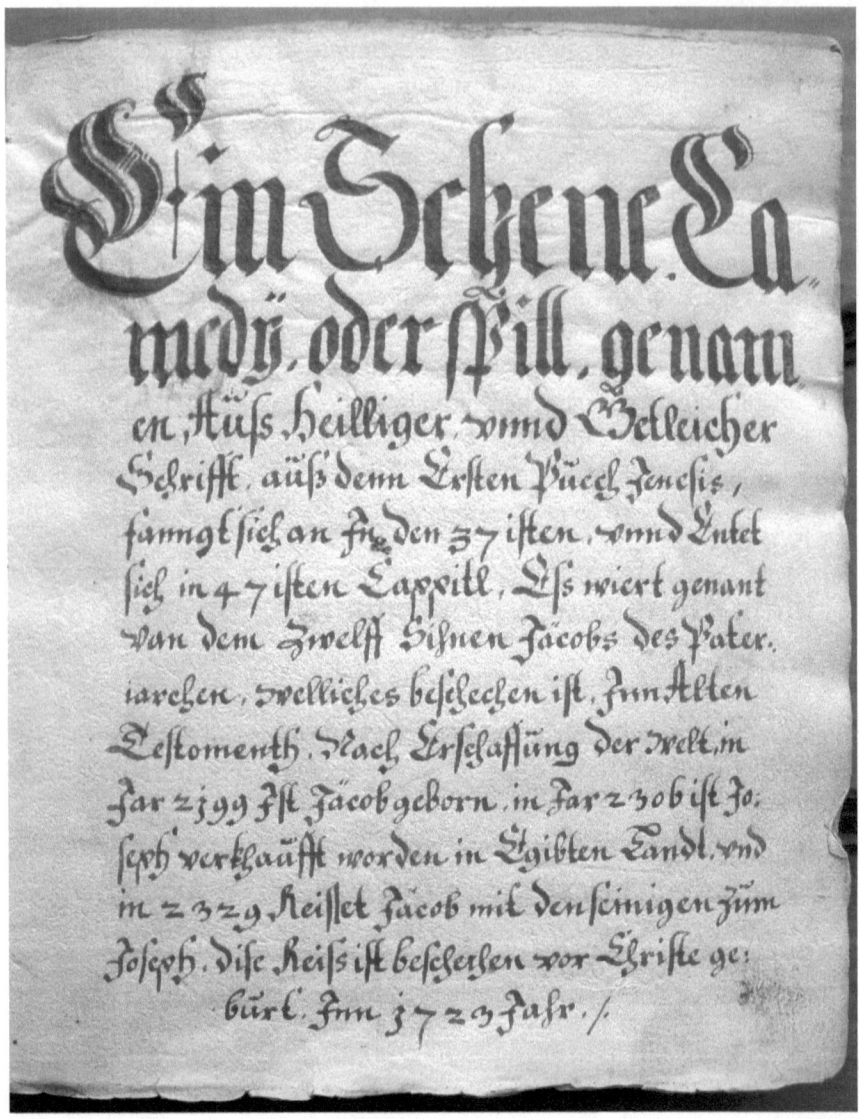

Fig. 1: Joseph Play of Axams (1677/78), TLMF Bibliothek FB 32070, title page.

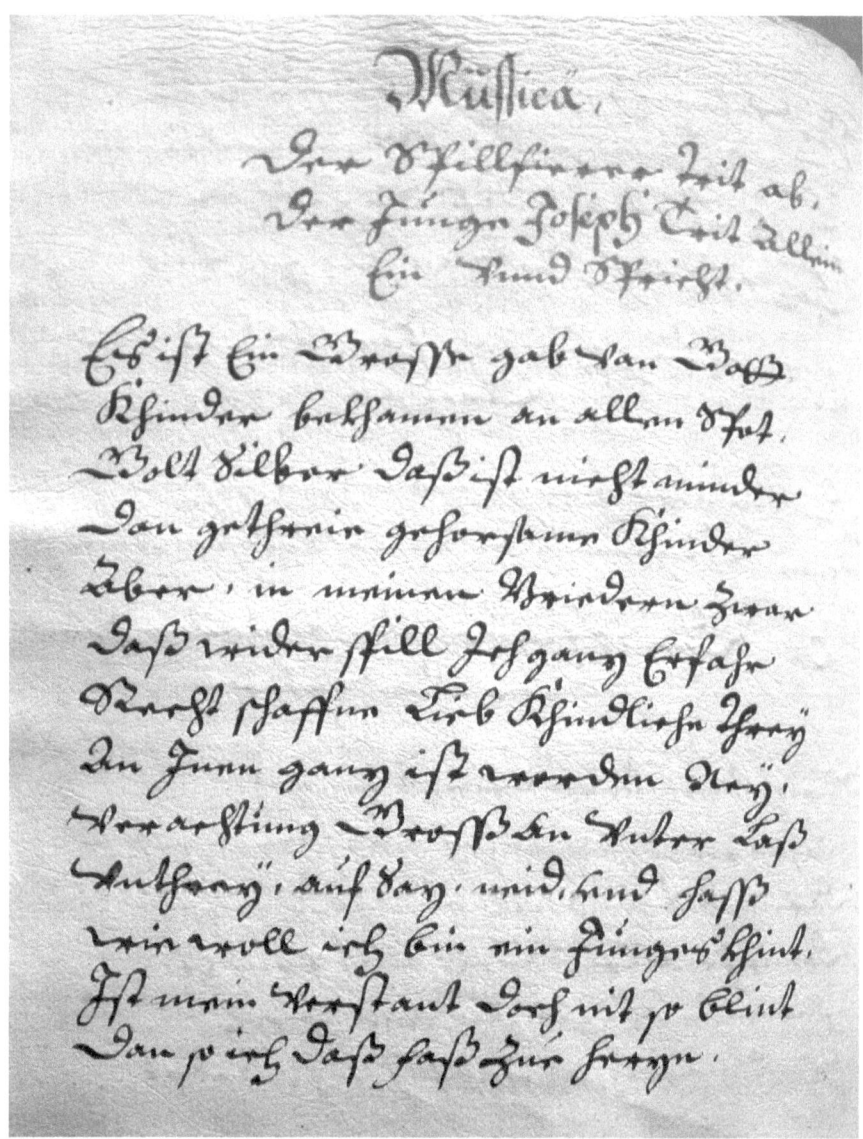

Fig. 2: Joseph Play of Axams (1677/78), TLMF Bibliothek FB 32070, detail: reference to "Mussica" accompanying the exit of the "Spielführer".

2.2 The Christmas / Three Kings Play, Matrei, eighteenth century, TLMF Bibliothek FB 32100

This play contains a rather extended musical scene which is dedicated to the episode of Joseph and Mary Asking for Lodging, a recurring theme in Tyrolean folk tradition. The musical episode bears the character of an *intermezzo* – it divides the play into two parts, in just the way comic *intermezzi* divided *opere serie* into two parts in the eighteenth century. The scene has distinct musical sections. Some sections are designated as "Recit.", an abbreviation for *Recitativo*, a common musical technique of "elevated speaking": the voice follows the rhythm of spoken language, but has fixed tone pitches, while one or more accompanying instruments mark the harmonic shifts. Recitative is a development by Italian composers active around 1600 (*recitar cantando*, monodic style), and is crucial for all the important genres of vocal music in the baroque period and beyond, above all for opera. Other sections are designated as "Aria" or "Duetto". The play is written in rhymed verse, but the "Aria" and "Duetto" sections are emphasized by a different layout – the lines ending with the rhymed words are arranged one below the other, as the following example shows:

> Maria
> Recit:
> *Ach wie so sehr ist mir das Herz, vor lauter Angst und großen Schmerz, betriebet, weil ich gar allzusehr in Gott, so ist mein Herr verliebet.*
>
> Aria
> *Ey dann Joseph laß uns wagen*
> *Um ein Herbrig umzufragen*
> *Schau! Ob eine findest bald,*
> *Und dich nicht zu lang aufhalt.*
> *Dan es ist bald an der Zeit,*
> *daß der Heyland uns erfreit.*

The musical intermezzo is rather long: It contains seven recitatives and eleven arias. The play ends with another "Aria". It is not clear whether this final section is intended to be sung by the "Engl", the role which has spoken the precedent words. It could also be a kind of concluding chorus, perhaps even including the audience, since the final "Aria" has strophic form and resembles a (hitherto unidentified) common Christmas carol. There are eighteenth-century plays beginning, if not ending, with hymn-like songs: Ellen Hastaba mentions a "Hymn to St. Genoveva" to be sung by "all the actors" at the beginning of a folk play from Mieming,[8] and the Nikolausspiel from Mutters

---

[8] Hastaba, *Das Volksschauspiel im Oberinntal*, pp. 46–47.

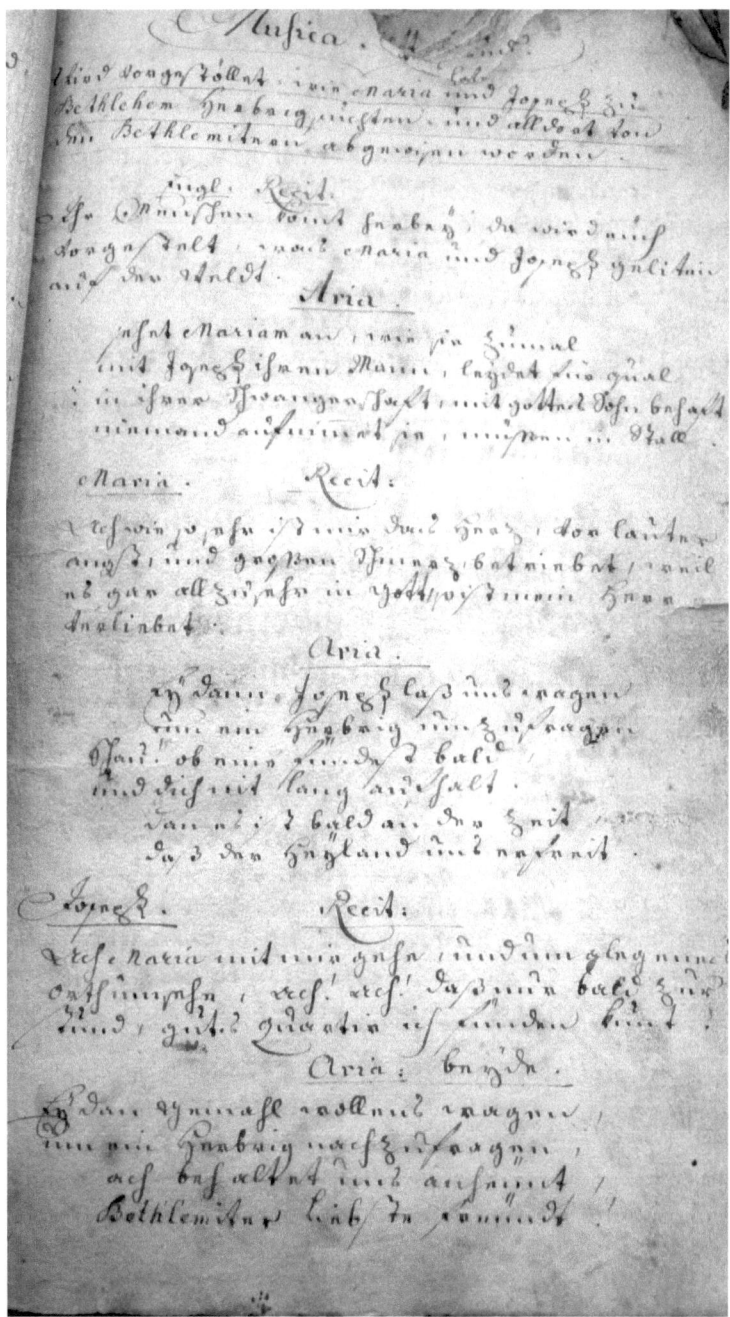

Fig. 3: Christmas / Three Kings Play, Matrei, eighteenth century, TLMF Bibliothek FB 32100, detail: musical intermezzo.

(1745) includes a strophic "Bith Ruef Vor den Spil" (Call for Mercy before the start).⁹

But let us return to the Christmas/Three Kings Play from Matrei. What do we learn about the music? The musical sources connected with the folk play seem to have been lost. We do not know exactly what the music sounded like, who performed, or who composed it. What we do know is that common musical forms were used – recitative, aria, and duetto – and that they were used in quite the same way as in existing compositions belonging to what could be described as "art music" of the eighteenth century. The play obviously does *not* call for genuine folk music. An observation is worth making: recitative, aria, and duet are the forms used in another genre of theater music: in Jesuit drama.

3 A non-musical source – and a supplementary musical one: The Mariahilf Play, eighteenth century, TLMF Bibliothek W 317/4, and a newly discovered music manuscript from Marienberg / South Tyrol

Here we have a situation similar to Jesuit drama: The sung texts and the spoken text are separated. In Jesuit drama, in addition to the "periochs" which are scripts containing the *argomento*, a summary of the plot, and lists of the roles and actors, often also the *Prologus and Chori Musici* was printed, i.e. the sung texts of the musical parts of the drama, which usually stood at the beginning and separated the several acts as *entr'actes*. The handwritten script of the Mariahilf Play preserved in the Ferdinandeum has a typically baroque, extensive title page, which includes the specification: "Die music hat componirt. der kunstreiche Herr Blasius Nezer, organist zu ampas". Here we have an indication of the composer. Sacred works by this Blasius Ne(t)zer can be found in the music archive of the Tiroler Landesmuseum Ferdinandeum. Recently Annemarie Bösch-Niederer found new documents concerning this composer and his family.¹⁰ She found out that Blasius Netzer (1728–1785) was the grandfather of

---

9 Ibid., pp. 8–49.
10 Annemarie Bösch-Niederer. "Vergessene Talente: Die Musikerfamilie Nezer (Netzer) in Bludenz." *Montfort: Zeitschrift für Geschichte Vorarlbergs*, vol. 64, no. 2, 2012, pp. 77–86.

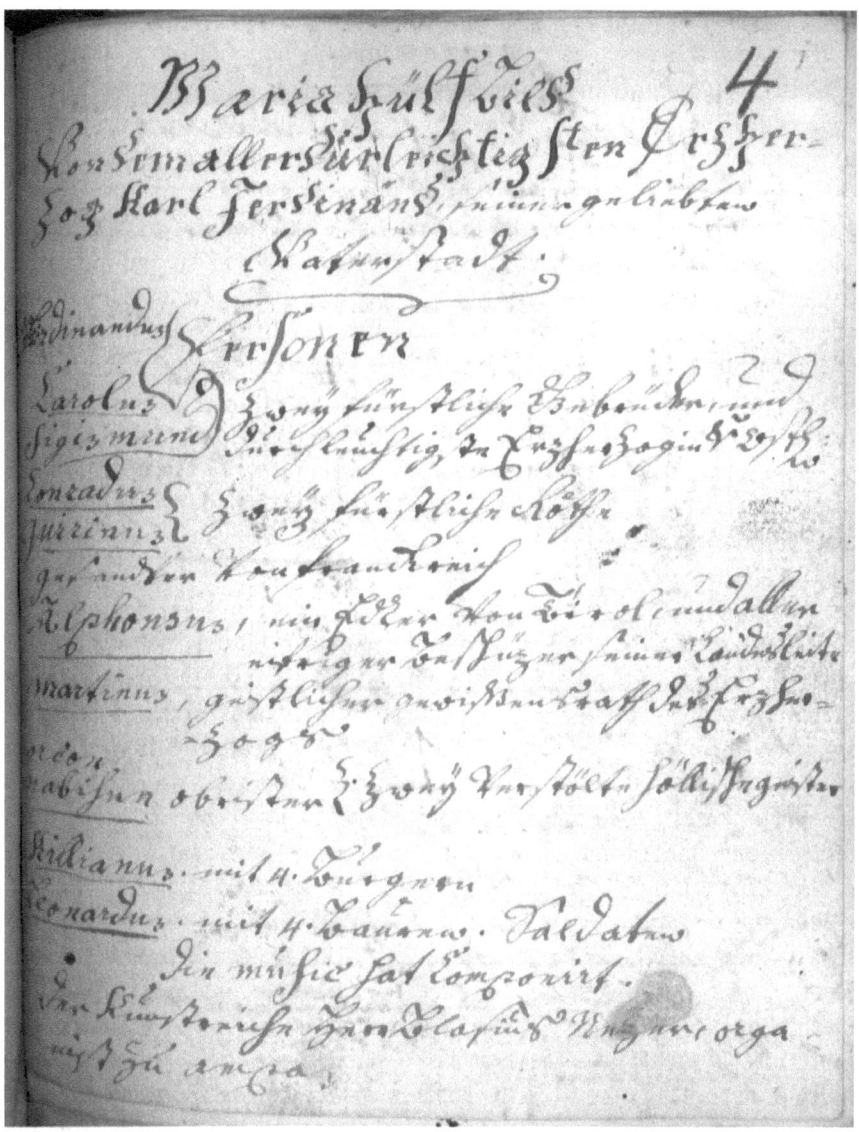

Fig. 4: Mariahilf Play, eighteenth century, TLMF Bibliothek W 317/4, title page.

the famous nineteenth-century Tyrolean composer Josef Netzer (1808–1864) from Zams. Blasius Netzer was active as teacher and organist in Ampass from 1751 to 1766.

His music to the Mariahilf Play has not come down to us, and Blasius Netzer's sacred music preserved in the Ferdinandeum and also in the Swiss Benedictine monastery of Müstair does not allow us to say anything about the style of his theater music, but there is another source which could give an impression: In the Benedictine monastery of Marienberg in the Upper Vinschgau (South Tyrol / Italy), I was lucky to find a treasury of music manuscripts of the late seventeenth to the late eighteenth century which contains sacred music, occasional music for festivities such as New Year and the nameday of the abbot, music to school plays for the Benedictine gymnasium in Meran, and other theater music.[11] Among the musical sources to plays that cannot be connected to the tradition of school plays in Meran, there is a remarkable, though incomplete set of parts belonging to an unidentified play which contained the roles "Vorsichtigkeit", "Liebe," "Eifer," "Tod," and "Teufel".

The music is by Blasius Ne(t)zer ("composuit Nezer") again, who, after some years in Bludenz, served as an organist in the village of Tschengls not far from Marienberg, an important pilgrimage destination in the eighteenth century. Netzer was in Tschengls from 1775 to 1779. We do not know whether the play and its music were performed in Marienberg, or perhaps in one of the surrounding villages; it is impossible to separate monastic theater tradition and school plays from folk-play tradition, since these three phenomena influenced each other strongly. But we can take this manuscript as a valuable source with regard to the style of Blasius Netzer's theater music. Again, we have recitatives, arias, duets, and one concluding chorus. The scoring includes strings, a pair of french horns, and figured bass (*basso continuo*), a standard scoring for monastic music as well as rural sacred music in the eighteenth century. The arias are in a galant *Singspiel* style, which is also typical of late eighteenth-century music in South Germany and Austria. It can be assumed that this was also the common style for music in eighteenth- and early nineteenth-century folk plays. Netzer is representative of the strong tradition of teacher-organists who served as the "general servants" for all musical needs in the rural Tyrol. Many of these teacher-organists were also composers, sometimes of remarkable ability.[12] This leads to the assumption that this group of musicians was primarily responsible for theater music in folk plays. There is some further evidence. Ellen Hastaba mentions the Holofernes *entr'acte* in the

---

11 See Gratl, "Musik zu Innsbrucker und Meraner Schulspielen."
12 See Franz Gratl. "Quellen zur ländlichen 'Schullehrermusik' des 19. Jahrhunderts in der Musiksammlung des Tiroler Landesmuseums Ferdinandeum." *Jahrbuch des RISM-Österreich* (Veröffentlichungen des RISM-Österreich, series A, vol. 14). Wien: Verlag Der Apfel, 2010, pp. 65–86.

The Role of Music in Folk Drama —— 195

Fig. 5: Music to an unidentified (folk) play, Marienberg Monastery, music archive, vocal Bass part (role: "Teufel"), detail: beginning of an Aria.

Antichrist Play from Silz: the music was composed by Josef Abenthung (1779–1860), teacher, organist, band leader, freedom fighter in the Napoleonic wars, farmer, merchant, and very productive composer.[13] The music to the passion play of Telfs (1812 and 1814) was composed by Wilhelm Lechleitner (1779–1827), choirmaster of the South Tyrolean Augustine abbey of Neustift up to the closing of the monastery by the Bavarian government, and, by the time he composed the music for Telfs, music teacher at the Royal Bavarian Gymnasium in Innsbruck.[14] Neither Abenthung nor Lechleitner had a strong connection to real folk music – in their works, they followed the models of "elevated" contemporary sacred and secular music, often in its rural form which proved very popular in South Germany and Austria in the eighteenth and nineteenth century. Lechleitner's ideal was the music of the Viennese classics: he was a "fan" of Joseph Haydn.[15]

4 Literary and pictorial sources

Finally, I would like to mention two examples of sources other than scripts and music manuscripts. One is the drawing by Jakob Placidus Altmutter, "Bauerntheater in der Höttinger Au," ca. 1809 (Tiroler Landesmuseum Ferdinandeum, Bibliothek, FB 4510/42b). Despite its origin in the first decade of the nineteenth century, the depiction represents folk drama in its typical form, perpetuating a baroque tradition. The clothing of the actors on stage is very baroque, with costumes *all'antica*, common in baroque and classical opera. The audience appears to be mixed in its social composition, with some people looking more like peasants and others with a bourgeois appearance. The musicians are quite prominent. They wear traditional costumes. They form an ensemble of the following instruments: two violins, flute (or *Schwegel*, a traditional type of flute), and double bass. These instruments were used in various musical genres, from

---

[13] Hastaba, *Das Volksschauspiel im Oberinntal*, p. 27. With regard to Josef Abenthung, see Franz Gratl. "Josef Abenthungs 'Pracktisches Handbuch für Cantor und Organisten': Eine neu entdeckte Quelle zur kirchenmusikalischen Praxis in Tiroler Dorfkirchen in der ersten Hälfte des 19. Jahrhunderts." *Veröffentlichungen des Tiroler Landesmuseums Ferdinandeum*, vol. 86, 2006, pp. 223–244.
[14] Hastaba, *Das Volksschauspiel im Oberinntal*, p. 27.
[15] In the "Sanctus" of his *Pastoral Mass for Christmastide* ("Pastorell-Meße"), Lechleitner cites Haydn's popular *"Surprise" Symphony No. 94*; two movements in this Mass setting are contrafacta of arias from Haydn's oratorio *The Seasons*. For a recording of Lechleitner's Mass, see: CD *Tiroler Weihnachtskonzert 2002*. Innsbruck: Institut für Tiroler Musikforschung, 2003.

church music to folk music. Altmutter's drawing is interesting because he clearly indicates that the musicians played from notated music. Genuine folk music would not have been written down – again, evidence for the assumption that the music in folk drama was composed and preserved in music manuscripts.

An interesting literary source on Tyrolean folk drama is the autobiography of the Italian musician and composer Giacomo Gotifredo Ferrari (Rovereto 1763 – London 1842).[16] Ferrari attended the gymnasium in Meran and lived in the Benedictine abbey of Marienberg in the 1780s; his autobiography offers lively descriptions of Tyrolean everyday life and customs. Ferrari describes a performance of a folk play on the Biblical theme of Noah's Ark in a village near Marienberg, which he calls "Slaunders"; Toni Bernhart suggests that Ferrari is referring to Schluderns.[17] Bernhart describes the performance at length, so I will concentrate on the musical aspects. The abbot of Marienberg and five monks attended the play; the performance started with the actors on stage singing "melodie nazionali, ma molto bene e con gusto naturale."[18] In this folk play, folk music – or music that Ferrari identified as local folk music – played a vital role. A very dramatic theatrical scene, the War in Heaven between Lucifer and Michael and Lucifer's final Fall, was concluded with the entry of two musicians, "ciascuno con una tromba, lunga dieci piedi, fatta di scorza d'albero, e che produce un suono simigliante al così chiamato Corno Inglese, o

---

[16] Giacomo Gotifredo Ferrari. *Aneddoti piacevoli e interessanti occorsi nella vita di Giacomo Gotifredo Ferrari da Rovereto: Operetta scritta da Lui medesimo e dedicata a sua Maestà Giorgio IV, Re della Gran Bretagna*. London: Autor/A. Seguin, 1830. New editions: *Aneddoti piacevoli e interessanti occorsi nella vita di Giacomo Gotifredo Ferrari da Rovereto*, edited by Salvatore di Giacomo. Palermo et al.: Remo Sandron, 1920 (Collezione Settecentesca); Giacomo Gotifredo Ferrari. *Aneddoti piacevoli e interessanti: Le avventure di un musicista italiano tra Rivoluzione Francese e Restaurazione 1763–1830*, edited by Mariasilvia Tatti. Bergamo: Lubrina, 1998. See also Georges de Saint-Foix and Arthur Mendel. "A Musical Traveler: Giacomo Gotifredo Ferrari (1759–1842)." *The Musical Quarterly*, vol. 25, no. 4, 1939, pp. 455–465; Sergio Durante. "Die Memoiren des ehemaligen Klosterschülers Giacomo Gotifredo Ferrari." *Musikgeschichte Tirols*, vol. 2, edited by Kurt Drexel and Monika Fink. Innsbruck: Universitätsverlag Wagner, 2004 (Schlern-Schriften, 322), pp. 161–172 (with a poor German translation of the original Italian text of Ferrari's *Aneddoti*); Toni Bernhart. "Das implizite Publikum im Laaser Spiel vom Eigenen Gericht (vor 1805)." *"Das Theater glich einem Irrenhause": Das Publikum im Theater des 18. und 19. Jahrhunderts*, edited by Hermann Korte and Hans-Joachim Jakob. Heidelberg: Universitätsverlag Winter, 2012 (Proszenium: Beiträge zur Theaterpublikumsforschung, 1), pp. 179–191, pp. 188–190.
[17] Bernhart, "Das implizite Publikum im Laaser Spiel vom Eigenen Gericht," p. 189.
[18] Ferrari, *Aneddoti piacevoli e interessanti*, p. 64. Translation: "singing national melodies, but very beautifully and with natural taste."

Voce umana, sonarono ammirabilmente una melodia patetica ed un valtzer vivace per esprimere, che essendo già il Diavolo nell'Inferno vi sarebbe tutto pace ed allegria su questa terra, e per annunziar nello stesso tempo il ritorno dei celesti viaggiatori."[19] Again, the music must have been folk-like: the long "trumpets" described by Ferrari must have been alphorns, typical Alpine folk instruments. If we take into consideration all the observations on music in folk drama, we have to class Ferrari's account as a testimonial to a non-mainstream tradition – or perhaps a tradition not equally well-documented because it does not depend on written sources.

5 Conclusions

The Tyrolean sources offer some valuable insights concerning the music in folk drama. Ellen Hastaba has stressed the crucial influence of Jesuit plays on folk drama.[20] Therefore, it is not surprising that the way music was integrated into Tyrolean folk plays shows remarkable similarities to Jesuit drama, with musical prologues, *intermezzi*, and epilogues, all consisting of recitatives, arias, and choruses. These musical forms are essential also for baroque opera and the German *Singspiel* of the late eighteenth century. We can assume that music in folk drama was usually composed and written down, except for some short acclamations which could have been improvised. Most of the identifiable composers were school teachers, the leading representatives of rural music-making in the Tyrol up to the twentieth century. Giacomo Gotifredo Ferrari's autobiography is the only source that describes the integration of real folk music into folk drama. Further research in the field should be guided by an interdisciplinary approach, bringing together the research results of theater scholars and musicologists. Up to now, musical sources have been neglected and slumber in the archives. Their systematic registration is a desideratum.

---

19 Ibid., p. 67. Translation: "both with a trumpet, ten feet long, made of tree bark, producing a sound that resembles the so called 'Corno inglese,' or the human voice. They played a pathetic melody and a merry, lively Waltz to express the complete joy on earth after the Fall to Hell of the Devil, and to announce the heavenly travelers."
20 Hastaba, *Das Volksschauspiel im Oberinntal*, pp. 23–30.

Erika Fischer-Lichte
From a Rhetorical to a 'Natural' Art of Acting: What the Networks of the Seventeenth and Eighteenth Centuries Achieved

Ever since the twentieth century, we have become used to regarding innovations in acting – and the concomitant novel acting styles – as inventions of particular individuals, such as Stanislavsky, Meyerhold, Brecht, Copeau, Artaud, Grotowski, to name just the most prominent ones. It is indeed true that they also drew on the ideas of others, sometimes even heavily, including the experiences of Far Eastern masters concerning acting as well as theories of Western scientists, such as psychologists, sociologists, anthropologists, and physiologists, which they applied – or exploited – in order to support and substantiate their own ideas on acting. However, it is justified to give credit for these innovations first and foremost to the individuals.

By contrast, in the seventeenth and eighteenth centuries, i.e. before the proclamation of the autonomy of art, ideas on acting and corresponding practices and theories were developed in certain networks. In the seventeenth century the most efficient network was that formed by the Jesuits all over Europe and even beyond. It included theoreticians and practitioners of the different arts as well as philosophers and scholars of antiquity. A similar network was formed during the next century by philosophers, theoreticians, dramatists, and actors, among them most prominently Aaron Hill, John Hill, David Garrick, and Henry Siddons in England; Raymond de Sainte-Albine, Antoine-François (or Antonio Francesco) Riccoboni, and Denis Diderot in France; and Gotthold Ephraim Lessing, Georg Christoph Lichtenberg, Conrad Ekhof, Friedrich Ludwig Schröder, and Johann Jakob Engel in Germany. In a sense, one could even include physiologists such as Louis Lacaze, Claude-Nicolas Le Cat, and Albrecht von Haller in this network.

At the center of the discussions in both networks was the question of the most efficient representation of a feeling or sentiment – preferably called affect in the seventeenth century – and of its capacity to trigger this very feeling in the spectator. Some of the most important differences between these two networks can be found (1) in their conceptualization of feelings, (2) in the sources they referred to in order to determine and describe the most efficient representation of each feeling, and (3) in their understanding and definition of the aims of the art of acting and theater in general.

One of the major aims of the Jesuit theater of the seventeenth century was to fight the Reformation. The performances strove to strengthen the Catholic faith of the spectators by ridding them of their doubts and returning them to the bosom of their Church. This purpose was best served by transforming the spectators into *viri perculsi* – deeply moved men – and was achieved through a corresponding dramaturgy coupled with a particular kind of acting, which was developed with the help of traditional knowledge on affects. The latter were not conceived as forces located within an individual but as afflicting a subject from the outside – he or she was seized and moved by the affect the same way a marionette is by the puppeteer. According to the traditional knowledge dating back to antiquity, there were only between eight and eleven affects. In his considerations on how music expresses and conjures affects in listeners, for example, the Jesuit music theorist Athanasius Kircher identifies eight such affects: "(1) Love; (2) Sorrow or pain; (3) Joy; (4) Anger or outrage; (5) Sympathy; (6) Fear or dejection; (7) Boldness; (8) Wonder."[1] Kircher assumes that there is both a compositional technique and a gesture suitable for portraying each affect to the listeners/spectators and, in turn, for triggering that affect in them.

In developing such gestures, the Jesuits referred to ancient books on rhetoric, in particular to Quintilian's works. On the one hand, this led to the creation of a repertoire of gestures that attributed to each affect one or several gestures as their perfect representation. On the other, it listed the gestures for the actor's initial stance for all roles – the *contrapposto* stance for the torso, arms, and legs, combined with the *crux scenica*, i.e. positioning the feet at a 90° angle to each other. This position was seen to represent a strong ego exercising complete self-control. If the dramatic character was, say, a martyr suffering for the Christian faith, the actor was not supposed to give up this basic stance: whatever the character was going through, s/he was never to be seized by the resulting affects to such an extent as to lose self-control; when portraying such a character, the actor always had to follow all the rules determining the representation of the affects. In the case of a weak dramatic character surrendering to the attack of the affects without being able to resist them, the actor was permitted and indeed required to give up the *contrapposto* stance and to break all the rules. The gestures relating to the *contrapposto* or the *crux scenica* were thus employed to represent the ego. In the following, my focus will be on those gestures that intended to represent the eight to eleven affects.

---

[1] Athanasius Kircher. *Musurgia universalis sive ars magna consoni et dissoni*. Rome: Corbeletti, 1650, p. 258.

In 1727, i.e. in the first decades of the eighteenth century, when the acting rules developed by the Jesuits over the course of the seventeenth century no longer held complete sway, although they were still dominant, the Jesuit priest Franciscus Lang published a book entitled *Dissertatio de Actione Scenica* in which he laid down these rules in order to emphasize their validity and authority, which were being challenged by new ideas. This book remains one of our main sources on the acting style developed and propagated by the Jesuits all over Europe. Lang proceeded from the common assumption that

> the stronger, more lively, and just gripping the art of acting of the person speaking on the stage is, the more powerful the affect triggered in the spectator will be. The senses are after all the gate to the soul, through which the appearances of things now also enter the chamber of affects.[2]

The perfection and strength of the representation is the condition for the represented affect to be aroused in the spectator. In accordance with the dominant notion of contagion, it was assumed that the represented affects would be transferred from the body of the actor to that of the spectator via their perception. The rules for such a representation of affects, for example, read as follows:

> 1. We *admire* by lifting both hands and bringing them close to the chest with the palms facing the audience.
>
> 2. We show *disdain* by turning the face to the left and, with extended and slightly raised hands, repel the object of our disdain, pushing it away from us. When showing that we despise something we do the same with the right hand alone, but slightly towards the wrist and simultaneously shooing, using a repeated shooing and defensive movement.
>
> 3. We *implore* either by raising or lowering or linking both hands with the palms turned to each other.
>
> 4. We suffer *anguish* or *grief* by folding the hands together like joined combs and either raising them towards the breast or lowering them to the waist. The same is conveyed by moderately stretching out the right hand while at the same time turning it towards the breast [...].[3]

The representation of these affects by an actor was seen to release certain forces within his body, which in that very moment of perception through the spectator invades the latter's body and transforms him or her. By way of a calculat-

---

[2] Franciscus Lang. *Dissertatio de actione scenica: Abhandlung über die Schauspielkunst*, translated and edited by Alexander Rudin. Bern: Francke, 1975, p. 200.
[3] Ibid., pp. 186 f.; Ronald Gene Engle. "Franz Lang and the Jesuit Stage." Dissertation, University of Illinois, 1968, p. 107.

ed and continuous attack of alternating affects, the spectators were to be transformed into *viri perculsi* and so driven to renew and strengthen their faith.

The tight and yet far-reaching network of the Jesuits guaranteed that wherever they exerted some influence on theater – i.e. at the courts and at schools – this style of acting was used even well into the eighteenth century.

Their relationship to the courts and their schools for young noblemen suggest that it was not only the predominance of the Catholic faith that was at stake here, but also a certain kind of courtly behavior. When we look at the rules of acting laid down by Lang we find some striking parallels to the sociogenesis of seventeenth-century court society as described by the sociologist Norbert Elias in his study *The Civilizing Process*. Elias notes that for the formation of this new society the individual was required to learn self-discipline, the calculation of future aims and purposes, and to control not only one's feelings but also one's whole body:

> In tracing the sociogenesis of the court, we find ourselves at the center of a civilizing transformation that is both particularly pronounced and an indispensable precondition for all subsequent spurts and counter-spurts in the civilizing process. We see how, step by step, a warrior nobility is replaced by a tamed nobility with more muted affects, a courtly nobility. Not only within the Western civilizing process, but as far as we can see within every major civilizing process, one of the most decisive transitions is that of *warriors to courtiers*.[4]

It need scarcely be said that, as Elias notes, "there are widely differing stages and degrees of this transition, this inner pacification of a society," but gradually a more complex social order for expressing power and controlling behavior develops:

> Competition for prestige and royal favour is intense. 'Affaires,' disputes over rank and favour, do not cease. If the sword no longer plays so great a role as the means of decision, it is replaced by intrigue, conflicts in which careers and social success are contested with words. They demand and produce other qualities than did the armed struggles that had to be fought out with weapons in one's hand. Continuous reflection, foresight, and calculation, self-control, precise and articulate regulation of one's own effects, knowledge of the whole terrain, human and nonhuman, in which one acts, become more and more indispensable preconditions of social success.[5]

The codes and proprieties of the required social behavior coincided with those promoted by the contemporaneous art of acting. Thus, the comportment of the

---

[4] Norbert Elias. *Power and Civility: The Civilizing Process*. Translated by Edmund Jephcott with some notes and revisions by the author. New York: Pantheon Books, 1982, vol. 2, p. 259.
[5] Ibid., p. 271.

actor could be presented and perceived as a generally acknowledged model to be copied.

The actor responded to this ideal of behavior in courtly society. Accordingly, the character presented by the actor who followed the rules was clearly marked as an ideal. Should the actor break those rules by running across the stage, falling down and rolling on the floor, lowering his hands below the waist, or keeping his feet parallel, he indicated to the audience that the character he embodied had a weak ego, as in the case of a fool, madman, or tyrant. Undoubtedly, the tyrant and the madman served as negative examples that were not to be emulated; the fool was meant to grant the spectators a feeling of superiority, to relieve them – at least temporarily – of the enormous pressures caused by the rigorous demands of self-control. Theater thus assumed the cultural function of conveying an ideal behavior pattern which individuals then had to internalize and practice in order to adapt to the challenges of everyday life at court.

The eighteenth century saw the rise not only of new ideas about sensibility and feelings but also of a particular social class – the bourgeoisie. The new ideal of 'natural behavior' propagated by its members set up a sharp contrast to the artificiality of the noblemen at the courts. Accordingly, the main purpose of theater and the role and function of sentiments within it changed. Human beings were now defined as sentient beings spanning the whole range of positive as well as negative feelings. One of theater's purposes was to endorse certain positive feelings. In a letter to Friedrich Nicolai in his correspondence on tragedy, Lessing explains:

> The meaning of tragedy is this: it should develop *our ability to feel empathy*. It should make us so empathetic that the most tragic character of all time and among all people overtakes our emotions. *The man of empathy is the most perfect man,* among all social virtues, among all kinds of generosity, he is the most outstanding. A person who can make us feel such empathy, therefore, makes us more perfect and more virtuous, and the tragedy which moves us makes us this – or, it moves us in order to be able to make us this.[6]

To be able to do so on stage required a new kind of acting – one that would take into account these new ideas of sensibility and feelings. Particularly after 1750, the idea gained ground that sentiments and feelings arise *within* people. Much physiological research during the eighteenth century centered on the relationship between body and soul. Leading physicians of the time such as

---

[6] Gotthold Ephraim Lessing. "To Friedrich Nicolai." Nov. 1756. *Werke*, edited by Herbert G. Göpfert. Munich: Hanser, 1973, vol. 4, p. 163.

Louis Lacaze, Claude-Nicolas Le Cat, and Albrecht von Haller all agreed – despite diverging in other aspects of their theories – that the body was directly influenced by mental states.[7] They came to the conclusion that there was a *natural law of analogy* according to which people's bodies are naturally active and changeable. Bodies are suited to expressing inner states and processes, especially feelings, and making them perceptible.

Around the same time (ca. 1750–1780), a fierce debate on acting ensued in England, France, and Germany.[8] The question at stake was how the actor could achieve a 'natural' portrayal of feelings. Should the actor conjure a feeling internally and then – according to the principle of analogy – automatically express it in 'natural' gestures (Aaron Hill, Sainte-Albine, John Hill)? Or should the actor study feelings precisely and then, following the principle of analogy, present them without actually feeling them (Diderot)? Lessing offered a middle ground. To Lessing, the principle of analogy functioned in two directions: "modifications of the soul that bring about certain changes in the body can in return be produced by those changes to the body."[9] Lessing assumes a psychosomatic interplay between the body and soul.

The historical parallel between physiological research and the debates of philosophers and theorists of theater might suggest that the philosophers and theorists were responding to the physiologists. However, the debate on the appropriate portrayal of feelings began before the first publications by physiologists. It is more likely that the changes in the art of acting that had already begun to occur were not simply stimulated by this scientific research. Yet there are many cross-references in the debates. In this sense, one could regard the physiologists as part of the network.

---

7 See Louis Lacaze. *L'idée de l'homme physique et moral.* Paris: Guérin & Delatour, 1755; Claude-Nicolas Le Cat. *Traité des sensations et passions en général, et des sens en particulier.* Paris: Vallat-La-Chapelle, 1767. 3 vols.; Albrecht von Haller. *Mémoire sur la nature sensible et irritable des parties du corps animal.* Lausanne: Bousquet, 1756–1760. 4 vols.; see also his *Biblioteca anatomica: Qua scripta ad anatomen et physiologiam facientia a rerum initiis recensentur.* Zurich: Orell, Gessner, Füssli und Co., 1774–1777. 2 vols.
8 Important works resulting from these debates include Aaron Hill, *The Prompter: A Theatrical Paper* (1734–1736); Raymond de Sainte-Albine, *Le Comédien* (1747); Antoine-François Riccoboni, *L'Art du Théâtre* (1750); Denis Diderot, *Paradoxe sur le Comédien* (1769–1778); Gotthold Ephraim Lessing, *Hamburgische Dramaturgie* (1767–1769); and Georg Friedrich Lichtenberg, *Physiognomische Fragmente zur Beförderung der Menschenkenntnis und Menschenliebe* (1775–1787).
9 Gotthold Ephraim Lessing. "Third Essay." *Hamburg Dramaturgy.* Translated by Wendy Arons and Sara Figal, edited by Natalya Baldyda. MediaCommons, 2012, mcpress.media-commons.org/hamburg/essay-3. Accessed 11 June 2018.

The English actor David Garrick (1717–1779) played a key role in the writings of English, French, and German theorists, including Diderot and Lichtenberg. In fact, his acting style was used to prove both sides of the debate. Diderot's accounts of Garrick's acting may clarify why this was the case. In his letter to Madame Riccoboni, Diderot describes a dispute over pantomime that took place during Garrick's first visit to Paris in 1751. In this dispute, Garrick argued that a person could make a great impression without words, a position that no one had anticipated. When others contradicted him, Garrick became animated. He grabbed a pillow and said:

> "Gentlemen, I am this child's father." Thereupon he opened a window, took his cushion, tossed it in the air, kissed it, caressed it, and imitated all the fooleries of a father playing with his child. But then came a moment when the cushion, or rather, the child slipped from his hand and fell through the window. Then Garrick began to mime the father's despair [...]. His audience was seized with such consternation and horror that most of them could not bear it and had to leave the room.[10]

Garrick's facial expressions, gestures, and movements captured a father's despair and elicited strong feelings from the spectators. They perceived these expressions, gestures, and movements as the manifestation of a deep despair. Nothing in this passage contradicts the idea that the actor may actually have felt a flash of despair.

In *The Paradox of Acting*, Diderot refers to one of Garrick's drawing-room circles in Paris to argue that the actor does not need to feel strong sentiments in order to trigger them in the spectators:

> Garrick will put his head between two folding doors, and in the course of five or six seconds his expression will change successively from wild delight to temperate pleasure, from this to tranquility, from tranquility to surprise, from surprise to blank astonishment, from that to sorrow, from sorrow to the air of one overwhelmed, from that to fright, from fright to horror, from horror to despair, and then, he will go up again to the point from which he started.[11]

This sort of quick transition from one feeling to the next is only possible through the controlled and intentional portrayal of facial expressions, gestures, and movements that are perceived as the complete expression for each sentiment. It would be impossible for the actor actually to experience such a range of feeling at will.

---

[10] Denis Diderot. "To Madame Riccoboni." 17 Nov. 1758. Quoted in Jean Benedetti. *David Garrick and the Birth of Modern Theatre*. London: Methuen, 2001, p. 188.
[11] Denis Diderot. *The Paradox of Acting*. Translated by Walter H. Pollock. London: Chatto & Windus, 1883, p. 63.

Garrick's art of acting does not prove or disprove whether the actor *must* or *need not* experience a feeling in order to portray it. Whatever his technique, Garrick had a strong effect on audiences. Since Garrick inspired both theorists of theater and everyday theatergoers, his acting provides us with a suitable case for exploring how the debates on the art of acting in the second half of the eighteenth century and the development of scientific knowledge about feelings not only went hand in hand with but cross-pollinated each other.

In this context, the change in key concepts is quite telling. In English, the terms *sentiment*, *affect*, and *passion* were all used in the seventeenth century, but the word *emotion* was not used at all until the middle of the eighteenth century. The concept of emotion first appeared in David Hume's *Treatise of Human Nature* (1739–1740), and was afterwards primarily used by the school of Scottish empiricist philosophers and mental scientists. The new concept of emotion was popularized above all by Thomas Brown's *Lectures on the Philosophy of the Human Mind* (1820), in which the term *emotion* was used to mean "all those feelings that were neither sensations nor intellectual states."[12] In contrast to earlier terms such as *affection* and *passion*, the concept of *emotion* did not carry specifically Christian associations and values. The concept of emotion was a *secular psychological category*, and we should therefore also regard these philosophers and scientists as part of the network.

Let us now take a closer look at the actor Garrick to see what was meant by the *natural expression* of an emotion. Garrick's acting debut in London took place prior to the intense preoccupation with the relationship between body and soul, and before the debates about the art of acting. In other words, Garrick's innovations in acting were not a direct response to these debates. As we have already seen with Diderot, Garrick and his art of acting rather formed a central element of the network.

Garrick debuted in the role of Richard III in Colley Cibber's 1700 version of Shakespeare's tragedy on 19 October 1741. His debut as an actor and Hume's *Treatise of Human Nature* (in which the term *emotion* was used for the first time) were exactly a year apart. At the beginning of the performance, Garrick's new way of acting astonished the audience. From the beginning of the performance, his acting put the audience in a state of wonder that quickly turned into rapture:

> Mr. Garrick's easy and familiar, yet forcible style in speaking and acting, at first threw the critics into some hesitation concerning the novelty as well as propriety of his manner.

---

[12] Thomas Dixon. *From Passions to Emotions: The Creation of a Secular Psychological Category*. Cambridge: Cambridge University Press, 2003, p. 23. See Thomas Brown. *Lectures on the Philosophy of the Human Mind*. Edinburgh: Tait, 1820.

They had long been accustomed to an elevation of the voice, with a sudden mechanical depression of its tones, calculated to excite admiration, and to entrap applause. To the just modulation of the words, and concurring expression of the features from the genuine workings of nature, they had been strangers, at least for some time. But after he had gone through a variety of scenes, in which he gave proof of consummate art, and perfect knowledge of character, their doubts were turned into surprise and amazement, from which they relieved themselves by loud and reiterated applause. [...] Mr. Garrick shone forth like a theatrical Newton; he threw new light on elocution and action.[13]

If the comparison to Newton seems far-fetched, a letter from the famous actor Charles Macklin to William Cooke supports this claim:

> It was amazing how without any example, but on the contrary with great prejudice against him, he could throw such spirit and novelty into the part as to convince every impartial person on the very first impression that he was right. In short, Sir, he at once decided the public taste; and though the players formed a cabal against him, [...] it was a puff to thunder.[14]

Even Garrick's first appearances on stage were revolutionary, as the reference to Newton suggests. It is unclear, though, what exactly constituted this revolution. Expressions such as "the genuine workings of nature" or "perfect knowledge of character" were also used in the first half of the eighteenth century in order to legitimate rhetorical gestures. The concepts of nature and the natural changed substantially over the course of the eighteenth century. The above descriptions of Garrick do not give us a very clear sense of how his art differed so radically from his predecessors.

To determine what was so 'revolutionary' in Garrick's acting, we need a more precise description of what Garrick did in these scenes, such as Diderot's account of Garrick's improvised pantomimes. These descriptions are not often found in reviews, which generally focus on Garrick's rendition of the dramatic character and the impression he made on critics and other spectators. A somewhat more precise description of one of the mad scenes in *King Lear* can be found in a review by John Hill, the translator of Sainte-Albine's treatise, which he had published under his own name with the title *The Actor: A Treatise on the Art of Playing* (1750). Hill writes:

> 'Tis an odd Effect of a Laugh to produce Tears; but I believe there was hardly a dry Eye in the House on his executing that first absolute Act of Madness in the Character. While I admired the action, I was almost at a Loss to comprehend in what Manner it was per-

---

13 Thomas Davies. *Memoirs of the Life of David Garrick*. London: Self-published, 1780, vol. 1, pp. 40–44.
14 William Cooke. *Memoirs of Charles Macklin*. London: Asperne, 1804, p. 99.

> formed: 'T was not anything like the Laugh of Mirth or Pleasantry, the Triumph of a happy Imagination; but seemed merely the Exertion of the Organs of the body, without any Connection with the Soul; an involuntary Emotion of the Muscles, while the Mind was fixed on something else. Upon the whole, other Lears I have seen, [...] Must pardon me, if I declare that the frantic Part of the character seems never to have been rightly understood till this gentleman studied it.[15]

Hill describes here how Garrick's laughter at the start of Lear's madness made a particularly strong impression on him as much as on the rest of the audience, rousing them to tears. Garrick's acting also shed a new light on madness for Hill. In other words, the acting taught Hill about the dramatic character. Garrick's acting does not present madness as a single affect that can always be expressed in the same way. Instead he shows a particular madness related to the character of the dramatic figure. The madness played here is not madness *per se*, but rather Lear's specific madness. What is remarkable in Hill's review is the use of the word *emotion*, which here is used in the sense of an uncontrollable muscle movement.

Of all the theater theorists, Lichtenberg emphasized most vehemently that actors must individualize the mental states they portray. During his stay in London in 1775, he saw Garrick in various roles. Lichtenberg's *Letters from England* offer the most precise portraits we have of Garrick's acting. In these letters, Lichtenberg extensively and in great detail describes Garrick's portrayals of Hamlet, Abel Drugger (from Ben Jonson's *The Alchemist*), and Sir John Brute (from Vanbrugh's *The Provoked Wife*). Lichtenberg describes in particular the scene in which the ghost of Hamlet's father appears to him for the first time:

> Hamlet appears in a black dress, the only one in the whole court, alas! still worn for his poor father [...]. Horatio and Marcellus, in uniform are with him [...]; Hamlet has folded his arms under his cloak and pulled his hat down over his eyes; it is a cold night and just twelve o'clock; the theater is darkened, and [...] quiet [...]. Suddenly, as Hamlet moves toward the back of the stage slightly to the left and turns his back on the audience, Horatio starts, and saying: "Look, My Lord, it comes," points to the right, where the ghost has already appeared and stands motionless, before anyone is aware of him. At these words Garrick turns sharply and at the same moment staggers back two or three paces with his knees giving way under him; his hat falls to the ground and both his arms, especially the left, are stretched out nearly full length, with the hands as high as his head, the right arm more bent and the hand lower, the fingers apart; his mouth is open: thus he stands rooted to the spot, with legs apart, but no loss of dignity, supported by his friends, who are better acquainted with the apparition and fear lest he should collapse. His whole

---

15 John Hill. Quoted in Charles Harold Gray. *Theatrical Criticism in London to 1795*. New York: Columbia University Press, 1931, p. 113.

demeanor is so expressive of terror that it made my flesh creep even before he began to speak. The almost terror-struck silence of the audience, which preceded this appearance and filled one with a sense of insecurity, probably did much to enhance this effect. At last he speaks, not at the beginning, but at the end of a breath, with a trembling voice, "Angels and ministers of Grace defend us!" words, which supply anything this scene may lack and make it one of the greatest and most terrible, which will ever be played on any stage. The ghost beckons him, I wish you could see him, with eyes fixed on the ghost, though he is speaking to his companions, freeing himself from their restraining hands [...]. [...] [H]e stands with his sword on guard against the specter, saying: "Go on, I follow thee," and the ghost goes on off stage. Hamlet still remains motionless [...] and at length, when the spectator can no longer see the ghost, he begins slowly to follow him, now standing still and then going on, with sword still upon guard, eyes fixed on the ghost, hair disordered, and out of breath, until he too is lost to sight. [...] What an amazing triumph.[16]

The expression of terror in Lichtenberg's account goes into such detail about elements and phases that it extends far beyond the codified expression that Lang had provided. It also goes beyond the descriptions in physiological textbooks and observations of actors in later tracts, such as Johann Jakob Engel's 1785–1786 work on acting, *Ideen zu einer Mimik*.[17] Lichtenberg describes the gestures, movements, and articulations that express terror itself. It also focuses on Hamlet's character traits – his particular sensibility as well as his social standing ("no loss of dignity") and his specific situation (still in mourning).

In Lichtenberg's description, Garrick's portrayal of Hamlet's reaction to the appearance of his father's ghost allows processes of the human *soul* to appear in ways that are not accounted for in either the physiology or the philosophy of the time. Hence, the art of acting opened up new dimensions of how to gain knowledge about people, their mental states, and their emotions. Garrick's art of acting was epoch-making from his very first appearances in 1741. Through Garrick, theater became a *psychological institution*, a laboratory for empirical psychology. It was able to function as such because by expressing very particu-

---

16 Georg Christoph Lichtenberg. *Lichtenberg's Visits to England, as Described in His Letters and Diaries.* Translated and edited by Margaret L. Mare and W. H. Quarrell. Oxford: Clarendon, 1938, pp. 9–11.
17 Engel's book was translated into English by Henry Siddons and appeared in 1815 titled *Practical Illustrations of Rhetorical Gesture and Action: Adapted To The English Drama; From A Work On The Subject by M. Engel, Member of The Royal Academy of Berlin; Embellished with sixty-nine Engravings, Expressive Of The Various Passions, And Representing The Modern Costume Of The London Theatres.* A second improved edition appeared in London in 1822, printed for Sherwood, Neely, and Jons, Paternoster Row. Remarkably, in this translation the gestures that accord to the physiological *law of analogy* are termed *rhetorical*, and the emotions that express them are termed *passions*.

lar emotions the art of acting not only aroused emotions in the spectators but at the same time broadened their knowledge of human beings and their psyche.

Garrick's early and remarkable achievement inspired other actors of his time, though without the same 'genius' and success. In his *Letters from England*, Lichtenberg expressly refers to the German actor Conrad Ekhof (1720–1778), who was not of the same caliber as Garrick but nevertheless by far surpassed some other celebrated London actors.

In fact, the first performance of Lessing's *Miß Sara Sampson*, which starred Ekhof as Mellefont, already deeply affected the spectators. In a letter to Johann Wilhelm Ludwig Gleim, Karl Wilhelm Ramler reports on the first performance of July 1755 in Frankfurt upon Oder: "Herr Lessing's tragedy was performed in Frankfurt, and the audience sat for three and a half hours, silent as statues, weeping."[18] Keeping in mind that in the middle of the eighteenth century audiences in the German states were rather noisy, coming and going as they pleased, eating, drinking, and conversing as the action unfolded on the stage, this seems to be an extraordinary response, which was due not only to the tragedy but also to a new style of acting. Friedrich Nicolai saw a performance in Berlin in October the following year and gave a detailed account of it in a letter to Lessing:

> Before I tell you about the performance in more detail, I must let you know that I was extremely affected; up to the beginning of the fifth act, I was often in tears, but by the end of the same act and throughout the whole scene with Sara, I was far too moved to be able to cry anymore. This has never happened to me at any other drama and confounds, to a certain extent, my own system, which generally resists being moved by tragedy. My feelings and my critical annotations on both your play and the actors were mixed in a wonderful confusion in my head.[19]

The emotions triggered in the spectators here and in other cases in the eighteenth century were still explained via the concept of contagion. As Johann Georg Sulzer writes about performances in his *Allgemeine Theorie der schönen Künste* in 1792: "It is certain that under no circumstances are human beings capable of more lively impressions and feelings than at public performances.

---

[18] Johann Wilhelm Ludwig Gleim. "To Karl Wilhelm Ramler." 25 July 1755. *Briefwechsel zwischen Gleim und Ramler: 1753–1759*, edited by Carl Schüddekopf. Tübingen: Bibliothek des litterarischen Vereins in Stuttgart 1907, vol. 2, p. 206.

[19] Friedrich Nicolai. "To Gotthold Ephraim Lessing." 3 Nov. 1756. G. E. Lessing. *Werke und Briefe*, edited by Wilfried Barner. Frankfurt: Deutscher Klassiker Verlag, 1987, vol. 11.1, pp. 111–116; pp. 111 f.

[...] Nothing in this world is more contagious or effective than emotions perceived from a crowd of people all at once."[20]

Usually, the network operated through an exchange of letters or through translations of essays and even whole books in which the 'members' of the network explained their view on acting. Detailed descriptions of acting and actors as in Lichtenberg's letters became increasingly common in German discussions of performances. Critics and theorists were no longer satisfied with individual descriptions, and compared how different actors performed the same roles and scenes. From these accounts we know, for example, that in Lear's mad scene Johann Franz Hieronymus Brockmann (1745–1812) climbed onto a tree stump as he proclaimed: "I will preach to thee: mark." In Friedrich Ludwig Schröder's (1744–1816) portrayal of Lear in the same scene, Lear attempted to climb the stump, but then collapsed. Contemporaries considered these variations *refinements*, because they revealed more about the 'truth' of Lear.

In his description of Schröder's portrayal of Hamlet, the critic of the *Litteratur- und Theaterzeitung* (1779) compared its details to Brockmann's portrayal of the same role in what became the first celebrated Hamlet on the German stage. He ended his report with a description of Act III, Scene 4 between Hamlet and his mother:

> When speaking the words, "How is it with you, lady?" Schröder avoided a mistake that Brockmann made. The latter looked at his mother as he spoke. The former spoke to his mother, whom he held with a shaking hand, without shifting his gaze away from the ghost.[21]

These *refinements* were not seen as expressing psychological 'truths' simply because they coincided with scientific knowledge about physiology. Rather, the art of acting enabled new scientific knowledge on emotions. In the second half of the eighteenth century it provided contemporaries with insights into the emotional states of the human soul, previously hidden and as yet undiscovered by either physiology or philosophy.

In his abovementioned book on acting, the philosopher – and later director of the Royal Theater in Berlin – Engel went so far [fig. 1] as to systematize the state of the human soul by considering single emotions alone.

---

[20] Johann Georg Sulzer. *Allgemeine Theorie der schönen Künste*. 2nd exp. ed., Leipzig: Weidmannsche Buchhandlung, 1794, vol. 4, pp. 254 f.
[21] Quoted in Berthold Litzmann. *Friedrich Ludwig Schröder: Ein Beitrag zur deutschen Literatur- und Theatergeschichte*. Hamburg: Voss, 1890 and 1894. 2 vols.

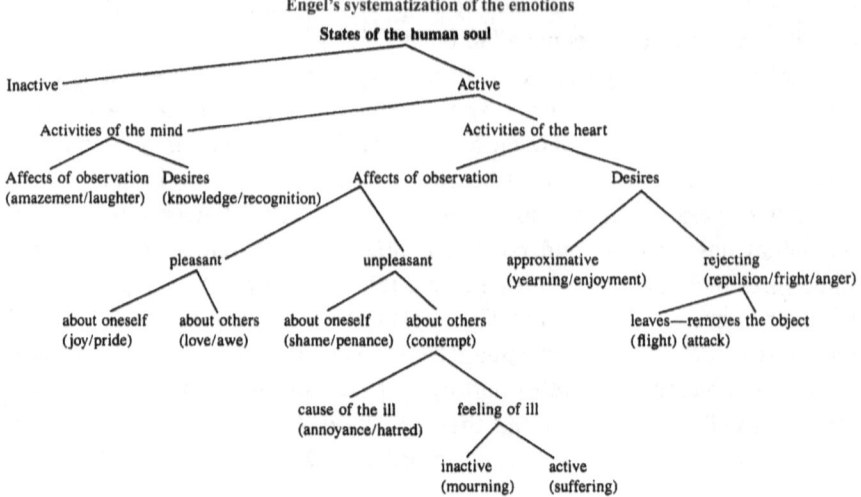

Fig. 1: My synopsis. See Erika Fischer-Lichte. *The Semiotics of Theater*. Translated by Jeremy Gaines and Doris L. Jones. Bloomington: Indiana University Press, 1992, p. 164.

The classification claims to take into account all single emotions that are not the product of combinations. All those that are not listed must thus be considered to be blended – i.e., combinations. Engel provided a detailed description of each state contained in the classification, and via the *natural law of analogy* formulated a corresponding gestural sign best suited to provide the perfect expression of each state. For example, he described anger as "the desire to remove, to destroy an ill," a desire which is "one with the desire to punish and take revenge:"[22]

> [A]ll Nature's energies stream outwards in order to transform the joy of what is Evil into Fear by the terrifying sight of it, into Pain by its destructive effect, and, by contrast, to turn our own bitter Annoyance into a pleasant feeling of our Strength, the Terror we instill in others [...].[23]

He identified the corresponding physical expression that derived analogously from this state as follows:

> Anger equips [...] all the external limbs with strength; pre-eminently arming those who are destined to destroy. If the external parts, overfilled with blood and juices, brim over and tremble, and the bloodshot, rolling eyes shoot glances like fiery daggers, then a certain indignation, a certain disquiet is also expressed by the hands and teeth: the former

---

22 Johann Jakob Engel. *Mimik*. 1804. Frankfurt: Athenäum, 1971, p. 285.
23 Ibid., p. 236 f.

are clenched convulsively, the latter are bared and gnashed [...] all movements are jerky and of extreme violence; the gait is heavy, forced, shattering.[24]

Each particular physical change was thus seen to have its cause in a certain emotion and, therefore, pointed back to that cause. Taken together, all these changes formed the gestural sign for anger, and so described the expression of the respective emotion perfectly. Whereas the corresponding modification generated by real anger collectively was to be understood as an indexical sign pointing to the underlying emotion, the gestures produced on stage according to Engel's rules constituted an imitation that perfected them. The result was a series of iconic signs, the suitable and perfect representation of the indexical signs of reality. They were neither a spontaneous expression of the emotion nor an arbitrary, conventional sign thereof, but, rather, adequate representations of the gestural sign observed in reality, a sign that had arisen as the spontaneous expression of the respective feeling.

'Mimic' knowledge and psychological knowledge here go hand in hand. In order to be able to constitute the 'correct' gestural signs, it is assumed that "the moral being is of just as much value to the observer as a polyp to Trembley or an aphid to Bonnet."[25] As this phrasing suggests, the development of this new kind of acting was regarded as a scientific undertaking, exploring hitherto unknown realms of the human soul.

At the beginning of the 1780s, Karl Philipp Moritz announced his plan to publish a *Journal for Empirical Psychology* dedicated to case studies, that is, to empirical material that could provide a basis for further research. The first part of the first volume appeared in 1783 and was titled *KNOW THYSELF, or Journal of Empirical Psychology, a reader for the learned and unlearned.*[26] Between 1783 and 1793, ten volumes were published that favored reports on certain mental states and 'sick' or deviant behavior. These reports were only possible through minute introspection, provoked and enhanced by the new art of acting. Knowledge of the human soul as promoted by the network of philosophers, actors, dramatists, and physiologists became one of the most important goals toward the end of the century. The art of acting and its theorization paved the way for the creation of a new academic discipline – empirical psychology – and played a significant role in establishing the concept of emotion as a secular one, indispensable for this new discipline.

---

24 Ibid., p. 238.
25 Ibid., p. 27.
26 See Hans Förstl, and Beate Rattay-Förstl. "Karl Philipp Moritz and the *Journal of Empirical Psychology*: An introductory note and a series of psychiatric case reports." *History of Psychiatry*, vol. 3, 1992, pp. 95 ff.

In conclusion: Although the two networks discussed here both identified gestures deemed to be the most adequate representations of certain emotions while at the same time being able to arouse those feelings in the spectators, the ways they proceeded and the goals they strove to realize differed enormously. The Jesuit network exposed the spectators to rhetorical representations of the canonical affects in order to transform them into *viri perculsi*, whose strong ego would not only keep them in the Catholic faith and prepare them to suffer for it without surrendering to all possible kinds of temptations, but would also, if not primarily, make them act as ideal courtiers.

The eighteenth-century network developed 'natural' signs for the most diverse emotions by following the principle of analogy in order to trigger strong feelings in the spectators, who predominantly hailed from the educated middle class. This meant pursuing a twofold purpose. One goal was the perfection of the human being by turning him/her into an empathetic being. The other was possible only on the basis of scientific knowledge of the mental and psychic states of human beings. This new kind of 'natural' acting was not only rooted in scientific knowledge. This form of acting itself brought forth new knowledge. The exposure to this new kind of acting thus contributed to human perfection also insofar as it enabled a much deeper and better knowledge of oneself and the other. Moreover, it furthered the process of shaping a new cultural identity of the educated middle class.

In both cases, the networks in question attributed to theater, and particularly to acting, a key role in the realization of their overall goals, however different they and the means of achieving them may have been. Both addressed audiences in different European countries and, as the available sources and documents suggest, were quite successful over a prolonged period of time. Both speak to the efficacy of networks if they are clearly structured with regard to their goals and the means necessary to achieve the envisaged developments and changes.

Jaša Drnovšek
Early Modern Religious Processions: The Rise and Fall of a Political Genre

Es ist Schande zu sagen – selbst seynwollende Katholiken werfen sich jetzt als Reformatoren auf, unterfangen sich ihre heilige Mutter, die christkatholische Kirche zu hofmeistern, und besonders ihre äußerliche Pracht, ihre Zeremonien und Feyerlichkeiten, als lauter Mißbräuche und Gauckelwerke, mit Mund und Feder zu beschnarchen und auszuzischen. [...] Ihr, meine Geliebtesten! Haltet euch unerschüttert an die alten Gewohnheiten und löblichen Gebräuche unserer christkatholischen Religion. [...] – Lasset euch doch von keinem Quacksalber, und Marktschreyer, von keinem heutigen Afterphilosophen – neue Begriffe von Gottesverehrung beybringen. Sie sind Leute eines gebrandmarkten Gewissens, Feinde der Religion, und der wahren Kirche, Selbstdenker, und Modewitzler, die eben so wenig zum Unterrichte des christlichen Volkes, als der Esel zum Lautenschlagen, berufen sind.[1]

It is a shame to say – even self-professed Catholics are acting up as reformers now, they dare to instruct their holy mother, the Catholic Church, and especially to criticize and hiss down, by tongue or pen, its external splendor, its ceremonies and festivities, as pure abuse and jugglery. [...] My dearest ones! Stick unbroken to the old habits and laudable customs of our Catholic church. [...] – Do not let any quack doctor, any market barker, any false philosopher of today – teach you new concepts of worshipping the Lord. These people have a corrupted conscience, they are enemies of religion, and of the true Church, self-thinkers, and modish wags, who are as little qualified to teach the Christian people as a donkey is to play the lute.

These highly passionate words, at once beseeching and despairing, belong to Albert Komploier, a Capuchin friar from Tyrol, who in the second half of the eighteenth century and the first decade of the nineteenth served as a preacher in the parishes of Brixen/Bressanone and Bozen/Bolzano. The passage is part of a sermon that he most likely gave during the last two decades of the eighteenth century and which he published in 1803 in a collection entitled *Das zerfallene Christenthum am Ende des achtzehnten Jahrhunderts oder Sonn- und Festpredigten wider die herrschenden Modelaster, falschen Grundsätze und*

---

1 Albert Komploier. "Auf das Fest des allerheiligsten Fronleichnams: Schutzrede für die Fronleichnamsprozeßion, und andere kirchliche Ceremonien." *Das zerfallene Christenthum am Ende des achtzehnten Jahrhunderts oder Sonn- und Festpredigten wider die herrschenden Modelaster, falschen Grundsätze und Scheintugenden unserer Zeiten.* Augsburg: Veith, 1803, vol. 2, pp. 164–179; p. 165, pp. 177 f.

Scheintugenden unserer Zeiten. In the second edition of the book, however, which was printed posthumously in 1846 and bears the significant addition "in zeitgemäßer Bearbeitung" ("updated version") on the first page, the appeal quoted above was radically changed: "Quacksalber" ("quack doctor") and "Marktschreyer" ("market barker") from the first edition of the book, for instance, were replaced by "Modeweise" ("modish wise men"), while "Afterphilosoph" ("false philosopher") was changed to "Aufklärer"² ("proponent of the Enlightenment"). In other words, the second edition attributes some sort of subtlety and craftiness in relation to the detractors of the Church.

In order to understand the aggressiveness, even ribaldry of Komploier's first version of the sermon, one needs to consider the great mental shift that affected the Catholic Church from the second half of the eighteenth century onward. It was precisely the 'false philosophy,' as Komploier had put it, the Enlightenment spirit, that provoked great and concrete political changes. In Austria, for instance, a church reform, started by the Empress Maria Theresia and continued by her son Joseph II, curbed the autonomy of the Church and diminished its political influence. Among other things, tax liability for the clergy was introduced; religious orders that were not considered economically productive, that is, not involved in charitable, educational, or other social activities, were abolished, and the number of their monasteries and convents was reduced; and, last but not least, a considerable number of religious festivals were banned, either, again, due to alleged economic reasons, or because the piety that manifested itself in such events was henceforth declared a "superstition."³ When Komploier talks of ceremonies, he is thinking first and foremost of religious processions. Historically, these fall into a long line of Christian tradition that began in late antiquity.⁴ However, it was not by accident that their golden age coincided with the age of the Counter-Reformation and Catholic renewal. In fact, in this period religious processions are often affiliated with

---

2 Albert Komploier. "Fronleichnamsfest. Widerlegung der Einwendungen gegen die Fronleichnamsfeier und andere kirchliche Ceremonien." *Das zerfallene Christentum am Ende des achtzehnten Jahrhunderts. Sonn- und Festtagspredigten wider die herrschenden Modelaster, falschen Grundsätze und Scheintugenden unserer Zeiten*. 2nd rev. ed., Lindau: Stettner, 1846, vol. 2, pp. 28–36; p. 35.

3 Significantly, the Enlightenment, according to Immanuel Kant, is nothing other than "[l]iberation from superstition" (Immanuel Kant. *Critique of Judgement*. Translated by Werner S. Pluhar. Indianapolis: Hackett, 1987, p. 161.).

4 One of the earliest recorded accounts of such processions appears in a fourth-century manuscript, the *Itinerarium Aetheriae*, written by a Galician woman who traveled to the Holy Land in about 381–384 (see *Egeria's Travels*, translated and edited by John Wilkinson. Oxford: Aris & Phillips, 1999).

two religious institutions that have been called "emblematic orders of the Catholic renewal:"[5] the order of Capuchin Friars Minor, and the Society of Jesus.

As different as these two orders may seem, they share at least three common traits that enabled them to become a new part of the clerical elite. First, at the time of the Council of Trent (1545–1563), when the process of the Counter-Reformation and Catholic renewal formally started, they were – or, at least, they figured as – new political players, carrying no baggage from the old Church; the Capuchins were established in 1528, while the Jesuits got their papal approval in 1540.[6] Second, from their very beginnings both orders distinguished themselves through a remarkably high mobility, which allowed them to build and maintain wide political networks. Third, numerous pastoral practices of these "mobilizers,"[7] including the staging of religious processions, coincided with the political views of the Tridentine Church.

One of the first documented processions, held by the Capuchins, was a penitential procession that took place on a hill near Montepulciano in Tuscany in the summer of 1539. Interestingly, it is described in a letter written by one of the very first Jesuits, Francisco Strada, addressed to the founder of the order, Ignatius de Loyola. Strada reports the following scene:

> [V]i venir una proçesión de çerca de treçientos niños desnudos y disciplinándose, los quales, como verdaderos soldados, seguían al capitán Xpo. crucifixo, el qual en lugar de bandera uno delante [de] todos llevava, cantando todos las letanías, y de poco en poco alta voçe exclamando: Misericordia, misericordia.
> Después desto, [...] se comineza á ordenar de comer, y los [...] capuchinos [...] salían [...] con unos canjstros de pedazos de pan, que [...] distribuyan por los niños, que de diçiplinarse cansados estavan.[8]
>
> I saw a procession of some three hundred naked children who were flagellating themselves, following like true soldiers their commander, Christ on the cross. He was borne by a child, instead of a flag, before all the others. All the while, the children were singing litanies and, from time to time, they would exclaim loudly: Mercy! Mercy! Afterwards [...] one was invited to have a meal and the [...] Capuchins [...] appeared [...] with some baskets

---

5 Ronnie Po-chia Hsia. *The World of Catholic Renewal: 1540–1770*. Cambridge: Cambridge University Press, 1998, p. 31.
6 Strictly speaking, the Capuchins were not an entirely new order in 1528. They had evolved from the Observants, one of the two branches of the Franciscan order (see Father Cuthbert. *The Capuchins: A Contribution to the History of the Counter-Reformation*. London: Sheed & Ward, 1928, pp. 85–120.).
7 Stephen Greenblatt. "A mobility study manifesto." *Cultural Mobility: A Manifesto*, edited by Stephen Greenblatt. Cambridge: Cambridge University Press, 2009, pp. 250–253; p. 251.
8 Francesco Strada. "To Ignatius de Loyola." 5 July 1539. *I frati cappuccini: Documenti e testimonianze del primo secolo*, edited by Costanzo Cargnoni. Perugia: EFI, 1988, pp. 321–325; pp. 322 f.

of bread, which [...] was given to the children, who were exhausted from flagellating themselves.

As plain as the procession depicted by Strada seems in its concept, it must have left a strong physio-psychological impact on its spectators. On the one hand, they could observe the penance in its most radical form, as mortification of the flesh. Since this was carried out by children, symbolic agents of innocence and purity, we can assume that the moral, pedagogical effect of the scene was accordingly intensified. In fact, Strada reports that the parents of the self-flagellating children were "confusos que los niños le enseñasen lo que ellos havían de hazer, se determjnaron de reformarse"[9] ("baffled as the children taught them what they themselves should do, [and] they decided to improve"). At the same time, however, one cannot miss the overall impression the procession left on Strada. He himself talks of "milagros"[10] ("wonders"). Considering the soldierly rhetoric he uses to describe the scene, and imagining children whipping themselves, singing, and shouting unanimously while marching lined up behind the moving statue of Christ, it must have been a highly unusual, yet not in the least repellent demonstration – and at the same time a production of power.[11]

As I have already mentioned, such religious processions were perfectly in tune with the politics of the Tridentine Church. In fact, its readiness to support such performances can already be traced in the decrees of the Council of Trent. For instance, in the decree entitled "On the invocation, veneration, and relics of saints, and on sacred images," one reads that "great profit is derived" from mimetic "representations" of the "mysteries of our Redemption," since they make people "excited to adore and love God, and to cultivate piety."[12] In addition, in the "Decree concerning the most holy sacrament of the eucharist," a fairly direct instruction is given, namely that in a procession to be held on the Feast of Corpus Christi, "truth" should "celebrate a triumph over falsehood and heresy," and "her adversaries [...] may either pine away weakened and broken; or, touched with shame and confounded, at length repent."[13] Considering this, it can be no coincidence that religious processions held by the Capu-

---

9 Ibid., p. 324.
10 Ibid., p. 325.
11 *Power* is here understood in the terms of Max Weber (see *Economy and Society: An Outline of Interpretive Sociology.* New York: Bedminster Press, 1968, p. 926.).
12 "On the invocation, veneration, and relics of saints, and on sacred images." *The Council of Trent: The Canons and Decrees of the Sacred and Oecumenical Council of Trent*, translated and edited by James Waterworth. London: Dolman, 1848, p. 232.
13 "Decree concerning the most holy sacrament of the eucharist." Ibid., p. 79.

Fig. 1: A drawing of the town of Škofja Loka from 1713. Oberösterreichisches Landesarchiv, Neuerwerbungen, Handschrift 140.

chins or the Jesuits began to flourish at the end of the sixteenth century. By then, most of the Council's decrees had not only been confirmed by the pope, but had also largely been put into practice.[14]

Aside from the Corpus Christi processions, which are explicitly encouraged in the decrees, another type of procession started to evolve in that period: the Good Friday processions. Like the procession Francisco Strada observed in Tuscany some forty years earlier, these processions were penitential in their character, too, and they would have provoked similar psycho-physiological effects in the spectators. Their production dimension, however, was much more sophisticated, and only kept growing during the next two centuries. If the initial Good Friday processions consisted of penitents who whipped themselves while marching solemnly through the streets, this initial phase was soon exceeded. Instead of penitents, it was laymen representing characters or dramatic scenes from the Passion of Christ who formed the core of these annual reenactments.[15] From this moment on, Good Friday processions can also be considered passion processions or passion procession plays.[16]

One of the best illustrations of what Good Friday processions looked like when fully developed is offered by the processions in the Slovenian town

---

[14] See Hubert Jedin. "Das Papsttum und die Durchführung des Tridentinums (1565–1605)". *Handbuch der Kirchengeschichte*, edited by Josef Glazik et al. Basel: Herder, 1975, vol. 4, pp. 521–560.

[15] For the term *reenactment* see Erika Fischer-Lichte. "Die Wiederholung als Ereignis: Reenactment als Aneignung von Geschichte." *Theater als Zeitmaschine*, edited by Ulf Otto et al. Bielefeld: Transcript, 2012, pp. 13–52.

[16] The distinction made here is a heuristic one; as opposed to passion processions, passion procession plays are those that include dramatic texts.

Škofja Loka in the first half of the eighteenth century [fig. 1]. These late performances reflect a tradition set up by the Capuchins one century previously on their missionary route from Innsbruck via Prague, Vienna, Graz, and Ljubljana.[17] The Good Friday processions of Škofja Loka, however, are documented not only by way of *periochae*, or, as is often the case with these performances, in the form of procession orders. Rather, a whole codex has been preserved, containing, among other things, a complete dramatic manuscript with 841 lines and stage directions written by Friar Romuald of Štandrež.

In this text, which originates in the years 1725–1727[18] and is called *Škofjeloški pasijon* (*The Passion of Škofja Loka*),[19] the whole action is structured into 13 'figures' (lat. *figurae*), that is, into 13 scenes, each concentrating on one self-contained event, such as the Last Supper, Flagellation, or Coronation of Christ.[20] These scenes were enacted either on large supporting frames carried through the streets, or on carts pulled by horses, or they were simply performed on foot. Within the scenes, the main narrative was accompanied by many other elements, embedded into the procession as collective bodies: angels, penitents, cross-draggers, eremites, local guilds, musicians, townsmen, town councillors, and the clergy. The last segment of the procession consisted of the common people.

The example of the *Škofjeloški pasijon* allows us to develop a good idea of the auditory and visual impact the procession must have had on the audience. If one looks at the lines the performers were to recite, it is striking how often the characters engage the audience. In almost every scene, the spectator is addressed in a lordly, disciplinary manner; sometimes, indeed, as *človek* (*man*), but far more frequently as *grešnik* (*sinner*), *grešni človek* (*man of sin*), or *grešna duša* (*sinner soul*). For instance, in the very first scene, "Paradise" (lat. *Paradisus*), the Third Angel, who has just been witness to the Fall of Man, speaks out:

---

[17] See Metod Benedik. *Die Kapuziner in Slowenien: 1600–1750*. Dissertation, Rome, Pontificia Universitas Gregoriana, 1973, pp. 51–63.

[18] See Matija Ogrin. "Tradicija in datacija Škofjeloškega pasijona. Ekdotična perspektiva". *Škofjeloški pasijon*, edited by Matija Ogrin. Celje: Celjska Mohorjeva družba, 2009, pp. 343–365.

[19] The manuscript itself does not bear any title. On a note added later, which is now lost, was once written: "Instructio pro Processione Locopolitana in die Parasceve Dni. (3. Die Martii 1721.)" (see Oče Romuald. *Škofjeloški pasijon*, edited by Matija Ogrin. Celje: Celjska Mohorjeva družba, 2009, p. 327).

[20] The scenes of the *Škofjeloški pasijon* are as follows: "Paradisus," "Mors," "Cæna Domini," a scene with Samson, "Sudor Sanguineus," "Flagelatio [sic] Christi," "Coronatio," a scene with Jerome, "Ecce Homo," "Christus in Cruce," "Mater Septem Dolorum," "Archa Fæderis" and "Sepulchrum Domini".

[21] Oče Romuald. *Škofjeloški pasijon*, edited by Matija Ogrin. Celje: Celjska Mohorjeva družba, 2009, p. 178 f., emphasis mine.

Grešna duša ti imaš poslušat,
ja, tojga Boga nikar taku skušat.
Ravnu tebi se ima tudi pərgoditi,
kir ti se na masaš to pregreho sturiti.
Zamoreš to nebešku kralestvu zgubiti
inu ta paklenski ogenj zaslužiti.
Odstopi tedaj od te pregrehe,
taku na prideš v te večne kehe.
Glihi viži se s tem *grešnikam* zgodi,
kateri zapovedi Božje na drži.[21]

The *sinner soul*, you have to listen
you should not tempt your God in such a manner.
Precisely to you this may happen as well,
since you do not refrain from sinning.
You might lose the kingdom of heaven
and deserve the infernal fire.
Therefore, renounce your sin
and in this way you will not come into the eternal jail.
The same will happen to the *sinners*
who will not keep the commandments.[22]

Only a few moments later, the Second Angel, who carries a moneybag, says:

O čudu čez vse čudesa,
čudite se vi v nebesa!
Srebrnikov trideseti
oče Judas za Jezusa vzeti.
Divica Marija bi ga na dala,
za vas volni svet nikar na predala.
Ti *grešnik*, ti ga pak predaš
ter za en majhen lušt ga kjekaj daš.
O *grešnik*, več, več je vreden!
Le-to dobru ve eden sleden!
Le-to, o *grešnik*, prov premisli
ter močnu v srce pərtisni. [fig. 2][23]

O wonder above all wonders,
you may wonder to the heaven!
Thirty silver coins
Judas will take for Jesus.
Virgin Mary would not give him away,
she would not turn him over for the whole world.

---

22 Literal translation, emphasis mine.
23 Oče, *Škofjeloški pasijon*, p. 180.

> But you, *sinner*, you will turn him over
> and give him away for a small pleasure.
> O *sinner*, but he is worth more, more than this!
> This knows everyman well!
> Think about this, o *sinner*, thoroughly,
> and impress it into your heart.[24]

On the other hand, the highly visual effect of the performance of the *Škofjeloški pasijon* can be surmised from the very length of the procession. Given that between 300 and 600 people, or one third to one half of the resident population of Škofja Loka, participated in it, it must have functioned as an impressive, identity-generating "closed crowd."[25]

While their main effect was produced in or during performance, Good Friday processions sometimes also resonated unintentionally beyond their initial frames. When Komploier in his sermon growls at the "reformers" who dared to hiss down the processions, his words may well have been aimed at the anticlerical satire of the time. Here, the most prominent example is the tract *Specimen monachologiæ methodo Linnæana*, written by a member of the Order of Illuminati, Ignaz von Born *alias* Johannes Physiophilius, in 1783, in which the religious orders are mocked as a species at the evolutionary level between monkey and man [fig. 3]. What is more, in *Entwurf einer ländlichen Charfreytagsprocession*, written by another Illuminatus, Anton von Bucher, in 1782, it is precisely the Good Friday processions that are under fire. Bucher attributed this book to the fictitious Pater Umgang (Father Procession), who in fear of the upcoming ban decides to sort out the best of many processions ("das beste heraus sortiren"[26]), and publish it for posterity. Yet what follows[27] is more than 80 pages in which characters and scenes are subjected to a most alienating satirical treatment. For instance, the scene of the sacrament of baptism is presented by the guild of bartenders ("Bierzapfler" and "Geiwirthe"[28]), who walk along carrying a plate with the inscription: "'Er aber taufete im Wasser.' Joh. 2,5."[29] ("'He, however, baptized in water.' Jo. 2:5."). Or, in another scene, the Jesuit missionaries, "voll christlicher Starkmuth" ("filled with Christian

---

24 Literal translation, emphasis mine.
25 Elias Canetti. *Crowds and Power*. New York: Continuum, 1981, p. 16–17.
26 Anton Bucher. *Entwurf einer ländlichen Charfreytagsprocession: Samt einem gar lustigen und geistlichen Vorspiel zur Passionsaction*. Munich: Fleischmann, 1782, p. 16.
27 In the preface, the narrator emphasizes that the text which follows was published exactly as delivered by Pater Umgang: "Ich habe nichts davon gethan, und nichts dazu." ("I did not remove or add anything.") (Ibid., unpaginated.)
28 Ibid., p. 23.
29 Ibid., p. 24.

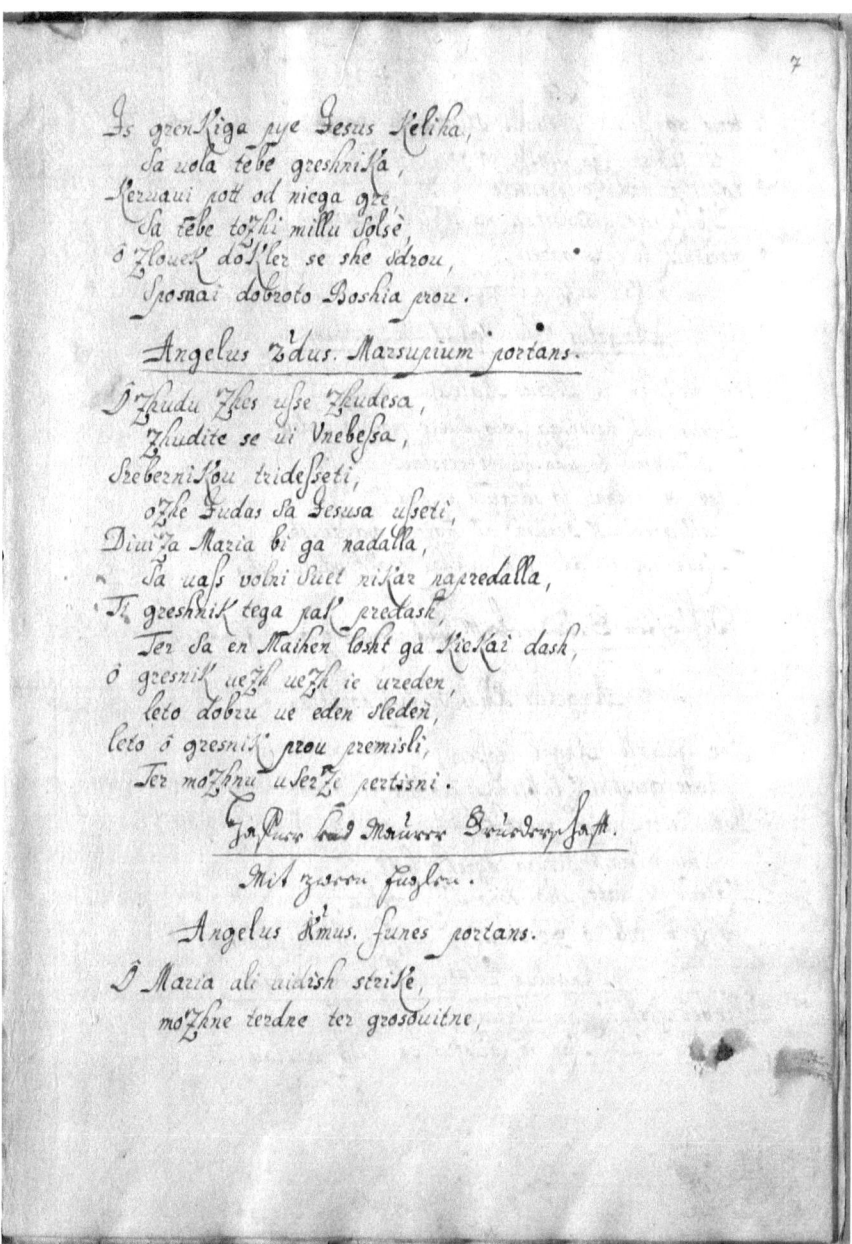

Fig. 2: The manuscript of the *Škofjeloški pasijon* (*The Passion of Škofja Loka*) from 1725–1727, fol. 7r. Slovenska kapucinska provinca, Kapucinski samostan Škofja Loka.

Fig. 3: A lithography made by Adam Arnst for the English edition of Johannes Physiophilius' tract *Specimen monachologiæ methodo Linnæana* from 1852.

courage"), who have been sent to India by the pope, are shown to strangle the unbelievers while reciting: "Die Götzenknecht und ihre Werke / Zuzernichten war unsere Stärke"[30] ("Our quality was to destroy / the idolaters and their works.").[31] The fact that the Good Friday processions are parodied, that the authority of the genre is exposed to ridicule and undermined, leads to the conclusion that Bucher perceived them in terms of power relations. Precisely by entering "the most political part of all literature,"[32] their political dimension became overt and explicit.

---

30 Ibid., p. 25.
31 Literal translation.
32 Matthew Hodgart. *Satire*. London: Weidenfels, 1969, p. 33.

Igor Grdina
Directions, Examples, and Incentives: Slovenian Playwriting in the Second Half of the Eighteenth Century

Around 1860 two distinguished Slovenian cultural and political figures discussed matters of a literary nature and national importance. One of them, the young and ambitious liberal Josip Vošnjak (1834–1911), had taken up writing a verse drama; the other, the somewhat older conservative Luka Svetec (1826–1921), thought it was too soon for such an endeavor.[1] In his opinion (which had been molded by the lyceum of the Austrian type) drama was the epitome of literature. Due to the complexity of its structure, the concentrated matter, and the necessary staging (i.e., all that went into a developed theater infrastructure), the tested capacity for reproduction, and the suitably cultured audience, drama always held a particularly representative place in the imagery and ideology of any Central European national space, transcending the artistic sphere. Impressive theatrical buildings of the nineteenth century, which were usually built in a historicizing fashion, were a monument of a sort to this very conception. They were meant to create an impression that it had always been thus.

However, only three generations earlier – a mere century – drama and theater were not concerned with such preconceptions. For Slovenes, who, as a modern national community, had not established themselves along the historicizing lines of a grand tradition and its associated appeal, but rather with a vision of an emancipated future, the forgetting of the past in the nineteenth century was somewhat understandable. Nationalistic leaders who often felt compelled to create dramatic oeuvres, thus expressing their cultural and political leadership and imposing personalities, found it helpful (at least initially) to treat the past as needing denial – and only denial. It was only later that they were able to acknowledge that they were not in fact the first to have done everything. Josip Vošnjak thus wrote a theatrical piece at the pinnacle of his career in which he quoted the entire comedy *Županova Micka* (*Micka, the Mayor's Daughter*) by Anton Tomaž Linhart (1756–1795) of 1789, adding an introduction and an ending which addressed the circumstances in which the comedy was premiered.[2]

---

[1] See Josip Vošnjak. *Spomini*. Ljubljana: Slovenska matica, 1982, p. 88.
[2] See ibid., p. 612.

Slovenian drama of the second half of the eighteenth century certainly differed from that of the high bourgeois era in respect to what it was supposed to represent. It was certainly not limited to the idea (and nor were its creators) that it had only a literary role. In this period marked by widespread illiteracy as well as sharp censorship, drama was a synonym for a regal form that could influence the widest audience of people of different classes. As such, it attracted very diverse minds – those who wanted to strengthen the foundations of the existing order as well as those who wished for changes of different kinds.

During the second half of the eighteenth century Slovenian drama, whose corpus comprised some 2000 texts, according to one of its greatest connoisseurs, Taras Kermauner (1930–2008), at the turn of the millennium, rather quickly invaded areas where it previously could not have succeeded, since it had only existed in the form of religious and school plays. In genre it first evolved towards libretto and comedy; at the time Slovene was asserting itself as drama's only expressive medium – the age of the previously common trilingualism (which never grew into a class triglossia) almost abruptly came to an end. Anton Tomaž Linhart, who wrote his earliest works in German – among them the tempestuous drama *Miss Jenny Love* (1780) – turned his attention to drama in the language of his fellow countrymen.

Two older contemporaries of Linhart's, the Barefoot monk Feliks Anton Dev (1732–1786) and the curate Jurij Japelj (1744–1807), who was even appointed the bishop of Trieste before his death, only used Slovene in stage-ready verse texts. The former of the two wrote the text for the short opera *Belin* (1780), while the latter tried to translate into Slovene the melodrama of Pietro Metastasio *Artaserse* from 1730.[3] Considering that Mozart was still trying to compose the music for a text of this well known Viennese court poet right before his death, i.e. *La clemenza di Tito* (*The Clemency of Titus*) which had first been used in 1734,[4] it is safe to say that Japelj – at least – was trying to keep up with the times. His translation work in drama reflects his desire to introduce the successful genre of melodrama to Slovene. Since Dev created his text for the short opera *Belin* in a totally different style – it was a baroque allegorical play in which a 'home version' of Apollo takes the lead role – there is an implicit yet palpable critical attitude in Japelj towards his older fellow clergyman. One should point out that Metastasio was at the time considered a great authority among Slovenes, since he commended the positive impression of their language just before his death: the Ljubljana dean and Viennese freemason

---

3 See France Kidrič. *Zgodovina slovenskega slovstva od začetkov do Zoisove smrti*. Ljubljana: Slovenska matica, 1929–1938, p. 178.
4 See Jože Sivec. *Opera skozi stoletja*. Ljubljana: Državna založba Slovenije, 1976, p. 102.

Janez Ricci (1745–1818), who ended his career as a titular bishop and was even awarded the *Légion d'honneur* in Paris during the period of the Illyrian Provinces (1809–1813), recited an Italian couplet in Linhart's translation in Metastasio's presence, which was received with great acclaim. Metastasio's verdict left a deep impression in Ljubljana.[5] This is probably why Dev's *Belin* – the older of the two texts – received much less attention than it otherwise would have. Eventually it received only limited attention in minor or private arrangements, where it was performed to the music of a Kamnik organ player and church choirmaster Jakob Frančišek Zupan (1734–1810) – the music was considered lost until 2008.[6] This lack of attention for *Belin* is further highlighted by the fact that it was of a decidedly cultural and reformatory character: it glorifies the victory of light over darkness, which symbolizes the introduction of Slovenian literature in the libretto.[7] On the other hand, Japelj never even finished his text, which has been supposed to reveal the lack of contemporary resonance of the first original Slovenian text for a short opera.

The destiny of both Slovene libretto texts from the second half of the eighteenth century is of particular interest because it points towards a highly evolved cultural standard and its great influence on newly forged traditions. Dev is fully aware that he stands at the beginning of a certain flow of events that is growing into a tradition, while Japelj immediately sets about introducing creative paradigms from elsewhere. Yes, Metastasio's melodrama from around 1780 was no longer the gold standard and was somewhat outdated, but it was not yet complete history either. The transition periods were inevitably separating themselves from the past in their awareness of the diversity and plurality of paradigms – regardless of the prevailing ideologies of modernity that so typically glorified a very specifically designed and planned future.

In Slovenian drama, this is most evident in the opus of Anton Tomaž Linhart. His youthful desire to merge the Italian and German taste in his homeland is witness to an ambitious creator endeavoring to build something new – but on the foundations of already extant and recognized traditions which provided a solid starting point and a good source of comparisons for his work – as well as a certain value. Linhart never intended to author works 'on a blank slate,' thus making things easy for himself by creating an entirely new, self-made tradition that would require new basic criteria; these were instead pro-

---

5 See Alfonz Gspan. "Ricci, Janez (Anton de)." *Slovenski biografski leksikon*. 1960.
6 See Milko Bizjak. "Prva slovenska opera *Belin*." *milko-bizjak*, www.milko-bizjak.page.tl.//Zupanova-opera-Belin.htm. Accessed 11 June 2018.
7 See Feliks Anton Dev. "Vesele krajnskeh modric na prihod njeh Belina." *Pisanice 1779–1782*, edited by Lino Legiša. Ljubljana: Slovenska akademija znanosti in umetnosti, 1977, pp. 54–65.

vided by an already valid qualitative standard. In one of his letters to Martin Kuralt (1757–1854) he maintains that he is not foolish or arrogant enough to claim an important title in Europe;[8] yet this was no obstacle to him adopting the highest examples, or rather their emblems, for his dramatic beginnings. His *Miss Jenny Love*, a tempestuous drama published in 1780 in Augsburg, was supposed to follow in Shakespeare's steps.[9] This applies particularly to the diversity of action (which leads to the tragic end of the main characters due to the demonic Lord Herington) and the use of external scenes, and quite possibly the setting of the textual microcosm in Britain – an homage, to be sure. However, the lack of long monologues steers away from the Shakespearean example.

In the spirit of his merging of German and Italian inspirations Linhart printed his collection of poems *Blumen aus Krain* (*Flowers from Carniola*) a year later; if *Miss Jenny Love* exhibited his knowledge of literary practices in the German north, he now turned his attention to the Latin south of Europe. This meant opening the doors to the more conservative conceptions of the stage. It seems that Linhart paused at Metastasio, too – but not at the historically 'grounded' melodrama (as Japelj did) but at the *azione teatrale*;[10] based on his two-act drama *L'isola disabitata* (*The Desert Island*), which is a prime example of the genre (and was also put to music by Franz Joseph Haydn), Linhart wrote the German text *Das öde Eiland* for a song play. However, by doing so he did not change his aesthetic credo: the rhythm of change in music theater is different from that in drama. The *Blumen aus Krain* collection is an interesting case of stylistic adaptation to other genres. Linhart's very diverse book exhibits texts of the 'last shift' style (a representative case is the German translation of the Slovenian romance *Pegam in Lambergar*; *Pegam and Lambergar*), but also some versifications done according to other ideals of form and thought. However, these were only the first steps on the author's path, which was paved by the need to unify the European republic of thought in his homeland. Following this path he also took into account some English (Pope) and French authors (Montesquieu, Beaumarchais).

Unfortunately, the next work by Linhart – a drama about an adventurous major John André, who was ordered to be hanged by George Washington in 1780 – is known by title alone.[11] It was entirely contemporary, but it also addressed interesting issues of loyalty and treason in a time of radical changes.

---

8 See Anton Tomaž Linhart. *Zbrano delo*. Ljubljana: Državna založba Slovenije, 1950, vol. 1, p. 408.
9 See ibid., p. 331.
10 See ibid., p. 498.
11 See Mirko Zupančič. *Literarno delo mladega A. T. Linharta*. Ljubljana: Slovenska matica, 1972, p. 98.

Yet Linhart, who subscribed to the enlightenment philosophy (even though he initially wanted to become a priest, he later doubted that just reading the Bible could make a man happy[12]), evidently could not find sufficient support for his literature – and his work was not financially viable enough to finance an independent publishing activity. If he wanted to maintain his literary activity (he was also interested in history), he desperately needed support. After his failed attempt to form an intellectual circle – a scientific academy whose members would be drawn from the local aristocratic and intellectual elite – his only remaining option was to join the circle of the baron Sigismund Zois (1747–1819). The wealthiest man in Carniola, Zois was a known supporter of the Muses whose rich library provided the basis for scientific and literary activity on the southeastern rim of the Austrian monarchy.

The baron Zois, who had been brought up intellectually in Italy, was a reformer.[13] Though he subscribed to some initiatives of French philosophers, he thought that circumstances at home needed special impetuses to make the world better. Linhart pictured his homeland as a junction of different cultures from which a new original tradition would spring up; however, despite some differing positions, he did not contest Zois's views. Zois's ardor for his mother tongue, which he understood as a tool for improving the microcosm, directed Linhart towards writing for the stage in Slovene. This was by no means a change of heart, since the last two plays written by Linhart still exhibit his devotion to the idea of a European synthesis in his homeland. However, what changed was the strategy that was supposed to lead to this effect: the need to change the world was directed to the most general addressee possible. His eagerness for his homeland, which was close to his heart even during the writing of the *Blumen aus Krain*, was now addressed to what was, linguistically and factually, its most numerous population. At first sight it seems paradoxical that Baron Zois, a descendant of a knighted bourgeois, directed Linhart towards the knowledge that changing the world starts with 'people without qualities'; yet the entrepreneur who only had the market to thank for his fortune could nurture no illusions about the quotidian source of his well-earned wealth, despite his belonging to the intellectual and class elite. Of course, the American and French revolutions, about which Ljubljana was well informed, as well as personal liberties – the most important result of the endeavors of the reformist emperor Joseph II – also produced their effects.

---

[12] See Anton Tomaž Linhart. *Zbrano delo*. Ljubljana: Državna založba Slovenije, 1950, vol. 1, p. 432.
[13] See Lino Legiša, and Alfonz Gspan. *Zgodovina slovenskega slovstva I.: Do začetkov romantike*. Ljubljana: Slovenska matica, 1956, pp. 379–382, p. 392.

The comedies *Županova Micka* and *Ta veseli dan ali Matiček se ženi* (*This Happy Day, or Matiček Gets Married*) were published in 1790 in Ljubljana; they are an expression of an eager, in many respects even combative literature which features emancipatory thinking. The *Županova Micka*, an adaptation of Joseph Richter's comedy *Die Feldmühle* (*The Country Mill*) of 1777 which was performed by traveling theater groups in Carniola on many occasions, is a critique of a morally depraved, frivolous nobleman which ends with mockery at his expense: it is peasants who set things straight with the aid of a 'noble lady.' The nobleman, however, is aided by a drunkard village scribe – which means there is no black-and-white division among characters according to class. Yet the aim of the play, which was first staged in 1789 in Ljubljana, was inevitably to point out that individual solutions to problems of dejectedness and dishonesty are basically impossible. Micka, who wants to be elevated in class, can only become a victim to a con-man.

Linhart's adaptation of Beaumarchais's comedy *La Folle Journée, ou le Mariage de Figaro* (*The Mad Day, or The Marriage of Figaro*) (which came just a year later) is much more ambitious. Since the Slovene version of this famous work, which Napoleon thought to be the revolution underway, was created in the period of increasing antagonisms between the French revolutionists and the *ancienne Europe*, additional attention was required from the Slovenian adaptor – and swiftness, too, since the text was published just in time before stricter censorship was enforced in the Habsburg Monarchy; the latter was a consequence of the growing fear of sympathies for the revolutionaries in Paris, whose incredible cruelty was dramatically reported even in Slovenian 'news poetry,' i.e. a sort of oral 'newspaper' for the illiterate peasantry. Singing inserts in the *Ta veseli dan ali Matiček se ženi* indicate the possibility that Linhart, a musical talent and himself a composer, followed the example of Lorenzo Da Ponte's libretto adaptation of Beaumarchais's work written for Mozart and his *Le nozze di Figaro* of 1786. The counter-feudal emphases in the Slovenian version are somewhat less pronounced than in the French original; however, they are still very explicit and visible also outside the stage situation. A recognizable feature is Linhart's aversion to German bureaucracy, which is obviously absent in Beaumarchais. In this respect the *Ta veseli dan ali Matiček se ženi* is more than a mere critique of aristocracy; it is also a critique of germanizing tendencies that became quite pronounced in the Austrian Monarchy during the reign of Emperor Joseph II. Linhart, who first enthusiastically supported the reforms of the enlightened monarch,[14] evidently came to realize that these

---

14 See Anton Tomaž Linhart. *Zbrano delo*. Ljubljana: Državna založba Slovenije, 1950, vol. 1, p. 450.

were ultimately condemned to fail due to the neglect of local circumstances. The unfortunate ruler, who was forced to overrule most of his reforms on his deathbed if he wanted his brother Leopold II to inherit anything other than complete chaos, met the limits of his absolutism – particularly in Hungary. The imagery and ideology of the emperor and those under him were now in almost complete opposition. The enforcing of German administration in the region that was in language exclusively Slovene pushed Linhart towards the circle of the counter-Josephine coalition shaped by conservative clergy and aristocracy from different provinces of the Habsburg Monarchy, together with enlightened counter-centralists and the advocates of the newly discovered spirit of nations. It is therefore far from odd that the comedy *Ta veseli dan ali Matiček se ženi* was first staged only on the eve of the March Revolution in 1848.[15] The regime of Leopold II was, despite its character of enlightened absolutism, already so afraid of people that it established a secret police for the purpose of control – a service that would later infiltrate all segments of the complex Austrian Monarchy. However, it failed to fulfill its purpose; Linhart's subversive version of *Figaro*, the *Ta veseli dan ali Matiček se ženi*, was reprinted even during the period of the strictest absolutism of Klemens Metternich (1773–1859) – for which a 'camouflage' as a grammar example came in very handy.

Slovenian drama of the second half of the eighteenth century decreased in activity considerably during the period of Metternich's absolutism, which treated very suspiciously any initiative 'from below,' yet it provided the basic platform for the subsequent playwriting in the region between the Alps and the Adriatic. While German and Italian stage managers usually drew on plays from elsewhere, Slovenes had no other options than to resort to domestic production, which consequently became nationally representative – the ideology of (high-)school poetics was not the only reason for this. Through the process of evolution from adaptation to originality, creative production for the stage remained mindful of qualitative standards, despite the performance amateurism that lasted almost until the end of the nineteenth century, even though it failed to become the European synthesis in Linhart's sense. But, then again – nobody managed to achieve that anywhere else either.

---

15 See Lino Legiša, and Alfonz Gspan. *Zgodovina slovenskega slovstva I.: Do začetkov romantike*. Ljubljana: Slovenska matica, 1956, p. 400.

DS Mayfield
Variants of *hypólepsis*: Rhetorical, Anthropistic, Dramatic (With Remarks on Terence, Machiavelli, Shakespeare)

1 The Dynamics of Cultural Networks: Floating *dicta*

ἄνθρωπός ἐστιν ὃ πάντες ἴδμεν ...
Democritus[1]

Everyone knows Protagoras' notorious assertion that 'man is the measure of all things' – an answer to the (implicit) question 'what is a human being'.[2] Democritus is taken to have said that 'man is a microcosm', that 'man is what

---

[1] *Die Fragmente der Vorsokratiker*, edited by Walther Kranz, translated by Hermann Diels, 3 vols. Zurich: Weidmann, 1985, vol. 2, pp. 177 f., 68B165). On 'floatation' in the '(virtual) cultural network', see Küpper (*The Cultural Net. Early Modern Drama as a Paradigm*. Berlin: de Gruyter, 2018; "Rhetoric and the Cultural Net: Transnational Agencies of Culture". *Rhetoric and Drama*, edited by DS Mayfield. Berlin: de Gruyter, 2017, pp. 151–175; Mayfield. "Proceedings". *Rhetoric and Drama*, pp. 203–229, pp. 220–222; "Interplay with Variation: Approaching Rhetoric and Drama". *Rhetoric and Drama*, pp. 3–52, spec. pp. 3–5, 9–10, 36–38).
[2] "πάντων χρημάτων μέτρον ἐστὶν ἄνθρωπος" (Protagoras, as per Sextus, in: *Vorsokratiker* 2, p. 263, 80B1; see Sextus Empiricus. *Against the Logicians*, edited and translated by R. G. Bury. Cambridge: Harvard UP, 1983, pp. 30–33, I.60–61); see also '*pánton chremáton métron ánthropon einai*' (Protagoras, as per Plato, in: *Vorsokratiker* 2, p. 263, 80B1); "Protagoras […] says somewhere that man is 'the measure of all things[']" (Plato. "Theaetetus". *Theaetetus. Sophist*, edited and translated by H. N. Fowler. Cambridge: Harvard UP, 2006, pp. 1–257, p. 41, 152A). Drawing on Aristotle, Cicero emphasizes (as does Quintilian): "*scriptasque fuisse et paratas a Protagora rerum inlustrium disputationes, quae nunc communes appellantur loci*" (*Vorsokratiker* 2, p. 266, 80B6); "Protagoras wrote out and furnished discussions of certain large general subjects such as we now call commonplaces" (Cicero. "Brutus." *Brutus. Orator*, edited and translated by H. M. Hubbell. Cambridge: Harvard UP, 1962, pp. 18–293, p. 49, xi.46).

Note: The paper from which this *essai* evolved was presented at Freie Universität Berlin on April 30, during the 2015 DramaNet conference; the author wishes to thank its organizers, as well as the editors of the present volume, especially Dr. Sven Thorsten Kilian. The article at hand benefitted from effectual comments on the part of Prof. Kathy Eden (Columbia University) and Prof. Joachim Küpper (Freie Universität Berlin).

https://doi.org/10.1515/9783110536690-014

everyone knows'.³ Virtually all of Aristotle's works open with a statement concerning the 'tò tí en einai' of human beings: de anima distinguishes man as 'the calculating animal'.⁴ The *Politics* offers 'man as a political animal' – more precisely: 'it is political more than any other gregarious animal, since it is capable of speech and reason'.⁵ The *Poetics* asserts: 'man is the most mimetic of all animals'.⁶ The first sentence of the *Metaphysics* reads: "All men naturally de-

---

3 "ἄνθρωπός ἐστιν ὃ πάντες ἴδμεν" (Democritus in: *Vorsokratiker* 2, pp. 177 f., 68B165; see Sextus. *Outlines of Pyrrhonism*, edited and translated by R. G. Bury. Cambridge: Harvard UP, p. 166, II.23); 'man, a microcosm,' '*mikrón kósmon*,' '*toi anthrópoi mikroi kósmoi*' (*Vorsokratiker* 2, p. 153, 68B34); see Hans Blumenberg's reference to Democritus' "Daß der Mensch eine kleine Welt sei" (*Theorie der Unbegrifflichkeit*, edited by Anselm Haverkamp. Frankfurt: Suhrkamp, p. 69).
4 "Imagination in the form of sense is found [...] in all animals, but deliberative imagination only in the calculative [animals: *zóois logistikois*]" ("On the Soul," *On the Soul. Parva Naturalia. On Breath*. Translated by W. S. Hett. Cambridge: Harvard UP, 2000, pp. 1–203, here p. 192 f., 434a, III.xi) – later termed "νοῦν κριτικόν", "a mind capable of judgement" (pp. 194 f., 434b, III.xii). For the phrase '*tò tí en einai*', see p. 70, 412b, II.i; Blumenberg considers it to be "untranslatable" (*Begriffe in Geschichten*. Frankfurt: Suhrkamp, 1998, p. 242; trans. dsm).
5 "why man is a political animal [πολιτικὸν ζῷον] in a greater measure than any bee or any gregarious animal is clear [...] man alone of the animals possesses speech [λόγον]" (*Politics*, edited and translated by H. Rackham. Cambridge: Harvard UP, 1944, pp. 8–11, 1253a, I.i.9–10); "for it is the special property of man in distinction from other animals that he alone has perception of good and bad and right and wrong" (pp. 9 f., 1253a, I.i.11). On the Stoic conception see e.g. Marcus Aurelius (*Meditations*, edited and translated by C. R. Haines. Cambridge: Harvard UP, 1930, p. 56, III.7; p. 58, III.9); the former is based on Aristotle, as per Sextus: "Others used to assert that 'Man is a rational mortal animal, receptive of intelligence and science'" (*Outlines*, p. 169, II.26; see 168n.). The latter aims to take such definitions apart (see pp. 286 f., II.211). Compare Blumenberg: "Das Merkmal der Vernünftigkeit steht in einer auflösbaren und der Funktion nach zweifelhaften Verbindung mit dem Leib als seinem Instrument. Mit anderen Worten: die klassische Definition des Menschen als des vernünftigen Lebewesens verpflichtet die Theorie nicht dazu, die Vernünftigkeit als eine gerade für dieses Lebewesen notwendige und integrale Leistung aus seinen Existenzbedingungen heraus zu verstehen. Dies wäre nur möglich, wenn Vernunft als das Minimum der Leistungsvoraussetzungen der Selbsterhaltung für dieses organische System, diesen Leib vom Eidos Mensch, erwiesen werden könnte. Die klassische Definition ist also nicht nur anthropologisch bedeutungslos, sondern geradezu Anthropologie verhindernd" (*Beschreibung des Menschen*, edited by Manfred Sommer. Frankfurt: Suhrkamp, 2006, p. 510).
6 "For it is an instinct of human beings, from childhood, to engage in mimesis (indeed, this distinguishes them from other animals: man is the most mimetic of all[)]" ("Poetics," edited and translated by Stephen Halliwell. *Aristotle. Poetics. Longinus. On the Sublime. Demetrius. On Style*, edited by W. H. Fyfe et al. Cambridge: Harvard UP, 1995, pp. 27–141, p. 37, 1448b, § 4) – a matter of gradation, not an absolute difference; man is indeed an animal (still); similarly, in the above definition (see *Politics*, pp. 8–11, 1253a, I.i.9–10).

sire knowledge" (*Metaphysics 1–9*, pp. 2 f., 980a, I.i.1).⁷ From suchlike statements, the Pyrrhonist Skeptic Sextus Empiricus inferred that 'man is not only unknowable, but even unthinkable'.⁸ In the twentieth century, Adorno asserted: 'One cannot state what man is, and this puts a veto on all anthropology'.⁹ Even so, the query 'what is a human being' persists. One reason may be Kant's assessing his catalog of questions – 'what can I know', 'what shall I do', 'what may I hope', 'what is man' – as coming down to the last item.¹⁰ One might

---

7 '*Pántes ánthropoi tou eidénai orégontai phýsei*' (*Metaphysics. Books 1–9*, edited and translated by Hugh Tredennick. Cambridge: Harvard UP, 1933, pp. 2 f., 980a, I.i.1). For Sextus' comment on the Aristotelian opening sentence, see Blumenberg (*Die Legitimität der Neuzeit*. Frankfurt: Suhrkamp, 1999, p. 314; see Sextus, *Outlines*, pp. 2–3, I.1); also as to Augustine, altering Aristotle's line (Blumenberg, *Legitimität*, p. 365); concerning the Medieval, Scholastic reception of Aristotle's introductory sentence (pp. 383, 405): "Bei Thomas von Aquino [...] ist der erste Satz der aristotelischen 'Metaphysik' zu einem der schlechthin gültigen und in vielfacher Argumentation genutzten Prinzipien des scholastischen Denkens erhoben. Die Natürlichkeit des Wissensstrebens impliziert die Wertung: *omnis scientia bona est*" (pp. 384; see 384n.–385n.).
8 See Sextus: "Now 'Man' [...] seems to me, so far as regards the statements made by the Dogmatists, to be not only non-apprehensible but also inconceivable. [...] when they wish to establish the concept of 'Man' they disagree in the first place, and in the second place they speak unintelligibly. Thus Democritus declares that 'Man is that which we all know'. Then, so far as his opinion goes, we shall not know Man, since we also know a dog, and consequently Dog too will be man. And some men we do not know, therefore they will not be men. Or rather, if we are to judge by this concept, no one will be a man; for since Democritus says that Man must be known by all, and all men know no one man, no one, according to him, will be a man" (*Outlines*, pp. 165–167, II.22–24). There appears to be a structural relation of Anselm of Canterbury's ontological proof of God to the initial sentence above; see Blumenberg: "der mittelalterliche Erfinder des Arguments unterscheidet selbst zwischen dem Gott seines Beweises, über den hinaus nichts Größeres gedacht werden kann, und dem Gott seines Offenbarungsglaubens, der größer sei als alles, was überhaupt gedacht werden könne" (*Legitimität*, p. 111); "*Ergo Domine, non solum es quo maius cogitari nequit sed es quiddam maius quam cogitari possit*" (Anselm, "Proslogion," chapter XV, cited by Blumenberg, *Legitimität*, p. 564); see what the latter calls "die Forcierung der negativen Sprache" (p. 565).
9 "*Was der Mensch sei, läßt sich nicht angeben.* [...] *Daß nicht sich sagen läßt, was der Mensch sei, ist keine besonders erhabene Anthropologie sondern ein Veto gegen jegliche*" (cited by Blumenberg, *Beschreibung*, pp. 487 f.); see "Die Erneuerung der philosophischen Anthropologie in den [1920ern] [...] begann nicht zufällig mit dem traditionell nur als Paradox möglichen Satz von Max Scheler: ... *die Undefinierbarkeit gehört zum Wesen des Menschen*" (p. 510).
10 "Kants berühmte[r] Katalog philosophischer Fragestellungen [...]: 1. Was kann ich wissen? 2. Was soll ich tun? 3. Was darf ich hoffen? 4. Was ist der Mensch? [...] *Im Grunde könnte man aber alles dieses zur Anthropologie rechnen, weil sich die drei ersten Fragen auf die letzte beziehen*" (Blumenberg, *Beschreibung*, pp. 500 f.); see Immanuel Kant. *Schriften zur Metaphysik und Logik 2. Werkausgabe*, 12 vols., edited by Wilhelm Weischedel, vol. 6. Frankfurt: Suhrkamp, 1977, p. 448, Einleitung III). These queries delineate philosophy "*in sensu cosmico*", the "field of philosophy in this cosmopolitan ['weltbürgerlichen'] sense" (p. 447; trans. dsm):

almost be tempted to submit that 'man is the animal that cannot stop asking and answering the question what man is'.[11]

This *essai* is structured as follows: a methodical second section ensues after the present exposition; the third part addresses the term '*hypólepsis*' from a rhetorical, anthropistic, and dramatic perspective; a fourth section tenders variations on the Terentian '*nihil humani*'; the conclusion is concerned with the most elemental level of the above query.

"1) What can I know? – / 2) What shall I do? / 3) What may I hope? / 4) What is man?" (p. 448; trans. dsm). Metaphysics answers the first, ethics the second, religion the third, anthropology the last query, as per Kant (see p. 448) – who tentatively subsumes the first three questions (hence their answers) under the last one: 'anthropology' as the subtending systematics. See Odo Marquard: "Es gibt kaum eine Philosophie, die nicht vom Menschen handelt" (*Glück im Unglück. Philosophische Überlegungen*. Munich: Fink, 2008, p. 142). As per Blumenberg, the question is distinguished by its indisputability, precision, 'lapidary' nature: "Keine der philosophischen Disziplinen hat eine so unbestrittene und eindeutige Fragestellung wie diese, nämlich die lapidare Frage: was ist der Mensch?" (*Beschreibung*, p. 499). Arguably, the query 'what is man' (and its various answers, hence anthropistics) is the (often tacit) foundation of any discourse, affecting the notional edifice on (virtually) all strata upward. Conspicuously, Blumenberg frequently begins chapters or segments with variants answering the formula 'what is man'; in his *Höhlenausgänge* (Frankfurt: Suhrkamp, 1996), see e.g. the first sentence of chapter III ("So wurde der Mensch, beim Durchgang durch die Höhle, das träumende Tier", p. 29) and chapter V ("Der Mensch ist das sichtbare Wesen in einem emphatischen Sinne", p. 55); likewise: "Der Mensch ist das Tier, das sich andere Tiere hält" (*Löwen*. Berlin: Suhrkamp, 2010, p. 89), opening a brief essay therein. Blumenberg employs variants of this template as a structuring device.

11 See Nietzsche's suggestive formulation: "Er ist das noch nicht festgestellte Thier" – man is the 'as yet undetermined animal' (*Kritische Studienausgabe* [*KSA*], edited by Giorgio Colli and Mazzino Montinari, 15 vols. Munich et al.: dtv and de Gruyter, 1999; here: vol. 11, p. 125; trans. dsm); see Karlheinz Stierle ("Was heißt Moralistik?" *Moralistik. Explorationen und Perspektiven*, edited by Rudolf Behrens and Maria Moog-Grünewald. Munich: Fink, 2010, pp. 1–22, here p. 20); Michel Foucault (*Einführung in Kants* Anthropologie. Translated by Ute Frietsch, Berlin: Suhrkamp, 2010, p. 118); Arnold Gehlen's reading: "Das ist ein guter Doppelsinn, denn der Mensch ist einmal irgendwie 'unfertig', nicht festgerückt, sich selbst noch Zweck und Ziel der Bearbeitung, und dann gibt es noch keine Feststellung dessen, was eigentlich der Mensch ist" (*Philosophische Anthropologie und Handlungslehre. Gesamtausgabe*, edited by Karl-Siegbert Rehberg, vol. 4. Frankfurt: Klostermann, 1983, p. 75; see pp. 86, 130); he adds: "das ist ein drohendes Wort" (p. 162). Generally thereto, see Mayfield (*Artful Immorality – Variants of Cynicism. Machiavelli, Gracián, Diderot, Nietzsche*. Berlin: de Gruyter, 2015, pp. 198, 391–402, spec. p. 395, 395n., 413n., 430n.).

2 The Method of Choice: Descriptivity

> Was zu beschreiben ist, stellt sich heraus,
> wenn man zu beschreiben begonnen hat.
> Blumenberg[12]

'What is a human being' – there have been and there will (in all probability) be an unlimited number of apparently finite answers to that boundless query.[13] No answer has superseded all others; arguably, none shall. Apart from a (Neo-)Nominalist *'nescio'*, the expedient approach to such plurality and diversity – one question, myriad and manifold answers – is descriptiveness, as practiced in Blumenberg's *Beschreibung des Menschen*. This method tends to be discursive, limitless; its objectives provisional, the path as such the primary concern.[14] Hence Blumenberg suggests the term *'Definitionsessay'* ('attempts at definition') – stressing the latter's tentative, heuristic character.[15]

---

12 (*Zu den Sachen und zurück*, edited by Manfred Sommer. Frankfurt: Suhrkamp, 2007, p. 173).
13 Blumenberg (as to Kant): "Freilich so, in der Art einer Metafrage, kann man erst ganz spät fragen, nachdem schon lange genug gefragt worden ist: was ist der Mensch? Aber was hatte man damit wissen wollen? Welche Antwort hätte genügt?" (*Beschreibung*, p. 502); the latter, being a suggestive question, may allude to the philosopher's earlier emphases as to inquisitive "*curiositas*" – of 'man as the being *plus ultra*' (see *Legitimität*, pp. 296, 296n.–297n., 314, 324; part three passim: pp. 261–528). The implied limitlessness (see Husserl's programmatically 'infinite labor', as referenced e.g. in *Beschreibung*, p. 441, and section 5 herein) leads to the question of method: in Blumenberg, *Beschreibung* (discursive descriptiveness), instead of yet another ‹-logy› (including, arguably, not another 'phenomenology'; see *Höhlenausgänge*, p. 15); and to a tentative, provisional objective: "die Ersetzung dieser Fragestellung ['was der Mensch sei'] durch eine andere, sie modifizierende [...] Fragestellung: *wie der Mensch möglich sei*. [...] Die Modifikation der Fragestellung kann zunächst und zumindest an die Kontingenz des Menschen heranführen: er muß nicht sein und er muß nicht so sein, wie er ist" (*Beschreibung*, p. 511).
14 As to the import of 'approximation' in Blumenberg, see these instances as indicative of his method: "Tendenzen bei Annäherung an" (*Die Lesbarkeit der Welt*. Frankfurt: Suhrkamp, 1986, p. 162); "Annäherung an" (*Lebenszeit und Weltzeit*. Frankfurt: Suhrkamp, 1986, p. 249); "provisorischen Annäherungen, [...] Leitfäden" (Hans Robert Jauß et al. "Sechste Sitzung: Gemeinsame Interpretation von Apollinaires *Arbre* [aus *Calligrammes*]". *Immanente Ästhetik – Ästhetische Reflexion. Lyrik als Paradigma der Moderne*, edited by Wolfgang Iser. Munich: Fink, 1966 [*Poetik und Hermeneutik*, 2], pp. 464–484, p. 483); see also the title of Blumenberg's respective article, and passim therein ("Anthropologische Annäherung an die Aktualität der Rhetorik [1971]". *Ästhetische und metaphorologische Schriften*, edited by Anselm Haverkamp. Frankfurt: Suhrkamp, 2001, pp. 406–431; "Approccio antropologico all'attualità della retorica". *Il Verri. Rivista di Letteratura* 35/36 [1971], pp. 49–72; "An Anthropological Approach to the Contemporary Significance of Rhetoric". *After Philosophy. End or Transformation?* [1987], edited by Kenneth Baynes et al. Cambridge: MIT P, 1993, pp. 429–458). Generally, see Heraclitus: "ἀγχιβασίην", "Annäherung" (*Vorsokratiker 1*, p. 178, 22B122).

To be speaking of 'human invariants' from a 'phenomenistic' perspective in the field of 'anthropistics' has the advantage of avoiding the implications of a deductive approach.[16] In this, the *essai* at hand follows Blumenberg, decidedly entitling his corresponding monograph *Description of Man*.[17] One reason he gives is this: "Every anthropology, including such as deny this [fact], is historical at core" (*Beschreibung*, p. 890; trans. dsm); in one sense, this signifies that opinions about man's '*tò tí en einai*' are variable.[18] His answer as to the utility of '(human) invariants' is twofold: "no science [or 'scholarship'] is at all able to operate rationally without introducing and establishing constants" (*Beschreibung*, p. 485; trans. dsm); and there can "be no theory of variants that

---

15 "Insofern sie Annäherungsversuche an die Definition sein könnten, will ich sie als 'Definitionsessays' bezeichnen. Was sie charakterisiert, ist die Verbindung zwischen dem formalen Anspruch auf Allgemeinheit und der materialen Resignation auf den partiellen Aspekt" (*Beschreibung*, p. 511) – perchance a form of Neo-Nominalism; some instances: "*Man is a being of poor intelligence, which is dominated by its wishes*" (Freud as quoted by Marcuse, cited in: Blumenberg *Beschreibung*, p. 513; trans. dsm); "*Mankind is a species of monkey suffering from megalomania*" (Vaihinger in: *Beschreibung*, p. 514; trans. dsm); "*I believe that man is ultimately so free a being that it is impossible to deny it the right to be what it believes to be*" (Lichtenberg in: *Beschreibung*, p. 516; trans. dsm); see also: "one is tempted to define man" (Oscar Wilde. "The Critic as Artist". *The Artist as Critic*, edited by Richard Ellmann. New York: Random House, 1982, pp. 340–408, here p. 388). '*Definitionsessay*' is 'paradoxical' (a contradiction in conventional terms), since 'definition' implies or claims finality (as do deductive approaches, typically ending in ‹-logy›), which is literally at variance with the tendency of an '*essai*'; for a factual implementation of the latter qua poetic program, see Montaigne qua 'source type'; for the latter term (*mutatis mutandis*), see Jurij M. Lotman (*Die Struktur literarischer Texte*. Translated by Rolf-Dietrich Keil, Munich: Fink: 1972, p. 151, 151n.). In general, see Holenstein (in another context): "In der Wissenschaftstheorie wird der teleologischen Fragestellung seit Kant ein heuristischer Wert zugestanden" ("Einführung: Von der Poesie und der Plurifunktionalität der Sprache". *Poetik. Ausgewählte Aufsätze 1921–1971*, edited by Elmar Holenstein and Tarcisius Schelbert. Frankfurt: Suhrkamp, 1979, pp. 7–57, p. 8) – emphasizing 'heuristic', rather than 'telic logic'.
16 So as not to turn this descriptive approach into yet another ‹-logy› (such as epistemology, anthropology, biology – let alone other notoriously ostensive logics). The expedient method in the field at hand is to proceed by induction, spec. qua (ac)cumulative analytics, detailed description; rather than by deduction, or analogous systematics – to say nothing of determining the supposed *télos a priori* and arriving at the apparently inevitable *quod erat demonstrandum*.
17 See Sommer's "Editorische Notiz": "'›Beschreibung des Menschen‹ ersetzt den Titel ›Phänomenologische Anthropologie‹' hat sich Hans Blumenberg (1920–1996) auf einem Blatt notiert" (in: *Beschreibung*, p. 897).
18 This implies that a plurality and variety of conceivably familiar (common, conventional, customary) anthropistic assumptions (as to 'what a human being is') are potentially in use (circulation, currency) during a certain period, and at different times; while diverse and variable on the whole, they may seem invariable or distinctive to a given time or discourse; from a diachronic perspective, multiple and manifold answers to the query 'what is man' have a tendency to coexist.

would not [simultaneously] advance the theory of *constants*" (*Beschreibung*, p. 487; trans. dsm). Blumenberg also employs the term "invariance" (*Beschreibung*, p. 484; trans. dsm), implying variation as the apparent state of affairs.[19] Assumptions concerning specific invariants will in fact vary over time: they are a matter of the *communis opinio* – hence changeable, (diachronically) sundry.

3 Variants of 'Taking Up and Tying in With'

Ὅτι πάντα ὑπόληψις.
Marcus Aurelius[20]

The theoretical concept herein suggested as expedient for describing also the aforesaid dynamics is '*hypólepsis*'.[21] Its (initial) meanings are disputed, and no

---

[19] Herein, this choice of terms ('variation', 'invariance') also follows Jakobson's approach, as applied in another field; see Holenstein's note: "*Das Verhältnis Invarianz – Variation, eines der Leitprinzipien der Jakobsonschen Linguistik, das die Sprache in verschiedener Hinsicht prägt [...]. Jede Variation ist auf dem Hintergrund der sie begrenzenden Invarianten zu sehen*" (in: Jakobson, *Poetik*, p. 83; compare also Holenstein's "Einführung," p. 21, therein; as well as his study, *Roman Jakobsons phänomenologischer Strukturalismus*. Frankfurt: Suhrkamp, 1975, pp. 101 ff.); see the linguist's specific formulation (the context being Poe, and Valéry's reading of the latter): "The invariance of the group is particularly stressed by the variation in its order" (Jakobson, *Language in Literature*, edited by Krystyna Pomorska and Stephen Rudy. Cambridge: Harvard UP, 1987, p. 87). See Blumenberg: "Aufschlußhaltigkeit [...] ergibt sich [...], wenn das Ineinandergreifen der formal entgegengesetzten Tendenzen von Konstanz und Variation [...] wahrgenommen wird" ("Wirklichkeitsbegriff und Wirkungspotential des Mythos [1971]". *Ästhetische und metaphorologische Schriften*, edited by Anselm Haverkamp. Frankfurt: Suhrkamp, 2001, pp. 327–405, here p. 348; initially in: *Terror und Spiel. Probleme der Mythenrezeption*, edited by Manfred Fuhrmann. [*Poetik und Hermeneutik*, 4]. München: Fink, 1983, pp. 11–66; here p. 26). See Marquard's employment of this notion (*de re*) in an ethical context (*sensu lato*): "Darum müssen wir herkömmlich leben: wir müssen stets überwiegend das bleiben, was wir schon waren; unsere Veränderungen werden getragen durch unsere Nichtveränderungen" (*Philosophie des Stattdessen*. Stuttgart: Reclam, 2009, p. 71).
[20] (*Meditations*, p. 326, XII.8; p. 330, XII.22; see p. 38, II.15; p. 70, IV.3).
[21] For the Stoic term "*Katalepsis*" qua "grasp" (including the Zenonic anecdote on the concept's coinage), see Blumenberg (*Legitimität*, pp. 298 f.; trans. dsm; compare p. 312). Among the books by the (unorthodox) Stoic Herillus of Carthage, D. Laertius notes one with the title "Περὶ ὑπολήψεως", which Hicks tellingly translates as "Concerning Opinion or Belief" (*Lives II*, pp. 270–271, VII.166; see p. 273, VII.167; and von Arnim, *Stoicorum Veterum Fragmenta* [*SVT*]. Vol. I. Stuttgart: Teubner, 1964, p. 91, §409; see also *SVT IV*, p. 150, s. v. "ὑπόληψις"). Similarly, two of Chrysippus' works on Logic contain the term: first, "Of the Arguments affecting Ordinary Suppositions ['*hypolépseis*']" (D. Laertius. *Lives of Eminent Philosophers*, edited and translated by R. D. Hicks. Cambridge: Harvard UP, 2006, vol. 2, pp. 310–311, VII.197); as well as one with the title "Περὶ ὑπολήψεως", which Hicks (using two English terms once more) renders

scholarly consensus appears to have been reached as to Aristotle's acceptations in particular.[22] The term has been conceived of as being primarily of

---

"Of Opinion or Assumption" (pp. 316–317, VII.201); thereto, see also von Arnim (*SVT II*, p. 8, § 15, and p. 9, § 17, respectively); the scholar adduces another intratextual occurrence of the term via a quotation in Plutarch (p. 291, § 994); similarly via Stobaeus (as '*hypolépseos*', *SVT III*, p. 92, § 378), and Aspasius (as '*hypólepsin*', p. 94, § 386); the latter's citation is taken up in Seneca's Latin as "opiniones" (*SVT I*, p. 81), "opinionibus" (p. 82, § 359; see Seneca, *Epistles 93–124*, p. 14, XCIV.6, and p. 18, XCIV.13); von Arnim also gives a long quote from Stobaeus, where Chrysippus uses the term three or four times (one may be an *erratum*, see *SVT III*, p. 147n.), in connection with various verbal forms (e.g. '*hypolambánein*', pp. 146–147), and affine terms such as '*katálepsis*' (here as '*akatalépto*', '*katalépseos*', and probably '*katálepsin*'), spec. in a context concerning common knowledge (using the terms '*doxázein*', '*dóxas*', '*pístin*', '*epistémen*', '*epístasthaî*', '*pisteúein*', for instance; p. 147, §548; see p. 147n.); in a comparable context, Sextus quotes Chrysippus as using the term "ὑπόληψις" (*SVT III*, p. 164, § 657; see Sextus, *Against the Logicians*, p. 230–231, I.432, where it is given as "conception"). For the later Stoic usage, see Marcus (*Meditations*, pp. 146, VI.30; p. 308, XI.18; p. 326, XII.7), also in connection with *hypólepsis*: "Ἀρκεῖ ἡ παροῦσα ὑπόληψις καταληπτική" (p. 236, IX.6); the Stoicizing use is (re)applied to Heraclitus in a Christianizing appropriation by Clement of Alexandria and Hippolytus of Rome: '*katalépsetai*' (see *Vorsokratiker 1*, p. 157, 22B28; p. 157n.; p. 165, 22B66; p. 165n.; Heraclitus. "On the Universe," edited and translated by W. H. S. Jones. *Hippocrates. Volume IV. Heracleitus. On the Universe*. Cambridge: Harvard UP, 1931, pp. 469–509, here pp. 478, XXVI, p. 478n.; p. 506, CXVIII, p. 506n.). In Epicurus' letter to Menoeceus, '*hypolépseis*' are contrasted with '*prolépseis*' – the former qua '*pseudeis*', being of the '*pollon*': "For the utterances of the multitude about the gods are not true preconceptions but false assumptions" (as given in: D. Laertius, *Lives*, vol. 2, pp. 650 f., X.124). For *prólepsis* (and several variants within a considerably dense space), see Epictetus (*The Discourses. Books III–IV*, edited and translated by W. A. Oldfather. Cambridge: Harvard UP, 1928, vol. 2, p. 256, IV.i.41–44; generally, see *Discourses I*, edited and translated by Robert F. Dobbin. Oxford: Clarendon, 2011, pp. 42–44, I.22; p. 47, I.25.6; and his "Commentary," pp. 188–193, 206).

22 In English, '*hypólepsis*' (and the respective paradigm) tends to be rendered as (*inter alia*) 'supposition', 'suspicion', 'judgment', 'conception', 'assumption', 'opinion', or 'acceptation' (the latter's Latin form being how Aquinas translates it) – which is apt, but may not convey the dynamic tendency of the term ('take up', 'tie in with'). As to Aquinas, see Günther Bien ("Hypolepsis". *Historisches Wörterbuch der Philosophie*, edited by Joachim Ritter et al. Darmstadt: Wissenschaftliche Buchgesellschaft, 2013, Vol. 3., pp. 1252–1254, here pp. 1252 f.). Werner Theobald ("Spuren des Mythos in der Aristotelischen Theorie der Erkenntnis. 'Hypolepsis' bei Aristoteles, *De anima* und *Anal. post.*" *Archiv für Begriffsgeschichte*, vol. 44, 2002, pp. 25–37, here p. 37). On *hypólepsis* qua rhetorical "strategy" of "indirect statement", and for a nexus with the term *hypónoia*, see Kathy Eden ("Hermeneutics and the Ancient Rhetorical Tradition". *Rhetorica: A Journal of the History of Rhetoric*, vol. 5, no. 1, 1987, pp. 59–86, here pp. 74 f.); as to the latter, rendered "innuendo", see Aristotle (*Nicomachean Ethics*, edited and translated by H. Rackham. Cambridge: Harvard UP, 1934, pp. 246 f., 1128a, IV.viii.6); for the philosopher's use, compare also (*Metaphysics*, p. 4, 981a, I.i.5; pp. 8–11, 982a, I.ii.1–4; pp. 18 f., 983b, I.iii.4), given as "take the opinion which we hold" (*Metaphysics*, p. 9), "opinions which we hold" (*Metaphysics*, p. 11); with reference to the Thalesian 'natural' *hypólepsis*, as "derived this assumption", "derived his assumption" (*Metaphysics*, p. 19) – i.e. directly from (the observation

mythical import and implication by Theobald; this may seem questionable.²³ Similarly problematic is Assmann's restrictive use: in his tripartite model, he

---

of) natural phenomena, implying a dynamic tendency. It is given as "suppositions", "supposition" ("Prior Analytics". Translated by Harold P. Cook. *The Categories. On Interpretation. Prior Analytics*, edited by Harold P. Cook and Hugh Tredennick. London: Heinemann, 1962, pp. 181–531, here pp. 502–505, 67a–67b, II.xxi), and appears in the forms '*hypolambáno*', '*hypolépsetai*' (and further variants), translated as "think," "thinks," "thinking" ("Prior Analytics," pp. 504–507, 67b, II.xxi). It is given as "judgement" – used in connection with, and as differentiated from, '*phantasía*' ("On the Soul," pp. 156–159, 427b, III.iii); as "belief" (p. 160, 428b, III.iii); and also offered as an overarching term: "Judgement ['*tes hypolépseos*'] itself, too, has various forms – knowledge, opinion, prudence, and their opposites, but their differences must be the subject of another discussion" (pp. 156 f., 427b, III.iii). The latter seems to refer to 1139b (see "On the Soul," p. 156n.), where it is given as "Conception" in connection with '*dóxe*' qua both "capable of error" – the context being '*epagogè*', "induction": "But all teaching starts from facts previously known" (*Nicomachean Ethics*, pp. 332 f., 1139b, VI.ii.1); and also as "belief," "beliefs," "mode of conception" (pp. 339–341, 1140b, VI.v.6). The form '*hypolepteón*' is given as "deem", '*apodekteón*' (in the same sentence) as "accept" (pp. 626 f., 1179a, X.viii.12). It is translated as "conception" ("Topica". Translated by E. S. Forster. *Posterior Analytics. Topica*, edited and translated by Hugh Tredennick and E. S. Forster. Cambridge: Harvard UP, 1960, pp. 263–739, here pp. 458–461, 125b–126a, IV.v), provisionally differentiated from *pístis*, here qua "belief" (pp. 458 f.); it is given as "opinion" (pp. 464 f.; see also: 300–301, 104b, I.xi.19 and I.xi.35), later as "conception" (pp. 628 f., 149a, VI.xi). It is also rendered "suspicion" (*The 'Art' of Rhetoric*, edited and translated by John Henry Freese. Cambridge: Harvard UP, 2006, pp. 436 f., 1416a, III.xiv.1), and "an inkling" (pp. 448 f., 1417b, III.xvi.10). There are other *loci*. Dionysius of Halicarnassus uses the term '*hypolépsetai*' in a context concerning '*enárgeia*' (sc. 'vivid description'; "Lysias", *Critical Essays. Volume I*, edited and translated by Stephen Usher. Cambridge: Harvard UP, 1974, pp. 20–99), where the translation as "feel" may seem somewhat infelicitous: "Nobody who applies his mind ['*diánoian*'] to the speeches of Lysias will be so obtuse, insensitive or slow-witted ['*bradỳs tòn noun*'] that he will not feel ['*ouch hypolépsetai*', perhaps: 'will not be able to adopt, take (sc. the mental image, hence the perspective, before his inner eye, that of the mind), tie in with (the vivid description)'] that he can see ['*horan*'] the actions which are being described ['*tà deloúmena*'] going on ['*ginómena*']" (pp. 32–33, § 7). As far as is assessible, the haptico-emotional connotations of the English 'to feel' are not covered by the concept of *hypólepsis*; more significantly, the abovecited sentence explicitly stresses the intellectual plane (see the terms *diánoia*, *nous*, the latter *ex negativo* in its context); the immediately preceding sentence had emphasized Lysias' "grasp ['*lépseos*'] of circumstantial detail" (pp. 32–33, § 7) – whereby the scholar's use of '*hypolépsetai*' in his own description ties in performatively with the same paradigm at a grammatico-verbal level. Naturally, the (intended, ultimate) effect of this process will then be *movere* (wherefore "to feel" is indeed applicable *de re*); but Dionysius' textual economy seems to focus on the (decidedly controlled, or rational) method by way of which this is produced.

23 In academic terms, Theobald's speculative, quasi-metaphysical approach may seem a cul-de-sac. Its stress is selective (not to say reductive), ignores the initial (and arguably crucial) rhetorical meaning of the term – as also in (ps.)Plato, which Theobald denies (see "Spuren," p. 26); it does not take Ritter's and Marquard's adoption of this rhetorical use into account – a brief reference to Bien's article remains without content-related consideration (see p. 25n.); it identifies the commenting mode of the "canon" and the imitative one of "classicism", both defined by "repetition" (p. 282; trans. dsm; see pp. 102, 285 f.) – as opposed to "referencing texts of the past in the form of a controlled variation", which 'critical' method he terms "'Hypolepse'" (p. 281; trans. dsm).[24]

---

also disregards Assmann's (re)application. Theobald's position is problematic in and of itself, particularly: "Und wie auch sonst, wenn nicht durch einen irgendwie als göttlich vorgestellten Eingriff" – including the ensuing speculations as to a Hegelian "Aufheben" being implied (p. 30). Theobald terms his approach "eine mythische Sichtweise" (p. 36), the implausibility of which he himself admits (p. 37). The tendency of Aristotle's overall œuvre is at variance with the Platonic approach, wherefore Theobald's vacillating attempt at drawing Aristotle closer to Plato (pp. 31–35) will not seem convincing *de re*. The decisive objection is posed by what Theobald treats to silence: *hypólepsis* is verifiably a rhapsodic, a rhetorical term (see Joachim Ritter. *Metaphysik und Politik. Studien zu Aristoteles und Hegel*, edited by Odo Marquard. Frankfurt: Suhrkamp, 2003, pp. 53, 64; Marquard, *Skeptische Methode im Blick auf Kant*. Freiburg: Alber, 1982, p. 76n.; *Abschied vom Prinzipiellen*, Stuttgart: Reclam, 2000, pp. 119, 139; Bien, "Hypolepsis," pp. 1253 f.; Jan Assmann. *Das kulturelle Gedächtnis. Schrift, Erinnerung und politische Identität in frühen Hochkulturen*. Munich: Beck, 2013, pp. 282 f.); moreover, the term retains a link to common usage in Aristotle's applications of the concept – referring to 'phenomenistic' assumptions, views commonly held (then 'taken up'), to acceptations, customary 'wisdom', tying in with the *communis opinio*. The possibility of Theobald's later, mythical construal Ritter had already disproven (if the text be the measure) by reading Aristotle *en détail*: "Thales [...] knüpft das Göttliche als den 'Grund' an die Erscheinungen an; er begreift das vorher mythisch Vorgestellte jetzt – wie Aristoteles sagt – 'aus dem Sehen'. Das Sehen sieht das sinnfällig Sichtbare" (Ritter, *Metaphysik*, p. 54); "[e]ntscheidend ist also für Aristoteles die Anknüpfung der alten Vorstellung an das Sinnfällige; diese Anknüpfung wird im Begriff des Grundes zusammengefaßt" (p. 54n.); Ritter's reference is to Aristotle (*Metaphysics*, pp. 18 f., 983b, I.iii.4; see pp. 8–11, 982a, I.ii.1–4).

24 "Eine neue Form kultureller Kontinuität und Kohärenz entsteht: die Bezugnahme auf Texte der Vergangenheit in der Form einer kontrollierten Variation, die wir 'Hypolepse' nennen wollen. Dabei müssen wir sogleich eingestehen, daß das keinem quellensprachlichen Wortgebrauch entspricht" (Assmann, *Gedächtnis*, p. 281) – he does log the literal sense: "hypoleptische [...] 'Aufnahme' (nichts anderes heißt 'hypólepsis' ihrem Wortsinn nach)" (p. 283). "Hier handelt es sich um eine dritte Form des Rückbezugs, die man von *Klassik* und *Kanon* scharf unterscheiden muß, auch wenn sich Querverbindungen herstellen können" (p. 285); "[d]er hypoleptische Prozeß [...] *Institutionalisierung von Autorität und Kritik*" (p. 286). Assmann refrains from tying in with either Ritter or Marquard in this respect. His rather schematic application takes the term in a foreshortened sense, assuming that the 'taking up' must be institutionally "controlled" (p. 281; trans. dsm; see pp. 285–289) – his prime example being the relationship of "the Platonic Academy and the Aristotelian Peripatos" (p. 285; trans. dsm); that it must generally agree as to "criteria" concerning "the truth claim" (p. 287; trans. dsm; see p. 283); that the hypoleptic form of reference may not "alter the function" (p. 289; trans. dsm); in general, he emphasizes (textual) "fixation" (p. 283; trans. dsm), a "situative framework" (p. 284; trans. dsm; see p. 283), speaking of "the principle [']hypolepsis[']" (p. 286; trans. dsm). Assmann's idealistic or ideological restrictions would seem to bar virtually any pragmatic application of the term. In another context (referring to Blumenberg and Adorno), Haverkamp offers an arguably foreshortened 'genealogy' and problematic teleology of the term in ques-

In contrast to Assmann's rather narrow, restrictive (and ideological) use, the *essai* at hand ties in with Ritter's reading of the term, as taken up and applied by Marquard, who describes *hypólepsis* as '*Anknüpfung*' ('tying in with').[25] Aristotle uses the concept to signify that philosophy proceeds inductively, taking its initial assumptions and taxonomies from (linguistic) conventions and common ken – current, circulating, 'floating' in (virtual) cultural networks.[26] It does not start from scratch (nor does it pretend to, like Des-

---

tion: "Die hermeneutische Tugend der 'Anknüpfung' und ihre spätere Vollendung zur Konsensfähigkeit, wie sie von Joachim Ritter erfunden, von Erich Rothacker befördert, von Hans-Georg Gadamer wirkungsgeschichtlich begründet und von Jürgen Habermas mit den höheren Weihen kritischer Theorie versehen wurde, steht noch in so unangefochtener Geltung, daß sie bis heute unhintergehbar erscheint" ("Das Skandalon der Metaphorologie. Prolegomena eines Kommentars". *Metaphorologie. Zur Praxis von Theorie*, edited by Anselm Haverkamp and Dirk Mende. Frankfurt: Suhrkamp, 2009, pp. 33–61, here p. 33). By contrast, the *essai* at hand aims at tentatively charting a non-teleological – or rather, a 'poly-telic' – horizon (emphatic of what would potentially be a 360-degree view). Sommer's assessment of the philosopher's project is pivotal in this respect: "Nicht zuletzt öffnet die Art, wie Blumenberg die freie Variation handhabt, die Phänomenologie für grundsätzlich alles, was in anderen Wissenschaften gleich welcher Ausrichtung Thema ist. Phänomenologie, so betrieben, ist nicht exklusiv, sondern rezeptiv, zieht nicht Grenzen, sondern nimmt auf und eignet an" ("Nachwort". *Beschreibung des Menschen*, pp. 897–906, here p. 902); "Wiederaufnahme von bereits Gesagtem ist [...] gelegentlich auch sachlich oder historisch vertiefte Neudurchdringung einer schon behandelten Thematik" (p. 906); arguably, (auto)*hypólepsis* with variation is a decisive Blumenbergian tool. Haverkamp does stress "Blumenbergs Tendenz zur Anknüpfung an Gegebenes" ("Nachwort. Die Technik der Rhetorik. Blumenbergs Projekt". *Ästhetische und metaphorologische Schriften*, edited by Anselm Haverkamp. Frankfurt: Suhrkamp, 2001, pp. 433–454, here p. 441), and his remark on Blumenberg's *modus* in a concrete case may seem plausible, on the whole (that is, when provisionally quarantining the tendency added by the critic's context): "Blumenberg sortiert hier wie so oft einen Gemeinplatz [sc. 'Metapher'] um: der Anknüpfung wegen wie auch zum Zweck der Durchkreuzung, die auf dem Fuße folgt" ("Skandalon," pp. 36 f.; employing the Derridean concept of 'paleonymy'; see "Technik," p. 441, where Haverkamp stresses Blumenberg's "proclivity [...] for paleonymic formulations"; trans. dsm; compare Jacques Derrida. *Dissemination*, edited and translated by Barbara Johnson. Chicago: U of Chicago P, 1981, pp. 3, 6n., 18n., 21); "Durchkreuzung" may seem overstated, since it is apparently intended here in the sense of 'thwarting' (rather than 'intersecting' or 'traversing', which would arguably allude to retaining, in some form, what is thus decussated). The concept of 'subtending' (respectively 'subtension') might be more expedient.

25 Marquard's (personal) *hypólepsis*: "von ihm [sc. Ritter] gelernt: [...] daß niemand von vorn anfangen kann, daß jeder anknüpfen muß" (*Abschied*, p. 7); "kein Mensch kann absolut von vorn anfangen, jeder muß – wie Joachim Ritter sagte: 'hypoleptisch' – an das anknüpfen, was schon da ist" (p. 78; see p. 90). Generally, see Blumenberg on the "Ökonomie des Nicht-mehr-anzufangen-brauchens" (*Lebenszeit*, p. 356).

26 See Aristotle: "no doubt it is proper to start from the known. [...] for us ['ἡμῖν'] at all events it is proper to start from what is known to us ['*apò ton hemin gnorímon*']" (*Nicomachean Ethics*, pp. 12–13, 1095b, I.iv.5). Generally thereto, see Wesley Trimpi (*Muses of One Mind. The Literary*

cartes or Husserl): "The load-bearing philosophical terms [...] are not posited by Aristotle. Philosophy takes them up 'hypoleptically' from preexisting linguistic usage" (Ritter, *Metaphysik*, p. 53; trans. dsm).²⁷

Analysis of Experience and Its Continuity. Eugene: Wipf & Stock, 2009), spec. "Aristotle maintains that we acquire knowledge by proceeding from what is more apprehensible to the senses [...]. We begin [...] inductively [...] these objects are more [...] intelligible to us (ἡμῖν)" (pp. 87–88; see p. 122; as well as Trimpi's article "Reason and the Classical Premises of Literary Decorum." *Independent Journal of Philosophy*, Vol. 5/6 (1988): pp. 103–111, here p. 108); "general concepts (τὸ καθόλου) are built up inductively from sensory perception (αἴσθησις)" (*Muses*, p. 92; compare pp. 47, 75–76, 119–123, 131–132, 232, 296–297, 331–332, 340, 367, passim). Accordingly, assumptions may also be derived from nature (respectively its observation) directly (as in Aristotle's example of the Thalesian 'natural' *hypólepsis*). Generally, see Kerferd: "What Aristotle does, almost regularly and as a matter of habit, is to take a current philosophical term or expression already in use, and then to refine it in such a way as to demonstrate that his own analyses and ideas were somehow already imperfectly present in earlier ideas already in currency" (*The Sophistic Movement*, Cambridge: Cambridge UP, 1999, p. 60). At times, Aristotle seems to limit the 'uptake' to the opinions of the wise (the latter valuation arguably being subject to variation, *de re*); *inter alia*, this is how Marcus uses it, particularly when quoting the term itself, taking up Democrates' statement "'ὁ κόσμος, ἀλλοίωσις· ὁ βίος, ὑπόληψις'", "'The Universe – mutation : Life – opinion'"; he places it in a Stoicizing context: "disturbances are but the outcome of that opinion ['ὑπολήψεως] which is within us" (*Meditations*, pp. 70 f., IV.3; see pp. 70n.–71n.). Likewise, Marcus explicitly ties in with "Monimus the Cynic" (p. 39, II.15; see pp. 38n.–39n.): "'Ὅτι πάνθ' ὑπόληψις", "that everything is but what we think it [sc. 'what we take it to be']'" (pp. 38 f., II.15); see D. Laertius, stating that Monimus was "mentioned by the comic poet Menander [...] in [...] *The Groom*", where he is quoted as "pronouncing wholly vain / All man's supposings", '*tò gàr hypolephthèn typhon einai pan éphe*' – said to surpass the '*gnothi sautón*' (*Lives II*, pp. 84–87, VI.83). The dramatist takes up the Cynic, who is taken up by the Stoic; in this respect, see Marcus' remark as to what is herein termed (rhetorical) *hypólepsis*, and with respect to drama in particular: "and the dramatic writers contain some serviceable sayings" (*Meditations*, p. 297, XI.6); "[f]or that some serviceable things are said even by the writers of these [sc. New Comedies] is recognized by all" (pp. 297–299, XI.6); such *hypólepsis* from drama is similarly defended in Augustine: "hinc et ille comicus [sc. Terence, here], sicut luculentis ingeniis non defit resplendentia ueritatis" ("[Epistula] CLV". *S. Aureli Augustini Operum Sectio II Pars III: Ep. CXXIV–CLXXXIV*, edited by Alois Goldbacher. *Corpus Scriptorum Ecclesiasticorum Latinorum*, Vol. 44. Vienna: Tempsky, 1904, pp. 430–447, here p. 444; see *Political Writings*, edited by E. M. Atkins and R. J. Dodaro. Cambridge: Cambridge UP, 2007, p. 97). The *hypólepsis* from Democrates (see also *Vorsokratiker 2*, p. 165, 68B115*85; as to the Pythagorean use, see *Vorsokratiker 1*, p. 473, 58D8), respectively Monimus, is referenced repeatedly in Marcus: "'Ὅτι πάντα ὑπόληψις" (*Meditations*, pp. 326, XII.8; p. 330, XII.22) – with this context: "that all is but as thy opinion of it, and that is in thy power. Efface thy opinion ['ὑπόληψιν'] then" (pp. 331–333, XII.22); see "[e]fface the opinion ['ὑπόληψιν']" (pp. 72 f., IV.7), "[t]ake away thy opinion ['ὑπόληψιν']" (pp. 216 f., VIII.40), "[o]verboard with opinion ['ὑπόληψιν'] and thou art safe ashore" (pp. 334 f., XII.25). Its meaning is not always negative: "Hold sacred thy capacity for forming opinion ['ὑποληπτικὴν']" (pp. 56 f., III.9). See the quantity of uses in Marcus passim (including the paradigm): "ὑπόληψις" (p. 58, III.9);

"ὑπολάμβανε" (p. 74, IV.11); "ὑπολαμβάνον", "ὑπολαμβανέτω", "ὑπολαμβάνον" (p. 88, IV.39); "ὑπολαμβάνει" (p. 160, VI.51); "ὑποληπτέον" (p. 112, V.12); "ὑπολαμβάνειν" (p. 160, VI.52); "ὑπολάβω", "ὑπολαβεῖν" (p. 170, VII.14); "ὑποληπτικῶς", "ὑπολαμβάνον" (p. 170, VII.16); "ὑπολήψεως" (p. 190, VII.62); "ὑπολαβέτω" (p. 216, VIII.40); "ὑπόληψιν" (p. 220, VIII.44), "ὑπόληψις καταληπτική" (p. 236, IX.6); "ὑπολήψει" (p. 262, X.3), "ὑπολήψεις" (p. 308, XI.18); "ὑπόληψις" (p. 320, XII.1). See the first paragraph of Epictetus' *Encheiridion*: "Some things are under our control, while others are not under our control. Under our control are conception ['ὑπόληψις'], choice, desire, aversion, and, in a word everything that is our own doing; not under our control are our body, our property, reputation ['δόξαι'], office, and, in a word, everything that is not our own doing" ("The Encheiridion", edited and translated by W. A. Oldfather. *The Discourses. Books 3–4*. Cambridge: Harvard UP, 1928, pp. 479–537, here pp. 482f., § 1). Via the two contrastive sets of enumerations, '*hypólepsis*' is thus expressly contrasted with '*dóxai*' (p. 482). The Stoa observes the difference in tendency: something that originates with another (the opinions of others) vs. what originates with or within oneself (one's own conceptions, assumptions). Naturally, the latter may also be (and usually, or often, is) an opinion seized from a common knowledge in circulation (general or particularized). As an offshoot of Platonic Socratism or Socratic Platonism, the Stoa may believe that it is possible to be taking one's conceptions from a realm removed from that of men and opinions. This is immaterial, here. As Karl Alfred Blüher notes (*Seneca in Spanien. Untersuchungen zur Geschichte der Seneca-Rezeption in Spanien vom 13. bis 17. Jahrhundert*. München: Francke, 1969), the aforequoted Epictetian sentence usually has "opinio" for "ὑπόληψις" in Latin translations (here by Hieronymus Wolf), while Sánchez de las Brozas, possibly influenced by Juan Luis Vives, gives it as "la opinion y juicio de las cosas" in Spanish – a formulation taken up by Quevedo verbatim (*Seneca in Spanien*, pp. 286–287, 287n.).

27 Ritter continues: "Die Zusammenhänge, mit denen Philosophie zu tun hat, sind schon in der Art und Weise ausgelegt, wie von ihnen vorphilosophisch die Rede ist" (*Metaphysik*, p. 53). "Daher beginnen die Kapitel des 5. Buchs je mit dem λέγεται; die Rede enthält die vorgegebene Auslegung" (p. 53n.). "Diese vorgegebene Auslegung wird für die wichtigsten Begriffe im 5. Buch durchgenommen und entwickelt, um so ihren philosophischen Sinn in der Anknüpfung an sie zu umreißen. So wird auch der philosophische Begriff ἀρχή hypoleptisch begründet. Mit 'Grund' hat der Mensch immer schon – erkennend und handelnd – zu tun" (p. 53). This general method is fundamentally inductive, hence at variance with the Platonic overall tendency at a basic (hence structurally decisive) level; see Ritter: "eine Philosophie, die sich im Verhältnis zu dem, was ist, jede Konstruktion und Deduktion aus reinen Begriffen versagt" (p. 63). In this respect, and to qualify the above parentheses thereto, see Blumenberg, quoting from and glossing Husserl (the latter cited in italics): "Es gibt einen Übergang aus der Gemeinsprache in die phänomenologische Sprache: *Die benutzten Wörter mögen aus der allgemeinen Sprache stammen, vieldeutig, ihrem wechselnden Sinne nach vage sein*, aber sie können mit *deutlichen und einzigen Bedeutungen* ausgestattet werden" ("Sprachsituation und immanente Poetik". *Immanente Ästhetik – Ästhetische Reflexion. Lyrik als Paradigma der Moderne*, edited by Wolfgang Iser. München: Fink, 1966 [*Poetik und Hermeneutik II*], pp. 145–155, here p. 146). In this regard, and with respect to the transmission of literary theory, see Trimpi ("adoption of terms", "a borrowed vocabulary", *Muses*, p. 5; compare also pp. 9, 244, 265n.). See Blumenberg for a similar structure of tapping into what a given community is already primed for (hence familiar with) at the nominal (sc. here: meta-)level: "der Begriff des Symbols – vorgeprägt durch den des Symptoms in der antiken Medizin" (*Schiffbruch mit Zuschauer. Paradigmen einer Daseinsmetapher*. Frankfurt: Suhrkamp, 1979, p. 90). In general, *hypólepsis* signifies that one

In line therewith, the concept's connective dynamics is accentuated herein.[28] Its tendency is that of 'taking up' something (where someone has left off), of 'tying in with' a common ground; in Ritter's words: "Anknüpfung an die üblichen Vorstellungen", "tying in with customary notions" (*Metaphysik* p. 58; trans. dsm). Assmann's definition of "Hypolepse" qua "controlled variation" (*Gedächtnis*, p. 281; trans. dsm) marks a restriction that virtually never applies: for a 'tying in with' need neither be explicit – it often is not; nor need it share the same 'criteria', 'truth claims', or 'principles' (as Assmann believes) – in fact, it usually does not.[29]

For (decidedly) heuristic purposes, the following will select and detail three conceivable forms of the concept at hand, while simultaneously demonstrating their reciprocities; for theatrical, oratorical, and anthropistic *hypolépseis* cannot be strictly separated: dramatic variants are typically rhetorical, though not necessarily (immediately) concerned with assumptions about what it means to be human.

3.1 With a View to Form and Function: Rhetorical *hypólepsis*

The term '*hypólepsis*' itself has a history of repeated 'uptakes'; in the context at hand, it will be needful to detail particularly the concept's rhetorical and philosophical '*vita*'.[30] Initially, it seems to have been used with reference to

---

has to start somewhere – meaning, with a common ground. In the final analysis, any such will do: taken formally, an 'everyone knows' (see Niccolò Machiavelli. *Il Principe*, edited by Giorgio Inglese. Turin: Einaudi, 1995, p. 115, XVIII) is itself a structuring device (compare Leo Strauss. *Thoughts on Machiavelli*. Chicago: U of Chicago P, 1978, pp. 101, 210, 313n., 314n., 320n.) – that is, regardless of whether or not something is in fact known (let alone 'understood').

28 In T. S. Eliot's *The Waste Land*, spec. the "The Fire Sermon" (edited by Michael North. New York: Norton, 2001), two lines may be illustrative in the present context: "I can connect / Nothing with nothing" (p. 15, III, verses 301 ff.) – a metapoetic irony, seeing that (in a type of kaleidoscopic neo-analogism) almost all this long poem seems to be performing is to tie virtually anything in with everything else. As to a rhetorical uptake of (folk)lore, see its reference to "[a] children's nursery rhyme" (p. 19n.), which 'everyone knows': "London Bridge is falling down falling down falling down" (p. 19, verse 426). Technically, Eliot's modernist poem is hypoleptic *kat' exochén*.

29 *Pace* Assmann (*Gedächtnis*, pp. 281–289), who speaks of "the principle [']hypolepsis[']" (p. 286; trans. dsm). See Marquard: "das 'Antiprinzip Anknüpfung'" (*Glück*, p. 67). Naturally, the receiving context differs from – or may be entirely at variance with – the (textual) environment of the respective source or emitting discourse. Generally, see Stierle: "Wiederholung ist prinzipiell vom Wiederholten unterschieden" ("Moralistik," p. 2).

30 As detailed above, Marcus takes up the term '*hypólepsis*' itself from Democrates (*Meditations*, pp. 70 f., IV.3; see pp. 70n.–71n.), and Monimus (see pp. 38 f., II.15), while integrating it

recitals of Homer – where one speaker follows after another, 'tying in with' him, 'taking up' where the other left off.³¹ As Aristotle's use demonstrates, *hy-*

---

into a receiving context of Stoicizing tendency. Given a different textual environment, a(ny) concept naturally assumes various functions (often at variance with the emitting context or discourse), taking on (diachronically) manifold additional nuances of meaning.

31 "Ritter spricht von ὑπόληψις: das Wort meint u. a.: 1. jemandem ins Wort fallen; 2. an den Vorredner anknüpfen; gemeint ist hier natürlich die zweite Bedeutung" (Marquard, *Skeptische Methode*, p. 76n.). See Assmann: "Das griechische Wort 'hypólepsis' wird in zwei typischen Kontexten verwendet, an die wir anknüpfen können. Der eine Kontext ist der Rhapsodenwettkampf. Hier bezeichnet man mit dem Wort 'hypólepsis' die Regel, daß der nächste Rhapsode genau dort in der Rezitation des Homertextes fortfahren muß, wo sein Vorgänger aufgehört hat. Der andere Kontext ist die Rhetorik. Hier bedeutet 'hypólepsis' die Anknüpfung an das, was der Vorredner gesagt hat. In beiden Fällen bezeichnet hypólepsis das Prinzip, nicht von vorn anzufangen, sondern sich in anknüpfender Aufnahme an Vorangegangenes anzuschließen und in ein laufendes Kommunikationsgeschehen einzuschalten. Dieses Kommunikationsgeschehen bildet, was man den 'hypoleptischen Horizont' nennen könnte" (*Gedächtnis*, pp. 282 f.) – apart from the last sentence (which may seem to have idealistic implications), this synopsis of rhetorical *hypólepsis* is expedient. See the (ps.)Platonic dialog "*Hipparchus*," where the 'Socrates' *persona* uses the term "ἐξ ὑπολήψεως" in the phrase '*toùs rhapsodoùs* [...] *ex hypolépseos ephexes autà diiénai*', translated as "the rhapsodes [...] recite them [sc. '*Homérou épe*'] in relay, one man following on another" (in: *Charmides. Alcibiades. Hipparchus. The Lovers. Theages. Minos. Epinomis*, edited and translated by W. R. M. Lamb. Cambridge: Harvard UP, 2005, pp. 278–305, here pp. 288 f., 228B) – a delegative process, incidentally. As Uwe Neumann shows *de re* (see "Agonistik." *Historisches Wörterbuch der Rhetorik. Band 1: A–Bib*, edited by Gert Ueding. Tübingen: Niemeyer, 1992, pp. 261–285), Homer's *Iliad* also features particular protagonists tying in with speeches made in earlier books (see p. 263), hence rhetorical *hypolépseis* that exceed an immediate verse-to-verse uptake: "Rede und Gegenrede wechseln auch im Wortkampf zwischen Thersites und Odysseus ab. [...] ein Vertreter des Volks ['mißt sich'] mit Odysseus. Thersites wird aber zugleich an Achilleus gemessen; denn er nimmt dessen Worte aus dem Streit mit Agamemnon genau auf (II, 240 = I, 356 u[nd] II, 242 = I, 232)" (p. 263). See Homer (*Iliad. Books 1–12*. Translated by A. T. Murray, and William F. Wyatt, edited by William F. Wyatt. Cambridge: Harvard UP, 2003, pp. 78–79, 2.240 and 241, with pp. 30–31, 1.232, as well as pp. 38–39, 1.356). In terms of versification, *stichomythía* has formal affinities to *hypólepsis*, while also conducing to the latter in terms of content and argumentative dynamics; for an Early Modern example in Gryphius, see Jörg Wesche ("Verse Games. Meter and Interactional German in the Baroque Plays of Andreas Gryphius", *Rhetoric and Drama*, edited by DS Mayfield. Berlin: de Gruyter, 2017, pp. 135–150, here p. 146; in the same volume, Jan Bloemendal, "Rhetoric and Early Modern Latin Drama. The Two Tragedies by the 'Polish Pindar' Simon Simonides (1558–1629): Castus Ioseph and Pentesilea", pp. 115–134, here p. 118; as well as Eden, "From the Refutation of Drama to the Drama of Refutation," pp. 55–70, here p. 59; see also Mayfield, "Interplay," pp. 16n., 20, 20n., 31, 34). A rhetorico-hypoleptic approach (qua 'taking up and tying in with') is particularly need- and feckful in all forms of contentious and controversial exchanges – that is, with a view to the opponent; Quintilian recommends drawing upon, and indirecting, the respective other's verbal force – "The most satisfactory thing is if you are in a position to derive an Argument from your opponent ['ex adversario ducere argumentum']" (*Institutio Oratoria 6–8*, edited and translated by Donald A. Russell. Cam-

pólepsis is not limited to a specific relay, exchange, or altercation; it may also involve longer distances between the time when a notion enters cultural circulation (in a context or discourse of emittance), and when it is (randomly) taken up again from common knowledge.[32] In a textual environment, *hypólepsis* may occur intra- and intertextually, hence trans-spatially, across languages, and naturally over time. Aristotle's descriptions of man have themselves become '*Anknüpfungspunkte*' (sc. 'points wherewith to tie in') – for implicit, typically unsystematic, nonlinear, uncontrolled, even entropic variations.[33]

---

bridge: Harvard UP, 2001, pp. 18–19, 6.1.4) – while also expressly tying in with the wording of the opposing party himself (see "ut ipsi vocant", "to use their own phrase", *Institutio Oratoria 3–5*, pp. 143–145, 3.8.58). Generally thereto, see Mayfield ("Otherwise. Rhetorical Techniques of Contradiction (With Remarks on Quintilian, Augustine, Machiavelli, Shakespeare, Gracián)." *Contradiction Studies: Mapping the Field. Proceedings of the international conference held at the University of Bremen, February 9–11, 2017*, edited by Gisela Febel, Cordula Nolte, and Ingo H. Warnke. Wiesbaden: Springer, forthcoming). See also the first sentence of the *Téchne rhetoriké*, where Aristotle uses the term "ἀντίστροφος" (*Rhetoric*, p. 2, 354a, I.i.1) to elucidate the relationship between rhetoric and dialectic (see p. 3); this may be described as a form of *hypólepsis*, the term being familiar from choral music (p. 2n.). Philosophical discourse 'takes up' or 'ties in with' terms (and assumptions) in circulation, i.e. from the fund of common knowledge or other (established) discourses (*sensu lato*); see Küpper's discursive description of literature ("Was ist Literatur?" *Zeitschrift für Ästhetik und Allgemeine Kunstwissenschaft*, vol. 45, no. 2, 2001, pp. 187–215; here pp. 194, 205n., 214 f.).

32 Assmann does submit this notion: "'Dehnung des hypoleptischen Horizonts' […], d.h. die Konstitution eines Beziehungsraums innerhalb dessen 'das, was der Vorredner gesagt hat', vor mehr als 2000 Jahren gesagt worden sein kann" (*Gedächtnis*, p. 283). He then rescinds the potential inherent in this insight by restricting the use of the term '*hypólepsis*' in such a way as arguably renders it sterile (being idealized, overly schematic) in terms of scholarly serviceability.

33 For more methodical forms of *hypólepsis* – decidedly varying, altering, even subverting the tendency of the emitting statement, *persona*, or discourse – compare e.g. the assorted textual practices of *sermocinatio*, 'putting words in the mouth of' (thereto, see Heinrich Lausberg. *Elemente der Literarischen Rhetorik*. Ismaning: Hueber, 1990, pp. 142 f., §§ 432–433; *Handbuch der literarischen Rhetorik. Eine Grundlegung der Literaturwissenschaft*. Stuttgart: Steiner, 2008, pp. 407–413, §§ 820–829; Strauss, *Thoughts*, pp. 42, 137–167; Mayfield, *Artful Immorality*, p. 91n.; "'Against the Dog only a dog'. Talking Canines Civilizing Cynicism in Cervantes' 'coloquio de los perros' (With Tentative Remarks on the Discourse and Method of Animal Studies)". *Humanities* 6.2.28. Special Issue Animal Narratology, June: 2017, pp. 1–39, here pp. 12n., 18, 18n.–19n., 21, 21n., passim; "Variants of Rhetorical Ventriloquism in the *Rhetorica ad Herennium*, Cicero, Dionysius of Halicarnassus, Quintilian, and Augustine (with Remarks on *sermocinatio*, *ethopoeia*, and *prosopopoeia*)". *History and Drama*, edited by Joachim Küpper et al. Berlin: de Gruyter, 2019); as well as the method of '*accommodatio*' (see 1Cor 9:19–27) and adaptation in rhetorical terms (see Kathy Eden. *Hermeneutics and the Rhetorical Tradition. Chapters in the Ancient Legacy and Its Humanist Reception*. New Haven: Yale UP, 1997, pp. 2, 14; Küpper, "Jesuitismus und Manierismus in Graciáns *Oráculo manual*". *Romanistisches Jahrbuch*, vol. 58, 2007, pp. 412–442, here pp. 428 f., 429n.; Mayfield, *Artful Immorality*, pp. 218, 218n.;

An oratorical angle on *hypólepsis* accentuates its form and function – the effectual application (also of anthropistic assertions) – in a specific (textual) environment (including dramatic works). It is grounded in the pervasiveness and prevalence of rhetoric as a multipurpose art, mediating between different cultural spheres (such as law, politics, etc.), and particularly until the Early Modern Age (also in the latter's drama).[34] Oratory – qua versatile, trans-temporal *téchne* – plays an enabling role prior to considerations of individual agency or particularized institutions (to say nothing of supposedly 'national' specifics).[35] The point of eloquence is ever (its) functionality, expediency: the "verità effettuale" (Machiavelli, *Il Principe*, p. 102, XV).[36]

Rhetorical *hypólepsis* is employed with a view to impact – as a feckful means for facilitating 'momentaneous evidence' in a given (and potentially any) addressee.[37] The (relatively stable) structure of such utterances is linked

---

"Interplay," pp. 18–20, 18n.–20n.). In general, the rhetorical *aptum* (see also "Interplay," pp. 18, 18n., 21n., 31, 37) is highly hypoleptic at the metalevel – a rhetorico-cultural interleaving that would require a separate study. For a nexus of *sermocinatio* and *hypólepsis* at the historiographico-poetical level, see Neumann: "Historischen Persönlichkeiten werden fiktive oder [...] überarbeitete Reden in den Mund gelegt; wobei die Argumente und der sprachliche Ausdruck der Redegegner deutlich aufeinander bezogen sind" ("Agonistik," p. 264). In general, the various forms of rhetorical *hypólepsis* 'take up (tie in with) and vary' foregoing instances (oral, textual, or otherwise). As to the random modes, the vector may indeed be a downright viral variation.

34 Generally thereto, see Bloemendal ("Rhetoric and Early Modern Latin Drama," pp. 115 f.); Küpper ("Rhetoric and the Cultural Net," pp. 151–152, 156, 165); Mayfield ("Interplay," pp. 5–8; see also "Talking Canines," pp. 12 f.).

35 See Küpper's description of rhetoric as "a trans-generic system of diction" (*Diskurs-Renovatio bei Lope de Vega und Calderón. Untersuchungen zum spanischen Barockdrama. Mit einer Skizze zur Evolution der Diskurse in Mittelalter, Renaissance und Manierismus*. Tübingen: Narr, 1990, p. 300; trans. dsm; see also the English version: *Discursive* Renovatio *in Lope de Vega and Calderón. Studies on Spanish Baroque Drama. With an Excursus on the Evolution of Discourse in the Middle Ages, the Renaissance, and Mannerism*. Berlin: de Gruyter, 2017, p. 289).

36 The "effectual truth" (*The Prince*, edited and translated by Harvey C. Mansfield. Chicago: U of Chicago P, 1998, p. 61); 'one cannot argue with results' (says Calvin *de re*, hence the American idiom). For a structural similarity with a Thalesian *hypólepsis* (as described by Aristotle), see Machiavelli's apparently inductive approach: "mi è parso piú conveniente andare dreto alla verità effettuale della cosa che alla immaginazione di essa" – i.e. not to the 'dogmatic' (Platonic, Augustinian, etc.) utopias of "immaginati republiche e principati che non si sono mai visti né conosciuti in vero essere" (*Il Principe*, p. 102, XV; see p. 102n.; thereto, see Mayfield, *Artful Immorality*, pp. 182n.–183n.).

37 Jakobson's 'conative' function; for the latter's terms, utilized passim in the *essai* at hand (see *Language*, spec. pp. 66–71). As to "momentane Evidenz" (here *mutatis mutandis*), see Blumenberg (*Arbeit am Mythos*. Frankfurt: Suhrkamp, 2006, p. 533; *Ein mögliches Selbstver-*

to their function, not least in that their form tends to effect an (apparent) recognition in the recipient (based on a perceived familiarity). While (latently) present, the content – reference(s), message, contexts, discourse(s) – is usually not immediately dominant: a rhetorico-persuasive purpose prevails.[38] Such hypoleptic statements are often artful – terse, maximatic, acute, incisive (in this sense, Jakobson's 'poetic' function applies) – hence have a tendency to appear

---

ständnis. Aus dem Nachlaß. Stuttgart: Reclam, 1997, pp. 111, 122f., 124; *Quellen, Ströme, Eisberge*, edited by Ulrich von Bülow and Dorit Krusche. Berlin: Suhrkamp, 2012, p. 43; *Theorie der Lebenswelt*, edited by Manfred Sommer. Berlin: Suhrkamp, 2010, p. 180; *Lebenszeit*, pp. 114, 127, 137, 139; *Beschreibung*, p. 161).

38 Hence the concept and study of 'anthropistics' (as suggested herein), a portmanteau of '*ánthropos*' and '*pístis*' (implying both 'persuaded of' and 'persuaded by'); as to the latter, see Lausberg (*Elemente*, p. 15, § 6; p. 33, § 65; *Handbuch*, p. 140, § 257; p. 190, §§ 348–349). In the *exordium* to Gorgias' "Encomium of Helen," "πίστις" is rendered "belief" in the translation (*The Texts of Early Greek Philosophy. The Complete Fragments and Selected Testimonies of the Major Presocratics*, edited and translated by Daniel W. Graham. Vol. 2. Cambridge: Cambridge UP, 2010, pp. 754–763; here pp. 754f., § 49.2); the context implies an 'opinion' (here qualified as "united and unanimous") or 'conviction' (an assumption, of which people had been persuaded previously, say by the poets): "the belief of those who heed the poets and the report of her name" (i.e. not a belief in the gods, here) – precisely since Gorgias is attempting "to refute [...] those blaming Helen, [...] to put an end to the blame [...] to put an end to their folly"; and this "by giving reasoning to my speech" – i.e. by being convincing, and persuading, if not the blamers and detractors, then those who matter, the people (p. 755, § 49.2). Later, in connection with *hypólepsis* (*de re*), the translation has: "to tell the knowers what they know produces credence ['*pístin*'], but does not bring delight ['*térpsin*']" (pp. 756f., § 49.5). In the "Encomium", the term for 'opinion' is '*dóxa*': "concerning most things most people take opinion ['*dóxan*'] as their soul's ['*psycheí*'] guide" (pp. 758f., § 49.11; the translation as 'soul' is problematic). The respective section culminates in a conjunction of both terms here at issue, accentuating them by end focus: "That persuasion proceeding via speech impresses the soul at will, can be seen by studying [...] the verbal competitions of philosophers, in which quick thinking is displayed, showing how changeable is the belief in an opinion ['δόξης πίστιν']" (pp. 758f., § 49.13). See the density of variants in the immediate vicinity: '*peithò*', '*dóxan antì dóxes*', '*ápista*', '*dóxes*', '*épeise*' (p. 758, § 49.13). Moreover, this entire segment (pp. 758f., § 49.8–13) is saturated with variants of '*peíthein*' (including '*pístis*') and '*dóxa*', concluding with both side by side in a sort of concise *peroratio* to this crucial part of the "Encomium". As to '*pístis*', see Aristotle, in particular ("Topica," pp. 292f., 103b, I.viii; *Politics*, pp. 554f., 1326a, VII.iv.5; *Rhetoric*, pp. 14f., 1355b, I.ii.2; pp. 150f., 1375a, I.xv.1), including a translation of '*pístis*' qua "sufficient grounds" ("Posterior Analytics," pp. 1–261, here pp. 180f., 90b, II.iii), as well as the remark: "But opinion ['*dóxe*'] implies belief ['*pístis*'] (for one cannot hold opinions in which one does not believe); and no animal has belief, but many have imagination" ("On the Soul," pp. 158f., 428a, III.iii) – while '*dóxa*' had been given as a (sub)form of '*hypólepsis*' before (p. 156, 427b, III.iii; with p. 160, 428b, III.iii). See Freese's gloss on *pístis*: "πίστις [...]: means of persuasion, 'probable' opposed to 'demonstrative' proof" (p. 479; compare *Rhetoric*, pp. 8–11, 1355a, I.i.11–12); see also: "πιστός" ("convincing") re "λόγον" qua "speech" (pp. 168f., 1877b, II.i.2). See Heinrich

'momentaneously evident'.[39] At times, they performatively emphasize their hypoleptic status itself.[40]

Niehues-Pröbsting: "True to its semantic origin, the term 'pistis' indicates [...] a work of the 'peitho'" ("Überredung zum Glauben". *Jahrbuch Rhetorik*, vol. 34, no. 1, 2015, pp. 13–44, here p. 13); "Der Glaube (*pistis*) ist für den Griechen schon rein sprachlich ein Werk der Überredung" (p. 14); he offers an example from Clement of Alexandria: "Clemens [stellt] *pistis* und *peithein* so zusammen, dass dem griechisch geschulten Ohr die etymologische Verwandtschaft nicht entgehen kann" (pp. 28 f.). His general *caveat* is crucial: "was *pistis* in der griechischen Philosophie bedeute[t] [...] [ist] mit dem christlichen Glauben [...] unvergleichbar. Aufgrund seines Inhalts erfährt im Christentum der Glaube eine einzigartige Aufwertung" (p. 15); "Die Aufwertung manifestiert sich in der Singularisierung des Begriffs [...]. Die *Rhetorik* des Aristoteles untersucht die Mittel, viele verschiedene Meinungen und Überzeugungen zu bewirken; sie kennt nicht die eine ausschließliche *pistis* [...] die Pluralbildung in der Rhetorik" (p. 21). For the latter: "Weil es das [sc. 'logische Evidenz'] in der Rhetorik nicht gibt, sind hier mehrere Gründe notwendig und möglich; solche nennt Aristoteles *pisteis*. Das Wort bezeichnet [...] die Gründe, aus denen die Hörer dem Redner glauben (*pisteuein*)" (p. 16). Generally, a scholarly description will ask '*cui bono*', inquire into the "*utilitas causae*" (Lausberg, *Handbuch*, p. 56, § 63; p. 230, § 417) – it will perform an analysis of function; in Blumenberg's words: "Funktionale Interpretation verlangt demgemäß die Zuordnung der uns vorliegenden Aussagen zu den je akuten Problemen und zwar inhaltlich *und* formal" ("Epochenschwelle und Rezeption". *Philosophische Rundschau*, vol. 6, 1958, pp. 94–120, here p. 102); this, as well as the ensuing, applies to the *essai* at hand: "es geht um funktionale, nicht nur um topologische Verhältnisse" (*Höhlenausgänge*, p. 341n.).

39 See Lausberg as to terseness (*Elemente*, p. 135, §§ 407–409) and acuteness (p. 23, § 37; p. 61, 61n., § 166).

40 As Strauss stresses, "[t]he first word of the *Prince* is *Sogliono* ('It is customary')" (*Thoughts*, p. 23) – a performative instance of *hypólepsis*: an explicit tying in with what 'everyone knows' (or is said to know), while simultaneously accentuating or appealing to that very fact. Likewise in Machiavelli's "ciascuno lo intende" (*Il Principe*, p. 115, XVIII; see Strauss, *Thoughts*, pp. 101, 210, 313n., 314n., 320n.) qua 'everyone knows', 'it is (generally) understood': behind which lurks a "Io credo che tu creda" (*Mandragola*, edited by Guido Davico Bonino. Turin: Einaudi, 1980, p. 43, III.x) – thus Sostrata to her daughter Lucrezia (a parallelism, with polyptoton: repetition with variation). See also: "It is the verdict of ancient writers" (*Discourses on Livy*. Translated by Harvey C. Mansfield and Nathan Tarkov. Chicago: U of Chicago P, 1998, p. 78, I.37); "Everyone can understand" (p. 303, III.43); "Prudent men are accustomed to say" (p. 302, III.43). Incidentally, the second sentence of Blumenberg's *Legitimacy of the Modern Age* commences with a "Jedermann kennt" (*Legitimität*, p. 11; see p. 16) – the reference being the term 'secularization' ("'Verweltlichung'"). He also indicates a rhetorically hypoleptic formula: "nicht erfunden, sondern vorgefunden" (*Präfiguration. Arbeit am politischen Mythos*, edited by Angus Nicholls and Felix Heidenreich. Berlin: Suhrkamp, 2014, p. 16); in the given context of prefiguration qua legitimization (concerning Alexander the Great), such 'rhetoric' need not be verbalized (albeit semioticized): "Kein Wort brauchte bei dieser Art der Rhetorik zu fallen [sc. inverting Xerxes' sacrifice]; sie war sinnfällig für jeden, der seinen Herodot und seinen Homer

3.2 Assumptions About Being Human: Anthropistic *hypólepsis*

When anthropistic statements are employed, it is not necessary for them to be distinctive, or reasonably applicable only to humans (let alone to all) – nor even simply to be rational; they are used for effect, and do not constitute a (deductive, systematically consistent) type of ‹-logy›; consequently, anthropistic *hypolépseis* are rhetorical, first and foremost: a provisional plausibility is requisite, their persuasiveness prevails.[41]

In terms of metastructure, such assertions (tacitly) refer to a *quaestio infinita* and represent its respective answer (usually a *tópos*) – with the qualification that these specific *loci* are 'more common' than others; they (claim to) refer to

---

gelesen hatte"; "Es ist die höchste Form der Selbstlegitimierung, an den vertrautesten Primärakt der griechischen Geschichte und des griechischen Selbstbewußtseins Anschluß zu gewinnen" (p. 16); "Ein schon gebahnter Weg wird benutzt, und nichts schließt aus, daß er in umgekehrter Richtung begangen werden kann" (p. 17). For a general assessment in this respect, see Küpper: "Im politischen Diskurs hat das Schema, etwas Neues nicht als neu, sondern als bessere Neuauflage und Einlösung von etwas Altem zu präsentieren, vor allem legitimierende Funktion" (*Diskurs-Renovatio*, p. 462n.; *Discursive* Renovatio 461n.); anthropologically put: "Es hatte der Menschheit allezeit genügt, das Unbekannte als das längst Bekannte 'wiederzuerkennen'" (Blumenberg, *Lebenszeit*, p. 192). Generally, see Küpper, as to 'investing' something with "eine[r] elementare[n] Transparenz, im Sinn eines Anknüpfens an bereits 'Gewußtes' und insofern Legitimiertes" (*Diskurs-Renovatio*, p. 232; *Discursive* Renovatio 224) – *de re*, the appearance of such transparency is a sufficient, perchance the desired effect (man being the provisional being). (The notion of) 'legitimacy' is (always) hypoleptic; it need not tie in with 'the truth', only with what is (or will be) believed to be factual – the effectual being the persuasive: '*pístis*' from '*peítho*' (as employed herein).

41 Generally speaking, instances of this form of *hypólepsis* 'take up and vary' statements that 'contain, carry, and convey' anthropistic ken (the latter meaning: of and by what human beings – at a given time or during certain periods – are persuaded with respect to the question 'what is human'). As a provisional assessment: deductive 'anthropo-logy' posits (supposed) constants; inductive anthropistics focuses on and studies notions as to 'human invariants' factually in circulation (which are needful: man being mortal, limited, having to arrange himself with the state of his knowledge; see part 5 below). In general, rhetoric accommodates circumstances, variants – also in its very form: "*variatio* [...] *varietas* [...] als Gesamterscheinung der Rhetorik" (Lausberg, *Handbuch*, p. 142, § 257); thereto, see Mayfield, including on oratory's polyfunctionality in this respect ("Interplay," pp. 5, 5n.–6n., 8, 8n., 31).

everyone.⁴² This gives them their 'conative' efficacy, their (often provocative) potential and (political) brisance.⁴³

Implying the general question 'what is (a) human (being)', said utterances tender a particular(ized) answer. These are comparable in form and function: such maximatic *sententiae* tend to assert their taking up and tying in with common anthropistic knowledge; and to have a universal (*kathólou*) claim.⁴⁴ Since

---

42 "Die *loci communes* [...] sind als solche Antworten auf (formulierte oder nicht formulierte) *quaestiones* [...] des judizialen [...] deliberativen [...] und epideiktischen [...] Bereichs" (Lausberg, *Elemente*, p. 130, § 393); a "*locus communis* (κοινὸς τόπος)" is preceded by a "*quaestio infinita*" (sc. "*quaestio generalis, thesis, propositum*; θέσις") (p. 38, § 83; see § 82.2). The query as to 'what a human being is' may be conceived as a *quaestio infinita* – both in the spec. rhetorical sense, and *de re*; as Lausberg indicates, such are often tacit or implicit (see Blumenberg's above remark as to 'meta-questions', *Beschreibung*, p. 502). 'Anthropistic' assertions are (or claim to be) 'phenomenistic', seeing that they state something (ostensively) general, universal – in the sense that potentially anyone might 'perceive' this (apparent) verity or state of affairs (concerning 'man's nature'). In the example Ritter selects from Aristotle, it is precisely not only common knowledge that philosophical discourse takes up (which a thinker may tie in with, or draw from), but also 'nature' itself (*Metaphysik*, p. 54, 54n.). This sense is present in Aristotle, who implies that Thales observed natural phenomena directly, 'tying in' therewith (see *Metaphysics*, pp. 18 f., 983b, I.iii.4).

43 In a context concerning a *rhétor*'s 'crafting' of '*ethos*' (see "ποιήσει τὸ ἦθος"), Aristotle observes: "the hearers also are impressed in a certain way by a device employed *ad nauseam* by writers of speeches: 'Who does not know?' 'Everyone knows ['ἅπαντες ἴσασιν']'; for the hearer agrees, because he is ashamed to appear not to share what is a matter of common knowledge" (Aristotle, *Rhetoric*, pp. 378–381, 1408a, III.vii.7).

44 "Ein in einem Satz [...] formulierter *locus communis*, der mit dem Anspruch auftritt, als anerkannte Norm der für die Lebensführung relevanten Weltkenntnis oder der Lebensführung selbst zu gelten, heißt *sententia* (γνώμη)" (Lausberg, *Elemente*, pp. 130 f., § 398); "Die auf Weltkenntnis bezüglichen Sentenzen [...] werden meist als Feststellungen [...] auftreten, während die auf die Lebensführung selbst bezüglichen Sentenzen [...] meist als Aufforderungen [...] formuliert sind. Die Grenzen in Inhalt und Formulierung sind fließend"; "Eine in besonders weitem Sinne infinite Sentenz wird (*propositio*) *maxima* genannt (fr. *maxime*, engl. *maxim*). – Eine in einer Sprachgemeinschaft als Volksweisheit verbreitete Sentenz wird 'Sprichwort' (*proverbium, adagium*, παροιμία) genannt" (p. 131n.). Distinctively, anthropistic *sententiae* asserting, or alluding to, human invariants display or imply a most universal claim; by necessity (given man's limitations in factual grasp vs. his at least potentially infinite notional reach), they have a tendency to be more frequently 'fabricated' (and then labeled as having been common ken and currency always already) than other maxims, in whose cases a (preceding) presence or prevalence may be verifiable to a certain extent; in other words: statements as to 'what man is' are (supposed or assumed) to be plausible quasi-*a priori*, since they (are taken to) tie in with what is accessible to anyone. Democritus' above remark is particularly pertinent, in baring said fact. Concerning the aspect of plausibility in rhetorical terms, see Gorgias: "εἰκὸς", "probably" ("Encomium of Helen," pp. 756 f., § 49.5); Aristotle accentuates the term "εἰκός" (*Rhetoric*, p. 26, 1357a–b, I.ii.15; therein, see also Freese's "Select Glossary of Technical and Other Terms," p. 475), precisely in a passage that ties in with "εἰκός" in a poetic context via '*tò*

the make or patterning of such remarks is relatively stable – hence memorable ('a human being is …', 'all men are …', 'man is the animal that …', etc.) – they may be altered paradigmatically, but also 'fabricated' all but entirely, and still retain much of the weight and (rhetorical) color of previous anthropistic *essais* (of acknowledged, or once current, 'attempts at defining human beings'), specifically due to their form itself.[45]

Anthropistic statements are hypoleptic in a most general sense: attempts at defining man's '*tò tí en einai*' take up and vary other floating *essais* (carrying and conveying notions as to 'human invariants') – explicitly, usually implicitly, and generally in 'free (uncontrolled) variation' (context and function will differ). Moreover, they might claim to be tying in with what is most accessible to all, what anyone may (allegedly) discern or experience for themselves: 'man is

---

kathólou', including a reference to "πιθανόν" ("Poetics," pp. 58–63, 1451a–b, § 9.1–18, 30–35). See Burckhardt: "das Geltendmachen des Plausiblen *(εἰκός)*" (*Griechische Kulturgeschichte. Gesammelte Werke* VII, vol. 3. Darmstadt: Wissenschaftliche Buchgesellschaft, 1962, p. 304); as to "*probabile, credibile, verisimile*", '*pithanón*', see Lausberg (*Elemente*, pp. 23 f., §§ 34–38); compare Glenn W. Most ("Rhetorik und Hermeneutik: Zur Konstitution der Neuzeitlichkeit". *Antike und Abendland*, vol. 30, no. 1, 1984, pp. 62–79, here p. 71).

45 In Poe's undulant formulation (from the ninth stanza of "The Raven"): "For we cannot help agreeing that no living human being" etc. (*Selected* Writings, edited by G. R. Thompson. New York: Norton, 2004, p. 59, verse 51) – the emphasis being on the immediacy of consent. As to '*color*' qua rhetorical term, see Lausberg (*Elemente*, p. 36, § 73.1; 36n.). These maxims are 'momentaneously evident', '*eingängig*' ('intuitive, memorable, captivating', implying 'common, customary', and including the dynamics inhering in the term 'current', from '*currere*') like rhythms; as to the latter, compare Wesche ("Verse Games," p. 137). See Blumenberg, for a particularly notorious case in point: "Das *Ich denke, ich bin* war einer der erfolgreichsten philosophischen Sätze. Nicht nur wegen der Hinzufügung des 'also', sondern wegen der vielfachen Abwandelbarkeit des formalen Schemas, das mit diesem Satz vorgegeben war, in den sich je nach systematischer Gewichtung anderer Akte und Inhalte immer neue Wörter einsetzen ließen" (*Lebensthemen. Aus dem Nachlaß*. Stuttgart: Reclam, 1998, p. 130 f.). As regards memorability, two things seem needful and one conducive: first, such *sententiae* refer – particularly in terms of form – to a previous proverb, maxim, saying, aphorism that is common knowledge *de facto*, or said or thought to be; secondly, they are formulated in a rhetorically polished (usually terse) manner, and often employ repetition with variation (via alliteration, assonance, polyptoton, *figura etymologica*, paronomasia, etc.): that is, they are (auto-)cohesive and self-contained, hence transportable if fragmented or severed from their source context; thirdly, it is helpful if they are in some way measured (with many being metrically patterned indeed); theirs is an aural plausibility (also), which need not be conceptual. In this sense, Jakobson's 'poetic' function applies. In turn, said aspects conduce to *hypólepsis*. As a particularly notable instance, see Poe's parody of (Diogenes' mockery of) Plato's definition of man (*Complete Stories and Poems*. New York: Doubleday, n.a., p. 358; thereto, see Mayfield, *Artful Immorality*, pp. 25n.–26n.).

what everyone knows' (as Democritus is said to have said).[46] This implies that they transcend or subtend virtually any conceivable discursive limits, and are transposable in terms of linguistic setting, hence intersect and supersede (supposed) 'national' or cultural boundaries; in this sense, they have a 'cosmopolitan' claim: they (are said to) refer, pertain, or appeal to all humankind. If at all present, epistemological, or similarly 'logical' considerations (to say nothing of metaphysical ones) are secondary, here.

Essais concerning 'human invariants' may (or claim to) be tying in with former 'definitional attempts' as to 'what man is'; anthropistic *hypólepsis* marks a (more or less specific) allusion (also *ex negativo*) to common knowledge about human beings, which is – or used (or is said) to be – common currency, 'floating' in (virtual) cultural networks.[47] Taking up a familiar form

---

46 On variants of *sermocinatio* (qua 'putting words into someone's mouth'), see Mayfield ("Variants of Rhetorical Ventriloquism" passim).
47 Machiavelli's *œuvre* is a particularly expedient example, in this respect. An explicit (albeit nonspecific, see *Il Principe*, p. 78n.) *hypólepsis* is used here: "It is the verdict of ancient writers that men are wont to worry in evil and to become bored with good, and that from both of these passions the same effects arise" (*Discourses On Livy*, p. 78, I.37); then follows an anthropistic appeal to a 'human invariant' ('man is the ambitious being'): "ambition [...] is so powerful in human breasts that it never abandons them at whatever rank they rise to. The cause is that nature has created men so that they are able to desire everything and are unable to attain everything" (*Discourses on Livy*, p. 78, I.37). Compare: "È cosa veramente molto naturale e ordinaria desiderare di acquistare" (*Il Principe*, p. 22, III) – the reference, context, or field of application ('man') being implied; an accentuation of human ambition is discernible in various discourses, also in *Scripture*, particularly in the Augustinian acceptation and emphasis – with Machiavelli inverting the valuative tendency. See also: "Besides this, human appetites are insatiable, for since from nature they have the ability and the wish to desire all things and from fortune the ability to achieve few of them, there continually results from this a discontent in human minds and a disgust with the things they possess" (*Discourses on Livy*, p. 125, II.Preface); see Callimaco's soliloquy (addressing himself): "Don't you know how little good a man finds in the things he has desired, compared to what the man supposed he'd find there?" (*Mandragola*, edited and translated by Mera J. Flaumenhaft. Long Grove: Waveland P, 1981, p. 39, IV.i). In the *Discorsi* and *Il Principe*, the (tacit) *quaestiones infinitae* – 'what are human beings (generally speaking)' – and the respective answers are both universal: 'human beings are insatiable, driven by their appetites, ambitious'. In *Mandragola*, this generalized answer is implied, in turn. Like Aristotle, Machiavelli's works typically begin with, and are passim grounded upon, a certain conception of man (the 'acquisitive, self-interested, etc. animal'). The first preface (a privileged locus) commences with the adversatively assertive statement: "Although the envious nature of men" (*Discourses on Livy*, p. 5, I.Preface). *Il Principe* particularly focuses on 'man as a self-seeking animal': "Perché degli uomini si può dire questo, generalmente, che sieno ingrati, volubili, simulatori e dissimulatori, fuggitori de' pericoli, cupidi del guadagno" (*Il Principe*, p. 110, XVII; the last name of 'Callimaco' is "Guadagno", *Mandragola*, p. 5, Prologo). Hence the reader is already primed for assessments such as "ogni occasione di propria utilità", stated in the vicinity of: "per essere gl'uomini tristi" (*Il Principe*, p. 111, XVII);

for asserting what everyone knows – or is said or thought to know – with regard to man, these claims (answers to the *quaestio infinita* 'what is human') are hypoleptic in both form and function.⁴⁸

Apart from (giving themselves the appearance of) being 'acceptations', anthropistic answers to the (tacit) *quaestio* 'what is a human being' tend to have a peculiar force or forte: they seem to immediately convey a sense of one's having been addressed (in 'conative' terms); such maxims (*loci communes, tópoi, sententiae*) are distinguished from other forms of common knowledge in that answers as to man's (peculiar) being have a general appeal (including such as may be per se appalling), being potentially directed at one and all.⁴⁹ This is particularly the case in drama, where the expediency of appealing to everyone – to what is (taken to be) common knowledge – will be patent as

---

this is stressed with a quasi 'general rule' as to an implied 'man is the greedy animal': "perché li uomini sdimenticano piú presto la morte del padre che la perdita del patrimonio" (pp. 111 f., XVII); a counterexample occurs when the context demands that this 'general rule' be mitigated: "e gli uomini non sono mai sí disonesti che con tanto esemplo di ingratitudine e' ti opprimessino" (pp. 150 f., XXI). The self-interested nature of human beings is then repeated with formulations such as: "quando tu vedi el ministro pensare piú a sé che a te", "l'utile suo" (p. 155, XXII), "de' consiglieri, ciascuno penserà alla proprietà sua" (p. 159, XXIII). It is arguably irrelevant whether or not the reader actually agrees, or wishes (or cares) to concur with such claims (let alone take delight in them); for it is assumed that 'everyone knows' this state of affairs (that 'it is understood'), wherefore such assertions tend to have 'momentaneous evidence' (also, and perhaps more effectually, *malgré soi*).

48 In this, anthropistic remarks are inevitably rhetorical, seeing that the arch-*téchne* works with, and insinuates (or engenders), 'familiarity' – a "Vertrautheitshorizont. Rhetorik arbeitet mit Vertrautheiten. Sie will nicht beweisen, sondern Widerspruch erschweren" (Blumenberg, *Quellen*, p. 212). Hence the recurrent formulation 'they say' is particularly applicable, here; see Ritter: "daß man [...] von dem ausgehen muß, 'was [...] gesagt wird'" (*Metaphysik*, p. 64); variants thereof are pervasive in *La Celestina* (edited by Dorothy S. Severin. Madrid: Cátedra, 2002), for instance – see (*inter alia*): "como dizen" (p. 107, I; compare p. 155, IV, p. 159, IV, p. 254, XI, p. 256, XII, p. 300, XV, p. 301, XVI, pp. 310–311, XVII), "dizen algunos" (p. 130, II; see p. 272, XII), "Pues dizen" (p. 137, II), "¿No has leýdo que dizen[?]" (p. 158, IV), "Por esto dizen" (p. 173, V), "bien dizen que" (p. 174, V), "No se dize embalde" (p. 256, XII), "No embalde dizen" (p. 265, XII), "No embalde se dize" (p. 307, XVII), "Todo el mundo lo sabe" (p. 342, XXI).

49 See Augustine's comment on the reception of the Terentian *dictum* (in part 4 herein). A maximal universality is their distinctive characteristic. Apart from being human oneself – and that everyone knows (and all have assumptions about) 'what man is' – virtually anyone will sense having been addressed, if a statement is of the form 'all human beings are'. The term 'rhetorical' signals 'purposiveness', expediency; here, the 'conative' is intricately interwoven with the 'poetic' function; the latter renders these remarks effortlessly transposable into other contexts; the 'referential', 'metalingual' functions (referring to the discourse, context, code) are typically not foregrounded; here and throughout, Jakobson's terms (see *Language*, pp. spec. 66–71) are used *mutatis mutandis*, as a heuristic device.

regards the intra- and extratextual recipients (qua addressees of an anthropistic message).⁵⁰

3.3 With a Difference: Dramatic *hypólepsis*

Due to its typically (including: virtually) dialogic form, rhetorical *hypólepsis* pertains to plays in particular (the anthropistic variant as the case may be).⁵¹ Certain oratorical devices are especially effective in dialog, hence in drama – above all, *distinctio*.⁵² Specifically theatrical and intratextual variants of *hypólepsis* may be encountered in comical exchanges – for instance in the form of dialogically productive (willful, accidental) misunderstandings, misnomers, or double entendre, where the 'metalingual' function is consequently express and

---

50 These or similar rhetorical appeals may bridge the 'horizon-related' gap between a text's time of production and the respective present (generally, see Hans-Georg Gadamer. *Wahrheit und Methode. Grundzüge einer philosophischen Hermeneutik. Gesammelte Werke* 1, Hermeneutik I. Tübingen: Mohr Siebeck, 2010, pp. 307–312, and passim; Hans Robert Jauß. "Literaturgeschichte als Provokation der Literaturwissenschaft". *Rezeptionsästhetik*, edited by Rainer Warning. Munich: Fink, 1994, pp. 126–162, here pp. 131–139). Apart from the always needful historico-philological considerations as to emitting and receiving horizon, 'reader response' would not be operational, if texts did not encompass a rhetorical potential to draw in virtually any recipient – simply on the basis that a text is written by humans, deals with things human, hence appeals to human beings (especially in terms of the Aristotelian '*kathólou*', *Poetics*, pp. 58–61, 1451b, § 9). Drama may be seen as a privileged locus for answering (and staging) the query 'what is man' in the particular.

51 See also the sample from Terence in section 4 (a rhetorical *hypólepsis*, with anthropistic tendency, in drama).

52 "*Prov.* [*advancing*] What's your will, father? / *Duke*. That, now you are come, you will be gone" (Shakespeare. *Measure for Measure*, edited by J. W. Lever. [*Arden*]. London: Thomson, 2004, p. 77, III.i.174–175; see *Measure for Measure*, edited by Mark Eccles. [*Variorum*]. New York: MLA, 1980, p. 149, TLN 1396–1397; the ensuing through line numbers refer to the latter edition); it may also have paronomastic color: "*Ang.* [...] Elbow is your name? Why dost thou not speak, Elbow? / *Pom*. He cannot, sir: he's out at elbow [sc. 'without the wit to reply']" (p. 30, II.i.58–60; see 30n.; TLN 513–516); "[*Esc.*] What was done to Elbow's wife, once more? / *Pom*. Once, sir? There was nothing done to her once" (p. 34, II.i.138–140; TLN 591–593). In dialog, *distinctio* is a form of rhetorical *hypólepsis*. One might also be said to 'tie in with oneself', e.g. in a *correctio*, or in a repetition (for emphasis, insinuation); see "look in this gentleman's face [...] look upon his honour [...] Doth your honour mark his face" (p. 34, II.i.144–147; TLN 598–600); and Pompey's echoing his own line with slight variation: "Why, very well: I hope here be truths", "Why, very well then: I hope here be truths" (p. 33, II.i.126, 132; TLN 579, 585). See also Othello's "Put out the light, and then put out the light! / [...] But once put out thy light", including the murderous–luminous isotopy overall (*Othello*, edited by E. A. J. Honigmann. [*Arden*]. London: Thomson, 2001, p. 306, V.ii.7, 10; see verses 7–13). As to '*distinctio*' – including '*antanáklasis*' ("die dialogische [...] Realisierung der *distinctio*"), '*dubitatio*',

tends to be dominant.⁵³ The following will stand in for countless possibilities in this respect:

> Elbow. My wife, sir, whom I detest before heaven and your honour –
> Esc. How? Thy wife?
> Elbow. Ay, sir: whom I thank heaven is an honest woman –
> Esc. Dost thou detest her therefore?
> Elbow. I say, sir, I will detest myself also, as well as she [...].
> (Shakespeare, *Measure*, p. 31, II.i.68–74; TLN 523–529)⁵³

The phrase "My wife" is here taken up and grammatically altered according to the situation of communication; the constable repeats his own "heaven", while

---

'*correctio*' – see Lausberg (*Elemente*, pp. 93–95, §§ 289–292, here: p. 95; see pp. 122–124, §§ 380–384). In general, a rhetorical *hypólepsis* (perchance particularly in dramatic dialog) may also use the devices of *figura etymologica* and paronomasia to effect a repetition with variation; or a polyptoton, as here: "*Esc.* [...] It is but heading and hanging. / *Pom.* If you head and hang all that offend" etc. (*Measure*, p. 37, II.i.233–235; TLN 683–684); and (with paronomasia): "*Esc.* [...] Is it a lawful trade? / *Pom.* If the law would allow it, sir. / *Esc.* But the law will not allow it [...] it shall not be allowed" (p. 36, II.i.221–226; TLN 671–675). In another context (concerning verse), Stempel speaks of something being "in kontaktfördernder Position am Zeilenende" (in: Jauß et al., "Arbre," p. 471); by and large, end focus tends to conduce to (rhetorical) *hypólepsis*; other such devices are anadiplosis, epi-, and anaphora, *inter alia* (generally thereto, see Lausberg, *Elemente*, pp. 82–83, § 250; pp. 86–89, §§ 265–273).

53 In this respect, see Jakobson's example of paradigmatic substitution in dominantly 'metalingual' dialogic contexts (*Language*, p. 69). The drama and its audience constitute a (virtual) *pólis* of sorts, naturally share 'currencies', establish commonalities, customary knowledge, conventions, for the duration of the particular play; this includes generic conventions concerning a kind of (explicit) contract between the actors and the audience (proposed, and usually entered into, in the exposition); see e.g. the prolog to *Henry V*, accentuating audience collaboration with regard to *evidentia*: "And let us [...] / On your imaginary forces work. / Suppose [...] / Piece out our imperfections with your thoughts. [...] / Think, when we talk of horses, that you see them [...] / For 'tis your thoughts that now must deck our kings [...] / Admit me Chorus [...] / Who prologue-like your humble patience pray" (*Henry V*, edited by T. W. Craik. [*Arden*]. London: Bloomsbury, 1995, pp. 120 f., Prologue 17–33). Generally, see Lausberg as to '*captatio benevolentiae*' with a view to '*delectatio*' (*Elemente*, p. 35, § 69; compare p. 25, § 43; *Handbuch*, pp. 158 f., § 277); see also: "captan la benevolencia" (Baltasar Gracián. *Oráculo manual y arte de prudencia*, edited by Emilio Blanco. Madrid: Cátedra, 2011, p. 139, § 67), "la semejança concilia benevolencia" (p. 145, § 77).

54 See the entire scene (*Measure*, pp. 29–38, II.i.41–272; TLN 495–718). The glosses suggest: "he means 'protest'" (p. 31n.); see "*Elbow.* [...] I do lean upon justice, sir, and do bring in here before your good honour two notorious benefactors. / *Ang.* Benefactors? Well, what benefactors are they? Are they not malefactors? / *Elbow.* If it please your honour, I know not well what they are. But precise villains they are, that I am sure of, and void of all profanation in the world, that good Christians ought to have" (p. 30, II.i.48–56; TLN 503–511). The rhetorical *hypolépseis* here present are repetition with metalingual correction ("benefactors", "malefactors"), followed by a paradigmatic replacement ("villains"); a hypoleptic rearrangement and

alluding to "honour" in "honest" (a *figura etymologica*); the "detest" is then given in antithetical terms ("thank heaven"), wherefore Escalus takes up "detest" with a view to effecting an auto-correction on the part of Elbow – who, echoing himself ("Ay, sir", "I say, sir"), does tie in therewith, but not in the manner likely to have been intended by the alderman.⁵⁵

In a serious context, Antony's oration – delivered after Brutus has spoken – is a specifically striking example as to how a particular 'tying in with' need not share the same assumptions (to say nothing of 'principles'), nor have exclusively textual implications.⁵⁶ Brutus' reasoning after the slaughter stress-

---

reapplication of the same terms ("Well, what [...] are they", "I know not well what they are. But [...] they are"). As to Elbow, the glosses refer to 'transpositions', 'ironic misplacings' (p. 30n.; see 31n., 32n.); in the text itself: "*Esc.* [*to Angelo*] Do you hear how he misplaces?" (p. 31, II.i.87; TLN 542); an apparent misnomer particularly to the point in that context: "a woman cardinally [sc. 'carnally'] given" (p. 31, II.i.78 f.; see 31n.; TLN 533–534; Elbow's misplaced term is capitalized in the Folio text – see *Measure* [*Variorum*], p. 64, with p. 64n.).

55 Generally speaking, *correctio* may be included as a variant in what one might term auto-*hypólepsis*. See a thematic 'tying in with oneself' in the *Rhetorica ad Herennium*: "quo facilius res cognosci possit, ne ab eadem sententia recedamus", "for the sake of greater clarity, to continue the same theme as above" (edited and translated by Harry Caplan. Cambridge: Harvard UP, 2004, pp. 366 f., IV.xliii.55); "ut ab eiusdem sententiae non recedamus exemplo", "to continue the use of the same theme for my example" (p. 370 f., IV.xliv.56). Likewise, an instance taken from Shakespearean (script) variants might be termed a form of auto-*hypólepsis* (effecting a polyptoton): "Q 'laid' may be an actor's echo from the previous line" – "I lay unto the grievous charge of others. / Clarence, whom I, indeed, have cast [or, as in Q, 'laid'] in darkness" (*Richard III*, edited by Anthony Hammond. [*Arden*]. London: Thomson, 2002, p. 169n.; re p. 169, I.iii.326–327). For a telling example of tying in with oneself (likely for reasons of legitimization), see Blumenberg: "Wahrscheinlich war es einer der fiktiven Antwortbriefe, die von ihm [sc. Descartes] in Umlauf gesetzt wurden, um auf gedachte oder indirekt übermittelte Einwände einzugehen" (*Höhlenausgänge*, p. 450). In this paradigmatic case, the intra-textual auto-*hypólepsis* is particularly patent: "*21 March, night*: Free. Soulfree and fancy-free. Let the dead bury the dead. Ay. And let the dead marry the dead" (James Joyce. *A Portrait of the Artist as a Young Man*, edited by John Paul Riquelme, Hans Walter Gabler and Walter Hettche. New York: Norton, 2007, p. 219, V.2630 f.); the glosses add: "Stephen cites and then transforms Luke 9:60" (p. 219n.).

56 Contrast Assmann (*Gedächtnis*, p. 283, with p. 281). If the environment is textual, the context cannot be identical, and the function will typically differ (at least in nuances), or be at variance entirely. For a historical example comparable to Antony's *modus operandi* in countering Brutus (as rendered in Shakespeare), see Quentin Skinner on Hobbes' technique: in *Leviathan*, the latter "picks up and deploys the distinctive vocabulary originally put into currency by the parliamentarian and radical writers of the 1640s" ("Hobbes on Persons, Authors and Representatives". *The Cambridge Companion to Hobbes's Leviathan*, edited by Patricia Springborg. Cambridge: Cambridge UP, 2007, pp. 157–180, here p. 159); "crucial is the extensive use he makes in the revised version of his theory of the distinctive vocabulary developed by the parliamentarian propagandists of the 1640s [...]. What Hobbes is doing [...] is seeking to discredit these writers by demonstrating that it is possible to accept the basic structure of their

es Caesar's '*plus ultra*': "Ambition's debt is paid" (*Caesar*, p. 238, III.i.83); it is also at the center of Brutus' speech to the public: "but as he was ambitious, I slew him [...] and death, for his ambition" (*Caesar*, p. 254, III.ii.26–28).[57]

In a rhetorical *hypólepsis*, Antony's speech explicitly takes up this term and charge on the assassinator's part, while redirecting its force via a series of slight variations, ultimately leading to an utter 'refunctionalization'.[58] Employ-

---

theory without in the least endorsing any of the radical implications they had drawn from it. [...] this new rhetorical strategy in *Leviathan*" (p. 161; see p. 176n.); as per Skinner, the Early Modern theorist uses the same tactic against the "House of Commons", who had 'denounced absolute power' as "'a strange *Monster* to be permitted by mankinde'": "Hobbes unhesitatingly picks up and hurls back the taunt" (p. 175; see Skinner. "Hobbes on Representation". *European Journal of Philosophy*, vol. 13, no. 2, 2005, pp. 155–184, here p. 179) – i.e. by employing the term 'leviathan' emphatically.

57 This emphasis on Caesar's ambition refers back to Brutus' earlier deliberative soliloquy (see *Julius Caesar*, edited by David Daniell. [Arden]. London: Thomson, 2006, pp. 197–199, II.i.10–34), including an appeal to what is deemed the general knowledge in this respect: "But 'tis a common proof" – after which follows an explanation of the method of ambition and of such natures (p. 198, II.i.21; see II.i.22–27).

58 Jakobson speaks of "successive transformations" (*Language*, p. 90); the glosses have: "Part of Antony's skill in manipulation is in being gradual" (Shakespeare, *Caesar*, p. 257n.). See the respective speeches by Brutus (pp. 253f., III.ii.13–40) and Antony (pp. 257f., III.ii.74–108); among other verses: "The noble Brutus / Hath told you Caesar was ambitious" (p. 258, III.ii.78–79); "But Brutus says, he was ambitious" (p. 258, III.ii.87); "Did this in Caesar seem ambitious" (p. 258, III.ii.91); "Yet Brutus says, he was ambitious" (p. 258, III.ii.94); "Was this ambition? / Yet Brutus says, he was ambitious" (p. 258, III.ii.98–99). For a detailed analysis of Antony's speech, see Jakobson (*Language*, pp. 90f.), especially: "Mark Antony lampoons Brutus' speech by changing the alleged reasons for Caesar's assassination into plain linguistic fictions. Brutus' accusation of Caesar, 'as he was ambitious, I slew him', undergoes successive transformations. First Antony reduces it to a mere quotation [...] The following polyptoton [...] presents the repeated allegation as mere reported speech [...] The most effective device of Antony's irony is the *modus obliquus* of Brutus' abstracts changed into a *modus rectus* to disclose that these reified attributes are nothing but linguistic fictions" (pp. 90f.); Jakobson then demonstrates the way in which Antony takes up individual phrases and words on Brutus' part, redirecting them (see p. 91); and shows how the "dramatic force of Antony's exordium [...] is achieved by [...] playing on grammatical categories and constructions" (p. 90). One might also accentuate the performative 'tying in with' as such – meaning, rhetorical (intratextual, here quasi-dialogic), and then also anthropistic (trans-temporal, intertextual, trans-linguistic) *hypolépseis*. In the context of his theory of metaphor, Blumenberg notes the transformative dynamics of (implicitly) hypoleptic 'refunctionalizations': "[es] ist für Wirkung aufschlußreich, was nicht nur Wiederholung, Zitat, Referat, also unbedingte Anerkennung der Verbindlichkeit des Vorliegenden ist, sondern die Mühe des Umgangs erkennen läßt: Arbeit der Verformung über die Gedächtnisleistung hinaus, aber auch Anspielung, die immer das Verständnis des anderen voraussetzt, ohne es bestimmen zu wollen. [...] Wirkung ist eben nicht die Aufbewahrung von Figuren, sondern der vertraute oder auch sperrige Umgang mit ihnen" (*Goethe zum Beispiel*, edited by Manfred Sommer et al. Berlin: Suhrkamp, 2014, p. 44). Moreover, any 'tying in with'

ing (*inter alia*) the rhetorical devices of parallelism, polyptoton, *figura etymologica*, antithesis, and irony, Antony's *hypolépseis* quasi-performatively keep

---

tends to be partial, poly-directional: "Was wir 'Hintergrundmetaphorik' genannt haben, der implizite Gebrauch einer Metapher, wird hier nochmals deutlich. Erst der Neuplatonismus hat diesen [Höhlen-]Mythos als 'absolute Metapher' genommen, teils anknüpfend an Empedokles und Plato, teils an die homerische Nymphengrotte, die in der Homer-Allegorese zu kosmischer Bedeutung aufgewachsen war, wie es des Porphyrios Traktat 'De antro nympharum' zeigt" (*Paradigmen zu einer Metaphorologie*. Frankfurt: Suhrkamp, 1998, p. 114). Such also yields formal or structural *hypolépseis*: "Am Höhlenmythos und mit dessen vorgeprägten Mitteln schafft Nietzsche die Rhetorik seines Antiplatonismus" (*Höhlenausgänge*, p. 627). As to Blumenberg's concept of "Umbesetzung" (sc. 'refunctionalization'), which reckons with (implicit, tacit) *hypolépseis de re*, see e.g. (*Matthäuspassion*. Frankfurt: Suhrkamp, 1991, p. 16; *Lebenszeit*, pp. 199, 203, 206; *Höhlenausgänge*, pp. 38, 296; *Legitimität*, pp. 52, 57 f.); particularly pertinent, here: "Der Gedanke der 'Umbesetzung' erklärt nicht, woher das neu eingesetzte Element stammt, nur welche Weihen es empfängt" (*Legitimität*, p. 60); "Die These von der funktionalen Umbesetzung als der Erzeugung des Scheins von substantieller Identität durch Säkularisierung ist eine Erklärung von Hartnäckigkeit, nicht deren Erleichterung oder Legitimierung" (p. 71; see pp. 75, 79, 89, 98 f., 157, 166 f., 257, 395, 399, 406); crucially (in that context, generally): "Es ist vor allem eine Ausdruckswelt, die sich durchhält. Die Sphäre der sakralen Sprache überlebt die der geweihten Sachen [...]. Die Umbesetzung von Systemfunktionen im Prozeß des Epochenwandels bedingt die sprachliche Konstanz in vielfältiger Weise" (pp. 87 f.; see also *Begriffe*, p. 17; "Wirkungspotential [2001]", pp. 380 f.; "Wirkungspotential [1983]", p. 49; *Arbeit*, p. 34; *Beschreibung*, p. 435; *Sachen*, p. 213; on the method of "Umbesetzungen", *Höhlenausgänge*, pp. 183–299; also on "Gegenbesetzungen", pp. 301–411; spec. pp. 303 f.); for applications of Blumenberg's concept, see Küpper (*Diskurs-Renovatio*, pp. 258, 274; *Discursive* Renovatio pp. 249, 265, 283; Mayfield, *Artful Immorality*, p. 170n.). For a particular case (as to Mach on Kant, infinitized here), see Blumenberg, noting "die formale Kontinuität der 'Umbesetzung' einer ihrer Funktion und theoretischen Leistung nach vorgegebenen Stelle im Text [...], obwohl der Autor gern von der Vorstellung des Bruches in seiner Entwicklung ausgehen möchte. [...] Umbesetzungen [...] sind nur vollziehbar oder nachweisbar, sofern Besetzungen stehenbleiben. Eine totale Umbesetzung ist ein Traum; wir würden nie erfahren, wenn sie vollzogen wäre" (*Quellen*, p. 160; see *Lebenszeit*, p. 51); the decisive statement in this respect (with the philosopher's reflections on his own concept): "Die 'Umbesetzungen', aus denen Geschichte besteht, werden rhetorisch vollzogen" ("Anthropologische Annäherung," p. 420), "Durchsetzung und Bestätigung der Umbesetzung sind rhetorische Akte" (p. 426). This ties in with his emphasizing "*consensus* als Ideal der Rhetorik" (p. 412); as a historical example: "Solche Rücksichten auf die Denkformen seines [sc. of Copernicus] Fachpublikums sind immer von der geringsten Schulspezifität – von Aristoteles oder Plato gerade so viel, wie zum Allgemeingut der Schulen geworden ist" (*Die Genesis der kopernikanischen Welt. Die Zweideutigkeit des Himmels. Eröffnung der Möglichkeit eines Kopernikus*. Frankfurt: Suhrkamp, 1996, 3 vols., vol. 2, p. 248; see p. 267). The latter marks a case in point for a decided functionalization of *hypólepsis*, and spec. with a view to (rhetorical) economy: "Die Komposition [...] ein Produkt der Assimilation", "eine höchst ökonomische Anpassung an die Rezeptionsbereitschaft der Zeitgenossen" (p. 297) – here as regards the relationship of Copernicus' *Revolutions* to Ptolemy's *Almagest*. As to rhetoric: "weil Überredung Gemeinsamkeit eines Horizontes voraussetzt, [...] Anspielung auf Prototypisches, [...] Orientierung an der Metapher, am Gleichnis" ("Annäherung," p. 412). Such

the very fact of his 'tying in with' Brutus' speech alive in the minds of his audience, by continually reaccentuating this *modus operandi* in a series of warily varied, increasingly adversative repetitions; Antony's sequence ultimately leads to a paronomastically incisive anthropistic *hypólepsis*: "O judgement, thou art fled to brutish beasts / And men have lost their reason" (*Caesar*, p. 258, III.ii.105–106).[59] The particularly "dramatic force" (Jakobson, *Language*, p. 90) of these terse and acute forms of *hypólepsis* heightens their 'momentaneous evidence' – both intratextually (with Antony's 'conative' appeal to the Romans including a form of stagecraft), and as regards the extratextual recipients.[60]

---

forms tie in with a given *Lebenswelt*, with what 'everyone knows' (or is said to know); they are universal (or give the impression of being so), hence portable (transferrable, translatable, as signaled by the term '*metaphérein*'), dynamic; Blumenberg accentuates this tendency when speaking of "Arbeit an den Bildern" (*Schiffbruch*, n.pag.; intro. abstract, corresponds to p. 2). See Harald Weinrich's statement: "Bildfelder [...] gehören zum sprachlichen Weltbild eines Kulturkreises. [...] Es gibt eine Harmonie der Bildfelder zwischen den einzelnen abendländischen Sprachen. Das Abendland ist eine Bildfeldgemeinschaft" (*Sprache in Texten*. Stuttgart: Klett, 1976, p. 287). See Konersmann: "Europa, mit diesen Worten leitete Harald Weinrich vor Jahren die Rehabilitation des Rhetorischen [...] ein, sei eine 'Bildfeldgemeinschaft'" ("Vorwort: Figuratives Wissen." *Wörterbuch der philosophischen Metaphern*, edited by Ralf Konersmann. Darmstadt: Wissenschaftliche Buchgesellschaft, 2014, pp. 7–20, here p. 11). Generally, Blumenberg notes: "Keine Erfahrung bewegt sich je in einem Raum völliger Unbestimmtheit" (*Lesbarkeit*, p. 16); the philosopher supposes an anthropogenic basis for the utilization (and 'endurance') of metaphors: "Lebensweltlich muss es immer schon Rückübertragungsverhältnisse der Anschauung gegeben haben, damit die Forcierung des Bewußtseins durch die Metapher ertragen werden konnte" (*Schiffbruch*, p. 79) – that is, a tying in with a basic structure or script pertaining to humankind, primed for various forms of *Anknüpfung*. With respect to a personal hypoleptic *praxis*, see Blumenberg's opening his contribution to the collaborative reading of Apollinaire's poem with the statement: "Ich möchte an die Äußerung von J. Taubes anknüpfen" (in: Jauß et al., "*Arbre*," p. 481).

59 It is not just "perhaps" the case that "brutish" is "a pun on Brutus, dehumanizing" him (*Caesar*, p. 258n.); see Jakobson's assessment: "this apostrophe with its murderous paronomasia *Brutus-brut*ish" (*Language*, p. 91).

60 The immediate reactions or effects are paramount; 'momentaneous evidence' is heightened in drama (especially if staged), since other factors will then conduce thereto, such as visual, auditory, 'emotive' stimuli, the overwhelming continuity, the drivenness of the plot; the latter in an Aristotelian sense: "tragedy is mimesis of an action [...] the plot is the mimesis of the action" ("Poetics," p. 49, 1449b–1450a, VI); "tragedy is mimesis not of persons but of action and life [...] and the goal ['*télos*'] is the most important thing of all" (pp. 50 f., 1450a, VI); "Plot [...] is the first principle and [...] soul of tragedy, while character is secondary" (pp. 53, 1450a, VI; see p. 57, 1451a, VIII).

Instances of the anthropistic variant are frequent in drama.[61] In addition to the innuendo in Antony's above statement, a reader or audience of Shakespeare might encounter other hypoleptic allusions to the Aristotelizing 'human invariant' of man qua *animal rationale* – for instance in Hamlet's invective

---

[61] Even so, it may not be expedient to refer to all humankind in all plots: some may require the staging of certain societal segments, at times gendered or profession-based, also for reasons of (sub)genre. *Mandragola* is built on the anthropistic assumption that 'all men are selfish'. The Prolog states an arguable verity about 'people in general' that might be translated into the definitional *essai* 'man is the finger-pointing animal' – here in a (self-interested) application by the speaker: "El premio che si spera è che ciascuno / si sta da canto e ghigna, / dicendo mal di ciò che vede o sente"; "che la gente, / vedendo ch'ognun biasma" (*Mandragola*, p. 6). Callimaco says about Ligurio: "I know that the likes of you live by cheating men" (p. 18, I.iii); the thesis might be: 'all parasites are fraudulent'. Naturally, the remark would be differently received in the form 'all human beings are leeches', or 'all men cheat'. When aiming to include the priest in the plot, Callimaco asks, Ligurio answers: "Chi disporrà el confessoro, tu? / Io, e denari, la cattività nostra, loro" (p. 30, II.vi) – i.e. 'everyone is greedy and wicked (perchance correlatively so)'. What receives a particularizing formulation here is generally articulated as 'all men are self-interested' in *The Prince*. In a soliloquy, the *Frate* gives the key to the play's conception of man indirectly: "Egli è vero che io ci sono suto giuntato; nondimeno, questo giunto è con mio utile" (pp. 42 f., III.ix) – the implicit *praemissa maior*: 'all men are eager for gain' (as *Il Principe* states expressly); the drama stages the universal *sententia* in (various) particulars. Later, Ligurio generalizes: "These *frati* are cunning, astute; and it stands to reason, because they know our sins and their own" (p. 29, III.2); 'all friars are sly' – a claim one of them later disavows: "Oh, how few brains are in these *frati* of mine!" (p. 49, V.i – says Timoteo). As a whole, and in all of its characters individually, this play stages the tacit *quaestio* 'what is man' with the (implicit) answer 'man is the (potentially consciously) self-interested animal' – express in the conduct of individual characters, and certain remarks on their part. The drama is not 'ahead of' theory or theoretical texts, as Paul Geyer believes (nor would such merit a 'value judgment'): "Literatur umschreibt immer das Selbstverständnis des Menschen. Als Wertkriterium für *Hohe* Literatur möchte ich ansehen, daß sie der zeitgenössischen *Theorie vom Menschen voraus* ist" ("Intertextuelle Bezüge zwischen dem theoretischen und dem literarischen Diskurs: Machiavellis *Il Principe* und seine Komödie *Mandragola*". *Italienische Studien*, vol. 18, 1997, pp. 91–102, here p. 91). Geyer's overstatement – "Eine Komödie ist dramatisierte Anthropologie" (p. 97) – contradicts his own thesis. Moreover, it is precisely not a ‹-logy› that is staged (neither here, nor does such seem possible); likewise, as to his second claim: "Machiavellis *Principe* konstatiert den Zerfall des mittelalterlichen Menschenbildes. Seine *Mandragola* zieht daraus die Konsequenz und legt damit den Grundstein für eine neue Anthropologie" (p. 101). Geyer's conclusions are not only inconsistent with respect to his own thesis, and the factual function in drama; they are also problematic discursively: "Machiavellis Beschreibung der Natur des Menschen als grundsätzlich moralisch verderbt, womit er übrigens in große gedankliche Nähe zu Luther und Calvin rückt" etc. (p. 96). Discursively, a common recourse may be found in the Bishop of Hippo; but the respective functionalizations are at variance with each other, seeing that Machiavelli reads Augustine against the latter's grain: tendency matters – and function in a given context; see Blumenberg, as quoted above ("Epochenschwelle," p. 102).

against his mother: "O God, a beast that wants discourse of reason / Would have mourn'd longer" (*Hamlet*, p. 189, I.ii.150–151); as well as in his later speech:

> What is a man / If his chief good and market of his time / Be but to sleep and feed? A beast, no more. / Sure he that made us with such large discourse [sc. 'power of reasoning'], / Looking before and after, gave us not / That capability and godlike reason / To fust [sc. 'become musty'] in us unus'd.
> (*Hamlet*, p. 345, IV.iv.33–39; see p. 345n.)[62]

The pun is in the particular application: reason is to lead to (more or less) bestial behavior by the end of this soliloquy: "O, from this time forth / My thoughts be bloody or be nothing worth" (*Hamlet*, p. 346, IV.iv.65–66). Behind these remarks lies the (tacit) *quaestio infinita* 'what is man', with one answer being hypoleptically alluded to: 'man is the rational animal' – which (implicit) claim is either denied outright, or subverted (in terms of its function in context).

One Shakespearean passage featuring an anthropistic *hypólepsis* all but suggests itself for closer scrutiny. Towards the climax of a longer monolog in the presence of, or addressed to, Rosencrantz and Guildenstern, Hamlet leaps (or lapses) into an apparently learned – Humanistic, Stoicizing, Neo-Platonic, Mirandolian – mélange, hardly distinguishable in precise discursive terms (while it is also doubtful whether such would aid discerning its function in this specific context):

> What piece of work is a man, / how noble in reason, how infinite in faculties, in form / and moving how express and admirable, in action / how like an angel, in apprehension how like a god: / the beauty of the world, the paragon of animals – / and yet, to me, what is this quintessence of dust? / Man delights not me[.]
> (*Hamlet*, pp. 253 f., II.ii.303–309)[63]

---

[62] Shakespeare (*Hamlet*, edited by Harold Jenkins. [Arden]. London: Thomson, 2003). In Aristotle, it is nature itself that does not perform anything sans reason, *télos*, or to no avail ('*máten*'): "For nature [...] does nothing without purpose" (*Politics*, pp. 10 f., 1253a, I.i.10).

[63] The foregoing passage had already confirmed Hamlet's mind as prone to *báthos* (in the literal sense), when he first praises the magnificence of the skies or heavens – "this majestical roof fretted with golden fire" (*Hamlet*, p. 253, II.ii.301) – to then state that, in his "disposition" (p. 253, II.ii.298), "it appeareth nothing [...] but a foul and pestilent congregation of vapours" (p. 253, II.ii.302–303). The language is in stark contrast to the coarseness of the content, and this applies also to the following 'descent', which increases the intratextual 'drop height' from which that poly-discursive, abstract 'fall of man' occurs. The above punctuation has caused controversy; it may be problematic as to the terms "action" and "apprehension" (see Jenkins' comment in: *Hamlet*, pp. 468n.–470n.).

Reasonably, this will not be received as an 'anthropological' consideration. Expressly, its function is 'emotive'. Obliquely (being directed at Rosencrantz and Guildenstern), it is 'conative', as the communicative situation bears out.[64] The reference to a self-definition of man as "the beauty of the world" does have allusive potentials with regard to certain discourses, taking on some (or perhaps much) of their (rhetorical) color; *inter alia*, Stoicizing, Neo-Platonic discursive affinities are non-distinctively meshed together with partly Christianizing, Humanist speculations concerning human dignity.[65] The particular application of this form, the function of this (mock-)appeal to man's grandeur, is the effect to be had – here by way of the anticlimax.[66] The initial, global assertion – with the implied *quaestio* 'what is man' (Hamlet's interjection, a quasi-imperative that almost looks like the corresponding query), and various replies by way of anthropistic *tópoi* 'under variation' – serves precisely the particular rhetorical purpose at hand. To be construing this as Hamlet's (let alone an author's) 'anthropology' would not only seem anachronistic; for there is no (deductive) logic involved here, but an (inductive) rhetorical one – with

---

[64] The rhetorical function is clear, both from the context and when taking this piece of verbal work in isolation.

[65] Intratextually, as well as to the audience, they are unlikely to be distinct. See Jenkins' gloss concerning an earlier passage: "The idea of man as partaking of both god and beast which thus underlies the play is very much the Renaissance concept. [...] see Pico [...] *De hominis dignitate*" (*Hamlet*, p. 438n.; see pp. 469n.–470n.); regarding Montaigne being "merely one example" for "a classical and Renaissance commonplace", see Jenkins' remark (p. 468n.) – here as to the description of the skies; while the superelevation of a particular author is problematic, the drift is pertinent: "Shakespeare is of course drawing on a common stock of ideas and terms [...] but the combination of them is quite his own" (p. 470n.). "As often Shakespeare achieves a magnificent result by combining elements, which, taken separately, are almost clichés" (p. 468n.) – that being precisely the point: their function is hypoleptic, seeing that 'everyone knows' (likewise as to most macrocosmic, or other discursive references, regarding astrology, humoral pathology, etc.). The 'conative' function – (self)persuasion (as implied in 'anthro-pistic') – is dominant (with a view to expediency). Any (supposed) 'agency' is subject to variation, rhetoric being an agent-indifferent, multipurpose *téchne* (see Küpper, *Diskurs-Renovatio*, p. 300; *Discursive* Renovatio, p. 289; "Rhetoric and the Cultural Net," passim; Mayfield, "Interplay," pp. 5–8, 8n., 29n., 37–38, with further references). The 'referential' (discursive, intertextual) or 'metalingual' functions recede for the particular purpose in the specific drama, the corresponding act and scene, and the context into which they are embedded (also extra-dramatically, as regards the cultural framework of the recipients).

[66] Couched in a statement to the effect that 'these are the private opinions held by the respective individual, and do not necessarily represent the state of either Denmark or the world' (*ut ita dicam*).

a view to functionality and impact.[67] The speaker is employing an anthropistic *hypólepsis* (distinctly dramatic in its textual environment).

On the whole, it must seem questionable to be positing an 'anthropology' based on suchlike assertions by characters embedded in plots and plays, in that the latter consist of multilateral contexts, differing causalities (whether apparently autotelic or ostensively manipulated), influencing what can at all, or will be said – as well as when, to whom and in whose presence, by which means, and to what end (that is, *cui bono* above all).[68] It will hardly seem plausible to construe a systematic 'anthropology' on the part of a (supposed) author – let alone of the Early Modern Age generally – based on such or similar passages, and by abstracting from the particular purposes in a given context. The foremost function of anthropistic statements (such as appeals to 'human invariants') is hypoleptic; and especially when embedded in dramatic works, where a particularly dynamic constellation of (interested) causalities – of *personae, nexus, utilitates* – determines their function. Primarily, the latter will be purposive: directed at the intra- and extratextual recipients (respectively the speaker himself), and always with a view to (immediate) effectuality.

By means of its context, and regulated thereby, Hamlet's speech not only stages the question 'what is man' (formulated as a half-imperative, query-like, interjective *thésis*); it also tenders an enumerative cascade of sundry answers – and not one.[69] The 'referential', contextual, discursive, epistemic, 'metalingual' functions seem to be in the background: the dominant purpose is impact (the 'conative' function, here specifically by means of an anthropistic *hypólepsis*, functionalized with a view to a persuasively effectual anticlimax), inextricably interwoven with the form itself (the 'poetic' function, linked to the dramatic genre, here).[70]

---

[67] It would also seem to strain the import of this passage in this particular drama from an extratextual viewpoint: for, like Polonius, the audience sees (and everyone knows by now) that 'there is method in this madness' (see *Hamlet*, p. 248, II.ii.205–206): much (rhetorical) practice, scholarly interest hardly – to say nothing of deductive 'anthropology'.

[68] See Lausberg, citing a twelfth-century Latin hexameter: "*quis, quid, ubi, quibus auxiliis, cur, quomodo, quando*" (*Elemente* 25, § 41; see *Handbuch* 183, §§ 328; p. 203, § 374).

[69] In anthropistics, one is dealing with 'quasi-definitional *essais*', not with 'definitions proper' (let alone '*sensu stricto*').

[70] See the Jakobsonian functions, *mutatis mutandis* (*Language*, spec. pp. 66–71). The emotive function of Hamlet's speech is connected to the conative one, seeing that it may seem to be auto-persuasive, as well (at least in part).

4 Nuances: 'Nothing Human Alien'

homo sum; humani nil a me alienum puto.
Terence[71]

At the outset of Terence's *Self-Tormentor*, the *senex* Chremes makes the above anthropistic statement. In Seneca, one encounters a rhetorical *hypólepsis* thereof: "Homo sum, humani nihil a me alienum puto".[72] Taking a larger temporal leap, one will find a truncated version of the maxim in Nietzsche's *Posthumous Fragments*: "nihil humani – ist antik" (*KSA 11*, p. 444, § 34.80, '*nihil humani* pertains to Antiquity'). Moreover, one might come across Jakobson's paradigmatically altered version of the dictum (a transtemporal rhetorical *hypólepsis*, not immediately anthropistic): "Linguista sum; linguistici nihil a me alienum puto" (*Language* p. 93; see p. 510n.).[73] Various other versions might be adduced.[74]

---

[71] ("Heauton Timorumenos / The Self-Tormentor". *The Woman of Andros. The Self-Tormentor. The Eunuch*, edited and translated by John Barsby. Cambridge: Harvard UP, 2001, pp. 171–303, here p. 186, I.i.77).

[72] "I am a man; and nothing in a man's lot / Do I deem foreign to me" (Seneca. *Epistles 93–124*. Translated by Richard M. Gummere, Cambridge: Harvard UP, 2006, pp. 90f., XCV.53). See Blumenberg for a reference to Voltaire on "Senecas [...] *Homo sum, humani nil a me alienum puto*" (*Lebenszeit*, p. 230, 230n.).

[73] Thus Jakobson, précising his position at a conference of anthropologists and linguists in 1953; this claim also concludes the corresponding essay, "Linguistics and Poetics" (of 1958/1960); see the gloss: "Lévi-Strauss, C., R. Jakobson, C. F. Voegelin und T. A. Sebeok, *Results of the Conference of Anthropologists and Linguists*, Baltimore 1953" (*Poetik*, p. 121n.; see p. 119).

[74] See Cicero, for instance, where the context is 'knowing one's duty', which may be obstructed by being "extremely self-centered": "est enim difficilis cura rerum alienarum. Quamquam Terentianus ille Chremes 'humani nihil a se alienum putat'" (*On Duties [De Officiis]*, edited and translated by Walter Miller. Cambridge: Harvard UP, 1913, pp. 30f., I.ix.29–30) – i.e. Cicero refunctionalizes (perchance, or rather likely, with a hint of irony) the decidedly self-interested quip on the part of Chremes (being inquisitive, intrusive, importunate) to show that other-than-selfish conduct is possible. See another refunctionalization of Terence's *dictum* by Cicero, which takes it as a merely notional (idealistic, utopian) remark (thereby implicitly disclosing its rhetorical quality): "if the judgments of men were in agreement with Nature, so that, as the poet says, they considered 'nothing alien to them which concerns mankind' ['humani', ut ait poeta, 'nihil a se alienum putarent'], then Justice would be equally observed by all" ("De Legibus," edited and translated by Clinton Walker Keyes. *De Re Publica [The Republic]. De Legibus [Laws]*. Cambridge: Harvard UP, 2000, pp. 287–519, here pp. 332 f., I.xii.33). Augustine takes up Menedemus' previous utterance also, thereby stressing the dialogic setting in the source (see "Epistle CLV," p. 444; *Political Writings*, p. 97); his *hypólepsis* ("Homo sum, humani nihil a me alienum puto") is notable in expressly highlighting the situation of reception, particularly the audience's reaction: "cui sententiae fuerunt etiam theatra tota plena stultis indoctisque plausisse" ("Epistle CLV," p. 445); this he uses for his specific purpose, decidedly refunctionalizing

Above, the *sententia* appears in four different genera (drama, specifically comedy; epistolary writing; fragmentary, momentary notations; a scholarly paper). Jakobson's version no longer answers the universal *quaestio* ('what is it to be human'). Nietzsche's context does not mention Terence, but Homer, Aristophanes, Horace, Petronius, La Rochefoucauld: the point being that the latter's contemporaries (and the Germans of the speaker's present) are said to have no patience for this "nihil humani" – here functionalized as signifying a "Genuß an niederen Sphären" (*KSA 11*, p. 444, § 34.80).[75]

It will be patent that Seneca would not employ the *sententia* in said fashion. His context reflects on the "way to worship the gods", answering "to believe in the gods"; then follows the query of "how to deal with men", to which a Stoicizing speaker replies with the equivalent of the Greek '*katà phýsin*': "Nature produces us related to one another, since she created us from the same source and to the same end"; the anthropistic Terentian verse follows, and is glossed as referring to a common humanity (*Epistles 93–124*, pp. 88–91, XCV.50–53).[76] This is far from Nietzsche's reapplication; and similarity with Jakobson's transtemporal rhetorical *hypólepsis* is in form only.

In Terence, Chremes is talking to the drama's titular self-tormentor Menedemus; the former opens the play with a self-important speech, in which he finds fault with the latter for working so hard being so old – instead of (delegatively) putting others to work in his stead. Menedemus replies rather reasonably, effectively telling the meddler to be minding his own business: "Chreme,

---

the anthropistic maxim: "Indeed, the fellowship of all human spirits naturally touched the hearts of everyone, so much that everyone there thought of himself precisely as the neighbour of every other human being" (*Political Writings*, p. 97, CLV; see "Epistle CLV," p. 445). See Montaigne: "*Humani a se nihil alienum putet*" (*Essais II*, edited by Emmanuel Naya et al. Paris: Gallimard, 2009, p. 32, II.ii). See also Marquard's connecting a variant thereof – "Nichts Menschliches sollte dem Schriftsteller fremd sein" – with an exposition drawing on one of Aristotle's definitions of man (*Skepsis in der Moderne. Philosophische Studien*. Stuttgart: Reclam, 2007, p. 22).

75 Euphemistically put: 'to be taking pleasure in bodily functions'. "Derbheit und Delikatesse zusammen bei Petronius, auch bei Horaz: mir am angenehmsten. Es gehört zum griechischen Geschmack. Homer war den Menschen um La Rochefoucauld herum zu derb, sie konnten das Triviale nicht genießen. Sie hielten eine gewisse hohe Empfindung bei sich fest, wie jetzt viele Deutsche, und verachte⟨te⟩n sich, wenn etwas wie Genuß an niederen Sphären in ihnen sich regt⟨e⟩. Aristophanes ist das Gegenstück: nihil humani – ist antik" (*KSA 11*, p. 444, § 34.80).

76 "Primus est deorum cultus deos credere" (Seneca. *Epistles 93–124*, pp. 88 f., XCV.50). "Ecce altera quaestio, quomodo hominibus sit utendum" (p. 90 f., XCV.51). "Natura nos cognatus edidit, cum ex isdem et in eadem gigneret" (pp. 90 f., XCV.52). "Homo sum, humani nihil a me alienum puto. / Habeamus in commune; nati sumus. Societas nostra" etc. (pp. 90 f., XCV.53).

tantumne ab re tuast oti tibi / aliena ut cures ea quae nil ad te attinent?" ("Self-Tormentor," p. 186, I.i.75 f.).[77] In rejoining, the quick-witted interlocutor makes use of an intratextual rhetorical *hypólepsis*; taking up a word ("aliena") and tying in with a phrase ("nil ad te") from Menedemus' response, Chremes turns them into said anthropistic *sententia*: "homo sum; humani nil a me alienum puto" (p. 186, I.i.76–77). The given context renders this remark a cunning defense of 'meddling with other people's business'.[78] This is a long way from Nietzsche's and Seneca's anthropistic *hypolépseis* – while Jakobson's rhetorical uptake (with paradigmatic alteration) actually stays closest to the tendency in Terence.[79]

On account of their structural equivalence, the above *Anknüpfungen* still seem similar to their maximatic 'source type', which remains recognizable formally (some elisions and variations notwithstanding). Even so, the respective contexts tend to differ – some of which have little (or almost nothing) to do with each other; or are downright at variance with the emitting discourse (as well as among one another).

Anthropistic assertions imply the (arguably indelible) query: 'what is (it to be) human'. The corresponding replies (including non-answers, rhetorical refusals to respond) – given at a particular time, in a specific context, containing, carrying, and conveying knowledge as to 'human invariants', for instance – may be taken up and varied in new contexts.[80] Hence the diversity of

---

[77] Compare and contrast Menedemus' (gullible) exclamation: "ita comparatam esse hominum naturam omnium / aliena ut melius videant et diiudicent / quam sua!" ("Self-Tormentor," p. 230, III.ii.503–505).

[78] Hence an idiomatic rendition is pertinent: "I'm human, and I regard no human business as other people's" ("Self-Tormentor," p. 187).

[79] The paradigmatic replacement performed by Jakobson – which particularizes the otherwise general *sententia* (hence limits or reduces its scope) – demonstrates the extent to which a recipient will sense having been addressed (when compared to assertions of the form 'all humans are'): "Linguista sum; linguistici nihil a me alienum puto" (*Language*, p. 93; see p. 510n.); with this statement, Jakobson defends against claims stating that he be overstepping the limits of the specialist province of linguistics, that he be meddling with other people's claimed and declared business – that he be overly interdisciplinary.

[80] Any '(re)uptake', (re)application, (re)placement – including what may appear as a 'mere' (or 'mimetic') repetition (thereto, see Borges' story "Pierre Menard, Author of the Quixote," *Collected Fictions*, edited and translated by Andrew Hurley. New York: Penguin, 1998, pp. 88–95) – will result in variation, variance. Likewise, the *hypólepsis* itself may have engendered or necessitated this new context first of all. Compare and contrast the tendency in Nietzsche's ensuing declaration: "Zwei Aufgaben: das Neue gegen das Alte zu defendiren und das Alte an das Neue anzuknüpfen" (*KSA 7*, p. 714, § 29.212) – the directedness is crucial, here: 'the old' is retroactively (or retrospectively) tied in with, or adapted to, 'the new'.

the (implicit) anthropistic answers above: in Terence, it is human to meddle; in Seneca, it is human to mingle; in Nietzsche, it is human to be corporeal.[81]

5 Elementally Speaking: 'Zitierende Tiere'

καὶ βραχὺς ὢν ὁ βίος τοῦ ἀνθρώπου.
Protagoras[82]

To distill the meta-theoretical yield of this *essai* so far: from a formal or structural perspective, *hypolépseis* tend to occur in grammatico-linguistic variants within immediate (dialogic, dramatic) exchanges, or intratextually associated contexts (including by the same speaker); in turn, transtemporal and intertextual uptakes typically have adaptive recourse to recognizable or familiar forms (such as the characteristic make of *sententiae*), refunctionalized with a view to (persuasive) effects in a receiving (often textual) environment; in terms of content, these *Anknüpfungen* may have a tendency to privilege broad-spectrum claims and appeals, for instance such as (are assumed to) pertain to all humankind.[83] The efficacy of the latter may seem to be grounded in the fact that 'taking up and tying in with' is a vital *modus operandi* for this animal.

To provisionally conclude the present *essai*, a certain anthropistic 'invariant' will be briefly invoked by recourse to Shakespeare's *King Lear*, in order to elucidate said reciprocity between a hypoleptic *héxis* and humankind. During their retreat, Edgar is speaking to Gloucester, whose strength and will are failing: "Away, old man, give me thy hand, away! / King Lear hath lost, he and his daughter ta'en"; the father responds with a fatalistic maxim, "No further, sir; a man may rot even here"; to which the son answers with another *sententia*, "What, in ill thoughts again? Men must endure / their going hence even as their coming hither. / Ripeness is all. Come on" – "And that's true too" rejoins Gloucester, who does not ignore either the rhetoricality of the exchange

---

81 For Jakobson's rhetorical, not immediately anthropistic *Anknüpfung*, one might submit this implied *essai*, describing man (emerging *kathólou*, from the function of his hypoleptic variant in context): 'man is the curious animal capable of speech and self-reflection' (in Aristotelizing terms) – 'wherefore it may also (self-reflexively) inquire into its particular (linguistic) capacities'.

82 (In: Kranz, *Vorsokratiker* 2, p. 265, 80B4; and D. Laertius, *Lives II*, p. 464, IX.51).

83 With respect to the reasons for a hypoleptic refunctionalization, one might add that, "as in every rhetorical figure, the *télos* is variable: legitimizing, continuing, shifting, defacing, ridiculing, polemicizing openly, staging oneself" (with thanks to Prof. Küpper for this suggestion in a handwritten comment from Jan 5, 2016; trans. dsm).

and its *dicta*, or the parity of their effective weight at the universal level (*Lear*, p. 363, V.ii.5–11).[84]

The various (implicitly anthropistic) *hypolépseis* here may be anything from a general 'man is a mortal being', to the *Scriptural* "There is a time for everything" (*Ecc* 3:1; *NIV*), Virgil's "stat sua cuique dies, breve et inreparabile tempus / omnibus est vitae" ("Aeneid VII–XII," p. 204, X.467–468), or to Stoic equanimity (as the glosses suggest, see *Lear*, pp. 363n.–364n.) and "indifference as to death" (in Melvillean terms) – as well as myriad other maxims and discourses.[85] The respective *sententiae* here deal with the conduct appertaining to, or effected by, this (anthropistic) knowledge: an (implicit) 'human invariant' – perchance, 'man is the being that potentially knows itself to be a dying animal' – serves as the hypoleptic 'anyone might know', 'it is understood'.[86]

As the Ancient Skeptics suggested (see Sextus, *Outlines*, p. 17, I.xi.23–24, for instance), it may be a viable (if temporary, tentative) solution to one's '*nes-*

---

84 (*King Lear*, edited by R. A. Foakes. [*Arden*]. London: Bloomsbury, 2013). The above echoes "The readiness is all" (*Hamlet*, p. 407, V.ii.218). The last remark is given despite the direness of the circumstances: (perchance) a comic relief, depending on the recipient's perspective, respectively on the particular performance.
85 "Each has his day appointed; short and irretrievable is the span of life for all" (Virgil. "Aeneid VII–XII". Translated by H. R. Fairclough, and G. P. Goold. *Aeneid VII–XII. Appendix Vergiliana*, edited by G. P. Goold. Cambridge: Harvard UP, 2002, pp. 1–367, here p. 205); "there is a time for everything [...] a time to be born and a time to die" (*Ecc* 3:1–2); see Melville (*Moby-Dick*, edited by Hershel Parker and Harrison Hayford. New York: Norton, 2002, p. 266, ch. 75).
86 As to the "dying animal" ("It knows not what it is"), see the third stanza of Yeats' poem "Sailing to Byzantium" (*Yeats's Poetry, Drama, And* Prose, edited by James Pethica. New York: Norton, 2000, p. 80, verses 22 f.). *Scripture* ascribes the above insight to another: "εἰδὼς ὅτι ὀλίγον καιρὸν ἔχει" (*SBLGNT*), "sciens quod modicum tempus habet" (*Apoc* 12:12; *Vulgate*) – see Blumenberg (*Schiffbruch*, pp. 85 f.; *Unbegrifflichkeit*, pp. 104 f.; *Lebenszeit*, p. 71, 71n.), who adds: "diese[r] Satz [...] ist [...] kaum an die kulturellen Bedingungen seiner Herkunft gebunden; er ließe sich in jede beliebige Sprache mit einem anderen Namen übersetzen" (*Schiffbruch*, p. 86). Generally, see Montaigne's *essai* "Que Philosopher, c'est apprendre à mourir" (*Essais I*, edited by Emmanuel Naya et al. Paris: Gallimard, 2009, pp. 221–241, I.xx), which ties in with Cicero's "*Tota* [...] *philosophorum vita* [...] *commentatio mortis est*" (*Tusculan Disputations*, edited and translated by J. E. King. Cambridge: Harvard UP, 1945, p. 86, I.xxx.74), taking up "Plato, *Phaedo* 67 D" (p. 87n.). See Epictetus: "Will you not, as Plato says, study not merely to die" (*Discourses III–IV*, p. 303, IV.i.172) – with references to "*Phaedo*, 64 A, and *Republic*, II. 361 E" (p. 303n.). See Seneca: "Epicurus [...]: 'Think on death' ['Meditare mortem'] [...] it is a wonderful thing to learn thoroughly how to die. [...] 'Think on death'. In saying this, he bids us think on freedom. He who has learned to die has unlearned slavery [...]. His way out is clear" (*Epistles 1–65*, edited and translated by Richard M. Gummere. Cambridge: Harvard UP, 1917, pp. 190–193, XXVI.8–10).

cio' to adopt – for the time being and the pragmatic affairs of life – the customs (the contingent *nómoi*, conventional *mores*, common usage) of a given time.[87] The corresponding, inductive methods of observation and description are an infinite task, 'limitless labor'.[88]

It is an arguable 'human invariant' that said being must always exceed itself (and all that has been) – 'man is the animal *plus ultra*'. In the context at hand, this may translate into "theory, which simply cannot cease" theorizing (Blumenberg, *Beschreibung*, p. 498; trans. dsm).[89] Yet it cannot always (nor

---

87 For the most part, this mode was adopted by Montaigne, one of the keenest Early Modern observers of humankind and its *mœurs*. See Heraclitus: "Therefore one must follow the common ['τῷ ξυνῷ']" ("On the Universe," pp. 498 f., XCII; see Kranz *Vorsokratiker 1*, p. 151, 22B2, where Sextus' gloss reads: '*xynòs gàr ho koinós*'; see the latter's *Against the Logicians*, pp. 72–73, I.133). Compare Blumenberg: "Die Menschheit hat den größten Teil ihrer Geschichte und des Volumens ihres Bewußtseins von unwiderlegbaren Annahmen gelebt und tut dies vielleicht – es ist ein Verdacht, des Beweises unfähig – immer noch" (*Arbeit*, p. 19). As to the function of assumptions in Blumenberg's thinking, see particularly: "Der Mensch ist ein Wesen der Ansichten mindestens ebenso, wie er eines der Einsichten sein oder werden mag. Wo er eine Welt hat oder sich gibt, hat er sich mit 'Weltansicht' begnügt und 'Welteinsicht' auch ohne Skepsis nicht in Aussicht. Erforschung der Metaphern hält inne im Vorfeld der Einsichten um den Ansichten ihr Recht widerfahren zu lassen" (*Lesbarkeit* n.pag.; foreword: "Über dieses Buch," third p. thereof). In other words: familiarities, commonplaces, acceptations, assumptions – variants of *hypólepsis*. In a larger framework, this pertains to the Blumenbergian ethics of 'culture qua detour': "Kultur besteht in der Auffindung und Anlage, der Beschreibung und Empfehlung, der Aufwertung und Prämierung der Umwege. [...] Die Umwege sind es aber, die der Kultur die Funktion der Humanisierung des Lebens geben. Die vermeintliche 'Lebenskunst' der kürzesten Wege ist in der Konsequenz ihrer Ausschlüsse Barbarei. [...] Umwegskultur [...] diese[s] Barbareiverschonungssystem, genannt Kultur [...]. Die Unversöhnlichkeit des Pluralismus der Weltansichten ist ein Risiko, aber ein zureichend begründetes" (*Die Sorge geht über den Fluß*. Frankfurt: Suhrkamp, 1987, pp. 137 f.). Seneca's radicalism – "Remove existimationem hominum" (*Epistles 1–65*, pp. 188 f., XXVI.6) – would leave humans with nothing to go on; in this respect, Marcus' nuanced stance seems more viable, and considerably more humane (see the notes in part 3).

88 As Husserl put it and Blumenberg practiced it; see "Husserliana VIII 352": "*Ich soll so leben, als ob ich unsterblich wäre und als ob ich wirklich ins Unendliche arbeiten könnte*" (cited in: *Beschreibung*, p. 441; compare Blumenberg *Genesis 2*, p. 473; *Höhlenausgänge*, p. 715; *Sachen*, pp. 112, 146; *Die Verführbarkeit des Philosophen*, edited by Manfred Sommer. Frankfurt: Suhrkamp, 2005, p. 148; *Schriften zur Technik*, edited by Alexander Schmitz and Bernd Stiegler. Berlin: Suhrkamp, 2015, pp. 193 f., 193n., 197 f., 201 f.); see Democritus' dictum: "ἐργαζόμενοι ὡς ἀεὶ βιωσόμενοι" (in: Kranz *Vorsokratiker 2*, p. 190, 68B227); the first paragraph of the preface to the first book of Livy's *Ab urbe condita*: "Res est praeterea et inmensi operis" (*History of Rome. Books 1–2*, edited and translated by B. O. Foster. Cambridge: Harvard UP, 1988, p. 2); the resigned variant in Nicolaus of Oresme: "*et labor interminabilis*" (cited in: Blumenberg *Legitimität*, p. 409); the term "unendliche Arbeit" also appears in Nietzsche (*KSA 11*, p. 20, § 25.36).

89 See Marquard (in another context): "Theorie meint dabei in Anknüpfung an den ursprünglichen Wortsinn: Sehen und sagen, wie es ist. Theoriefähigkeit ist dementsprechend die Fähig-

does it ever altogether) start from scratch (as Descartes and Husserl apparently tried) – 'life is short' and 'men limited'.[90] Hence Marquard's describing 'man as the *zoon hypoleptikón*' (see *Apologie*, p. 68) – a 'hypoleptic animal' that 'takes up, ties in with, and varies' – is tentatively applicable, and perchance in the *studia humanitatis* above all: "human beings are beings that quote" (*Abschied*, p. 105; trans. dsm), 'man is a quotational animal' of necessity.[91]

Variants of (rhetorical, anthropistic, dramatic) *hypólepsis* were accentuated herein, particularly in terms of their artful form and function. Other empha-

---

keit, illusionsresistent zu sehen und zu sagen: So ist es" (*Stattdessen*, p. 135); "also der Sieg des So-ist-es über das So-hat-es-zu-sein" (p. 137). Given the plurality, diversity, contingency of the factual, this descriptive task is unlikely to be otherwise than endless.

90 As to Cartesian attempts: "Analog zu [...] Descartes [...] stilisiert Lichtenberg seinen Kopernikus, indem er ihm den Willen zuschreibt, *den ganzen Plunder einmal wegzuwerfen und von neuem anzufangen*. Fast wörtlich so hatte Descartes [...] sein Programm bestimmt: *funditus omnia semel in vita evertenda*" (Blumenberg, *Genesis 2*, p. 368); see other anti-hypoleptic examples: "*die Nachwelt von der Überlieferung zu befreien*" (Regiomontan, cited in: *Lebenszeit*, p. 128); in a context referring to Melanchthon: "das Bewußtsein von der Notwendigkeit, der Reformation ihre von Luther verachtete, aber nach der 'eschatologischen Phase' unvermeidbare Kulturfähigkeit zu geben und dafür den Schulrahmen der tradierten Bildung zu respektieren" (Blumenberg, *Genesis 2*, p. 387) – prior, the philosopher had offered Melanchthon as an exemplar for a perceptively simulative *hypólepsis*: "In dem Kapitel mit der lapidaren Überschrift *Quis est motus mundi?* knüpft Melanchthon, so könnte man denken, an Luthers Neuerungsvorwurf an" (p. 378). As to human limits: "Der Mensch ist kein absolutes Wesen" (Marquard, *Stattdessen*, p. 7; see pp. 26, 45); Blumenberg: "Nicht die Trägheit macht die Tradition, sondern die Verlegenheit" ("Annäherung," p. 427). Naturally, man is the being that refuses its limitations.

91 They are (actively) hypoleptic, (consciously) citational, (inevitably) referential beings: "denn die Menschen sind zitierende Lebewesen" (Marquard, *Abschied*, p. 105); "[d]enn die Menschen sind 'hypoleptische', sie sind anknüpfende Lebewesen" (*Stattdessen*, p. 42); "kein Mensch kann absolut von vorn anfangen, jeder muß – wie Joachim Ritter sagte: 'hypoleptisch' – an das anknüpfen, was schon da ist: Zukunft braucht Herkunft. Diese hermeneutische Einsicht" (*Abschied*, p. 78; see p. 90); "daß die Menschen nie von Anfang an anfangen. [...] Denn die Wirklichkeit ist [...] stets schon da, und sie müssen anknüpfen" (p. 76); "das Leben des Menschen [ist] stets zu kurz, um sich von dem, was er schon ist, in beliebigem Umfang durch Ändern zu lösen: er hat schlichtweg keine Zeit dazu. Darum muß er [...] 'anknüpfen'" (p. 16); "das Leben ist kurz, darum müssen wir [...] anknüpfen an Vorgegebenes" (*Apologie des Zufälligen*. Stuttgart: Reclam, 2008, p. 67); "Denn der Mensch ist – sterblichkeitsbedingt unvermeidlich – der wandlungsträge Anknüpfungmüsser, das Zoon hypoleptikon" (p. 68); "[j]ede Veränderung muß an Vorhandenes anknüpfen [...] hypoleptisch [...] das 'Antiprinzip Anknüpfung'. Anknüpfung – Hypolepsis – besagt: Das, was bleibt, ist die Möglichkeitsbedingung von Veränderung [...] Die Menschen können – wegen ihrer Sterblichkeit nie [...] in beliebigem Umfang von ihrem je besonderen Anknüpfungspunkt entfernt werden: Sonst zerstört man sie. Darum ist Ethik unvermeidlich Hypoleptik oder illusionär" (*Glück*, pp. 67 f.).

ses and contextual embedments are conceivable and merit attention, given the time – as everyone knows: *'humana vita brevis'*.[92]

---

[92] Machiavelli's *Mandragola* commences with a Canzone, the first words of which are the *tópos* "Perché la vita è brieve" (p. 3); see the above quote from Protagoras (in: Kranz *Vorsokratiker* 2, p. 265, 80B4); Marcus has: "βραχὺς ὁ βίος" (*Meditations*, pp. 82, IV.26; p. 144, VI.30; p. 326, XII.7), and the variant "ἀκαριαῖος ὁ ἀνθρώπειος βίος" (p. 308, XI.18). The (endlessly varied) 'source type' naturally being this Hippocratic aphorism: "Life is short, the Art long, opportunity ['*kairòs*'] fleeting, experiment ['*peira*'] treacherous, judgment ['*krísis*'] difficult" – variants usually take up and alter only the first dicolon ('*Ho bíos brachýs, he dè téchne makré*'), and omit the medical context (98 f., I.i); see Seneca's "de brevitate vitae": "'vitam brevem esse, longam artem'" (*Moral Essays*, edited and translated by John W. Basore. Cambridge: Harvard UP, 1932, vol. 2, p. 286, X; see p. 287n.). Referring to the *Stoicorum Veterum Fragmenta*, Pohlenz (*Stoa und Stoiker. Die Gründer. Panaitios. Poseidonios*, edited and translated by Max Pohlenz. Zurich: Artemis, 1950) tenders the following: "Zenon sagte, an nichts seien wir so arm wie an Zeit ['*chrónou*']. Denn wahr ist das Wort (*des Hippokrates*): 'Das Leben ist kurz und lang die Kunst ['*brachỳs gàr óntos ho bíos, he dè téchne makré*']', am meisten diejenige, die seelische Krankheiten ['*tes psyches nósous*'] zu heilen unternimmt" (p. 11; see p. 360n.; for the Greek, see von Arnim *SVT I*, p. 70, § 323, who cites from Stobaeus); in the Modern Age, translating '*psyches*' as "seelischen" is problematic – the point being ethical (hence this-worldly), not metaphysico-speculative. By and large, selectivity and truncation have a tendency of conducing to *hypólepsis*. For references, variants, see Blumenberg (*Lebenszeit*, p. 72); Goethe (*Faust. Der Tragödie erster und zweiter Teil*. Munich: dtv, 1962, p. 54, verses 1786 f.).

Index

Academia de los Nocturnos 172–173, 175–176, 178–179, 182–183
Académie Française 23, 169–170, 172
Accademia degli Addormentati 122
Accademia degli Illustrati 122
Accademia dei Pastori frattegiani 122
Admiral's Men 58
Adorno, Theodor W. 235
Alberti, Leon Battista 104
Albury, W. R. 103
Alexander the Great 20
Altenburg, Detlef 185
Altmutter, Jakob Placidus 196
Anderson, Miranda 76
André, John 228
Apollinaire, Guillaume 25
Aretino, Pietro 119
Argensola, Lupercio Leonardo de 179, 181–183
Ariosto, Ludovico 78, 105, 119
– Cinque Canti 120
– I Suppositi 78
– La Lena 78
– Negromante 106
Aristophanes 268
Aristotle 20, 39, 41–51, 69–70, 84, 108, 126–127, 134–136, 139, 149, 151, 153–155, 157, 159–161, 163–165, 170, 234–235, 240, 242–244, 247–248, 268
– Economics 45
– Ethics 42
– Metaphysics 234
– Nicomachean Ethics 45, 159
– Politics 20, 41, 43–45, 234
Arnim, Achim von 64
Artaud, Antonin 199
Assmann, Jan 241, 243, 246
Australian Opera Company 65
Ayrer, Jacob 54

Balzac, Honoré de 30
– Le Lys dans la vallée 34
– Père Goriot 31, 34
Bandello, Matteo 128, 130–131, 133
Barkan, Leonard 10

Barthes, Roland 3, 10
Batman, Stephen 10
Baxandall, Michael 104
Beaumarchais 228
– La Folle Journée, ou le Mariage de Figaro 230
Bembo, Pietro 132–134, 137–138
– Prose 137–138
– Rime 132
Benedictine Gymnasium of Meran 194
Benedictine Monastery of Marienberg 194, 197
Benedictine Monastery of Müstair 194
Bernhart, Toni 197
Bierbach, Christine 177
Bishop, Henry R. 65
Bismarck, Otto von 31
Blanchard, Edward 65
Blumenberg, Hans 237–239, 272
Boccaccio, Giovanni 9, 22, 137–138, 155
– Decameron 22, 85, 120, 155
Borges, Luis 28, 32
Born, Ignaz von
– Specimen monachologiæ methodo Linnæana 222
Borromeo, Carlo 72
Bösch-Niederer, Annemarie 192
Bracy, Henry 65
Brecht, Bertolt 199
Brockmann, Johann Franz Hieronymus 211
Brown, Thomas
– Lectures on the Philosophy of the Human Mind 206
Browne, Robert 63
Browne, Thomas 4, 7
– Religio Medici 4
Brunelleschi, Filippo 95, 108
Bucher, Anton von 224
– Entwurf einer ländlichen Charfreytagsprocession 222
Burke, Peter 101
Burton, Francis
– Anatomy of Melancholy 11

Calderón de la Barca, Pedro
– La vida es sueño 32

Campbell, Stephen 103
Canossa, Ludovico 102, 106, 110, 112–113, 115
Cardinal Richelieu 169
Castelvetro, Lodovico 162–164
Castiglione, Baldassare 77, 177–178, 183
Cathalán, Bernardo 174–175
Cervantes, Miguel de
– Don Quijote 2
Chamisso, Adalbert
– Fortunati Glücksekel und Wunschütlein 64
– Peter Schlemihl's wundersame Geschichte 64
Charlemagne 30
Charles V, Holy Roman Emperor 101
Charles V of France 39–43, 45–47, 51
Charles X of France 31
Chateaubriand, François-René de 28
Chaucer, Geoffrey 9
Cheney, Patrick 11
Cicero 7, 48, 267
Collège de Navarre 42
Comenius, Amos 60
Comoedia von Fortunato 60, 62
Connell, Michael 73
Cooke, William 207
Copeau, Jacques 199
Corneille, Pierre 32, 162, 169
– Cid 32
– Examen de Polyeucte 162
Covent Garden 65

Da Ponte, Lorenzo 230
Da Porto, Luigi 128, 131, 133
Damrosch, David 66
D'Ancona, Alessandro
– Origini del teatro italiano 102
Dante Alighieri 21–22, 119, 138, 156–158, 164
– Commedia 21
– De vulgari eloquentia 21–22
Davies, John 9
De' Pazzi, Alessandro 135
Dekker, Thomas 55, 58, 60–63, 65–66
– Pleasant Comedie of Old Fortunatus 58
Democritus 233, 255
Denores, Giason 164

Descartes, René 244, 273
Dev, Feliks Anton 227
– Belin 226
Diccionario de autoridades 171
Dickens, Charles 30
Diderot, Denis 199, 204–207
– Paradoxe sur le comédien 205
Diez, Friedrich 28
Dionysius of Halicarnassus
– De compositione verborum 137
Dörrer, Anton 186
Drnovšek, Jaša 4
Dromgoole, Dominic 87–88, 90–91, 97
Drury Lane Theater 65
Du Chesne, François 41
DuLaurens, André 10

Eagleton, Terry 166
Ekhof, Conrad 199, 210
Elias, Norbert 202
– Über den Prozeß der Zivilisation 202
Elizabeth I of England 58
Engel, Johann Jakob 199, 211, 213
– Ideen zu einer Mimik 209

Federico da Montefeltro 103, 107
Felipe II of Spain 180
Felipe IV of Spain 173
Ferrari, Giacomo Gotifredo 197–198
Ficino, Marsilio 9
Fitzgerald, F. Scott
– The Great Gatsby 68
Flaubert, Gustave 30, 33–35
– Madame Bovary 31, 33–34
Fontane, Theodor 30, 33–35
– Effi Briest 31, 33–34
Foucault, Michel 103
Fraternity of Saint George 180
Fregoso, Ottaviano 103

Garrick, David 199, 205–210
Giolito, Gabriel 114
Giraldi Cinzio, Giambattista 122, 136, 152
– Discorso intorno al comporre delle commedie e delle tragedie 154
– Giuditio 152–153
– Orbecche 127–128, 130

Gleim, Johann Wilhelm Ludwig 210
Goethe, Johann Wolfgang von 55, 274
Goldoni, Carlo
- L'impresario delle Smirne 115
Gonzaga, Elisabetta 177
Grandes chroniques de France 39
Green, John 60–61
Greenblatt, Stephen 89
Greene, Robert 108
Greider, William 37
Grillparzer, Franz
- Fortunatus Wunschhütlein 65
Grotowski, Jerzy 199
Guarini, Giovanni Battista 119
Guazzo, Stefano 183
Guillaume de Dormans 39–40, 42
Gulizia, Stefano 77, 96

Haller, Albrecht von 199, 204
Hamburg National Theater 53
Haß, Ulrike 94
Hastaba, Ellen 186, 190, 194, 198
Hauser, Arnold 126
Haydn, Joseph 196, 228
Hegel, Georg Wilhelm Friedrich
- Vorlesungen über die Ästhetik 166
Heinrich Julius of Brunswick-
   Wolfenbüttel 54–55
Henslowe, Philip 58
Herder, Johann Gottfried 6–7, 23–28, 33
Heywood, Thomas 71
- Apology for Actors 100
Hill, Aaron 199, 204
Hill, John 199, 204, 208
- The Actor 207
Homer 247, 268
Horace 268
- Ars poetica 147
Hörmann, Ludwig von 186
Hulsmann, Guido
- The Ethics of Money Production 47
Hume, David
- Treatise of Human Nature 206
Husserl, Edmund 91, 244

Ibsen, Henrik 32
Ignatius de Loyola 217
Inghirami, Tommaso 102

Jacobs, Helmut C. 173
Jakobson, Roman 250, 262, 268
Japelj, Jurij 226
Javitch, Daniel 153
Jean de Dormans 39
Jonson, Ben 58
- The Alchemist 208
- Volpone 119
Joseph II, Holy Roman Emperor 216, 229–230
Journal for Empirical Psychology 213

Kant, Immanuel 235
Kantorowicz, Ernst 48
Kappl, Brigitte 151
Kasseler Fortunatusdrama 63
Kermauner, Taras 226
Komploier, Albert 215–216, 222
- Das zerfallene Christenthum 215
Küpper, Joachim 2
Kuralt, Martin 228
Kyd, Thomas
- Spanish Tragedy 54

La Academia del Buen Retiro 173
La Pléiade 9
La Rochefoucauld, François de 268
Lacaze, Louis 199, 204
Lamartine, Alphonse de 28
Lamb, Charles 65
Landino, Cristoforo 9
Lang, Franciscus
- Dissertatio de Actione Scenica 201
Le Cat, Claude-Nicolas 199, 204
Lechleitner, Wilhelm 196
Leonardo da Vinci 108–109
Leopold II, Holy Roman Emperor 231
Lessing, Gotthold Ephraim 53, 67, 199, 203–204, 210
- Miß Sara Sampson 210
Lichtenberg, Georg Christoph 199, 204–205, 208–211
Linhart, Anton Tomaž 227, 229
- Blumen aus Krain 228–229
- Das öde Eiland 228
- Miss Jenny Love 226, 228
- Ta veseli dan ali Matiček se ženi 230–231
- Županova Micka 225, 230

Litteratur- und Theaterzeitung 211
Lohse, Rolf 123, 125, 161
Lombardi, Bartolomeo 135
Lope de Vega
– Arte Nuevo 170
Louis Philippe I of France 31
Louis XIII of France 169
Luce, Siméon 40
Lucretius
– De rerum natura 8

Machado de Assis, Joaquim Maria 28, 32
Machiavelli, Niccolò 78, 82, 105, 246, 249, 255, 274
– Mandragola 78, 82, 263
Macklin, Charles 207
MacPherson, James
– Ossian 65
Magelone 57
Maggi, Vincenzo 135–136, 155, 157, 159
Mann, Thomas
– Buddenbrooks 68
Manzoni, Alessandro
– Promessi sposi 33
Maria Theresia, Holy Roman Empress 216
Marlowe, Christopher 55
Marquard, Odo 243, 273
Martinez, Ronald 103
Marx, Karl 38
Maurer, Joseph and Hanns Dollinger
– The Joseph Play of Axams 187
Melbourne Liedertafel Harmonia 65
Melbourne Opera 65
Menander 113
Mendelssohn, Moses 53
Menius, Friedrich 60–64
Metastasio, Pietro
– Artaserse 226
– L'isola disabitata 228
Metternich, Klemens Wenzel Lothar von 231
Meyerhold, Vsevolod 199
Michel, Francisque 29
Minturno, Antonio
– De poeta 161
Montaigne, Michel de 4
Montesquieu 228
Moritz, Karl Philipp 213

Mowat, Barbara 9
Mozart, Wolfgang Amadeus
– La clemenza di Tito 226
– Le nozze di Figaro 230

Nebrija, Antonio de 23
Netzer, Blasius 192–194
Netzer, Josef 193
Newton, Isaac 207
Nicolai, Friedrich 53, 203, 210
Nicolas de Villemer 40–41, 44
Nicole Oresme 42–43, 45
Nietzsche, Friedrich 267–270

Opitz, Martin 60
Oresme, Nicole 41–42, 44–51
– De moneta 47
– Livre de Politiques d'Aristote 46–47
Ovid 9, 108
– Heroides 153

Pacioli, Luca 101
Parabosco, Girolamo
– Il Pellegrino 114
Paris, Gaston 29
Parker, Jamie 91
Pegam in Lambergar 228
Petrarch 22, 119, 124, 132–134, 137–139, 141
– Rerum vulgarium fragmenta 131–132, 142
Petronius 268
Pia, Emilia 177
Pieri, Marzia 124
Pierre d'Orgement 40, 42–43, 48, 50
Pineda, Juan de
– Monarchia Ecclesiastica 7
Pino da Cagli
– Breve considerazione intorno al componimento de la Comedia de' nostri tempi 72
Pinós y Castro, Gaspar Galcerán de 176
Pippin, Robert 38, 65
Plato 5, 38, 48, 69–70, 119, 154, 171, 241
– Ion 6
– Politeia 84
Plautus
– Menaechmi 80
– Poenulus 102

Plutarch 9, 240
– De Alexandri magni fortuna aut virtute 20
Pope, Alexander 228
Protagoras 233

Quintilian 200

Racine, Jean 32
– Phèdre 32
Rainolde, John
– Th'overthrow of stage-playes 71
Ramler, Karl Wilhelm 210
Raynouard, François-Juste-Marie 29
Real Academia Española 170, 172, 182
Rehberg, August Wilhelm 64, 66
Reynolds, Robert 55
Ricci, Janez 227
Riccoboni, Antoine-François 199
Richter, Joseph
– Die Feldmühle 230
Ritter, Joachim 243, 246
Robortello, Francesco 159–161, 163
Rojas, Fernando de
– Celestina 106, 256
Romuald of Štandrež 220
Rousseau, Jean-Jacques 6
Royal Bavarian Gymnasium of Innsbruck 196
Royal Theater of Berlin 211
Ruggirello, Fabio 126

Sachs, Hans 63
– Tragedia mit 22 personen, der Fortunatus mit dem wunschseckel 57
Sackville, Thomas 54
Said, Edward 3
Sainte-Albine, Raymond de 199, 204, 207
Sanders, Bernie 37–38
Schiller, Friedrich 27
– On Naïve and Sentimental Poetry 27
Schmitt, Arbogast 134
Schönwiese, Ekkehard 186
Schröder, Friedrich Ludwig 199, 211
Scot, Reginald
– The Discoverie of Witchcraft 9
Seneca 268–270
– De brevitate vitae 180
Sextus Empiricus 235, 271

Shakespeare, William 10–11, 26, 32, 53–55, 60, 67, 89, 91, 93, 104, 108, 121, 144, 228, 263
– As You Like It 89
– Hamlet 10, 32, 73, 92, 142, 208–209, 211, 263–266
– Julius Caesar 32, 260, 262
– King Lear 8, 207, 211, 270
– Love's Labour's Lost 89
– Macbeth 32
– Measure for Measure 258
– Midsummer Night's Dream 7, 10–11
– Much Ado About Nothing 89
– Othello 8, 32, 73
– Richard III 206
– Romeo and Juliet 32, 121
– The Twelfth Night 89
– The Winter's Tale 108
Siddons, Henry 199
Sidney, Philip 11
– Astrophil and Stella 10
Simonde de Sismondi, Jean-Charles-Léonard 29
Singer, Wolf 5
Smith, Bruce R. 104–105
Socrates 6
Soll, Jacob 101, 103
Sophocles
– Ajax 161
– King Oedipus 122, 159–160
Spencer, John 55
Speroni, Sperone 127, 131, 136, 139, 142, 152–159, 164
– Canace 127, 131, 136, 139, 142, 152–155, 157, 159, 164
Spies, Johann
– Historia von D. Johann Fausten 55, 67
Staël, Germaine de 29
Stanislavsky, Konstantin 199
Stewart, Pamela 80, 82–83
Strada, Francisco 217–219
Strindberg, August 32
Sulzer, Johann Georg
– Allgemeine Theorie der schönen Künste 210
Surphlet, Richard 10
Svetec, Luka 225
Szondi, Peter 151

Taine, Hyppolite 25
Tasso, Torquato 119
– Il re Torrismondo 141
Taylor, Charles 6
Teatro Olimpico 122
Terence 268, 270
– Self-Tormentor 267–268
The Christmas / Three Kings Play, Matrei 190
The Mariahilf Play 192
Theobald, Werner 241
Thurnher, Eugen 186
Tieck, Ludwig
– Deutsches Theater 64
– Fortunat 64
Tiroler Landesmuseum Ferdinandeum 186, 192, 194, 196
Tolstoy, Leo 30
Tragödia von des Fortunati Wunschhute und Seckel 64
Trissino, Giovan Giorgio
– Sofonisba 128
Trump, Donald 37–38
Twain, Mark
– A Connecticut Yankee at King Arthur's Court 37

Uhland, Ludwig
– Fortunat und seine Söhne 64

Vadian, Joachim 9
Vanbrugh, John
– The Provoked Wife 208
Virgil 21, 138
– Aeneid 21, 133, 271
Visconti, Luchino 115
Voltaire 53
Vošnjak, Josip 225

Warner, Michael 112
Warning, Rainer 142
Washington, George 228
Wasserman, Earl 6
Weaver, James B. 37
Webb, Jennifer 103
Weimann, Robert 114

Zelman, Alberto 65
Zingerle, Ignaz Vinzenz 186
Žižek, Slavoj 3
Zois, Sigismund 229
Zola, Émile
– L'Argent 68
Zorzi Pugliese, Olga 103
Zupan, Jakob Frančišek 227

www.ingramcontent.com/pod-product-compliance
Lightning Source LLC
Chambersburg PA
CBHW031801220426
43662CB00007B/490